SHOOTING
007

SHOOTING
007
AND OTHER CELLULOID ADVENTURES

ALEC MILLS

The
History
Press

For Lil

First published 2014

The History Press
The Mill, Brimscombe Port
Stroud, Gloucestershire, GL5 2QG
www.thehistorypress.co.uk

© Alec Mills, 2014

British Library Cataloguing in Publication Data.
A catalogue record for this book is available from the British
Library.

ISBN 978 0 7509 5363 4

Typesetting and origination by The History Press
Printed in Great Britain

CONTENTS

FOREWORD

by Sir Roger Moore

I can't think how long I've known Alec; it feels like forever – and I mean that in the nicest possible way! We've shared some interesting times, whether it was hundreds of feet underground in a South African goldmine, on an orbiting space station or on a nuclear submarine planning to destroy western civilisation as we know it.

The one thing I enjoyed most about the Bond films was coming together with a family to make the movies, and Alec was a long-standing member of that family. Well, not long standing in the vertical sense as he isn't that tall, as the box he often stood on to help him reach his camera viewfinder will testify. But in terms of talent and personality, Alec is a big man.

At the time of writing, I haven't yet read my old friend's autobiography, so I cannot really make any comment about its readability. However, if he tells the truth about the shocking way I behaved on film sets over the years, on various continents, above water and below, above and below ground, then I think you will be amused and appalled at the disgraceful way some actors behave because of the inflated egos that they develop due to their good fortune.

If, on the other hand, Alec just boasts of his artistic achievements in the world of cinematography you will have to believe it, because Alec does not lie ... except when he is writing or talking, as I discovered on the ten or so happy occasions we worked together.

Knowing Alec, I can safely promise you a good read, and I always tell the truth.

Sir Roger Moore

PREFACE

I well remember my mother, Lil, reading fairy tales to me in bed to try to get me off to sleep. I was young and believed everything she read from the book to be true. Mouth wide open and totally convinced that all this could be a way of life, I slept well. Many years later I wondered if I had been brainwashed and had had my future played out before me on the 10-inch black-and-white Murphy television set which my parents somehow managed to buy. Lil smiled when she reminded me of those past early years as we strolled down memory lane. In a strange way, those scenes reflected both my life and career, somehow mirroring those fairy tales.

I had to think carefully about how I would write about my life and profession. I want not only to write about the film world – so unlike the current technology of high-definition digital cameras – but also to share my hidden emotions, which may be difficult to explain. But I will try ...

Autobiographies of my predecessors, the people who contributed much to my filming education over the years, were useful, as were my personal experiences in a fast-changing film industry. Those experiences are not easy to describe now, with new technology moving on and leaving behind a generation of 'oldies' to salvage past memories. With my generation of film people now fast in decline, I suddenly felt the need to explain my own images, particularly when reading Sir Roger Moore's memories of me; indeed, I have memories of Sir Roger, which I will come back to later. It is also necessary to establish personal images of my early background which may be of interest to others. My story is one of a retired generation and it may be difficult for the modern reader to understand our environment. I and others came from a world that is now seen as past history as the evolution of the film industry continues on its journey with its fast-changing technology.

'Past history ... that's right, accept it's too late to argue about that now – we are what we are,' Suzy quickly pointed out, looking over my shoulder as I made a few notes. Suzy was always ready with her opinion, even when discussing my possible retirement. At the time I had hated the very idea but my caring wife thought it would be worth considering and that I should wake up to the fact that the phone had finally stopped ringing.

'But I'm not dead yet!' I said, fighting back.

This issue inevitably brought up the subject of my appalling memory, an unfortunate inheritance handed down from Lil and now more noticeable as I struggled to recall fast-fading reminiscences while keeping alive the idea of writing an autobiography – private moments for the family to enjoy before all are lost to memory. We were both aware that I would need to do something in retirement, more than likely retelling past adventures and experiences. Even if they were recorded out of sequence, my accounts would remain as honest as memory allowed.

Then I asked why an old fool would want to reveal his private life – exciting as it was – when it would be easy to disguise the reality to his advantage. In all likelihood all those who take on the challenge of writing their memoirs are tempted by this.

'I assume you mean taking licence?' Suzy asked, reading over my shoulder ... wish she wouldn't do that!

I enjoy reading autobiographies, usually of those with whom I worked in the past, though there were times when I hardly recognised the author, the person I thought I knew. So now I wonder if the writer had an outside influence suggesting that a little exaggeration of past experiences would be accepted – even if it was not entirely honest. With this in mind, I felt I must look carefully to what I write, should I take up the challenge. My book should be interesting to read, perhaps entertaining, while at the same time it would need some licence to flow, to keep the reader's interest – which is easier said than done. Should the thought of retirement finally become reality, we would probably move to Devon, where Suzy and I could look out across the glistening water breaking over the rocks bordering our garden – the perfect atmosphere for ageing memories to flow back. Again, this is easier said than done; in truth, I would always be captive to an occupation that dominated my life.

There are many better qualified in putting pen to paper with their entertaining wit while remaining comfortable in their humility; at this early stage I'm not sure where I stand on this one. With these humble thoughts in mind and the constant maltreatment of my wife who bullied me into accepting this late challenge to write of past experiences, I knew it would be a difficult task to face up to, even more so should I tell the 'whole truth'. I suppose the only reason I accepted this challenge was in part my refusal to accept any awareness of passing years. Like friends and colleagues before me, I am well into the chapter of holding a pension book, so perhaps delaying acknowledging the truth was my denial of growing old, hoping to delay the inevitability of my retirement. Be that as it may, my physical condition remained good for my age – brain still functioning normally, my enthusiasm and energy have never faded. It was there for all to see. The problem now was that the phone had stopped ringing. Suzy was right – I had been rumbled ... What to do?

It would be easy to sit down in a comfortable armchair and reflect on days gone by, making notes or perhaps watching one of my old films on the telly, if only to lift my morale, my self-esteem. But this would inevitably depress me too, knowing that my work could have been better had it not been compromised by schedules which were more important for the director; at least I could improve the lighting in my head. I supposed I could also do a little gardening, which I really hate. More than likely I would just sit there dozing, waiting for the Grim Reaper to come calling. Obviously, my thinking was becoming negative, allowing depression to set in.

As a result, I decided to take a second glance at my colleagues' autobiographies – those directors and cinematographers with whom I had the pleasure to work. I had gained knowledge through these people's kindness when I pestered them for information – how they did this or why they did that – hoping not to become a pain in the bum! My options remained open about what I thought I should do, or perhaps what I should not do. There was a long way to go and I was still not confident about writing a book.

Slowly a more optimistic attitude grew within me and I felt positive about the challenge to join this well-known club of authors, but this was soon followed with disturbing negative feelings when I reminded myself of the famous names who had already and successfully taken up the challenge to write of their personal experiences; I doubted I could match their accomplishments. Again I was quickly reminded this was 'unhelpful' to the cause. I pressed on despite my concerns, while at the same time knowing that my attempt would produce much the same subject matter as other books, scripting the same theme but with different labels attached. Already I was convinced that my efforts would be a waste of time, and possibly less interesting anyway.

'That's not the point of this exercise!' Suzy whispered in my ear.

So now I considered being more controversial, writing kindly of those whom I respected and had the pleasure of working with, while others would be treated with the contempt they deserved – diplomatically, of course. In the end both would feature in my story, leaving me grateful for their part in my challenging career.

Here I should point out that it was never my style to sit back and say nothing when an honest opinion ought to be voiced, if necessary disagreeing with an egotistic authority and questioning his opinion. Silly me, thinking I would be safe with this approach! There were times when it would have been wiser – indeed safer – to remain silent when sensing disagreement, allowing others to dictate the conversation without reasonable discussion. However, this was not in my character and sometimes it resulted in people having a negative attitude towards me personally, but even at the time I knew that I would have hated myself for not voicing an honest opinion. I will come back to this later, along with the ensuing consequences.

After all the problems that came my way in this ever-changing industry, it was now time to look back on my small part and see how 'my scene' had played out in this special profession. If I am honest, my career seemed to come my way by chance. Later, I came to believe that things in life do not necessarily just happen by accident!

With my working days now over, I started to ask questions of myself – had I achieved all that I hoped and worked so hard for? On balance, I believe that I have, and happy I am to admit this, in spite of my failings – which I also intend to share with anyone who might be interested. My aim is to hold the reader's interest by telling my version of the truth, or at least as near to the facts as memory allows.

I was advised to keep my account of my personal life to a minimum, as readers would be more interested in my film work. While I believe this to be true, on thinking about it further, I decided that it would be dishonest to the reader if the real Alec Mills did not surface or was not even recognisable. I decided not to go along with that false image. 'I am what I am,' for better or worse, come what may. This personal account will be a private evaluation of both my life and career.

It was my good fortune that life pointed me to an industry which is so out of the ordinary, action packed and rewarding that after sixty years of working in the world of films I cannot recall a day when I did not look forward to going to work. In all probability, that is true for many who work in the British film industry. Fortune surely smiled on me in allowing me to progress with some of the great British and European cinematographers of my time, not forgetting those directors who played their part in influencing my work later on. From the age of 14 my career was completely dominated by these incredible people who were so generous in their support to this young fool, so if I claim some measure of success through idol-worship, then so be it! I would happily plead guilty to that.

The observations you will read come from a selection of personal experiences which over the years have given pain, joy, tears and laughter, all of which gave me much to reflect on as I wrote. More than likely some of the continuity will be awry but – with apologies to Eric Morecambe – I'm playing all the right notes, but not necessarily in the right order!

However, before my film career comes to dominate the book, there is a part of my history which can only be established in my own way: my early background, where I came from with recollections from my early years during the war. In a strange way these experiences would point me towards where my future would eventually take me. A humble life with a happy ending – a real fairy tale!

Should you decide to read on, you will learn how a foolish young boy ceased to exist the day his schooling came to an end, and all because of a woman going by the name of Lil. However, for you to understand this sequence of events in their proper context, I would ask your patience, with the need to go back to school, where my story really begins, and where to this day I still remember my teacher saying ...

THE EARLY YEARS

'Mills ... this is just awful ... really awful!'

Mr Lee, my long-suffering school teacher carefully studied my paper, occasionally changing his vision by taking off his spectacles to study my nervous state as I stood in front of his desk. He tapped his ruler on the small table in the way we students recognised as a bad omen and he followed the gesture with the predictable overstated deep sigh before returning to read the drivel in front of him – my 'composition', as it was called in those days.

He was right, of course; we both knew that. His comment simply underlined an attitude that I had to my early schooling in the years during the Second World War, now long past. It would be fair to say that under the teaching skills of Mr Lee my school days could be described as nothing short of disastrous. Now, seventy years later, I sit in front of the computer facing up to the reality of his teaching, hoping to reclaim past history which at times may well be embarrassing. I still remember the grin on his face, the nodding head suggesting that I was doomed to fail in life. At the time I would have agreed with his judgement; I was without doubt a terrible student. To complete the image I paint of my teacher, a veteran of the First World War, this sad human being had a dreadful habit of spitting into the coal fire that warmed the classroom, claiming this peculiarity to be the result of a gas attack during the conflict. I can offer no such excuse to salvage my lack of interest in his teachings.

The groundwork of my education continued to drag on with little expectation of achieving medals of any kind, either academic or on the sporting field – just another frail specimen of youth who struggled to keep up with other athletes at school. In my defence, this was partly due to bad attacks of asthma, most of which were blamed on the black and yellow smoke pouring out of the tall chimneys that spread their pollution across the capital, the main contributor to the famous London fogs. Even so, it cannot really be used as an excuse as I do not recall ever staying away from school because of my condition – Lil would make sure of that. Should I look for any excuse for my academic failings, I would point to Hitler's never-ending bombing of London and the changing of schools with different teachers due to the bomb damage, which I hope gives some explanation for the continual interruptions in my education. In all honesty, I should also admit to a certain lack of self-discipline. Whatever excuse I may offer, there was little continuity in my schooling during those dark days when living in the capital was dangerous, although for a youngster it could also be exciting. Now, of course, I regret those wasted years; I am what I am and the clock cannot be turned back.

Even so, images from those war-torn years would linger, and still remain in my memory. One recollection was of Lil with concern on her face as she put her comforting arms around me as the bombs of the nightly visits of the Luftwaffe fell around us. It is an unfading image of a loving mother which is perhaps difficult for the current generation to understand.

I was relating these experiences to Suzy, who threw down the gauntlet challenging me to mention these experiences in these memoirs.

'Did you tell Simon or Belinda about your war?' she asked, using my children to highlight my parental failings.

Strangely enough, I had never considered it. Suzy made an interesting point with that comment, so now it was necessary for me to think more about my offspring and give them something of my past history to remember me by, digging

deeper into the library of memories where I hoped something would remain from my early years. Faint they may be, but they are necessary, otherwise my story would make little sense. Bear with me ...

I remember little of my early childhood, apart from the occasional flashback triggered by a photograph in the family album. As a child I never had my own bedroom. I slept in the sitting room on a put-u-up, as they were called – a couch during the day opening out to a double bed at night. When I lay in bed everything seemed scary as I stared at the distorted shadows flickering on the ceiling, projected images from the paraffin oil heater that took the chill off the cold room – central heating did not exist in humble homes then – leaving cold, unpleasant memories. My

'England expects ...' Even in my early days it looks as if my mum and dad had me singled out as officer material.

Margate beach in the 1950s. This had always been a popular holiday resort for the Mills family and my parents would eventually retire to this town in the 1960s.

eyes scanned the dark surroundings for unwelcome ghosts who might be present, perhaps exaggerated by the crying wind coming through the poorly fitting windows. Pulling up the eiderdown, I would cover my face and I could at least take comfort from the hot-water bottle. It was frightening, but this is how things seem to a small boy.

Lil was a tailor's assistant in London's Savile Row, where her working life was spent making trousers for the wealthy. Mum took pride in her work and was pleased to be associated with the elite tailors, but with the passing of time her hands became arthritic and her tailoring days were no more. She was a mother who scrubbed the front stone doorstep once a week, suggesting the cleanliness of the inhabitants within – a habit not uncommon in those days. Luxuries were few and far between, but a certain dignity existed in working-class families. Alf, my dad, a porter and decorator by trade, came home from work on a Friday night and gave Mum her 'weekly allowance' to feed and clothe us, while I would be spoilt with a small bar of Cadbury's milk chocolate – a joy that has never left me.

My two older brothers, Alfie and John, were vaguely around. I say 'vaguely' with respect to them both, particularly Alfie. He died early, as a 16-year-old, having suffered the agony of infantile paralysis, which was not uncommon in those days. I remember little of Alfie, but what I do recall is the pain my parents went through when he passed away. Alfie was a much-loved son but due to his condition his legs were fitted with callipers (braces) so he could only walk with the aid of crutches.

I can only imagine how life was for this young man. Should his name come up in a casual conversation, you could be sure that tears would appear in Lil's eyes, even many years after his passing.

Yet, in spite of all the difficulties described, a highlight was the yearly ritual of going on holiday to Margate, where we would meet up with other family members to enjoy the wonders of the sea air. A daily ritual of hired deckchairs on the beach would take place as the family claimed our spot in a circle, warding off others from intruding on our territory. To complete this idyllic scene, loudspeakers on the sea front would play 'I Do Like to be Beside the Seaside' – such joy! With the sun slowly burning its way into flesh, handkerchiefs now suddenly appear with four corners tied in knots fitting snugly on heads to give added protection from the fierce rays, our red faces suggesting we had had a wonderful holiday. Images still remain of ladies' skirts pulled above the knees, their brown linen stockings allowed to roll down to their ankles – memories now long past ...

Strangely enough, I still have pictures in my mind of visiting my grandparents. Ted Hodgson was a giant of a man, who to a small boy appeared to rule his household with great authority. Their home was always impeccably clean and had a strong Dickensian atmosphere: a mantelpiece with a dark green pelmet covering a highly polished black-leaded fireplace, not forgetting the traditional aspidistra plant housed in a flowered china pot – a typical feature of the time. Gas mantles complete the image – electricity had yet to arrive in their house. Ted Hodgson was king in his castle, while my grandmother Mary, a sweet kindly lady, appeared to know her place; but, again, all this was seen through young eyes.

WAR AND PEACE

The year 1939 saw the outbreak of war, which to a 7-year-old would mean little. To be honest, I don't recall Lil or Alf being too concerned about it at the time; if they were, they certainly didn't show it. Anyway, I had my own problems to deal with in the daily ritual of going to school – war or no war, nothing would change that!

Family discussions about the conflict remained frequent, where Dad would tell of his involvement in the First World War. If pressed, he would tell his part in the Battle of the Somme, his memories of the dreadful conditions in the trenches. Regrettably,

I paid little attention to his wartime exploits, although it will be necessary to return to this sad history when I later discover more about my hero.

Home was a small ground-floor flat in a three-storey Victorian dwelling in Croxley Road, housing three families. The house had a small backyard with sheds for storing coal for the fires – the main source of heating in the home. In consultation with the other families, Alf built a small air-raid shelter in the yard which we could all squeeze into should it be necessary. Constructed of corrugated iron and concrete and fitted with basic wooden benches, the shelter would be strong enough to save our lives should the house be hit during the Blitz. As our family was housed on the ground floor we were also supplied with a Morrison shelter – an iron frame covering the bed with wire mesh to the sides – though everyone preferred to visit Alf's work of art in the backyard.

With the Luftwaffe losing the Battle of Britain to the Royal Air Force, Hitler decided to bomb London into submission at night, the only way the Luftwaffe could protect their bombers from the British fighter pilots. This was a strange and interesting episode, if seen through young eyes. With the radar system picking up the German aircraft crossing the English Channel, an air-raid siren would tell of an imminent attack on the capital, forewarning families to rush to Alf's safe haven. There we would all squeeze into the cramped shelter, soon to hear the pulsing sound of the German aircraft arriving above.

The bombers' arrival automatically brought a nervous silence; no one spoke as the bombs rained down, fingers crossed as one or two exploded nearby – another even closer! This may seem strange, but I don't recall ever being frightened by this: concerned possibly, interested certainly, but terrified – I don't think so. Everything seemed unreal ... A strange atmosphere now takes over as ladies silently pray under their breath, their moving lips betraying their inner thoughts; God's protection was needed now more than ever! One night their prayers failed when relatives living in nearby in Woodchester Street were killed in the bombing; their home was flattened by a German bomb. My cousin Brian was the only survivor from the devastation, and he would help me later with these recollections.

The bombing of London continued, and my ninth birthday present from Hitler was the heaviest night of destruction recorded on London. As the clock passed midnight, Lil led the way with a subdued verse of 'Happy Birthday': a weird moment as bombs fell around us. With the sound of aircraft moving away, the tension finally started to ease, the concern now was for others with all the destruction going on around us. I leave the rest to the imagination.

When the dreaded school day was over I would amuse myself playing around on an old upright piano which, believe me, had seen better days. While my attempt at playing was not serious, I quickly mastered 'Chopsticks', before the reality of the night bombers returned. Self-taught, I was soon able to play the popular tunes of the day, which somehow came easily to me. 'God's gift', Lil claimed, with this sudden talent emerging, and another sacrifice would be made for my piano lessons.

The selected tutor, Mr Braithwaite, was impressed with my playing by ear, but it would be a different matter when a sheet of music was placed in front of me. In spite of this, after a period of his expert tuition my never-say-die tutor was convinced that I should go the Royal Academy of Music in London and try for their junior exam. Lil was pleased that I did 'reasonably well', but with a changed music sheet put in front of me I was slow in transferring the challenge to the keyboard. To everyone's surprise – not least my own – I passed the exam, if not enough to win their 'plaudit of merit'.

Although this was an achievement, even with this so-called 'gift' I really wanted to give up the piano lessons, knowing that I was a 'tinkler' rather than a real pianist. Lil later came to accept the inevitable, realising it was a waste of time and money, though probably more noticeable was my lack of interest in becoming a musician. If truth be known, not at any time was my heart set on a music career and with a little nudge I was allowed to abandon that most unlikely idea. Perhaps in time I might have achieved Lil's ambition, but this young lad was not appreciative of the possibilities put his way.

Lil had not given up that easily. With the accolade of my achievement at the Royal Academy, she now planned her next overconfident move, this time without telling me what she had in mind. It was time to prove what her son could do on *Opportunity Knocks*, the famed talent show in the days before the *X Factor* or *Britain's Got Talent*, compered by Hughie Green. Auditions for those to take part in the show would be held at the London Palladium; it appeared that confirmation of my entry had already arrived in the post.

Lil's big day finally arrived. With the other young hopefuls – and their equally doting parents – we all stood in an orderly line in the wings of the vast London Palladium stage, waiting for our names to be called out. Parents prayed that their offspring would win a place on the show and I shook nervously in the background, thinking of the disaster which surely lies ahead.

At the time, Richard Addinsell's *Warsaw Concerto* was a popular piece which had captured the nation's imagination. In all humility, I suppose I played the concerto reasonably well, though apparently not as well as Anton Walbrook who in the film played a shell-shocked Polish pilot who also happened to be a famous pianist. I had practised hard to get the concerto as near to perfection as my tiny hands could stretch.

The routine was simple. When your name was called by the 'talent master' – an indistinct figure sitting in the shadows of the auditorium – you walked to centre stage, confirming your name and what you were going to do; then you got on with it without further ado. With over a hundred auditions to be held, limited time was allocated to each 'artiste': a singer might get an opportunity to prove their worth, a musician possibly got a little extra time to play his piece, while a comedian's 'jokes' would allow the poor talent master to cringe further into the shadows.

Slowly the queue moved forward as we watched the hopefuls performing their various talents to the talent master, whose sighs at the torment he was suffering were clearly audible before he yelled out, 'NEXT!' The obvious failure would then quietly exit stage right in tears as the next package of talent took centre stage and the ritual started over again, as the hopefuls indicated what particular gift they had to offer to the world of show business before proving it.

With Lil and her favourite musician at last reaching the front of the queue, the moment of truth had come. Carefully watching those who went before, Lil was convinced that the talent master would appreciate the value of this young artiste and would allow the concerto to be played without interruption. The moment Lil had been dreaming of finally arrived.

'ALEC MILLS!' the shadowy figure called out from the darkness.

With a squeeze of the hand for good luck, Lil eased my small reluctant frame forwards. I walked slowly to the centre of the enormous Palladium stage, where nervous tension now started to rise. Swallowing hard, I whispered my name before moving to the massive Steinway grand piano, dwarfing our old upright back home. Out there all alone where my feet barely managed to reach the pedals, and now feeling well below par, I quietly paused to compose myself (as rehearsed with Lil) as my clammy hands touched the keys ready to attack Addinsell's masterpiece. A deep breath and I was ready for the challenge ahead ...

Before I continue, I should first explain for those who are not familiar with the *Warsaw Concerto* that the music starts with heavy chords: twenty, possibly thirty, fortissimo chords.

My tiny hands struck the keys perfectly with the required passion. I suppose I had got as far as about the twentieth chord or so – certainly no more – when the talent master yelled out, 'NEXT!' with great gusto. Although this came as a relief to me, sadly the shock was too much for Lil to accept as there was no doubt in her mind, and mine, that the chords had been played immaculately. However, the decision had been made, and her darling son's musical career was cut brutally short simply because this silly 'tosser' didn't appreciate real talent – at least as Lil saw it. More embarrassment would follow when Lil crossed the stage to join me on the way to the nearest exit – the notorious stage right – pausing for a brief moment to give a cruel stare to the indistinct figure cowering from her in the shadows.

Now we turn away from the world of showbiz to the world where my interest really lay.

My passion for the cinema came early at the local church hall watching silent films of Charlie Chaplin, Buster Keaton, Laurel and Hardy and other comedians of that era. It was free and therefore acceptable for the family budget to cope with.

However, to visit a real cinema, to enter the sanctuary of the auditorium, required money and was a domestic luxury unaffordable in the Mills household.

Following my failure to become a musician, I decided to focus instead on other strategies that would enable me to enjoy the expense of an afternoon at the local fleapit along with my roguish pals. If we emptied our pockets, the few pennies collected would be enough to buy one ticket for a shilling to sit close to the screen. Entering the darkened hall, the holder of the precious permit would find a seat close to a side exit and, after five minutes or so, he would go to the toilet, which was usually situated by an exit door. Opening the door would allow the rest of the waiting criminals loitering outside to creep silently into the darkened auditorium, one at a time, suggesting that we had come from the toilet. This unlawful exercise usually worked well, but inevitably there came the time when the usherette's torch was pointed directly in my face, caught out for not being in possession of a ticket. My plea of losing the receipt failed to impress the lady and I was quickly shown the exit door – the same door by which I had entered; it would seem that I was on their wanted list!

The only reason I tell this sad account was because of one occasion when we went to the cinema on a Sunday afternoon, entering the hallowed hall in the usual rehearsed illegal manner. The film – a musical, I seem to recall – ran longer than usual, making it necessary for me to run home very fast. Perspiring like mad, I swallowed a quick cup of tea forced on me by Lil before dashing out to the local church of St Simon for Evensong, where one of my many labours was to sing in the church choir, earning money for my visits to the cinema. With the film having run late, I made the service with seconds to spare. Rushing into the vestry, with the help of the elderly choristers, I quickly put on my black cassock and white surplice, possibly wearing a tilted halo after cheating my way into the cinema. With the organ already playing, a Bible was thrust into my hands and it was time to adopt the customary slow pace on entering God's house. Mr Elliott, organist and choirmaster, cast a glance in my direction and was obviously displeased with my late arrival and flushed appearance. Even so, I quickly adopted the required angelic look for the measured walk to the choir's pews, where, along with the congregation, we sang our hearts out to the Almighty. But the Lord was not pleased with Alec this day, nor was this the first time I had been late for my religious duties, and now, finding myself further in debt on my account with Him, it was time for the reckoning; time to teach Alec a lesson.

The evening service usually ran for an hour or so but soon a call of nature would make the point that it had been a mistake to drink the tea Lil had forced on me. At first I was not too concerned about the problem: an hour was not long to control myself. But before long it was necessary to review the situation, which was now becoming desperate. Mr Elliott was already annoyed by my arriving late for the service – rightly so, as we were paid for singing in the choir – so with this in mind I decided not to disturb my fellow choristers, who would come to regret this decision. With the priest now well into his sermon and his attentive parishioners holding to his every word, I knew that if I climbed over the other members of the choir seated behind the cleric, the congregation would turn their attention to me. This was not school so I could not put my hand up and ask the vicar if I could go to the toilet without his sermon ending in disaster, but it was about to do so anyway as nature took its course.

With twenty minutes of the service remaining and no chance of easing my way past the choir, the hint of acid urine on clothes soon attracted the attention of my fellow choristers and the elderly vicar. The situation now turned into a Brian Rix farce, where the audience – sorry, congregation – were still unaware of what was going on as the unusual fragrance had yet to reach them. Sadly this was not so for the poor old vicar, who probably thought it could be emanating from himself. The elderly members in the choir, who most likely had similar problems in life, recognised this particular aroma and sat there, hoping it was not them relieving themselves, while others had no idea where this strange scent came from and quietly looked around to see who it could be. Eventually all looks turned in my direction, leaving my wretched life hanging in shreds. Fortunately, the choristers – bless them – reminded themselves where they were, so my assassination took place after the film – sorry, the service – was over; not that it mattered now – I would be dead when Alf heard about this!

At the conclusion of the service we walked back to the vestry, the pace possibly rather quicker than usual. Aware of my imminent demise, I rushed to the toilet and locked myself in, leaving the choir with bowed heads in final prayer to the Almighty. I too prayed, asking for divine forgiveness, protection and mercy. Then I made sure that everyone had left before leaving the sanctuary of the church.

Taking my cassock and surplice home to be washed, I had to face up to the anger of Alf, who found all this to be 'f***ing embarrassing' or, as Dad put to Lil, 'It's that f***ing film stuff he goes on abart!' How could I challenge Dad's wisdom – a true Cockney through and through! Speaking of my dad here, I write of a tough man who was quiet and polite in company but an entirely different animal as a soldier, which I will come back to later.

To bring this sad episode to an end: Mr Elliott decided that my services would no longer be required in the choir, so now it was necessary to find another source of income to help finance my legal visits to the cinema – which Alf kept on 'abart'!

The year 1945 would bring the end to the war, with street parties all over London. Croxley Road was no exception and I would be required to play all the popular tunes of the day on the piano: 'We'll Meet Again', 'She's my Lady Love', 'Lily of Laguna' – all Lil's favourites. Rationed food suddenly appeared on linen-covered tables and there was beer a-plenty. We also remembered those who had not survived, and some gave silent prayers for those who never came home, while others reflected on what could have happened had we failed. The high mix of emotions around the table is impossible to describe; the joy full of sadness even though we had won the war.

After the celebrations, my school days would also soon come to an end, leaving me with little idea of what I would do in the workplace. It is possible that I would have given way to the idea of being a musician, but even Lil had given up on that unlikely idea, perhaps realising that the answer was already planted in her son's dreams, even if he didn't recognise it. In the meantime, I would wait and see what came along – what life had planned for me ...

CARLTON HILL STUDIOS

I hesitated about giving this honest assessment of my early background. I was risking making a fool of myself. What would be the point? Perhaps it was a necessary part of life's journey that pointed me in the direction of my future. At the same time it is a personal responsibility to tell of the background from which I came, if only to keep the record straight. As you see, I have no problem with this and hope to continue this way for the rest of the book.

It was 1946: one year after the end of the war, when I finally reached the age of 14. My schooldays were over and now I was ready to join the world of the working man. Liberated from the disciplines of school life, I could earn a wage. Small it may have been, but at least it allowed me to visit the cinema without sneaking in through the back door. Those days had passed; I would pay from now on.

It was possible to stay on at school until the age of 15, should I have decided to, but there was little chance of that happening with this young man. My incarceration at Essendine School was over, I was out of jail. A pleased smile on the headmaster's face suggested he agreed enthusiastically with my decision; I knew we had something in common.

It is interesting – if not downright strange – that, with my love of the cinema, it had never occurred to me to be a part of it, in whatever capacity. However, it had not escaped Lil's attention that this industry had given me so much pleasure and, realising where my interest really lay, she decided to do something about it. Without telling me of her latest plan, Lil found a small film studio in Maida Vale, Carlton Hill Film Studios, where the manager, Mr Robert King, agreed to interview me. As I waited for this 'miracle' to happen, the inevitable lecture quickly came: 'Alec, this interview is very important. Now make sure you get this right!' The message was loud and clear; Lil knew well that I was a cheeky little bugger who could easily spoil my own chances of winning the position.

Hair combed, smartly dressed, sitting upright, I was on my very best behaviour as I sat opposite the studio manager in his office at 72a Carlton Hill. The interview appeared to go well as I worked at convincing Mr King that I would be an asset to the studio in any capacity he may offer – clapper boy, stills cameraman ... I showed him the Kodak Box Brownie camera I carried, hoping this would impress him. It didn't. We settled for tea boy!

Smiling, the kindly manager put his hand up, interrupting the obviously rehearsed chat I had practised with Lil. He was suitably impressed with my cheeky performance.

'You can start in three weeks; your wage will be one guinea per week.'

A fortune – twenty-one visits to the cinema, sitting in the front seats! To my relief – and Lil's – no questions were asked about academic qualifications; perhaps the gentleman had been thrown off guard by this small talkative lad. Even so, he

Carlton Hill Studios in 1947. Early memories of a 14-year-old tea boy and occasional clapper boy who had the audacity to ask if he could put the clapperboard in to see himself on the screen (front row first from left). Names I remember include George Bull (gaffer, third row second from right), Donald Wynn (smiling with moustache, fourth row third from left) and sound mixer Charlie Parkhouse, standing next to Donald Wynn.

made it clear that I would need to wait a little longer before I became a cameraman, or even part of a camera crew, although that would possibly come in time.

The weeks before I started work passed slowly, giving me time to consider what I would do when the big day arrived. The image in my mind was working on the studio stage with famous actors, directors shouting through a bull horn, 'Action! – Cut!', cameramen with caps back to front, a Charlie Chaplin image, of course.

When the big day finally arrived I found myself working in a department called 'filmstrips'. Filmstrips were strips of film used for educational purposes, to project images at venues where lectures were held for the government's Central Office of Information. Essentially, a series of photographs are transferred on to a 35mm negative via a rostrum camera from which positives are made, finally ending as projected images. This was definitely not what I had had in mind and far from what I had expected, but at least it was a beginning, where I would have the thrill of seeing real films being made, if only from distance. Eventually my patience would be rewarded, though it would be five long months before I finally arrived on a film set – a frustrating time for a 14-year-old lad desperately in need of becoming a tea boy! But at least the long journey had started. John Campbell, a school friend and fellow conspirator in the art of cheating ways into the cinema whose passion for films matched my own, asked me about vacancies at the studio; with my promotion to the film set the studio manger agreed to meet John.

At last my moment arrived; now came the start of a career which I would be totally committed to, and I believed this was life's plan for me on planet Earth. The first thing to do was to join the film technicians' trade union, the Association of Cine-Technicians (ACT). My membership number was 10578 – Brother Mills had arrived!

To repeat myself – which you will note I am prone to do – I was a small lad whom ladies described as 'that sweet little boy'. It was a terrible start: I was a man now, a fellow worker. Even so, I quickly realised that this 'sweet little boy' thing could be turned to my advantage and that perhaps going along with this awful outrage could be useful. One fast learns the need for friends in the film business.

In my new surroundings I was polite and courteous to everyone on the set; if asked, I would get the ladies' tea. Deep inside, though, something was starting to bother me. In my world of actors and technicians, not one had a cockney accent, which – to my shame – concerned me, giving me with a feeling of being left out in the cold, excluded from the circle of all these exciting people. Was this another mountain to climb? I now realise how stupid and ridiculous this was, but having grown up in a typical London family it was inevitable that I would have developed the cockney slang, along with its quips – inherited from Alf, of course. Although my accent was not particularly heavy, I was aware that a strong cockney manner could at times sound aggressive, even if softened with its traditional sense of humour. My problem was whether anyone would take me seriously.

Carlton Hill Studios in 1947, working on *Vengeance is Mine* using an old Vinten camera. Valentine Dyall was the star of the picture (seated in front of the camera), with cinematographer Jimmy Wilson (second row, first from left), George Bull (gaffer, second row second from left), Charlie Parkhouse (sound mixer, to the right of the lamp), Bill Oxley (camera operator) and the focus puller known as 'Mo' Pierrepoint because he had the same surname as the last British hangman.

Confirmation of this came when actresses moved from that 'sweet little boy' to 'that sweet little cockney boy'. Obviously I had to do something to sort out this personal problem. I would hate to be called a snob, which most certainly I am not, but at the time I foolishly believed that my tone of voice together with my cheeky cockney manner was not helpful to me or my career. So came the 'Rain in Spain' consciousness, where a slow transition would take place. With hand on heart, I can honestly say that this was a natural fine-tuning rather than a corrective phase. I knew that I would never completely lose my cockney accent.

Of course, there are many in the film industry with different tones of voice, but for me it was a question of being labelled as different from my colleagues – stupid, I know! One successful cockney in the public eye was the hairdresser Vidal Sassoon, who came from an East End background. Please make allowances for my bad memory, but I seem to recall Sassoon admitting to having elocution lessons in order to lose his cockney accent to help him achieve success in the world of hairdressing. Like the hairdresser, I recognised the hidden rules of life, the need to adapt and work hard to climb up the invisible ladder which – as you will read later – was difficult enough, anyway, while at the same time, quietly admitting that I couldn't afford elocution lessons. Alf would have killed me if I had asked his help in this.

Carlton Hill Studios started life as a church before its transformation into a small film studio. Here our lives were dedicated to making second feature films or short musical performances used as fill-in breaks between time-scheduled televisions programmes on the BBC. Viewers would be entertained with pretty chorus girls singing and dancing to pre-recorded playback music. This young tea boy gazed at them with mouth wide open, enjoying the moment as my dreams suffered in silence. Children's programmes would find Annette Mills playing the piano with her puppet friend Muffin the Mule dancing on top; commercial television had yet to arrive in the UK. As I write this I suddenly realise how old I am – so be it.

Carlton Hill in 1949. Another musical slot for television with a famous personality of the day playing the piano. This time Robert Ziller was cinematographer, George Bull (holding lamp) was once again the gaffer and 'Mo' Pierrepoint has moved up to camera operator. By this time I was now pulling focus.

On my graduation from tea boy to innocent clapper boy, like those before me I was required to do the shopping for the camera crew's needs or to do anything else asked of me. Nothing would stand in the way of my progress and I drank in without question or hesitation the traditions to which all newcomers to the camera department are exposed. It was my turn now.

Reading Ronald Neame's autobiography, *The Horse's Mouth*, it would seem that I graduated from the same school of innocence as that director, where we would always do what we were told, unquestioningly. He wrote in his book that as a young boy he was sent to get a 'sky hook', only to be passed on from one person to another until the rude awakening dawned that there was no such thing. Eventually the kindly cinematographer Jack Cox explained the joke to the innocent clapper boy. In Christopher Challis's wonderful autobiography, *Are they Really so Awful?*, he wrote of his early days as a junior assistant where he was sent shopping for the camera crew's needs, with no questions asked, and so the tradition would continue with me.

One errand which I was sent on came from a camera operator who, you will appreciate, remains anonymous. He gave me his list of 'requirements' for the local chemist. Off I went, not bothering to read his list ...

'What can I get you, sonny?' the tall lady asked, looking down at me from behind the counter.

That hurt, I'm a man now – a worker! Biting my lip, I gave her the list, which she read out.

'Aspirin ... tin of Vaseline ... throat pastilles ...' she looked at me '... DUREX?'

Her eyes fixed on me. 'Are they for you, sonny?' The discourtesy continued.

'Err ... no ... that's ... a mistake,' I said, biting my lip and pretending I did not know what they were. Quickly paying up, I made a hurried exit with the shopping list suddenly shortened.

Now a confirmed member of the 'Mug's Club', I was sent to the paint shop to collect a tube of 'anti-shadow paint', '... preferably grey, sir, if you have it.'

Apparently it was difficult to get hold of; with a smile on his face, the man sent me on my way as the tradition carried on. 'Try the art department, son, they may have some!'

From one department to another, I toured the studio before another kind soul came to my rescue, explaining the joys of humour. I was now on my way to manhood – wonderful, memorable days!

With the war now past history, film studios came alive with stories about the conflict. One of Carlton Hill's contributions was *Eyes that Kill*, which brings to mind a scene of Martin Bormann (the secretary of the Nazi Party) planning his escape to England hoping to set up a Fourth Reich – something ridiculous like that. Outside the studio a dense London fog was fast descending over the city; soon the yellow smog would creep its way into the studio before finally arriving on our set. The cinematographer, Ray Densham, decided he couldn't handle this any longer and suggested that we stop for the day – the usual practice on such occasions, which helped those who travelled home by bus or train. However, Ray's suggestion would not work this time. The director, Richard M. Grey, hearing his cinematographer's plea, decided to change the action in the script; the scene would now read, 'A German corporal enters the bunker informing Martin Bormann of a heavy fog creeping into the bunker: "Heil Hitler!"' To everyone's disbelief, filming would now continue with no one getting away early that night. Naturally, this juvenile nonentity thought it was a fantastic suggestion, and how clever it was of the director who wrote the screenplay in the first place to suddenly come up with this idea.

Truth be known, I would have happily gone on all night, fog or no fog, but on this occasion I thought it best to remain silent; it was definitely not the right time to rock the boat. Sadly, the cinematographer was unable to relish this wonderful opportunity as the director and I did!

Another 'masterpiece' was *A Gunman Escaped*, with the same Richard M. Grey directing. This time I would have the pleasure of working with a different cameraman, Cedric Williams, a highly respected cinematographer of the time.

Even when film production was at its peak, dark clouds started to form on the distant horizon, hints that we were heading for a serious recession which would hit the film industry; again something new for this teenager to experience – another part of growing up. Inevitably it encouraged the voices of gloom to be more vocal in their opinions that there would be little or no future for a film industry in Britain, their assertion based entirely on the advent of commercial television, which was then soon to appear in the UK. A sense of doom lingered in the background as the industry remained quiet; the naysayers started to grow louder, suggesting my dream world would soon come to an end. This was confirmed with the news that Carlton Hill Studios would soon close down, leaving many out of work as the recession slowly bit.

For the past three years I had felt secure at the friendly little studio where I experienced a taste of the good life, working with interesting people. Suddenly there was the reality of an industry in doubt with everyone confused about the future. All change! With no films in the so-called pipeline I expected to find myself out of work; the few connections gained at Carlton Hill would mean little now and I would disappear without trace.

I knew I would miss this pleasant studio and the wonderful memories as seen through young eyes. I hoped that one day I would meet the right people who would help me on the long journey ahead. It happened that there was such a person in Michael Reed, a tall camera assistant at the studio with whom I felt totally at ease. A patient colleague with strong principles and qualities I could only hope to match up to, he would play a key role in the progress of my career.

THE NAVY LARK

The year 1950 was a difficult one, with the film industry going through a period of change as it slowly evolved. What some see as terminal, others see as modernisation. With confusion dominating the atmosphere, everyone was unsure in which direction the industry would go.

In my short working life I had experienced wonderful moments where I enjoyed the sweet taste of the good life working in an industry which had changed me beyond all recognition. Was this to be my lot? Although little had been achieved so far, one thing was certain: whatever the future held, I would remain involved with photography one way or another. Life's script was placed before me at Carlton Hill Film Studios.

I had never experienced or even heard of a recession before, but it would seem that when times were bad the film industry would be among the first to suffer the consequences. Already I was hearing voices of doom expanding on their opinions about the state of the business, eventually reaching apocalyptic proportions. It happened that this disaster occurred when I was due for my conscription into one of the armed services, 'National Service', as it was called in those days. For some time after the war young men reaching the age of 18 would spend two years in the army, navy or air force – more often in the army.

I considered the past three years where much of my time had been spent in the studio darkroom, developing black and white negative tests for the cinematographer, followed by making a print on bromide paper to satisfy my cameraman that all was well with his lighting. Should the result offered not be to his satisfaction, I would be sent back to the darkroom to 'improve' his lighting by wiggling my hand in front of the enlarger lens, masking the areas which the cameraman thought he had over-lit; in effect I was cheating on his behalf! Finally satisfied with my efforts, the print would be offered to the director, now confident of his approval.

With all this darkroom skulduggery experience behind me, I could at least hope to serve my National Service in the navy's photographic branch, as others had before. However, I was told I had been misinformed and this was unlikely to happen unless I volunteered for a longer period of service. I was told that if I did so, with my past experience, I would almost certainly be accepted into my 'branch of choice', which made my decision easy.

Passing out photograph (1950).

With the so-called demise of the film industry I could see no alternative but to sign on in the Royal Navy – to be precise, the Fleet Air Arm – where on the given day I would report to HMS *Daedalus* at Lee-on-Solent with FX886962 Naval Airman Mills in full expectation of going into the 'branch of choice'.

They had lied!

The authorities were aware of my background in the film industry: I had made that very clear on my application form, if a little exaggeratedly. However, it seemed that this meant little now. What I had not realised was that few ratings get into the photographic branch even if they did volunteer; I certainly don't recall anyone suggesting that my chances would be slim. Suddenly I found myself being trained as an aircraft mechanic servicing aircraft.

After a short time I was posted to the aircraft carrier HMS *Illustrious*. The idea was to give new recruits a taste of life at sea on a floating runway where we would observe the expertise of the pilots practising their take-offs and landings, assisted by their experienced aircraft handlers, with whom I would be associated in time. In the meantime, my immediate task on board was to make sure everything was shipshape for the Captain's Rounds, where the officer of the day inspected the mess deck below, where ratings lived and slept in hammocks.

Below deck the conditions were awful: over-crowded and smoky. An old sea dog suggested that, if I wanted, I could sling my hammock up on the cable deck, which

I did with great relish, preferring the sweet fresh air to the smoky atmosphere below. It was summer with the weather remaining fine as I slept comfortably in my hammock as *Illustrious* cruised through the night in home waters.

This would be my first experience of a hammock, where I learned of an unsuspecting chill which could penetrate through the heavy material before carrying on into one's bladder. Should this happen, you would wake up the next morning to realise that you had urinated in your sleep, which of course is what happened now, making my life even more miserable than it already was. When I returned to the mess deck below, the old hand was waiting for me. He smiled at the sprog's (new rating) innocence, which obviously gave him much to delight in as he added one more victim to his list of idiots. It was Carlton Hill Studios all over again! How on earth did I get into this dreadful situation? Already I was counting the years.

With onboard training completed, I was posted to HMS *Peregrine* in Sussex, attached to 603 Squadron. Ratings on a ship (a camp is called a ship) are divided into four watches: Port 1, Port 2, Starboard 1 and Starboard 2; my watch was Port 2. I had experienced a relatively sheltered existence at Carlton Hill; I would suggest that my adult education really began now.

From time to time I found myself on Guard Watch, where six ratings slept in the guardhouse overnight and remained on call should disturbances take place in

Practising how to start the propeller of an aircraft manually without losing your arm.

FX886962 Naval
Airman Mills – Britain's
last line of defence ...

the local town of Littlehampton, which usually occurred when drunken ratings ended up fighting with the local residents. This duty was undertaken once a month (more or less), but it was possible to have a substitute take your place with a written request submitted to the duty officer; if signed by the substitute this would normally be granted.

Why, you may ask, would any idiot want to be a substitute to have a punch-up with drunken sailors? I can only suggest that the secret of this lies in naval history. There was a tradition in the navy of 'splicing the main brace', which I believe began in Lord Nelson's time when sailors were given a measured tumbler of rum celebrating victory at Trafalgar. As I hate rum or spirits of any kind, I could give my 'tot' away or collect sixpence every time rum was issued. With my shipmates aware that extra rum was available to them in return for a favour, there would always be a willing hand to replace me for my weekend duties, to take over my Guard Watch.

With my application granted, I could now go home for the weekend, far away from the madness of this self-inflicted navy lark. However, there were times when my request for a replacement would be denied and I was required to do my duty in the guardhouse – as I was one Saturday night ...

It was in the quiet early hours when the duty watch were hastily woken up and quickly dispatched into Littlehampton, a town where frustrated sailors went for a change of scenery – probably looking for girls – which inevitably ended in a fight. We sat sleepily in the back of the 'tilly van' (utility) resentful at being disturbed from our slumber, when the petty officer informed us why we had been woken up. It seemed that a rating had been arrested by the police for violent assault and put in a cell, so our job was to take him back to camp. He went on to describe the rating as a 'total nutcase' with the potential of being violent; we might need to restrain him. Following this report we quickly woke up, wondering what ape-like monster lay ahead. As I was the smallest in the patrol I could hardly see myself being useful if there was 'a bit of a do'.

There he was, our bruised monster, lying crumpled in the corner of the cell, black-and-blue from the fight he had been in, though more likely this came from the three coppers standing guard over him – they did not look too good either. Fortunately our man was too weak to give any trouble. This was the moment when I decided only a fruit case would volunteer for a life such as this!

Although I make light of my short service in the navy, there were times when events captured my interest, as it was when applications for weekend substitutes were denied for reasons unknown. Suddenly a strange sense of secrecy hung in the air. Reporting to the guardhouse of my latest posting back at Lee-on-Solent, the duty watch were suddenly informed of an 'invasion' taking place that night; a military exercise designed to check on HMS *Daedalus*'s defences, with the RAF regiment playing the role of the enemy.

Exercises like this were necessary, if only to find out where the camp's Achilles' heel may perhaps lie. The officer went on to explain that the RAF regiment were commandos who would treat this exercise as if their lives depended on it, reminding us that this was not a game. Facing up to this challenge would require both watches, Port 1 and Port 2 (roughly 200 officers and men) to remain on call ready to defend our 'ship'. We assembled in the canteen and the duty officer laid out his plan to outsmart the enemy.

'Gentlemen' – a rare compliment from an officer to the lower deck – 'we will scatter our men around the camp's perimeter; if the enemy are spotted whistles will be blown, showing which direction they are coming from. I am not anticipating any problems – any questions?'

None.

He continued, 'In the unlikely event of breaching our defences the enemy will stick yellow labels on the target, showing that it has been blown up.'

The plan seemed fair enough, with everyone convinced we could handle this if only by weight of numbers. No problem! My nominated position was to guard the hangar on the south side and defend its valuable residents.

It was a clear moonlit night and one could see almost as well as by daylight – a bad night for an invasion, I thought to myself. With the long night carrying on into the early hours, perhaps the regiment would consider this unhelpful to their war games. With this in mind, I retreated into the shadows of the hangar, where I planned my next leave with friends back home, my thoughts allowing me to wallow in self-pity with Carlton Hill still lingering in the background. My dreams of the past were soon interrupted by a new challenge.

It was around three in the morning when war broke out, with whistles suddenly coming from all directions, guaranteeing pandemonium. I remained alert, ready to defend my hangar if necessary. The battle plan seemed to be going well, with receding whistles suggesting that the enemy were being driven back by the overwhelming force of Port Watch ... when suddenly my attention was drawn to movement near the transport section where the petrol tankers were parked. Obviously we had fallen for the old five-card trick – an obvious lure, I thought to myself. I could now see legs moving around beneath the tankers as the regiment casually blew them up with their dangerous yellow labels. Could this, I wondered, be Naval Airman Mills's big moment?

With my rifle raised – I had a rifle, no bullets – I approached the enemy, carefully watching their movements under the tankers. Clearly they had not seen my approach in this strange game we were playing. Finally I cornered them; it was movie time!

'STICK 'EM UP!' I said, with great authority.

The two 6-foot-plus giants looked down at me, their camouflaged faces unable to disguise their anger at being caught out. Receiving no response, I repeated my challenge, perhaps a little more anxious in the voice this time. Still no response came, so I reasoned that they had a different script to the one I had, a thought reinforced by the action they took next. Pointing their bayonets in my direction, they slowly moved towards me. At first I could not be sure if they were surrendering or what, but they gave me a clue when they removed my rifle from my clammy hands. It would seem that any further discussion was clearly out the question so I legged it. The bastards cheated; after all, I could hardly say, 'Bang, bang! You're dead!'

Worse was to come when I reported back to the officer in charge, the author of our brilliant tactics, explaining I had been robbed of my rifle. For one brief moment he reminded me of my old school teacher Mr Lee with his salty reply!

With the war games over we found ourselves drinking hot cocoa with the 'enemy' in the NAAFI, where we would now find out from the referees how we had fared in the exercise. Needless to say, we were sunk out of sight time and time again with their dangerous yellow labels. The two towering giants returned my 'stolen' rifle, which could only make my embarrassment more public, adding even more reason for the 'pig' to scowl at me.

I should explain that the term 'pig' is a rating's word for an officer. I first learned this when the wardroom (officers) were playing a hockey match against the ratings. The 'pigs' arrived with only ten men, complaining they were at a disadvantage and would need someone to fill the position. Obviously they turned their attention to someone they considered officer material – me! Although I explained that I was not any good at the game, pointing out that was the reason why I was the linesman, they refused to listen to my feeble excuses. So now I found myself playing for the wardroom, a situation where I could not win, whatever the result: if the ratings won, my team had lost; if the officers won, I had betrayed my fellow ratings. My problem would quickly be resolved when the hard ball, travelling at speed, collided with my testicles! Lying on the grass in excruciating pain with blurred vision, the venom directed at me was reduced, if only for a brief moment. My shipmates had little sympathy to my crisis, preferring to laugh at my agony, until I was dragged to the side of the pitch to allow play to continue.

Here I should perhaps add that there was a tradition in the Royal Navy where ratings had to run across the quarterdeck (a small or large parade ground) while officers were allowed to walk. So now came a critical moment where this miserable human being from the lower deck approached this sacred area in excruciating pain. I could barely walk, let alone run, so my next challenge would come from the guardhouse on the other side of the holy ground which I was standing on.

Through my double vision I tried to attract the attention of the military police, waving my arm to seek their permission to drag myself across the hallowed ground. Of course I was ignored. I begged their understanding – their mercy – still with no helpful response coming to my aid. There would be no alternative but to take a chance and limp across the sanctum, holding my injured parts from rubbing against my legs. I suppose I had taken three or four steps, certainly no more, when the predictable scream rang out.

'THAT RATING, COME HERE AT THE DOUBLE! – I SAID DOUBLE!'

The military police screamed their abuse at me, forcing a slight increase in speed, which caused even more pain as I dragged myself across the danger zone. It was only after a medical report that I was told I would not be put on a charge.

DELIVERANCE

It was 1952. Two long years had passed, with everyone enjoying hot dry dusty summers, the humid conditions creating a stifling atmosphere which would bring on a strange attack of the asthma which I had believed had disappeared long ago in youth. I was on leave at the time, trying to control my breathing before going back to *Daedalus*. On my return to camp the doctor, seeing my condition, transferred me to Haslar Naval Hospital in Portsmouth, where I was given injections to calm the spasms. Checking my breathing, the doctor put a strange question to me: 'Take your time, Mills. Do you like being in the navy?'

It was an odd question, coming from an officer. I was not really sure where he was heading with this remark – 'pigs' were not to be trusted. Even so, the medic's enquiry had aroused the interest of the other patients in the ward, who eagerly awaited my reply as I struggled with my breathing to answer him. The stethoscope moved slowly across my chest and back; two fingers tapped my upper body. The wheezing was still there and certainly was not helpful as he waited patiently for my reply to his question. What could be behind this? I wanted to answer, but with the shortness of breath I found it difficult to speak. Every question demanded an answer, every answer used energy. I played it safe, nervous of the hidden repercussions. One last check would prove that the wheezing was still there, impossible to disguise. He paused ... a beaten man.

'Mills, I'm afraid you will not be in the navy much longer; we will be discharging you.'

At no time during my illness had I imagined that my services to the navy would no longer be required – not that I could find any fault with the doctor's assessment. On the medic's departure a confused mumbling came from the other patients in the ward. They eagerly gathered around my bed, and now for the first time I realised that they were trying to 'work their tickets', claiming to be unfit for service.

With little chance of any sleep, I lay in bed, planning the rebirth of my career in a film industry which had now recovered from its recession. It was a cycle which apparently happened from time to time – something new to learn from for the future.

Everything now moved fast. The navy could not get rid of me quickly enough. I was handed a demob suit and a train ticket, both parties were happy with our divorce. It was October 1952 when Naval Airman Mills became a civilian. It was a fresh beginning and I had new contacts to meet, hoping that this would be the resumption of a film career which would soon take off.

As I write, Wagner's *Tannhäuser* overture comes to mind, though I am not sure why. Perhaps the drama in the music echoes the moment for me.

It was necessary to pause and take stock with all that had happened over the past two years. My life had been put on hold until this miracle came to my rescue. Thinking about this later I would ask myself if this experience was a necessary part of my 'personal journey', but again only a higher authority would know the answer to that question.

My active chattering mind worked overtime as the reality of my absence from the filming community dawned. The few connections I had gained at Carlton Hill would mean little now. In all this excitement I was reminded that I was still a member of a trade union, which would help me find employment. With Carlton Hill no longer an option, I needed a fresh start where I would hope to meet new friends and make fresh contacts.

The opportunity to resurrect my career came more quickly than I could reasonably have expected. Suddenly I found myself working on a film already in production at Riverside Studios. While I cannot remember the name of the film, I would always keep in mind the name of the director – John Gilling. Perhaps my dreams were somewhat clouded in the mist of my return to the film world, where I still held an image of gentle filmmakers working with civilised people, a wonderful atmosphere with kind understanding people in support, as helpful as those gentle souls at Carlton Hill had been. Not so with Mr Gilling, a director who seemed to regard the clapper boy as the lowest form of life in the extreme, which quickly dispelled the joys of returning to 'my' film world. Be that as it may, I knew my place and paid due respect to the gentleman, even though I despised his manner to a humble camera assistant. However, all became clear when a colleague mentioned that our director was a retired naval officer, confirming a rating's impression of officers: 'Once a pig always a pig!' I was grateful that this man had no idea I had just been invalided out the service; or perhaps he did. Perhaps it would help if I saluted him in future. Although all this nonsense would be no more than a tiny drop in the ocean, a sad backdrop to human nature, it came as a timely reminder that the long journey ahead would not come easily for me – if the face doesn't fit ... In the end I put the attitude down to my own insecurity.

In contrast to all this, the cinematograpapher Harry Waxman was a kind and helpful gentleman who welcomed me as part of his team as I settled into my new surroundings. My good fortune would continue with Harry's offer to work with him on his next film, a genuine act of kindness which was much needed at that difficult time. Little did we know at the time that this would lead to a professional relationship which would continue long into the future. Now all my hopes and expectations would be placed in Harry's hands. With my career back on course, life was looking healthy once more – Harry would make sure of that!

For the next nine years my career would be under Harry's Waxman's controlling influence. He was a no-nonsense cameraman who insisted on his authority with everything I did, but his was also a name I would learn to respect: what Harry didn't know about cinematography would hardly be worth knowing anyway.

THE SLEEPING TIGER

With my happy return to the world of films I would hold on to my untarnished image of the beautiful industry with its wonderful atmosphere, though, if past experience had taught me anything, it was important – indeed necessary – to make friends with those who might show an interest in the development of my career – contacts! Harry Waxman would be the leader in this and pointed the way forward, if with a few hiccups on the way. To me everything about the film industry was exciting, both good and bad. I would even put up with the egotism of a self-opinionated ex-serviceman preferring to retain his rank in civilian life, knowing well that others could be waiting in the shadows if my face did not fit. This was not a question of bitterness, but a fact for us all.

So now it was time to meet the director of *The Sleeping Tiger*, Joseph Losey, who arrived from the United States as one of the many victims of Senator Joe McCarthy, the American politician who in the 1950s purged many in the entertainment world as communist sympathisers. Actors and directors alike were forced to take their talents to foreign shores.

My impression of our director was of a quiet, pleasant gentleman who appeared to go about his work with little fuss. He retained a personal dignity residing here in the UK, this England – this tranquil isle. I doubt that Joe Losey had met Harry Waxman before.

The Sleeping Tiger enjoyed the early signs of having a wonderful atmosphere, with Dirk Bogarde and the American actress Alexis Smith giving an impression reminiscent of my early Carlton Hill days; I would feel very much at home here. However, this would prove to be a false image when suddenly the joys of filming shattered my private world of dreams. It all stemmed from a misunderstanding between the director and cinematographer.

It started with Harry going to the toilet after a rehearsal and line-up; the set was now handed over to the cinematographer for lighting – a normal procedure on a film set. On Harry's return to the set, however, everything had changed, including the set-up, without any consideration of all the problems involved – for example, lamps had been moved in his absence. *Sleeping Tiger* would be an appropriate title. Without warning, Harry launched a verbal attack on Joe which seemed unending, his sudden outrage going seriously over the top for all to witness. With nowhere to hide, onlookers watched an embarrassing scene played out to its end, leaving both director and cinematographer just 'existing' with each other in an ice-cold atmosphere until the end of filming, with the director wisely deciding not to respond in the same manner.

Unfortunately, Harry was not in a forgiving mood that day and allowed the atmosphere to remain tense as everyone quietly melted into the background. The resulting silence hung in the air – a truly awkward scene for us all. In the aftermath of all this personal temperament, a cold atmosphere would now take over our filming, where one wrong word would leave a feeling of treading on glass for fear of suddenly reigniting the situation. It could never have happened at Carlton Hill; my beautiful dream world finally died.

I doubt that *The Sleeping Tiger* attained any critical acclaim for Joe Losey, even with Bogarde's and Smith's contributions – just another one of the many *film noir* psychological thrillers which came from the 1950s, but again, who was I to judge? I was just a silly clapper boy! Joe Losey went on to make other films in the UK, including *The Servant*, *The Go-Between* and *The Gypsy and the Gentleman*, which I worked on later, but, as you might expect, this time with a different cinematographer: Jack Hildyard BSC.

HARRY WAXMAN BSC

In the excitement of establishing myself as Harry's junior assistant I would soon learn why the cinematographer was highly respected. Harry was a knowledgeable cameraman who would willingly share his expertise with anyone who cared to ask; to this day I still remember listening to Harry on the phone, discussing a problem from an enquiring cameraman seeking his help. That tells the real story of the man I knew.

This was the 1950s. Cinematographers to some degree were still pioneering technicians, experimenting at times, motivated to accomplish something different within the camera itself, as with Gilbert Taylor's demonstration of the old Schüfftan process even as late as the seventies on *Macbeth* – which I describe later. Perhaps the same can be said of today's cinematographers experimenting with the current digital technology. This was Harry's gift; he was a teacher, a cinematographer who generously allowed me to take written notes while under his wing.

'Alec, if you don't ask why I do this or that you will learn nothing from me; look, listen and observe!'

Harry's comment would stay with me throughout my working life as his assistant, but I would also remember those nameless ones who were unwilling to share their expertise with me or anyone who cared to ask.

As Harry's keen student, it was necessary that I remain 'uncomfortable' with the 'guv'. He was the master of the foot-candle system, his preferred way of measuring light, which he considered more accurate than F or T stops. Digital light meters were not around in those days – now, of course, both systems are available at the flick of a switch. As a result of Harry's teachings and discipline I was happy to follow in the master's footsteps, carefully taking notes of his daily tutorials on the set.

Now confirmed as the cinematographer's loyal apprentice, I would soon be recognised as a regular member of Harry's crew. The cameraman's generosity in his teaching would be repaid by my undying loyalty when, over the following years, Harry's skills rubbed off on me; he would make sure of that. Should I become a cinematographer in time, I would gladly apply Harry's preferences, doing it his way. Never would I regret this – except on one occasion that comes up later, when I really let Harry down.

The other side of Harry's personality was his wonderful sense of humour, which he enjoyed sharing with his crew: Jimmy Bawden (camera operator), Paul Wilson (camera assistant) and yours truly now established as Harry's clapper boy – who still fetched the tea! In time Paul moved on to work with other cinematographers, giving me the opportunity to move up the ladder and become Harry's camera assistant – slowly, slowly moving forward ...

Although I shower praise on my champion, the problem of Harry's short temper, which first came to light on *The Sleeping Tiger*, would remain in the background. At the time I had thought that Harry's outburst with Joe Losey was a one-off, an unfortunate moment of folly which would never happen again. It was not, but even this problem could not change my loyalty to the guv, though it would be necessary to understand him and stay alert to his ever-changing moods.

For the record, I remained Harry's camera assistant for nine years from 1952 to 1961, working on productions including *The Sleeping Tiger, Father Brown, Lost, Contraband Spain, House of Secrets, Robbery Under Arms, Third Man on the Mountain* and finally *The Roman Spring of Mrs Stone*.

Fate dealt me a good hand when I met up with Harry Waxman BSC.

FATHER BROWN

Earlier, I mentioned the problem I had in writing of friends and colleagues, knowing that this would not always tally easily with the challenge of telling the truth – at least the truth as I see it. Writing an autobiography makes it necessary to camouflage an account here and there, so take what you will from this private account.

Pressing on and hoping not to cause offence, unlike the Losey affair, Harry's next film would be a pleasant experience, with Alec Guinness playing the title role of *Father Brown*, a kindly priest-cum-amateur sleuth. In the film, Father Brown tracks down Flambeau (Peter Finch), a well-to-do thief who stole a famous cross from the priest's church. It is a wonderful tale with an interesting script, the interplay between priest and thief becomes a challenge for the minister as he sets out to reform the criminal. Our location filming would take the unit to Paris and Cluny, a small wine-growing town hidden somewhere in the countryside. It was a taste of wonderful things to come. More important, Paris was my first experience of foreign

On location in France with *Father Brown* in 1954. Alec Guinness, leaning on an umbrella, plays the lead role of God's detective, discussing a scene with director Robert Hamer. I am the camera assistant standing behind the camera operator. The big lamp, known as an 'arc' lamp, housed carbon rods with negative and positive poles, creating an 'arc' of light when the lamp was switched on. The carbons had to be adjusted from time to time as they burned down, before they were eventually changed, a process that could take up to ten minutes per lamp.

travel, so it was necessary to further my education with a visit to the Folies Bergère, with my graduation taking place at the Moulin Rouge, where one could appreciate the female form.

With a happy relaxed atmosphere on the set I became interested in the director's role. I suddenly realised that I had an enquiring mind which had somehow been

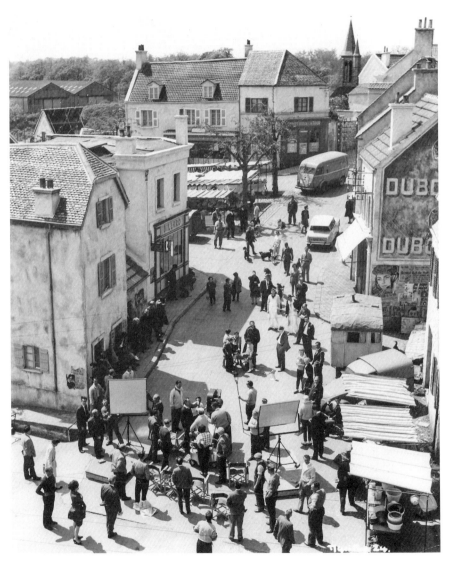

On *Father Brown* the bright French sun meant that very often a simple reflector would suffice to light the scene, with only a few reflectors being needed overall.

hidden during my schooling years; it would seem that I was becoming more inquisitive. This miracle came about while listening in to a low-key conversation between the director Robert Hamer and Alec Guinness, discussing the scene while the set was being lit.

Standing close to my camera, where the camera assistant normally exists – my domain – made it impossible not to eavesdrop on their discreet conversation. I became intrigued by the actor's reading of the scene, or – dare I say – his confusion. This humble nonentity had the impertinence to listen in and had a silent opinion of his own; they didn't ask and I didn't tell.

I listened and took note of the skills of good directing, where the director's authority faces the challenge of doubting actors. With Harry's advice to 'look, listen and observe', I found myself totally absorbed with the director's approach to what he required from the scene, his sensitive timing. The actors' concerns were politely listened to and then they found themselves playing the scene – more often than not in the director's preferred way. I believe this was when I first began to understand what made a good director: in part it is his relationship with actors and, if necessary, an ability to gently disarm the overconfident performer who had other ideas of how the scene should be played.

Of course, it goes deeper than that, but in the unlikely event that I would ever achieve status as a director I would probably model myself on a gentleman by the name of José Quintero, a director who in the future would make a big impression on me, as did Roman Polanski's directing of *The Tragedy of Macbeth*.

Alec Guinness, Joan Greenwood and Cecil Parker had no problems with Robert Hamer's ability, having worked with the director before during their Ealing Studio days; nor would Bernard Lee, Sid James or Peter Finch.

Harry was very excited about his next film, where he would be working with the Oscar-winning cinematographer Guy Green. Guy had won the award for his black-and-white cinematography (in those days there were separate prizes for colour and black-and-white films) on David Lean's *Great Expectations*. Other images by Guy which will stay long in British cinema history are *Oliver Twist, Captain Horatio Hornblower* and *The Way Ahead,* to name but a few.

Lost was the story of a baby who disappears from his pram, with Inspector Craig (David Farrar) setting out to find the child with few clues to go on; David Knight and Julia Arnall played the stricken parents while Thora Hird contributed to the drama.

Guy would be the director of *Lost*, with Harry Waxman his preferred cinematographer. It was a partnership which created much discussion within the filming community as two respected cinematographers would be working closely together. Harry sang loud in praise of Guy's work; he was excited about this new partnership. If truth be told, I could hardly wait to meet this highly respected gentleman: he had a reputation for being quiet and polite to all. At the same time, I wondered if I should be concerned about the different opinions that they might have – another *Sleeping Tiger* for Harry ...

Guy Green now arrived wearing a different hat and with different responsibilities resulting from the many pressures put on a director due to production demands, not least with scheduling. Directors are not alone in this problem: cinematographers also get tangled up in these situations when schedules start to slip, resulting in the sacrifice of creative art in favour of speed, which I suggest was the situation on *Lost*.

One day as we approached lunch Guy was clearly behind on the day's dreaded call sheet. The pressure was slowly building, with the director hoping to complete the sequence before the break in order to stay on schedule. Guy's unease was no help to Harry, who was feeling the pressure the director was putting on him. Past experience suggested that this rolling snowball was now fast approaching. With the clock ticking, the director's frustration was clear for all to see, as was his cinematographer's; his face was starting to redden – a sure sign from past experience that Harry was close to exploding and speaking his mind about all the pressure Guy was putting on him. Even so, Harry held his peace and I quietly prayed to myself, knowing that the scene could not possibly be completed before the lunch break. In spite of this the director tried once more, pleading to a fellow cinematographer.

'Harry, just light it, please!'

I closed my eyes, holding my breath as I listened to this sudden increase in the level of Guy's appeal. The set went quiet. It was as if all sound had been switched off as we waited on Harry's reaction. It had to come – this had not been a gentle tone from the Guy Green we all loved and respected. To be honest, Guy's remark was unfair to a fellow cinematographer who was doing his utmost to meet Guy's deadline; with my past experience of Harry and Joe Losey's encounter I waited nervously for Harry's likely response to Guy's unfortunate lack of tact.

Harry's face now moved from red to crimson, confirming my assessment that the volcano was close to erupting. However, this time the expected outburst would be different – controlled and extremely professional. The cinematographer looked at the director firmly, quietly reminding him that as a cinematographer at no time in his illustrious career did he 'just light' his artistes or his sets; with that we broke for lunch.

After that stand-off I was left speechless at Harry's discretion, unsure whether to praise his diplomacy or to be wounded at Guy's unwelcome proposal to a friend and colleague. I played it safe, calling it a draw. To his credit, Harry's wise control saved the incident from getting out of hand and prevented a cloud forming over his relationship with Guy, whom he truly respected. For the record, they did get on well together. No doubt Guy felt uncomfortable with his comment in the first place, undoubtedly sparked off by the insane pressures put on directors and cinematographers which can be difficult to accept. Again, one might ask, would the film suffer as a consequence of 'just lighting it'? Of course it would; my money would be on Harry this time.

Cinematographers are aware of their responsibilities and what the photography adds to the drama and how it helps the storyline. The 'look' of the film is discussed between director and cinematographer before filming takes place and if that look or other creative elements are sacrificed then the plan slowly starts to diminish. So now I wondered how I would react should a challenge be placed on me in that same manner. To be honest, I really did not know, but again there would always be something new to learn from in this dream world where I existed. No doubt time would tell ...

CONTRABAND SPAIN

Writing of concerns about directors and cinematographers brings to mind an uncomfortable situation when I once asked myself who was right and who was wrong.

As Harry's camera assistant I quickly recognised the good and the not-so-good side of his character. Perhaps his temper was a legacy from family genes, though in hindsight this problem possibly came from not understanding others' difficulties – it was usually the difficulties of those accountable for the daily call sheet schedules that were perennial hotbeds for the guv. The few words that Harry sparred with Guy would be a spit in the ocean.

Even so, my allegiance to Harry would remain steadfast whatever the cost; others would scoff at this but I believe my observations are fair and unbiased. From all I witnessed over the years, I feel that Harry was right in most situations which irritated him, but with his hidden frustration burning away inside he found it difficult to control his inner feelings, which could quickly turn to resentment, finally boiling over to anger in seconds. Should a repeated 'how long, Harry?' enquiry be made concerning the lighting time, a terse quick reply would come, resentful and irritated whether justified or not. This was soon followed by genuine regret at his initial reaction, which had probably been over the top, now too late to repair the damage. I could read Harry's mind when his behaviour suggested something was irritating him; others would hardly recognise the danger signals.

Contraband Spain was directed by Lawrence Huntington, with Richard Greene, the hero in the story, assisted by the pretty Anouk Aimée, going in pursuit of the smugglers and counterfeiters on the French–Spanish border responsible for his brother's murder.

With our filming completed in Spain, we travelled to Dover to complete our location work. As we were filming in the docks at night it soon became clear that things were not going well for Harry, with the tell-tale signs of his frustration giving cause for increasing alarm. The night of the long knives would soon be with us!

The first assistant director, Denis Johnson, was a big man in stature; he was a polite, friendly colleague, liked by everyone and could take the odd unpleasant remark from Harry in his stride without getting too upset. It was well into the early hours when Harry's latest crisis finally surfaced, certainly not helped by Denis's enquiry, 'How long, Harry?'

Unable to control his frustration any longer and troubled by the usual problem of an over-ambitious call sheet – Denis's call sheet – Harry finally snapped, verbally attacking the one person he held responsible for this unachievable schedule. Denis would now suffer the spite of Harry's tongue, which would prove to be a terrible mistake for Harry. The normally polite, calm and unassuming Denis suddenly turned on him, furious at the disrespect shown in front of the unit. He was not prepared to take any more of Harry's rudeness and the resulting embarrassing scene would play out to its end. In the aftermath of Denis calming down it was clear to all where the general sympathy would lie, leaving Harry to suffer in his own discomfort. Personally, I was shaken by the madness of it all, which made it impossible for me to defend Harry's latest outburst, but with dawn – the guilty party responsible for the latest scheduling crisis – breaking on the horizon, Harry's position was not a happy one.

There were many reasons why *Contraband Spain* would leave a bad taste in the mouth, most of which came from production demands with the scheduling, hence my reasoning about who was right and who was wrong. Other concerns would inevitably surface which I dare not go into, though there were times when the scene behind the camera was more interesting than the one we were filming. Temperaments are difficult to handle in a highly charged industry when you are constantly under pressure in one way or another, yet somehow we manage to survive, shrugging it off like water falling off a duck's back.

I was both surprised and disappointed when Harry went off to film *The Secret Tent* without his usual camera crew, but obviously he was embarrassed about all that had gone on before and needed time to get over it. With the sudden disappearance of my only contact I was left wondering if it would mean starting all over again.

Fortunately, this happened at a time when the film industry was busy, with opportunities to work on other films and meet up with new colleagues – names that I could add to my short list of contacts, which was always an important issue for me. However, on this occasion the number of new contacts would be extremely limited as I instead found myself on one of the many two-man camera crews working on John Huston's *Moby Dick* – a massive film by any scale.

Although my contribution would be small I would experience the rare opportunity of whale hunting, with stuntmen doubling for key actors, their sole intention being the killing of one whale in particular, given the name Moby Dick. Filming in a turbulent Irish Sea made handheld camera work extremely difficult if not virtually impossible to control; at times the only thing I could do would be to support the camera operator who had the near-impossible task of capturing the spearing of Herman Melville's legendary whale. Although the rough sea was of little help to the killing of Moby Dick it certainly made the sequence visually more interesting, with the waves battering our little boat as it pitched up and down. At least this offered a rare exciting experience of the chase, even if it was with an artificial whale.

Our tall sailing ship, Captain Ahab's *Pequod*, had restrictions on when she could or could not put to sea. Should the wind speed be above 10 knots the ship would remain in harbour as filming was not possible. Memories come to mind now of the gambling that took place on board. There were three card schools, the top school with the likes of John Huston, Gregory Peck and others all playing poker, wagering a small fortune. Moving along the deck one would find a school of moderation for the less wealthy, before finally coming down to the lowest form of life – camera crews with a top bet of two shillings, which probably suggested that you had a very good hand.

When my small effort was completed, it was followed by a trip to the Canary Islands, where I would join up with the main unit who were already filming there, and my first experience as part of Oswald Morris's camera crew.

As for the film, I loved it – simply brilliant, even if that is to disagree with the odd biased commentator who for reasons of their own could not shower praise on this masterpiece. *Moby Dick* was a classic of its time: an ambitious, challenging epic with wonderful performances enhanced with Oswald Morris's cinematography. The film was loaded with well-known names and played to full houses wherever it was shown. Gregory Peck's Captain Ahab was a man determined to kill Moby Dick whatever the consequences, in a personal vendetta after losing his leg in a previous encounter with the great white whale. With Richard Basehart, Leo Genn, James Robertson Justice, Harry Andrews and Bernard Miles, the cast goes on and on with this memorable movie.

The phone rang! It would seem that Harry Waxman was back in town, asking me to meet him at Pinewood Studios. Apparently *Contraband Spain* was now past history, conveniently forgotten with the passing of time, and still no explanation as to why I had been dumped in the first place. I thought it best not to ask and just act as if nothing had happened. Even so, Harry was clearly embarrassed by that unfortunate incident – could this be a new dawn breaking with the guv?

All of the madness had come from trying to meet what Harry considered an impossible schedule at the expense of the quality of his work. It was a compromise which Harry always struggled with but now left me wondering where his next challenge would come from.

Once again Harry would team up with Guy Green for *House of Secrets*, in a period where films could now be made in a number of different formats. Hollywood's CinemaScope system was clearly ahead in this race but soon competition would arrive with the new VistaVision process favoured by the Rank Organisation; with our interiors being filmed at Rank's Pinewood Studios this guaranteed VistaVision getting the nod for the film – one of the first British films to use this new process.

To reduce the noise of the camera motor, VistaVision cameras were housed in large cumbersome blimps – nearly impossible tools to work with. The poor camera operator almost needed an extension implant in his neck just to operate this ridiculous tool. However, that problem would quickly be resolved with a periscope viewfinder which was hurriedly designed to ease the camera operator's pain.

On location in France filming *House of Secrets* (1956). Guy Green directs at right (crouching forward), with actor Michael Craig in the light overcoat standing behind Guy. Jimmy Bawden was camera operator with cinematographer Harry Waxman standing to the left of the camera. Other recognisable technicians include continuity lady Tilly Day (silver hair, wearing sunglasses) and Bob Asher, the first assistant director, standing with hand on his hip, while I crouch beneath the Vistavision camera. My personal moment from hell came on this picture, where I was responsible for an entire day's filming being ruined.

The film ran through the camera gate from side to side (each frame now eight perforations long instead of the usual four), which would present new challenges for the camera assistants, and, as with all new equipment, other problems would inevitably surface.

Harry Waxman, who always enjoyed the challenge of technical debate, disagreed with Guy regarding the size of close-ups in this new format. I tuned in to this interesting discussion as two respected cinematographers offered differing opinions. Sitting on the fence, I could see both points of view, though in the end silently favoured Guy's visual explanation over Harry's theoretical one; the camera operator would compose the framing to the director's liking.

Our filming started in Paris, where the first scene required the camera to hang over the edge of the first stage of the Eiffel Tower. The thought of this new and expensive piece of equipment falling from that height was really terrifying, particularly as the cost of the camera alone was rumoured to be in excess of seven hundred thousand pounds. With all the security ropes which the cautious grip used in tying it down, the camera operator could barely get near the camera, but this was understandable and we were all very paranoid when using this new, very expensive, equipment before returning it to ground level.

I promised earlier that my story would remain as honest as memory allows. With this in mind I am now obliged to tell of a sickening incident where there is no disguising what really happened. In short, I was responsible for ruining an entire day's filming. My feeble excuse was to put the blame on the new VistaVision camera – it was a different monster from a camera assistant's point of view – but even that pathetic explanation could not be a defence when you consider how the problem could have been prevented. It is necessary that I mention this horrible incident, which still haunts me even in retirement; it requires as honest an explanation as possible.

We were filming in the departure lounge of Le Bourget Airport; the same lens had remained on the camera throughout the entire day of filming. Behind the lens the 85 gelatine filter was sitting comfortably inside the camera; the filter was safe and well protected so there would be no reason to touch it again throughout the day.

My excuse: at the time, gelatine filters were regarded as expensive items, with camera assistants at Pinewood encouraged to be economical with them, which is exactly what this diligent assistant was doing by cutting the filter to cover the gate's aperture before sealing it down with Sellotape to prevent the filter from moving.

The day's filming went smoothly, with Harry grateful for a sensible schedule to meet, as was Guy – who successfully completed his call sheet that day with everything appearing to be well. However, in the process of breaking down the camera, I removed the lens to discover – to my horror– that the gelatine filter had moved and now covered only half of the camera gate aperture! One could not imagine a worse disaster for a camera assistant – truly shock-horror time. I froze in total disbelief at what faced me as we had been filming like this all day. Presumably the filter had become dislodged when first inserted into the camera, so one thing was certain: I had not checked the filter through the lens port when it had been inserted. It was a simple, basic elementary requirement and clearly an inexcusable mistake for Harry's so-called diligent camera assistant to make, but also one I could not hide from!

So came the moment of truth. A feeling of being alone, out in the cold, total anxiety, happy to die there and then, preferably while listening to Mozart's Requiem to help me on my way. With no music, I needed to face up to the consequences. With no defence to offer, I straight away explained to Harry what had happened, admitting my mistake in forgetting the obvious routine check, knowing well that

The Gypsy and the Gentleman (1958). From left to right: Patrick McGoohan and Melina Mercouri on the horse, with Keith Michell in the white shirt holding her hand. I was focus assistant, with Jimmy Bawden operating the camera; cinematographer Jack Hildyard stands behind the camera with director Joe Losey.

The unit poses on a stage at Pinewood Studios in front of a painting of the German pocket battleship *Admiral Graf Spee* for the end-of-picture unit still on *Battle of the River Plate* (1956), where the lowest form of life sits in the front row clinging on to his trusty clapperboard. Cinematographer Chris Challis stands in front of the ship with director Michael Powell seated behind me. I think the woman on my right is the continuity lady Bette Harley.

he would remind me of that responsibility. Now I expected the worst to happen, with Harry's loud opinion of me echoing around the airport as I fully anticipated being fired.

However, my expectations were not met by the reality. To my surprise, Harry was calm, in total self-control. Quietly he spoke to me, making sure he understood how this had occurred, though still doubting that I could make such a silly mistake as this. It was as if Harry was looking for a way to divert the blame. Was the guv trying to protect me? If so, I was not helping by admitting it was my mistake.

After accepting the situation, Harry walked over to Guy, who was now some distance away enjoying the day's successful shoot, chatting with artistes while I waited nervously by my camera, where soon I would learn of my expected fate. Watching the expressions on their faces from a distance, I could only imagine what the two were talking about, with the obvious repercussions which would surely follow from this terrible disaster. Although I could not hear their words, their faces clearly suggested that my career was about to end. A lifetime seemed to pass before Guy walked over to me with Harry a few steps behind. He looked directly at me and put a reassuring hand on my shoulder.

'Alec ... Don't worry about this; sometimes these things happen.' He smiled. 'We will try to catch up tomorrow!'

To this day, even as I write of this episode many years later, tears comes to my eyes as I think back to Guy's compassion towards a junior assistant, his understanding of my pain when he probably had other ideas as to what he would really like to do to me. I would understand that, but that was not Guy Green's way. Perhaps it was Harry and Guy's understanding of a tricky situation and their sympathy for a junior assistant who had made an elementary mistake that did not allow him to end up as the sacrificial lamb.

It is necessary that I include this item in my career history – a narrow escape not forgotten. Even so, it could not end there; at the appropriate time, out of earshot, Harry would let me know what he really thought of my lack of diligence and of course I would have expected no less from the guv! Although this tragedy would haunt me through the years I would surely learn from that experience;

On location in Canada in 1957, while filming *High Tide at Noon*, directed by Philip Leacock with Eric Cross as the cinematographer.

mistakes would never happen again through my lack of concentration. Yet with all that happened, whether it was fate or good fortune, luck or Divine intervention, whatever excuse I may offer, a trump card came to my rescue.

The next morning we were scheduled to film exteriors alongside the aircraft on the tarmac. It was raining hard with the forecast expecting the conditions to persist all day, making exteriors no longer possible. Guy quickly decided to move back into the departure lounge and retake the previous day's work, which allowed me to believe that it was only the price of film stock wasted – a poor excuse, I know, but at the time I needed to believe this. However, the mental charge I placed on myself would be far greater. As you see, it still haunts me to this day. I'm truly sorry Guy ... Harry ... I let you both down!

House of Secrets was a story of counterfeiting with spying set in Paris. A cruel press called the film a 'box-officer sleeper', with the director described as 'one of David Lean's cinematographers'. Michael Craig played the role of the hero, with support coming from Anton Diffring, Gerrard Oury, Geoffrey Keen, Brenda De Banzie and David Kossoff, all well-known names from a past era. However, my heroes were Harry and Guy, who I truly believe saved my career.

It was necessary to pause and think twice before writing this next chapter of my life, particularly after my admission of guilt, which inevitably brings the challenge to be more open with my 'private journey'. I am what I am, a human being who made a mistake, but we all make mistakes from which we learn, accept the experience and move on. I have promised to be honest and clear in my writing and so it now becomes necessary for me to revisit the past and tell of a personal experience that some will surely scoff at, while others who have experienced similar events would prefer to remain silent.

Flashback: our lives are a series of events. One thing that came from the hostilities of war and the bombing of London was a sense of togetherness, a bonding of neighbours and friends sharing their concerns with each other during those dark days. Should a neighbour pass you in the street, you would get a smile or a nod of recognition, a friendly gesture before night fell, when the German bombers would return to do their worst.

With this in mind, let me tell of a polite old gentleman, easily recognisable, bent over his walking stick as he shuffled along the pavement. Although we never knew his name, this kindly man always turned his head and smiled in acknowledgement as he went on his way. Ten years had passed since the war had come to an end; life had returned to normal and the old man was still living nearby, close to a skeleton church which had been destroyed by incendiary bombs during the Blitz.

Although visits to the cinema were principally for entertainment, for me they were also a source of learning; to some extent they were my private film school. Sharing in this dream world my girlfriend Lesley would join me on visits to the cinema, or we might go dancing or to other leisure pursuits with friends. Slowly we were becoming creatures of habit – wonderful days of youth. With the entertainment over, we would end the evening at our favourite spot to continue our courting, parking the car outside the same burnt-out church; the ruined building was close to both our homes. As you would imagine, in the early hours there would be no one around in these quiet peaceful surroundings – the perfect setting for romance while others slept in their warm beds.

One night we came out of the dance hall to find it was snowing hard. With conditions deteriorating fast, we drove slowly back to 'our' church. Even with no let-up from the snowstorm, I was still determined that nothing would deter me from the wicked intentions I had planned that night. Later Lesley reminded me this was wishful thinking on my part, which was probably true – I am a dreamer, after all! The falling snow and soft music coming from the car radio helped to create the perfect romantic scene, and I occasionally cleared the windscreen with the wipers to enjoy the beautiful picture painted before us. With the heat on full and aided by the passion within, the windows quickly steamed up, the extreme conditions making sure of that. It was in this relaxed state that we cuddled up to each other; now time to make my move.

We were in a close embrace, with Lesley looking over my shoulder, when she gasped and quickly pulled back – I hadn't touched her yet – claiming she had seen a face peering through the steamed-up window behind me. I quickly turned to see the peeping Tom, and we both immediately recognised the face of the kindly old man with the stoop before it quickly withdrew from the window. My first reaction was to get out of the car and confront him, but Lesley was unhappy about me leaving her alone. Putting the headlights on would not help the situation as the face had disappeared without trace, leaving a silent, empty street, with only the pulsing sound of the beating wipers clearing the snow from the windscreen, much slower than our racing heartbeats. A total mystery ...

Could all this be in our imagination? Absolutely not! Both Lesley and I agreed that the face we saw that night was of our stooped neighbour, the same old man who used to totter up the street, who had died a few weeks earlier. It is true that we did not immediately think of the poor soul's passing as he gazed through the window, but with both of us recognising the face it put paid to the plans I had had that night. Needless to say, there would be no more 'threesomes' outside that church. Leaving the scene as quickly as possible, we left the spirit to do his haunting by himself.

I have no intention of going into what or who we saw through the car window that night, but in that short time I sensed a troubled, lost expression on his face. This happened so fleetingly that one might question how we could take all this in. I don't know; I cannot answer that. These were our feelings at that moment and to this day neither Lesley nor I would change our minds on this matter.

I questioned whether I should mention this experience in these memoirs, knowing the reaction of doubters on such matters, but with Lesley also seeing the apparition before us we can both bear witness to the moment. Whether Lesley sensed that 'lost' look on the old man's face is not something I recall talking about; even so, this incident should be recorded because it really happened. It was some years later that I watched a television programme about the paranormal where Arthur C. Clarke, the well-known science fiction author, claimed that it was rare for two people to see a ghost at the same time. Well, Arthur, Lesley and I did, and both of us would swear to it happening; as for me, the experience would leave many questions unanswered about the afterlife – if there is such a thing.

I accept that many will find this subject difficult to understand, particularly with reference to the afterlife, but as with all strange events they fade over time, sometimes to the point where you end up doubting your own sanity. This might also have been doubted when I volunteered for the navy, as I stubbornly refused to listen to good counsel when advised to think twice about my decision – no chance, with my obstinate personality! Could this be a peculiarity in my character, shaping my fate? Whatever the deal was, in the future I would keep an open mind on unexplained events that made little sense, and I would be reunited with Harry Waxman – or could it be that I was 'destined' to work with him? It would seem that we were fated to share a part of the long journey together.

Harry's next challenge, *Robbery Under Arms*, brings back memories courtesy of the Rank Organisation, which had decided to send their camera crews around the world – genuine locations for reality, we were told. The film industry was entering

The Hotel Augusta. We stayed in this dump overnight, where the rowdy ranchers got drunk, boasting to see who could drink more and stay upright. I didn't get much sleep, trying to keep track of the huge spiders in my room. The next day we headed for the outback, where the accommodation was even more basic.

exciting times and Harry and crew were flying off to Australia. The long flight to Down Under would find us stopping off at many countries along the way before finally reaching Darwin, where we first experienced the big change in temperature. Our next stop was Alice Springs in the heart of Australia, where the humidity becomes even higher. On opening the cabin door a buzzing black cloud entered our temporary habitat as billions of flies moved in to explore our transitory home. The excitement of visiting Australia was fast losing its appeal and there was one more stop still to come before we reached our destination.

Close to the Flinders mountain ranges, Port Augusta was then a small town in South Australia, where one was reminded of a small settlement as portrayed in American cowboy films. I stayed overnight in what was laughingly called a hotel due to the fact that it had one bedroom available for a weary traveller passing that way. The small box room had a high ceiling with all four corners housing large cobwebs probably spun over many years; the well-entrenched spiders probably resented my presence. The rowdy Aussies in the saloon bar next to my room did not help matters, with their boisterous challenges to see who could stay on their feet the longest.

The next day we moved to our final destination, where our tenancy resembled an old rundown holiday camp. The local Aboriginals had managed to tidy up it before our arrival, though it was still obvious that the place had not been used for some time. Suddenly, we found ourselves trapped in the middle of nowhere for the next six weeks, with little to do after a day's filming; our isolation was complete. The excitement of foreign travel and the glamour of filming were fast losing their appeal as we sweated in the daytime heat in the unpleasant surroundings. Should any comfort come from all this it was that *Robbery* had taken me to the other side of the world, even if it aroused little desire to return to this vast continent.

With nothing to do after the day's filming, Bert Batt, the assistant director, attempted to relieve the monotony by tinkling on a dusty old upright piano which had seen better days. I would try to help Bert out, suffering its dreadful tone – not helped with the odd key missing here and there – but at least the unit appreciated

While filming on *Robbery Under Arms* one of our Aboriginal trackers who knew how to handle a bullwhip boasted that he could remove the cigarette from my mouth without touching me – even though I didn't smoke. I was shaking like a leaf but fortunately it was no idle boast. Not surprisingly, I kept my eyes shut!

these attempts to break up the boredom with a little light entertainment. Harry, for reasons known only to him, appeared to resent these social activities; recognising the signs, I decided to pull back from helping Bert. It seemed that the endless heat was having a strange effect on Harry's frame of mind, somehow affecting his attitude. Every day I would learn something new about the guv – some good, some bad – but nothing would change my attitude towards him.

Although set in Australia, *Robbery Under Arms* was an interesting story similar to the early American cowboy films with armed gangs holding up stagecoaches. Peter Finch enjoyed the lead role of Captain Starlight, the gentleman cattle rustler/ bank robber; the supporting cowboys were Ronald Lewis, Laurence Naismith and David McCallum, not forgetting the pretty Jill Ireland and Maureen Swanson, all under the baton of director Jack Lee.

The director's homework had probably been based on American cowboy films, one of which may have been *Stagecoach* with John Wayne. I mention *Stagecoach* as the film features a well-known scene with a carriage pulled by four horses galloping hard to outrun a hold-up, probably helped with a little under-cranking with the camera, seen from the coach driver's point of view. Our film also required

One of our more reliable vehicles in the Australian bush, and a perfect opportunity for the Keystone Camera Crew to pose for an unusual unit still.

From left to right: the grip, Ronnie Anscombe (clapper loader) with me seated beneath the parasol on the camera dolly. Harry Waxman leans in the background, wearing the checked shirt.

a four-horse coach to evade the hold-ups featured in the story. Although action scenes like this are exciting to watch – sweating horses with a swaying coach, noise and dust adding to the drama – they can be dangerous to film and so inevitably take time to organise and set up, usually ending as a second-unit sequence. However, our director decided that we would recreate this drama ourselves for his robbery, without a second unit ...

Perhaps I should briefly explain the term 'second unit', which usually works with doubles for the action sequences which take time and money with its preparation. These technicians are experts in their own field and their work usually fits seamlessly into the scenes already filmed by the first unit – or vice versa.

Our stagecoach was loaned from a museum and had the usual handrail on top where luggage would normally be stowed. This was to be my position, from where I could support the camera operator Jimmy Bawden, who was safely strapped down next to the driver. With Jimmy in position, I put one reassuring arm around his waist to give extra support – for him and for me – while at the same time my other hand held on to the luggage rack to aid my own security.

Off we went with everything going well for a minute or so, when suddenly the swaying movement of the coach started to increase. No longer was it possible to support Jimmy, whom I knew was safely strapped to his seat; it was now time to think more about my own survival. Our filming suddenly bordered on madness as I was paralysed, unable to move, holding on to anything available. All the time I

In spite of our isolated position, the sparks still had to manhandle the customary lights to the filming location – no easy task in the Australian bush.

The Flinders Mountains gave *Robbery Under Arms* a totally authentic look and feel, exactly as the Rank Organisation producers had wanted.

retained my faith in the driver's skills, his expertise – none of which appeared to be forthcoming – and still no signal yet to abandon ship!

Unknown to Jimmy or me, the director was standing on the back of the coach, screaming at the driver to go 'faster, faster!' Unhappy with all the madness, the poor man still did his best to push the horses to the limit, which it seems was not enough to satisfy our director. Eventually a loud gunshot came from the rear of the coach, making the horses bolt, producing a state of shock in our traumatised driver, who was now screaming.

'They're out of control; I can't stop them!' Apparently it was every man for himself time!

With Jimmy strapped to the seat and me just about hanging on to the swaying coach, there was little chance of anyone being able to jump off; we were frozen to our positions with no intention of breaking our necks – we had to accept our fates. This frightening experience finally came to an end when one of the rear horses in the team fell, so putting a brake on the other three; later it was revealed that the two lead horses were galloping animals and had never been used in teamwork.

A real-life drama would now play out with Harry Waxman – BSC and animal lover – now offering his opinion on all this. Within seconds of the stagecoach coming to a halt my champion could barely contain himself; with steam coming out of ears, he rushed over to Jack Lee, who now got a dose of the well-known Waxman treatment: *Contraband Spain* take two! Visibly shaking from all this, Harry confirmed that 'someone' had fired a gun, making the horses bolt – yet another dangerous self-inflicted incident to record in a camera crew's experience. However, the real tragedy of all this nonsense came with the final editing of the film, where the scene of galloping horses that I remember so well was cut from the film.

Another Harry 'moment' came when the unit carried the heavy equipment with all the necessary paraphernalia to film a scene at the summit of a steep rock-strewn hill. In the heat of the midday sun this was no small effort on everyone's part, including the make-up department, who struggled up the hill carrying their make-up bags, chairs and umbrellas – apparently necessary protection from the burning sun for artistes. With more sweat called for, Harry asked for Vaseline. Looking into the make-up department's bags, it would seem that they had forgotten to bring it with them as it was not really seen as a priority. Although words failed Jack Lee, the same cannot be said of my hero. I think it best to leave it there. Life could never be dull working with Harry Waxman.

The Internet Movie Database, better known to those in the industry as the IMDb, makes interesting reading in praise of the film: 'Many of Britain's top players and technicians travelled half-way across the world to film this Australian classic of daring adventure in its authentic locales. The result is an outdoor film of rare sweep and power which stirringly and convincingly recreates the roaring pioneer days where life was lived close to nature.'

At least this would have put a smile on Harry's face.

THIRD MAN ON THE MOUNTAIN

The name Harry Waxman comes from my early years in the film industry; in today's film world the name is hardly known or remembered. Even so I write here of a cinematographer who would not – could not – accept anything less than his own professional benchmark, which in hindsight is a discipline he made sure I understood. Harry's commitment to his work was one of total dedication, an

The Third Man on the Mountain (1959). Filming in the Swiss mountains without the luxury of a camera truck meant using a variety of logistical techniques to transport the equipment to the shooting location. The mountain in the background is the Matterhorn.

obsession which at times could go too far. Be that as it may, I still respected the guv, even understanding his fiery moments. The harmony we shared would be instrumental in the forming of my own career, not forgetting how I failed him on *House of Secrets*. Later, as a cinematographer, I would understand why certain issues drive a cameraman to frustration, though in my case with less anger.

One day I heard a well-known cinematographer speaking unkindly of Harry; he suggested that Harry was not a good cinematographer – very good technically, of course, but not visually. This personal opinion came from a colleague whose work I also admired, even if I thought his opinion cruel. So then it was necessary for me to defend Harry's labours; it was a short debate where I found myself totally on Harry's side, but at the same time I wondered if there could be some truth in the man's comments.

There is a fine line in our profession where we are judged for our work or, in Harry's case, his personal temperament. Admittedly, Harry's irritations were no help to him, but one cannot deny that he was a clever technician, a cinematographer who would do his utmost to help a fellow colleague, as he did with me and others before me. Others whom I worked with would give you nothing, as you will read later in my account.

Harry's next challenge would come while working on a film for Walt Disney, *Third Man on the Mountain*, with our location based in Zermatt, Switzerland. With Ken Annakin directing, we found ourselves filming in the shadow of the Matterhorn, a snow-covered mountain where the cool climate would always please.

One short scene required the camera to be lowered down a crevasse, pointing up at our lead actor, Michael Rennie. Due to the narrowness of the fissure, our filming window was restricted to when the sun finally hit the cinematographer's desired position for maximum effect. With all the difficulties of capturing this in its magnificence this short scene would require careful planning before the sun finally reached the optimum position. The gap above slowly closed; already I smelt danger approaching for Harry ...

A small platform built by the riggers with tubular scaffolding to support the camera was lowered down into the crevasse, along with the minimum camera equipment and four people. Looking down at what seemed a bottomless black pit – it was a long way down – Ken Annakin, Harry Waxman, Alan Hume (camera operator) and I climbed down to the rig; when the stepladder was removed our lives were in the hand of God – and the riggers' work of art.

On our overcrowded platform any unnecessary movement would be seriously frowned upon by the riggers above, who were already concerned about this silly routine of moving around. With time getting short for Harry's masterpiece to happen, not forgetting the constant problem of the ice moving, all that remained was to hold that position until the sun finally appeared where Harry required it.

With the tripod placed at the centre of the small platform, we all positioned ourselves around the camera, allowing the director to check Alan's framing through the camera before carefully moving around for Harry's check, then moving once more for me to check that everything was set correctly before finally allowing Alan to move back to his position to operate the camera.

Alas, there was one unforeseen setback still to come. Harry gave me the lens aperture, which I dutifully set, making sure everything was in place. At this point the director decided on one more check through the camera; Alan moved away and we moved around one more time before we were ready to start filming. With the sun finally arriving at Harry's required position he was over the moon; the timing was perfect.

'ACTION! Action ... action ... action ...' The repeated echoes of the director's instruction bounced off the surrounding ice walls, signalling Rennie to do his acting bit, before 'CUT ... cut ... cut ... cut ...' Alan gave the thumbs-up – a great shot! Harry beamed with satisfaction as the dodgy dance routine on the platform allowed me to move back to my position to check the camera gate, only to find that, unknown to me or anyone else, the director had opened the aperture to see through the camera with his final check and had forgotten to mention it!

Now, for those who have not been fortunate enough to find themselves down a crevasse, I should first explain that it can become a cosmic echo chamber where sounds become louder before fading, repeating themselves more than once. This had to be the perfect scenario for Harry's 'volcano' to erupt. He had to have a go at someone. Anyone could be blamed for the terrible disaster – for political reasons he could not point the finger directly at the wicked director, Alan or me – which could only leave those poor souls above, who had nothing to do with this catastrophic situation. Even as nature's echo chamber repeated Harry's misuse of the English language, we still had enough time to rebuild the ice set before the sun disappeared from sight, even if it was not in the perfect position for the cinematographer.

To this day I still remember the visual spectacle below the surface, of the gentle gradation of blue ice slowly fading to black in depth. In this wonderful industry camera crews often find themselves in unusual situations, dangerous at times, others simply beautiful. Both came my way with my crevasse experience, leaving me with a memory that would stay over many years.

In this film Michael Rennie was joined by the young American actor James MacArthur, who would feature in other Disney films. A young Janet Munro claimed the female lead, with the usual names in supporting roles: James Donald, Herbert Lom, Laurence Naismith, Dorothy Maguire and Walter Fitzgerald, truly one of the great American old-timers.

Lesley and I finally decided to get married, and the wedding took place at the same church where I had sung as a choir boy. The elderly verger greeted me with my best man John Campbell, his expression clearly registering that we had met somewhere before, though he was not sure where – he didn't ask and I didn't tell! Sadly my old choirmaster Mr Elliott was no longer around to discuss the good old days.

It was sod's law that soon after we had got married the film industry entered one of its periodic slumps, which happen from time to time. However, this time the camera crews at Pinewood Studios would be made redundant; 'Last in, first out!' came the cry, and I was the first to leave the studio. Fortunately, the head of Pinewood's camera department, Bert Easey, offered me a second unit working on *Sea Fury* as a sort-of wedding present, which would help to boost our meagre funds after the nuptials. So now I found myself working on a Dutch tug filming in the North Sea, assisting my camera operator Austin Dempster, with whom I had worked before on *The Battle of the River Plate*.

Filming in the North Sea in February guarantees relentless seas, but these were the ideal conditions required for our back-projection plates for the film. Throughout the day our little tug battled its way through mountainous waves, leaving me permanently nauseous and soaked to the skin. Austin, of course, loved the experience; he enjoyed sailing.

One memory which stands out from this dreadful experience is of Austin standing at the bow of the tug, clutching his handheld camera as the little boat pitched up and down in the waves. Undaunted, my fearless camera operator carried on filming, his only comfort coming from smoking his ever-present pipe, with my soaked body giving support to his bulky frame as the conditions continued to deteriorate. Eventually an enormous wave came over the bow with such force that I was picked up and tossed down the deck, leaving Austin to his fate. Soaked to the skin, I looked around to see if Austin was still with me; there he was, standing upright – magnificent, imperial – as if nothing could move him, totally unaware of what was happening around him, pipe in mouth, still grasping his camera and filming. I doubt he even realised that I was no longer supporting him.

My friendly camera operator adored the sea. The same could not be said of his assistant, who would remember this experience as the perfect storm where most of the time was spent cleaning the camera of the salt water that found its way through the protective covers wrapped around the equipment. I decided that this would be my last adventure at sea, a promise which I have managed to keep to this day.

The only reason I include this small item in my story is to show the nature of our employment, where camera crews are sometimes asked to do the most ridiculous and at times dangerous things without question or hesitation. Later you look back and wonder if you were mad, or could it be that we are privileged to be part of this beautiful industry?

SWISS FAMILY ROBINSON

Walt Disney's exciting family adventure would take Harry with crew to the tropical island of Tobago, where sunshine comes guaranteed every day, with John Mills as the father of the Robinson family enjoying the company of Dorothy McGuire as his on-screen wife, as well as the usual Disney favourites completing the family Robinson. These included James MacArthur, Janet Munro, Tommy Kirk and Kevin Corcoran, with Cecil Parker playing Captain Moreland and Sessue Hayakawa joining in the fun as the wicked pirate chief.

Writing about famous actors and the joys of travelling around the world, one easily forgets the price that you pay with your family life. In my defence, generous financial compensations were awarded as some recompense for these separations, which contributed much to the family bank balance in the hope that one day we would be able to buy our first home. This was the case with *Swiss Family Robinson*.

Often the loser in this arrangement, this time Lesley, now my wife, joined me in Tobago while the house-hunting took a backseat. Settling down in the surroundings of the Blue Haven Hotel, Lesley would get on with the business of working on her suntan, allowing me to play on the right wing of the Walt Disney football team. On rest days we played so-called 'friendly' games with over-enthusiastic local teams who were committed to beat the Brits, come what may, which usually ended up in a physical do-or-die encounter on the field of battle. The star of the film, John Mills, was team manager and occasional cheerleader. However, my tale stars the second-unit camera assistant, Jimmy Devis, our strong, reliable right back who held the

The Disney football team in Tobago while filming *Swiss Family Robinson* (1960). John Mills (team manager in the white shirt) stands on the right; I'm crouching second from the left in the front row, with Jimmy Devis standing behind me. The man standing on the left was the unit stunt arranger – obviously expecting a dirty game!

Disney line in defence as we faced up to the notorious Tobago Marauders, who were rather inclined to take all this much too seriously.

One game stands out when Jim claimed that he was constantly being kicked by an opponent, which the local referee apparently saw as normal, choosing to ignore Jim's plea for protection. With no help coming from the ref, Jimmy decided to blow the whistle himself and went seeking retribution. Recognising Jim's outrage, the laughing villain decided it might be wiser to stay clear of our wounded hero and quickly took flight. Our champion had other ideas and went off in hot pursuit of the bare-footed scoundrel. Jim was now desperate for revenge.

At this point both teams were more than happy to take the opportunity to rest from the scorching sun, with play set to continue once Jim and friend had run out of steam, kissed and made up, so keeping everyone happy. Eventually, our wilting champion, unable to keep up with his fleeing adversary, returned covered in sweat. Slumping beside me, he struggled to suck in air, catching his breath and claiming that he was dying. No volunteers came forward to give him mouth-to-mouth resuscitation. Fortunately Jim survived the ordeal while his opponent, still full of energy, continued to run off into the distant horizon and was not seen again.

Swiss Family Robinson was a big film by any standard, which required two full units; at the request of director Ken Annakin, Ernie Day now joined Harry Waxman's team as first-unit camera operator, while the second-unit cinematographer, Paul Beeson, also enjoyed the benefit of a full camera crew. In keeping with the spirit of a Walt Disney movie, the film had a variety of animals running around the island, drunken pirates fighting each other, the normal family quarrels of young love with the rivalry of brothers, tigers trapped in pits and, not least, an adventure with a giant 20-foot anaconda waiting in the jungle should anyone be foolish enough to get near him – which brings to mind a terrifying close encounter while filming the snake.

On location with Ernie Day (camera operator) and Harry Waxman sitting in the background with the dark glasses while Ted Underwood (grip) relaxes on the grass.

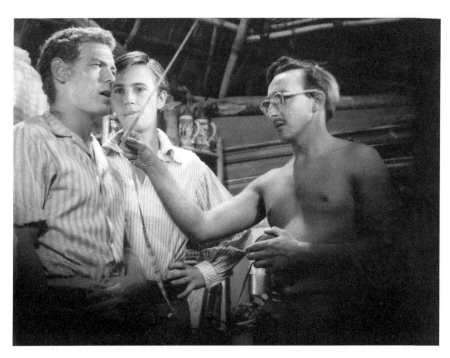

James MacArthur as Fritz and Tommy Kirk as Ernst, with their focus puller trying to grow a moustache.

In one scene James MacArthur was wrestling the snake in a leech-infested swamp, but while the anaconda was supposedly tranquillised it was still alert enough to have a go at the actor, who had been advised to keep the snake's head down in the filthy water. With the struggle taking place not helped with the actor's greasy hands, the snake managed to wriggle free from his grasp and was lost from sight; at this point the actor sensibly made a very hasty retreat from the swamp.

A nervous silence fell as we all looked around, wondering where the snake would eventually surface – not least Ernie and me, who were filming close to the action when the reptile disappeared from sight. Suddenly a splash came with the snake's head reappearing roughly 6 feet from the camera lens. I did not have time to check the distance as this re-emergence guaranteed instant pandemonium, with Ernie and me back-pedalling fast in retreat from its jaws – what fun!

So much happened in a Disney script that putting all this action together required both units to work closely together, which, I am sorry to say, did not happen. What soon became clear was that the combination of Harry Waxman and Paul Beeson working together had all the signs of bad chemistry. Even more worrying was that the two cinematographers could barely 'exist' with each other, let alone discuss mutual problems, which in turn would be unhelpful to our filming.

Obviously this suggested that both parties had crossed paths before and now they found themselves working together on the same film.

Problems started to emerge from a lack of doubling-up on several pieces of equipment, nothing too serious, I hasten to add, but the situation was not helped by Harry's insistence that the main unit should take preference – a comment which could only add more fuel to the silence of the two similar-minded cinematographers. Knowing Harry as I did, I knew it would be necessary to tread carefully before releasing any equipment to the second unit without Harry's authority, but unknown to both Harry or Paul, Jimmy Devis and I decided to handle this delicate problem of sharing equipment quietly by ourselves. Now I was back on my 'beware watch', praying that nothing would go wrong, and somehow we managed to get away from all this madness around us. Harry controlled his feelings and kept them to himself, which again was unusual for the guv; even so, I had my reservations about all this nonsense and stayed alert to the situation.

When they had completed their filming the second unit returned to the UK, but even with the atmosphere now more relaxed it never became clear why Harry and Paul, two knowledgeable cinematographers, had so much ill-feeling towards each other. The reality is that I cannot remember the two speaking to each other throughout the entire film – past history alone would have the answer to this sad chemistry.

It was some years later and long after Harry had passed away that I visited Paul in hospital, still curious for an answer to this question of ill-feeling between the two. Tactlessly, I popped the question: 'Why?' The pleasant atmosphere suddenly cooled as the conversation went quiet. Paul thought about this before turning his piercing eyes straight at me. Had I overstepped the mark in asking that stupid question? Paul eventually smiled – more a grin, I thought – as he thought about my question. Sadly no further comment came, suggesting that there were past issues which Paul was not prepared to discuss, and I would never know the reason for the terrible atmosphere between them. To be honest, I found it disturbing that two such distinguished cinematographers were unable resolve an issue so damaging to them both. No winner would come from this clash of personalities.

Now the only reason I tell this sad account is that later something happened which would eventually change Harry's attitude towards me personally, damaging our long-standing professional relationship after years of loyalty to each other. Even so, my thanks go to the Robinson family and to other Disney productions; the Mills family now had enough money for a down-payment on Cherry Trees, our new home.

THE ROMAN SPRING OF MRS STONE

With filming scheduled to start in Rome, Harry suddenly became worried about the cost of air freight, which would not normally be a concern for him. However, this sudden money-saving initiative was put to the production office, with the result that the equipment would now travel to Rome by lorry, with Harry insisting that I travelled in the passenger seat next to the driver, who I well remember had personal problems with BO!

My hotel was close to the Via Veneto, and I was relaxing there in comfort waiting on the unit's arrival when suddenly I had reason for concern. As I lay on the sun terrace, I noticed someone staring at me, but on making eye contact he at once turned away. Immediately this brought to mind problems other film companies had experienced while filming in Rome, where the Mafia was known to get involved with foreign companies working there, wanting their pay-offs or whatever the local Dons demanded. With this in mind I kept a cautious eye open to see if I was being watched – or was all this my imagination?

Later, a phone call from the production office back in the UK explained that there would be a delay with the unit's arrival, which would be a few days later than originally planned. Apart from the odd call checking on my safe arrival, so far I had not met or spoken with anyone from the Italian production office, so it would seem that they knew even less about the delay of the English unit than I did. For all I knew they could be the Mafia! Either way, I was not too concerned about the hold-up, which gave me more time to explore the city, starting with a stroll down the Appian Way and twice to the Colosseum, casually looking over my shoulder to see if I was being followed. Everyone in Rome now came under my discreet examination ...

In the end I would never know the truth about the men in black as the problem would be resolved when I was summoned back to the UK and told to bring all the equipment with me. The schedule had changed, with the Rome experience happening after our filming in Elstree Studios. Life was always full of surprises and suddenly I was to return to England by air, much to the lorry driver's dismay at losing a return trip and Harry's frustration at learning that the expense was no longer an issue.

The director of *Roman Spring*, José Quintero, was unknown to many apart from our leading lady, Vivien Leigh. A quiet, gentle human being, Quintero surprised his key technicians on the first morning of filming when he politely explained that he had never directed a film before, nor was he a technical director, and that therefore he would need their support. We would come to see that José's gift was his ability to get exciting performances from his actors. Later I learned that his directing skills came from working in the theatre and television.

The carefully selected technicians were Harry Waxman, camera operator Ernie Day and Peter Yates, the first assistant director who in time became a director – one of Peter's best known films is *Bullitt*. Last but not least was June Faithful,

The end-of-picture party on *The Roman Spring of Mrs Stone*. I was asked to present Vivien Leigh with a small gift from the company, for which she gave me a kiss. The film's director, José Quintero, was one of the best I worked with, with the crew enjoying a happy atmosphere throughout the production.

an experienced continuity lady. These were the key people who surrounded José on that first morning of filming. The director did not lose his authority through his openness; José instantly held both actors and hardened key technicians in the palms of his hands as they gave in to the director's genuine honesty. With no ego problems left to deal with, the Quintero chemistry was complete.

The normal procedure for a film sequence is for the director to run through a scene with the actors, allowing the key technicians to observe how the scene plays out. It happened that the first morning this involved our two stars, Vivien Leigh and Warren Beatty. To satisfy my ever-present curiosity of director/actor relationships I now experienced a demonstration of perfect handling.

Red light on, the stage went quiet; one could hear a pin drop as we watched these two giants of cinema quietly displaying their word-perfect reading of the scene. Possibly an hour passed before José decided that he would like to spend more time with his actors, suggesting everyone else should go for tea in the canteen. Peter Yates duly removed everyone from the set, allowing only the key technicians to remain with José as he continued with his 'private' rehearsal. The unit did not need telling twice, and everyone went off to the canteen, knowing that they would be summoned back once they were ready on the stage. Needless to say, I was disappointed with this idea and now came up with a cunning plan, explaining to Peter: 'I'm bringing tea back for Harry, Ernie and June. Would you like one?'

After delivering the refreshments I quietly melted into the background, silently watching the magic of this director at work with his actors. I believe this was the first time that I honestly appreciated what genuine heartfelt directing was all about – the director's influence over the actors' performance, their reaction to his judgement with requests for clarification, before ending up with something truly wonderful. Before the crew were removed to the canteen I had already been impressed with the actors' reading of the scene, so it had made little sense to me that it was necessary to keep rehearsing these talented people. Not for this director: he expected more from them, convinced there was more still to come.

This was the first morning of filming and the director's opportunity to develop that all-important building block with his two stars. By the time the rehearsal had finished, Vivien and Warren were both also aware that this man knew his business, their elated faces confirming they could rely on his judgement. They could trust him. Of course, many would claim this was normal for a director, but José Quintero was not looking for normal; he was looking for perfection!

A strong rumour suggested that Vivien Leigh's contract included the name José Quintero as director for *The Roman Spring of Mrs Stone*. You may also wonder how I know this; the truth is I was a nosey little bugger, though I prefer to call this natural curiosity, especially when listening in to careless conversations whispered near the camera. This was my domain, and it really is amazing what one learns there, as you will read later ...

The press reports were generally complimentary about the film, which was the story of an ageing actress (Vivien Leigh) whose husband suddenly dies, leaving her alone in Rome – the perfect scenario for an Italian gigolo (Warren Beatty) to make his move. Harry's photography of Vivien was simply gorgeous, with a cast including Coral Browne, Jill St John, Carl Jaffe and the fabulous singer Cleo Lane, while not forgetting Lotte Lenya, who won a nomination for best supporting actress. *Roman Spring* gave me an interesting experience of watching the skills of a little-known director's handling of actors and a lesson in how to win over hard-bitten professional technicians.

Yet, with all this happening, at no time did I have reason to believe this would be the last time that Harry and I would work together. The guv always had my unending loyalty for his support towards me, our professional relationship had never been closer. Should there have been a formal parting of ways, *The Roman Spring of Mrs Stone* would have been the film where we would both have chosen to say our goodbyes, particularly in the harmony of Harry Waxman showing such respect to this unknown director.

Harry went off filming with a different camera crew, which by now I had accepted as the norm in our relationship. Past experience suggested that we would get together again on his return. With me now available for work, a surprise call came from Paul Beeson, offering me a film.

It was some weeks later that Harry returned from his latest trip and decided to ignore me for reasons known only to himself. He even went so far as to look the other way, making it difficult to ask why he was acting in this manner. I admired Harry, he knew this, so why this sudden change of attitude towards me? Obviously it could only be due to Paul offering me a film while Harry was away. When *Roman Spring* finished, we had all left on the best terms, so this made little sense, but it would seem that Harry had regarded my working with Paul as my personal disloyalty to him. If so, Harry had seriously misjudged me.

Sadly this juvenile situation continued for some time before Harry's attitude mellowed – a little – though even with the passing of time this damaged relationship would never be healed completely, leaving another silly situation the

Working on Robert Louis Stephenson's *Kidnapped* in 1960. As you can tell, it was high summer in Scotland. James MacArthur (centre) played the role of Davy Balfour; I would work on three films for Walt Disney with James, including *Third Man on the Mountain* and *Swiss Family Robinson*, but he will always be best remembered for his role as Danny Williams in *Hawaii Five-O*. 'Book him, Danno!'

guv had created for himself. There was still one brief moment that I would hold on to and remember him by. Eventually Harry managed a smile towards me ... from a distance ... nothing more. Regrettably, we would never get round to talking about this nonsense before Harry passed away. God bless you, guv! You played an important role in the development of my career. Later I would ask myself if I had also been playing my part in Harry's 'private script' – could this be true of us all?

There are many questions in life to which we will never know the answer. Private relationships don't necessarily make interesting reading, although later I would reflect on why some influenced me over the years. I believe my experience with Harry was the key that kept my career on course. Paul was a hiccup which did not help matters and Harry unfortunately misread the script, not understanding that I only chose to work with Paul – someone I hardly knew – while the guv was away. Suddenly I found myself standing between two stools with all this nonsense making little sense to me.

So now a new era begins with Paul Beeson, working on films for Walt Disney: *Greyfriars Bobby*, *The Prince and the Pauper*, *In Search of the Castaways*, *Three Lives of Thomasina*, *Dr Syn*, *Alias the Scarecrow* and *Moon-Spinners*. Others included *Tarzan Goes to India* and *Monster of Terror*, the latter with an ageing Boris Karloff.

Disney films always featured family entertainment with colourful cinematography and bold filter combinations creating a 'fantasy-land' appearance. With this in mind, I hoped to gain more from working with Paul and take notes about what he did before asking why, looking to learn from his imaginative lighting. This would not happen. Unlike Harry Waxman, Paul was not one to share his expertise with me or anyone who cared to ask, although this should not detract from the fact that Paul was a fine cinematographer.

Looking back on my Beeson era, two private moments come to mind, both of which have stayed with me and both from the *Tarzan* film, leaving a respectful memory of Paul.

Greyfriars Bobby was filmed in 1961 for Walt Disney at Shepperton Studios, the story of a faithful dog which stayed by his master's grave for years after his death. From left to right: Don Chaffey (director), Herbert Smith (camera operator) and yours truly as focus puller, now slowly working his way up the ladder.

Working on *In Search of the Castaways* in 1962. Maurice Chevalier with Hayley Mills standing in front of camera. I am holding the essential focus puller's tape with David Harcourt behind camera.

It was late, on a hot sticky summer night when I arrived in Bombay (Mumbai today). The atmosphere was humid and the odd shop remained open to compete for the few customers who might still be around. Godfrey Godar, Paul's camera operator, met me at the airport and suggested that we purchased practical clothing for the location where we would be filming. Although I was tired we went shopping to buy khaki jackets with shorts to match, white socks and boots – 'uniforms the Brits wear in India', the tailor suggested. He was mocking, of course; they were the uniforms the colonials had dressed in.

That colonial image quickly disappeared as reality sank in. Kitted out in my stylish new clothing, an early call required me to make a long trek carrying the camera equipment through thick bush – I hesitate to call it jungle but the foliage was too thick for transport of any kind, with everyone staying in single file close together. I was the last in line, carrying the camera.

Fifteen minutes or so of carrying heavy equipment would inevitably take its toll as I fell behind the rest of the party. Suddenly I came across a mound of earth where a young woman sat, cradling her arms around a tiny child drinking water from a Coca-Cola tin. I stopped ... the sight startled me. The young woman looked at me and smiled before turning her attention back to the child without a word spoken between us. I cannot explain why, but that image remains with me to this day, possibly a reminder of how lucky I have been in life and how fortunate the Mills family are. Then an afterthought struck me – what an idiot I looked in my smart new clothes! It was something else to consider after this meeting. Was this pre-set by destiny to make me think, or just another chance encounter?

On another occasion we were filming in a remote part of India when the generator driver told the production office that his wife had died and he asked to be allowed to return home to cremate his wife. The man was very upset. Although the Indian production manager was sympathetic to the driver's problem and agreed to let him go, he refused to pay his fare. The electrician could not afford the price so Paul generously gave the man cash for the round trip.

When he returned to work, the electrician remained inconsolable. One day, driving at speed, whether by accident or a deliberate act, he crashed the generator and died in the incident. Paul represented the British crew and attended the funeral pyre, paying his respects to a colleague. Where did Paul's compassion come from? I

Hayley Mills snapped while looking over my shoulder – she was probably checking to make sure that I was lacing it correctly!

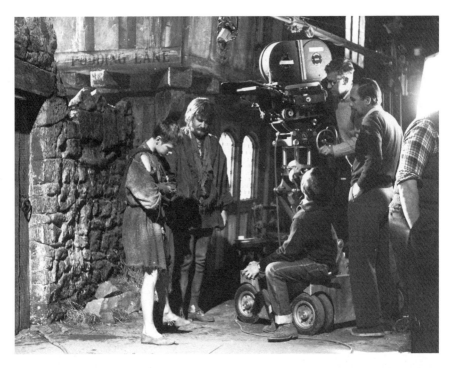

Working on *The Prince and the Pauper* (1961) for Walt Disney at Shepperton Studios. The young lad in front of the camera was Sean Scully, a Walt Disney mainstay of the time who would also appear in *Dr Syn, Alias the Scarecrow*. David Harcourt is operating the camera while I sit on the front of the camera dolly, hoping that one day someone will invent a remote focus control!

Tarzan in India (1962), with Jock Mahoney in the lead role of Tarzan.

On location for *Tarzan in India*. I'm the one adjusting the camera for camera operator Godfrey Godar (seated with cap).

would later learn that Paul had been an officer in the navy, so perhaps it was time to reappraise those wardroom 'pigs' and ask questions about my own moral fibre.

Jock Mahoney was the latest Tarzan, with Jai the ever-present elephant boy helping him. The story in this film concerned the building of a dam servicing a power plant which would inevitably flood the land and kill many elephants in the process. Our hero would, of course, require an adversary, and Leo Gordon played the customary villain in the piece.

The director, John Guillermin, with whom I had worked in the past, continued to impress me with his animated drive and energy; this lively approach to filming was John's particular style. In the future we would work on other films, in particular one by the name *King Kong Lives*, although that was still a long way off. By that time I would be John's cinematographer, which in turn would lead to a very important step in my career.

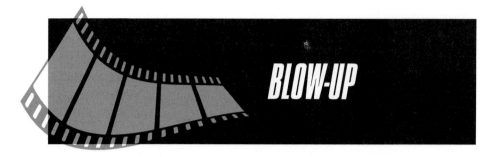

Perhaps with my frankness and personal beliefs I could be labelled an oddball; no longer does that bother me, so take what you will from negative thoughts or comments. Let me make this clear: I believe in fate, my destiny – call it what you will – as you will have picked up from the odd clue in my writing. The reality is that I am comfortable admitting to this, providing that fate or coincidence do not become entangled.

The next family milestone was to buy Cherry Trees, a sixteenth-century thatched cottage in a pretty Buckinghamshire village, where the property sat high on a hill overlooking the landscape of the beautiful Chiltern Hills – truly a joy to wake up to. Although the property was expensive for our insufficient finances there was something 'different' about Cherry Trees which in a strange way attracted our attention. It was certainly different from other properties we visited. We decided to go ahead and buy it, come what may, and to take the risk of unforeseen financial problems which might occur later. However, the financial worries quickly passed when I received an unexpected call from a gentleman suggesting that I should meet the cinematographer Carlo di Palma at a small studio in Holland Park. It was a name that I had not heard before, although it was obviously not English, leaving me to wonder how my name had come into this strange story.

It was a pleasant interview with Carlo. He was a quiet gentleman who carefully considered me and left me with me a sense of being 'sized-up' as we chatted away, before finally deciding that I would be the 'chosen one' to meet the director of *Blow-Up*.

'Alec, meet Michelangelo Antonioni!'

I was announced as if I was about to meet royalty. A face turned to me, and I was introduced to an equally quiet man with even less to say to me; his facial expression gave little away, making it difficult to describe Antonioni – aloof would be my early choice.

'Hello, Alec, welcome to *Blow-Up*.'

He then turned away and went back to his script. That was it – the sum of my interview with Antonioni! I had been given an opportunity to study this fêted director in close detail, allowed a small peep into the workings of this strange, unusual man.

Back at home I settled down to read the script of *Blow-Up*, a weird and complicated story about photography with pretty young models cavorting around posing for an energetic fashion photographer in the guise of David Hemmings, who captured their skills – or anything which attracted his interest – through his camera lens.

The overlong opening sequence to *Blow-Up* introduces the audience to the strange world of young models living their dreams, pretty to look at and desperate for fame. The story eventually moves on to Antonioni's deeper understanding of the script, where this unusual director could be described as the 'thinking' man. He was a director with an inventive mind who set out to challenge the audience with his extraordinary story, if necessary putting something completely unrelated into the scene just to tease their curiosity – a deliberate distraction, while at the same time allowing his fussy talent slowly to develop the plot. To be honest, I never worked Antonioni out – much as I tried – but the experience alone was memorable.

Antonioni would take great care with all the colours and dressings on his sets – exterior or interior – everything would be dressed to his complete satisfaction through the camera frame before the camera turned over. Filming one particular night scene on location in London, the director suddenly decided to have a section of the road surface painted black – at night – which made little sense to a humble camera assistant who was in no position to ask why this was necessary. Could this be art for art's sake gone mad? When I saw the film on its release I believe – at least I think – I understood what Antonioni was trying to achieve; it would seem that our director was deliberately trying to confuse his audience – certainly me – before ending with a surprise finale.

Try as hard as one may, it would be impossible to read Antonioni's mind or even his way of thinking. I doubt anyone who saw the film, even critics, would notice a visual detail such as this, which left me asking myself if his black-painted road helped. A gentle wind blowing on the soundtrack added to the possible murder scene the director created, while at the same time he guided his audiences into a semi-hypnotic state. That's all I have on this one – heavy stuff this!

Another striking scene was of young people enjoying themselves at a rave-up which would stretch Antonioni's set dressing to the outrageous. The selected location was a big house at Cheyne Walk on the Chelsea embankment, even though a scene of this nature would have been easier to control in the studio. Then again, *Blow-Up* was no ordinary film; nor was Antonioni an ordinary director, so came the perfect demonstration of the art of realism.

We arrived early to set up for a gathering of beautiful young women with their enthusiastic partners, all happy and willing to take part in the scene. With Carlo's lighting completed, the scene fully rehearsed and the set dressed to Antonioni's complete satisfaction, we were ready to start filming. The props department then began to hand out the usual drinks and smokes, creating the right atmosphere. After

Working with Antonioni (with curly hair) on *Blow-Up* in 1966. Camera operator Ray Parslow stands next to him while I was the camera assistant. This was the only picture I ever managed to get, given the tight security about the film, which was especially important for Antonioni, who preferred to film as near to reality as possible – including the drug scenes!

a short time a horrible smell started to circulate among the relaxed partygoers. It might have been dreadful to me, but at least it helped our carefully selected guests to get into the right frame of mind, to be more relaxed for the scene. Through the haze it was now clear why this scene was not being filmed in a studio. Obviously someone knew someone else, who happened to know a crowd of people who would enjoy a party such as this, who probably knew someone who knew others who would know where to obtain the necessary 'something' for a party such as this ... Who else but Antonioni would go to such extremes with his set dressings?

Moving to the Maryon Park sequences, the photographer's interest falls on a couple in the distance who appear to be arguing. His professional curiosity takes over and he decides to photograph them, at which point the lady sees him. Developing the film in the darkroom later, he sees what might be a possible murder scene which could incriminate Vanessa Redgrave, who would do anything to retrieve the *Blow-Up* print and negative.

The climax to Antonioni's film ends with David Hemmings watching a tennis match being played by two mime artistes who are playing without a ball. The weird, doped onlookers watch an imaginary ball bouncing from side to side over the net, leaving the audience wondering if there was a ball, or indeed if there was a murder after all.

Antonioni deservedly received acclaim for *Blow-Up*, as did Carlo di Palma's cinematography, which contributed much to the dark atmosphere of the script. A pleasant man, Carlo was in complete harmony with all of the demands placed on him by Antonioni, helped in no short measure by another Brit, Ray Parslow, the camera operator, and of course yours truly, who would try to keep everything sharp through the haze. The stars were David Hemmings, Vanessa Redgrave, Sarah Miles, Jane Birkin and John Castle.

David gave a lively performance as an animated photographer who was tough on the young models while at the same time retaining his interest in collecting antiques. Foraging around a traditional second-hand shop, his eye is caught by a propeller, which he buys. Again it had nothing whatsoever to do with the story – pure Antonioni. If it did have some meaning, then I missed it!

To be honest, I never mastered the art of understanding the silent Antonioni, a director who gave little away, not allowing one to learn from him. Even so, the opportunity to experience and work with this man would make this a worthwhile cause and one forever remembered.

Jogging the memory of this fast-fading chapter now more than forty years past, it was necessary to remind myself of this unusual experience on DVD. With *Blow-Up* now outdated as technology has changed, I imagine today's critics would slaughter Antonioni's effort, though at the time I seem to recall *Blow-Up* being referred to as 'a classic work of art'. How quickly times change.

David Hemmings came under the spell of the 'Antonioni technique'. It was years later when directing his film *Running Scared* that David tried to follow in his master's footsteps. Precise with his set dressings and with beautiful visuals, David emulated his hero, this time helped by Ernie Day's expertise with the photography, and of course yours truly, now established as Ernie's camera operator. However, like others before him, David would learn that imitation rarely works; things are never quite the same the second time round, even with Antonioni's influence hovering in the background. Without the master's label David's film would be lost on most, but even so the Antonioni flavour would probably be recognised in David's tribute to the grand master.

The Antonioni story was set around the Swinging Sixties, with *Blow-Up* reflecting that period, but would anyone enjoy the film today? I found myself on the not-totally-convinced side, but again, who am I to judge? No doubt the Chelsea gathering would remember this film, even though it would be necessary to plough on through to the end before making up their minds if there was a murder after all.

I was pleased to meet the director Michelangelo Antonioni.

MOVING ON ...
MOVING UP

Generally, we are inclined to judge others from our own observations, which could be wrong – possibly even unfair – leaving me wondering how others considered me. With *Blow-Up* soon to end, Michael Reed called with a new challenge.

'Alec, would you be interested in operating the camera on *The Saint?*'

Mike had offered me this opportunity before but at the time my courage had failed me, knowing that I was not ready for the challenge. This would not happen again.

Aware of the task ahead of me, my last weeks of filming on *Blow-Up* were spent practising the art of using a geared head – a worthwhile tool that any camera operator would choose. Should anyone pass through the stage at lunchtime they could be sure that the camera would follow them until they were out of sight, a wry smile on their faces would warn of a challenge ahead for me. When filming was over for the day, more time was spent mastering the art of this professional tool so that I was ready for the real test.

To this day, I still remember my first scene operating the camera for the director Roy Ward Baker, a simple task as written in the script: 'The Saint tied down on a table dressed as a Roman Soldier at a fancy dress party; the camera moves from tied hands to a face with the heavy standing guard over him.'

Take one: 'Action!'

'CUT!' the director shouted. With satisfaction he turned directly towards his camera operator, obviously testing me out.

'How was that for you?' Mr Baker's preference was to address me as 'you'!

I gave an equally firm reply: 'It was fine, thank you.'

'Do you want to go again?'

Already he's testing me ... 'No, that was fine for me.'

Michael smiled, pleased at my response to an unconvinced director, having warned me earlier to be positive in my decisions, whether good or bad. Nothing gets up a director's nose more than a camera operator who wavers, unable to make decisions!

What should also be remembered was that in those days reflex cameras were not available; instead, the parallax viewfinder on the left side of the camera blimp would guide the operator's efforts, which again was partly in the hands of the camera assistant. One would hate to think of the consequences for the poor camera operator should his focus change.

Over the following year Michael would be responsible for sharpening my skills as a camera operator. An unassuming gentleman who used his influence over my limited ability, he was also someone to whom I would forever be in debt. Much would be learned from working on a television series with Michael Reed.

Roger Moore – the Saint – was also generous in his understanding to this new camera operator, whose head was clearly on the chopping block should anything go wrong. In Roger's foreword to this book he jokingly refers to the fact that I am not tall and stood on a box to reach the camera viewfinder. With his giant 6-foot frame, he reminded me of the famous 1966 class sketch from *The Frost Report*, with John Cleese (tall, upper class), Ronnie Barker (medium height, middle class) and Ronnie Corbett (short, lower class – like me), each looking up to or down at each other depending on their social status. In time, Roger and I would become good friends and colleagues ... but, as Ronnie Corbett said: 'I knew my place!'

Yes, at times Roger would be my 'pain in the neck', but we would always remain good friends. In the future we would meet again with another screen legend going by the name James Bond – but at least I was there first!

ON HER MAJESTY'S SECRET SERVICE

Looking back on past experiences as youth gives way to awareness, perhaps *The Saint* was a necessary learning curve that taught me to accept disappointment even while I was enjoying a small measure of success. Operating the camera on a television series would bring out the confidence in me which had somehow been missing; a year's experience behind the camera sorted that trouble out before the series finally came to an end. I now look upon it as my dress rehearsal.

Michael had worked for Peter Hunt before. Peter, an editor of much repute for his slick work on the James Bond films, was now directing the opening sequence of *Chitty Chitty Bang Bang* while I tagged along as camera operator. You can probably understand my frustration when Peter suggested that I should operate the camera 'badly', allowing the racing cars to disappear out of frame before panning to catch them up, which happened to cameramen in days gone by and was probably just as frustrating for the viewers. We also filmed speed trials at a Formula One race in Monte Carlo for a film soon to start; my position was in the tunnel, where I remember experiencing the pain of the unbelievable noise even when wearing ear defenders for protection. It was another rare and unforgettable experience – but sadly the film never happened in the end.

The *Chitty Chitty Bang Bang* sequence would take a month to film, allowing time for Peter and Michael to build a strong professional relationship, with Peter offering Michael his next film *On Her Majesty's Secret Service*. This film would be the turning point in both our careers, although in the end it would not work out as we would have wished or hoped. Even so, our careers were now moving to a different level, working with a gentleman going by the name of James Bond.

Before this excitement could be realised, Sean Connery, tired of the part after five films, decided to abandon the coveted role of agent 007. So a new James Bond needed to be found, tested and photographed for looks, physique and personality –

Filming in the cable car winding house of Blofeld's Piz Gloria lair. This sequence was actually filmed on a mechanism designed by special effects supervisor John Stears on a stage at Pinewood Studios, so I was not quite so high off the ground as it appears, but when being winched towards the giant cog wheels at 15mph. I still needed to be confident that the cable would stop at exactly the right time and place. (© 1969 Danjaq, LLC and United Artists Corporation. All rights reserved)

all the qualities of his predecessor. It was even more important to see how the new secret agent came across on the screen, with three candidates being put to the test before an unknown Australian model was named 'the chosen one'.

George Lazenby's claim to fame may have come from a television commercial featuring images of a handsome man carrying a big wooden crate of Big Fry chocolate on his shoulder; another account suggests that Cubby Broccoli had met George in a barber's shop somewhere in London. Whatever the truth, this would be something of a gamble with George now suddenly in the public eye. From now on a hungry press would follow his every move as the new 007, which sadly ended in his downfall. Peter Hunt tried to protect him from all of the negative publicity to which he would be exposed, but George ignored the director's protection by playing James Bond off screen as well as on, making himself an easy target for the press – game over!

George's transgressions may have been forgiven and put down to inexperience, but he would seal his own fate while on location in Portugal when he decided to go horse riding. Cubby Broccoli paced up and down waiting on George's return to the set, breathing fire and speaking to no one, his expression clearly suggesting that George was in big trouble for his irresponsible behaviour, the consequence of which would not bear thinking about should he have had an accident. Actors have personal responsibilities to look after themselves when working on films, considering all that could happen should anything go wrong; George's immature folly had also kept the entire unit and the professional Diana Rigg waiting on set for his return.

It would not come as a surprise to learn that George would not appear a second time as agent 007. Given time and coaching, he might have developed further as an actor and gained an understanding and respect of the responsibilities to which all actors must adhere. George would perhaps have made a great James Bond, but his temperament and this thoughtless act of riding a horse would only leave him with wonderful memories and time to reflect on all of the possibilities.

Lazenby's Bond received mixed reviews from the press, which at the time I believed to be fair, while Diana Rigg's Tracy would keep our hero's sexual activities restrained before they got married. The dramatic ending comes with Mr and Mrs Bond driving off on their honeymoon, where Tracy is murdered by 007's arch-enemy Ernst Stavro Blofeld, played by Telly Savalas.

Of the many countries and locations I had the privilege of visiting throughout my career, the Switzerland location of Murren-Schilthorn will be one best remembered, not only for its perfect climate but also for the fantastic atmosphere in this fabulous skiing resort. Suzy and I recently returned to the Jungfrau mountain where we filmed the sequences and destruction of Blofeld's lair Piz Gloria – memory lane time! The slowly revolving restaurant at the summit now treats visitors to the beauty of the surrounding snow-covered mountains, majestic in their glory, allowing those wonderful memories to flow back.

In today's film industry the name Michael Reed hardly features in the minds of young wannabe cinematographers, but what they will remember was Michael's stunning cinematography of *On Her Majesty's Secret Service*, which was as beautiful as the compliments shown him on both sides of the Atlantic.

I should also mention Willy Bogner's skiing skills on the second unit. His work was truly outstanding at times, with the camera strapped between his legs while he was towed behind a bobsleigh on a bob run. His efforts must be seen to be believed.

THE HUNTING PARTY

Over the years, Michael and I shared a wonderful working relationship, with our families also enjoying the good times together, but December brings a period in the calendar when film production remains traditionally quiet – a situation that could perhaps go on well into the New Year! With little prospect of work, it is necessary to tighten belts as the Christmas holiday gets closer, which could be particularly worrying when there were rumours that it could be the spring before the industry returned to normal. Even so, an upbeat Michael called me with the news of the offer of a film in Spain, which would start early in the New Year. It was called *The Hunting Party*.

Having read the script – a western – Michael thought it was an exciting story with a strong cast, including Gene Hackman, Candice Bergen and Oliver Reed. In this positive mood he arranged for a script to be sent to me from Madrid, which arrived a few days later. I phoned Michael, agreeing that it was an exciting idea, although privately I was surprised that he would be interested in a subject such as this. Anyway, no more attention was paid to this particular observation.

When Mike and wife Jill joined the Mills family in celebration over dinner the atmosphere was relaxed with the prospect of a film in the New Year. The contented smiles around the table reflected that belts could now be loosened. All seemed well, until during the meal Michael asked my opinion of the script. I had of course assumed my copy to be the same as his, and I carefully mentioned that I was surprised he would be interested in a subject such as this. My honest reply came as a surprise to Michael, who looked at me, uncertain why I would say this, leaving me in a tight corner with his next obvious question.

'Why do you say that?'

The McKenzie Break filmed in Ireland in 1968 was a happier production with Mike Reed compared to the misery of *The Hunting Party*. Ireland has always been famous for its rain and the camera cover, if not comfortable, at least kept me dry!

The table went quiet waiting on my nervous reply.

'Well ... I suppose it was the rape scene, the scenes with the kidnapping of ...'

He stopped me before I went any further, wanting to see my script.

At first Michael had thought I was pulling his leg, he was well aware of my weird sense of humour and that I could have been playing one of my silly games on him, but not this time. This time I was serious. Michael quickly flipped through the pages before deciding that it was not the time or place to read the script and said that he would take it home to read later. At this point alarm bells were ringing.

The next morning Michael called with the news that he had already phoned the production office in Madrid and pulled out of the project! I could hardly believe what I was hearing as neither of us could afford the luxury of losing a film such as this; times had been quiet and we both had mortgages to consider, so none of this made any sense. More questions – selfish questions.

Michael clearly understood what had happened. It would seem that the production company had sent a script to Michael that was considerably different to mine. We never knew if this was intentional on their part or not, but either way it did not matter now as my friend had withdrawn from the film out of personal principles concerning the subject matter, beliefs which would not allow

The nose gets more bent as time moves on, though still quite handsome. It's curious how so many people have said that I reminded them of Peter Sellers.

him to pursue this project any further. He immediately suggested that I should not withdraw from the film just because of his moral viewpoint – his personal commitment. Perhaps my dedication to principle was not as strong as Michael's, which in time I will surely pay for, but I really could not afford to lose the work, believing that my family came first, which no doubt makes me the lesser man.

It happened that in the end Michael was very fortunate in his decision not to take the job, leaving me to wonder if an outside force was protecting my friend while my penance would be to work on the film and experience the consequences.

The Hunting Party was by far the most unhappy film I ever worked on, with a dreadful atmosphere existing throughout our filming – a situation created entirely by the director, Don Medford. The chemistry between Dick Bush, Michael's replacement as cameraman, and Medford was next to zero and within two weeks Dick had been replaced with the Spanish cinematographer Cecilio Paniagua. The new arrival, a quiet, pleasant gentleman, appeared to meet the director's approval by sensibly staying clear of Medford's dangerous shadow, but even so the story does not end there. The American actor Mitchell Ryan, with whom we had filmed for the past two weeks, was next in line for the chop. Like Dick Bush, he would suddenly disappear overnight, so that at breakfast the crew would look around the table to see who was missing.

The saga was now in full swing. Oliver Reed was next, threatening to walk off the film, claiming that he could not stand working with Ryan's replacement, another American actor allegedly recommended by Candice Bergen. 'All change!' a wag remarked, with Mitchell Ryan being recalled to the set, probably on a better deal this time, with his family now in close attendance.

With all this uncertainty going on I expected to be next in line for the hatchet – heads or tails time – however, I managed to struggle on through to the end of this dreadful ordeal, completing my punishment for not resigning as Michael had done in the first place. As luck would have it, Michael would have hated working with this director; his concerns with the script had protected him from this awful person. Now I was left with a sad experience to reflect on – possibly something I would need to learn from.

As filming eventually got back to normal there was one more questionable moment as we moved to Almería. The production company hired an aircraft to

While filming *The McKenzie Break* we found ourselves on location in Kensal Green Cemetery, which was a little scary as I found myself standing in a grave only yards from where my elder brother Alfie had been laid to rest in 1938. My expression clearly explains this moment with director Lamont Johnson.

A posed photograph for the album! The camera crew included Ron Drinkwater (focus puller), Michael Reed (cinematographer), myself (operating) and a young Malcolm Mackintosh (clappers) standing behind Michael.

take the unit and equipment to the new location. Oliver Reed, Don Medford and the minor roles joined us on the trip, but for reasons known only to himself, the producer decided to travel by road. The flight went well enough until we were making our final approach to the airport, when the starboard engine suddenly caught fire. Through the windows we could see flames pouring from the engine, made worse as the propeller was still working, fanning the burning oil over the wing – a fireball in the making! Although there were no immediate signs of panic on board you could be sure our heartbeats were racing faster than normal; fortunately the engine's fire extinguisher still worked and the pilot managed to land on one engine.

It was later established that the aircraft was on its last flight before being scrapped. The obvious conclusion was that it had been rented out cheaply to the production company. When we heard this, you could be sure that the matter would not end there; Oliver Reed personally threatened the demise of the producer, although by the time he finally arrived in his car Ollie had calmed down. After the aeroplane incident the unit seemed to receive more respect and I do not recall seeing the producer after that episode – he suddenly disappeared from the scene without a trace.

The Hunting Party was about abduction. Outlaw Frank Calder (Oliver Reed) kidnaps Brandt Ruger's wife (Candice Bergen) and Ruger (Gene Hackman) forms a posse to go after them, which of course ends with the predictable bloodbath. The supporting cowboys were recognisable names from a past era, probably cast more for their horse-riding skills. Although L.Q. Jones, Simon Oakland and Mitchell Ryan were now visibly slower on the draw, they were still happy to go down memory lane as we sat around the crackling fire at night, listening to the spitting wood and reliving memories past.

Yep – happy days, returning to the past!

There is a strange excitement in a profession where you can never be sure where the next challenge might come from, dealing with many egos and trying to win over new faces, or perhaps unpleasant people to work for. Be that as it may, fresh connections would always be useful, even if they sometimes left a bad taste in the mouth.

My next challenge would bring an entirely different problem to the last experience. It was the early spring when I returned to the UK and film production remained quiet. Even so, that did not matter: I was just happy to be back in civilisation after the insanity of *The Hunting Party* experience.

The expected rest would not last long. Within days a call came from producer Timothy Burrill, asking me to meet the director of a film soon to start in Shepperton Studios. No name was mentioned and at the time I could not be sure if I would be happy or not working again so soon after my recent experience in Spain. Out of curiosity I went anyway.

It turned out that the next director whom I would be shaking hands with was Roman Polanski, who had lately featured in the headlines around the world and was now here in England to direct *The Tragedy of Macbeth*. At first I felt uneasy as to how I would handle this very delicate interview, bearing in mind the recent murder by the Manson Family of Polanski's wife, the actress Sharon Tate. I sat there feeling uncomfortable and ill-at-ease as the director carefully weighed me up, considering me. Would I be the right person for Roman Polanski? This unease would pass after a lengthy interview with the director, who invited me to be his camera operator on

Shooting *Macbeth* (1975) on location in Snowdonia with Roman Polanski making sure that I understand what he wants – or else goodbye Alec!

Shakespeare's masterpiece. Once the cross-examination was over it was clear there would be none of that 'Action – Cut – Over here, boys' attitude with this director – quite the reverse. Roman Polanski knew precisely what he wanted to see on the screen, down to the smallest detail; get it wrong and you would surely hear from him before being shown the nearest exit.

The director made it clear that he would be making great use of camera movement to add drama to the subject, which so far was in step with my own thoughts on the matter. Looking directly at me, he added, 'There will be no limits to the challenge to your skills as camera operator.'

Not knowing exactly what Polanski had in mind, this bothered me. The director's comments would be repeated and underlined at his first pre-production meeting with all departments coming together.

'We will be filming direct sound with a BNC camera ...'

No problem. However, my comfort would quickly pass when Roman looked straight at me. 'The BNC camera will be in handheld mode!'

I now understood what Roman meant by 'no limits' in challenging my skills. My obvious reaction was to explain the physical impossibility of handholding a BNC camera, but sensibly I decided to remain silent, if only to see where he was heading before the director could point me to the nearest exit! Already I had visions of the muscular camera operator Bob Kindred waiting outside in the corridor in anticipation of my early departure – I had seen Bob hanging around in the canteen earlier – but all became clear when I learned what the director's definition of a handheld camera was.

Roman's idea was to install an overhead tracking rail above a large courtyard set in the studio, leaving me to assume that the camera would be coupled to a telescopic harness hanging from the track. Still unconvinced by this, and with the thought of losing the luxury of my geared head – which made operating a camera so much smoother – I could only assume that it would be necessary for me to guide the heavy camera with my hands, with my framing coming from the parallax viewfinder. No way – the idea was ridiculous; I had no chance of winning that battle.

Then again, I reasoned that Roman's idea could possibly work, but it would depend on how steady the overhead mechanism was and how much control I would have at my end of the apparatus. I certainly had my doubts with all this and at this point it was anyone's guess what the final outcome would be. I wanted to work for Roman Polanski, so it was important not to sound negative at such an early stage; even so, it would not be easy to tell him that what he was asking was impossible.

I believe this discussion was about the forthcoming battle sequence.

At the same meeting we discussed the handheld filming on location in Snowdonia. To help with this problem Roman suggested a harness for the Arriflex IIC camera, which would help with the scenes he required. His idea – if not original – involved two strips of 4 x 2 wood resting on my shoulders, strong enough to support the camera with accessories and counterbalanced by the weight of the battery at the other end of 'Roman's harness'. Bearing in mind that, like Roman, I am small in build, my concern was more about the overall weight of the equipment, plus the heavy wooden harness, which would not be helpful to my operating. This idea would make it impossible for me to satisfy the standards which the director was demanding from me. Bob Kindred was now back in the frame, but Roman suggested I had time to play around with his idea.

Working from Roman's basic description, I decided to design my own lightweight alloy harness, made to my own specifications. It was a good deal lighter than Roman's planks of wood – stronger and easily more manageable – so now the celebrated Mills Handheld Harness was born. My director was suitably impressed, insisting that I also had one made for him. As it happened I had already asked for four to be prepared.

Roman Polanski and Gil Taylor experimenting with my camera harness.

95 WEST EATON PLACE MEWS
LONDON · SW1

9th July, 1971.

Dear Alec,

Just as well we parted without a hand-shake -
because parting, as the French say, is to die a little.

Anyway, I'd like to tell you that it's not only
been an excitement and a satisfaction working with you,
but also a lot of fun.   I hope the film will be a
success - not only for me, but for all of us.

See you at the premiere in your best bib and
tucker.

With best wishes,

Roman

P.S.   Alas I can't let you have the camera sling, but
it's yours whenever you want to use it.

Roman's personal *au revoir* at the end of *Macbeth*. He liked the camera harness so much that he refused to let me have it back.

Macbeth would lay down a challenge for any camera operator working with a demanding director such as Roman Polanski, who somehow drags you along to achieve his ambitious ideas, which I trust showed in the final result on the screen. One critic suggested that Polanski's *Macbeth* mirrored the personal tragedy of his wife's murder – an unmentionable subject on the set – while I would always remain cautious as to how I handled this extraordinary situation. Roman, however, was ready for the task ahead with his unbelievable energy now focused entirely on Shakespeare's play, although perhaps in hindsight the Tate murder may have influenced the director's filming, one way or another. In a strange way it may have helped him to exorcise his personal tragedy.

On a personal note, I enjoyed working with and for Roman Polanski, a challenging director with unbelievable energy which always indicated that we would get on well with each other. Happily we did; one day Roman suddenly decided to share his thoughts with me.

'Alec, did I tell you why I chose you as my camera operator?'

Apparently it was because we were both exactly the same height and I would see everything from the same viewpoint as he did. While I found this to be an extraordinary reason for choosing me, I was more than happy to go along with the director's very clever insight.

Driving to work in the morning I would wonder what Roman's challenge of the day would be; his demanding mind never stopped working. One day I enjoyed a particular Polanski experience which more than likely came from Roman's chosen cinematographer Gilbert Taylor. I would now learn an old trick, which in time I would gladly pass on in demonstrations to the students at the National Film and Television School.

Back in 1926 – long before I was born – the German cinematographer Eugen Schüfftan was credited with inventing a process of filming through a sheet of optical glass silvered on one of its surfaces – a technique which became known as the Schüfftan process. Although this technique is rarely used or even heard of these days, it is worth recording how Gil and Roman used the system to great effect, bearing in mind that this was pre-computer-generated imagery – not to mention that it was much cheaper.

There is a scene in the film where Macbeth sees an imaginary dagger in front of him, tempting him to kill Duncan, the king. To achieve this image, Gil put the mirrored glass in front of the camera lens, which was angled to reflect the ghostly floating blade positioned against a black background to the side of the camera. Looking through the viewfinder, the image I saw was of Macbeth trying to reach out to the dagger – which the actor could not see. The reflection of the ghostly blade kept appearing and disappearing before Macbeth's eyes as he reached out to grab the weapon, which vanished when Gil dimmed the reflected light on the dagger. The Schüfftan magic was achieved without the aid of today's technology and was captured on the original negative, allowing the result to be seen at rushes the next morning. It is a wonderful memory, if only in that it helps us to appreciate the challenges which early cinematographers had to employ; it is a sadly forgotten technique in today's CGI world.

Polanski's memorable version of *Macbeth* was famous for Lady Macbeth's sleep-walking scene, with Francesca Annis being entirely naked and the stage cleared of unnecessary personnel. Prior to shooting the scene Francesca confided in me in a casual conversation over a cup of tea in the canteen, perhaps looking for comfort as to how Roman would handle this. I assured her he would handle it with taste, which of course he did.

Alfie Darling (1974). Your job is finished – now get out! Robert Watts, the production manager, hands out the 'Chinese handbills' to the crew, the normal notice of your services no longer being required given to every member two weeks before the end of filming.

From the personal view of someone trying to appreciate the works of Shakespeare, I found Polanski's version of *Macbeth* to be a rewarding experience, considering the good-for-nothing slob I had been at school. Roman's interpretation of the play gave me pause for thought, changing my attitude to the arts so that now I could smell and breathe the atmosphere which Roman created with his masterpiece.

Jon Finch played Macbeth in this screen adaptation with Francesca Annis contributing much to the drama with her beauty and dangerous charm. Martin Shaw's Banquo would always please, as would John Stride's Ross, with other well-known names to delight the Bard's audiences. However, Roman Polanski would be my star, a director who set out to challenge his camera operator so that at the end of each day I was mentally and physically exhausted. Although the dialogue was Shakespeare's, under Roman's direction it was performed in a modern manner that made it easier to understand.

However, my own personal tragedy was now close at hand; now would be the start of my own heartbreak. Trying not to be too dramatic with this, family issues in the wake of *Macbeth* would change my life. Life had not been easy for Lesley, with my career taking me around the world and problems inevitably arose from these separations, finally ending in our divorce. The guilty party named was the love of my work along with long hours and foreign locations. I would now pay the price.

A FORMER DWELLER

Flashback: Mr and Mrs Metcalf, a delightful retired elderly couple, accepted our offer for their beautiful thatched cottage Cherry Trees over two other buyers. However, this came with a condition of mortgage which required alterations in the attic and the restoration of the old plasterwork. This work would reveal a deep opening which on closer inspection was discovered to be a priest hole – a seventeenth-century hiding place for Catholic priests – skilfully concealed behind the inglenook fireplace in the sitting room below.

At first we assumed the Metcalfs knew nothing of this secret hideaway and there was no suggestion of a 'former dweller' who shared the cottage with them; but to be fair, the priest hole was only exposed by accident, so perhaps it was unknown to them. Later, however, we would learn they were aware of a 'presence'. Clearly this old property had an interesting tale to tell and on further research we would probably uncover more of Cherry Trees' past history, learn more of the resident guest we inherited – a lady who had shared the company of previous owners over many years past ...

All this came from a casual get-to-know-you chat Lesley had with our new neighbour, Sue Ash. During the exchange Sue's children hinted of a 'presence' in Cherry Trees, but, before there was time to find out more, the subject was conveniently changed – which did not go unnoticed by Lesley. Curiosity now took over and the matter was brought up at a more suitable time, with the neighbour's reluctant explanation going along these lines.

A short history of Cherry Trees: The Metcalf family had lived in the cottage for twenty years prior to the Mills family moving in. They were well-off business people and the cottage was well furnished, giving an appearance of material comfort with a happy atmosphere – the same impression Lesley and I had shared when we first viewed the property.

One day when her husband away on business, the lady of the house was enjoying a quiet moment with her thoughts. Gazing out the window, she saw an old man walking around the garden. When she asked him what he was doing on the property, the man explained that he had been the gardener some years earlier and was interested to see the garden. The old man went on to engage Mrs Metcalf

Cherry Trees, our family home in the Chiltern Hills which came complete with its own resident spirit...

in conversation and seemed curious to know if she had had visitors to the cottage. Not satisfied with her initial reply, he pressed on.

'Any... unusual visitors?' A strange question indeed ...

Mrs Metcalf thought carefully about this and recalled something odd which had happened shortly after they had moved into the cottage, when she had sensed a strange feeling of someone behind her. She turned to see an old lady standing at the open door, asking her if she liked the cottage. Surprised, not knowing who the person was, Mrs Metcalf went to speak to her but the lady disappeared – gone without a trace! Mrs Metcalf looked outside but there was still no sign of the lady and the visitor had not been seen since, though there were times when she had a feeling of a 'presence'.

The old gardener smiled knowingly; this was the answer he was hoping for. Intrigued by all this, Mrs Metcalf asked for an explanation. It would seem that the mysterious lady had lived in the cottage many years past, where she died, but came back to visit the new owners of the property. However, she would only reveal herself if there was a happy atmosphere from within – an odd phrase which was passed on to Lesley later. It was a questionable tale indeed, but with all the weird and wonderful stories handed down over the years we would never get an exact account of this past history, which was probably exaggerated over time.

I struggled while writing about this episode, which partly concerns the afterlife – something which has always interested me. With this strange account this interest would continue when the Mills family moved into Cherry Trees, where we would first learn of the permanent guest we inherited. Although I cannot claim this explanation to be verbatim, you will notice that the visitor 'spoke' to Mrs Metcalf. Following our earlier experience outside the bombed-out church during our courting days, Lesley and I would keep an open mind on all this, with no reason to doubt this account of something which had happened many years prior to our arrival. Nor have I added anything extra to make this explanation more interesting, but I will admit to taking a little licence to make this disclosure easier to understand.

Now the only reason I tell of this handed-down account was when something strange happened to me when Lesley moved away from Cherry Trees after our divorce.

With our children Simon and Belinda both away at their boarding schools I was now alone in the cottage, feeling very sorry for myself, very depressed. One night, sitting up into the early hours, deep in thought about the family break-up, I suddenly became aware of the old beams creaking above me, something I could not recall happening before. Why now in the early hours? Could this be our friendly visitor moving around? Listening to the movement, I was convinced the old woman was with me, probably even watching me; it could only be her. But again, can you hear a ghost or was I going mad in my loneliness?

Remembering the previous owner, I tried to have a conversation with my invisible friend. Would she reveal herself? Would I drop dead from the shock if she did? In the madness of it all I spoke to the lady with all sincerity of our wonderful home, anything to get her attention, even suggesting that we could share this beautiful cottage, which of course she could claim we already did.

In the uneasy calm of awaiting a reply nothing happened, except that the creaking beams had noticeably stopped before continuing from different parts of the room, as if my invisible companion was moving around. Even more convincing was that the beams stopped creaking when I was speaking to her, suggesting that the old woman was listening to me. But again, did I imagine all this?

The lady never materialised, which was probably a good thing anyway as I was not sure what would happen if she had – apart from my dying-of-shock scene, but at least that would solve the pain of the divorce. Later I recalled that the spirit would only reveal herself if a happy atmosphere existed in the cottage, which I could not claim with Lesley's departure. As a consequence I would never meet the dear soul – perhaps in time, who knows ...

Thirty years later would bring an interesting twist to this account, which for reasons of continuity will appear later in this memoir.

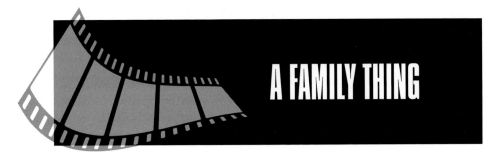

A FAMILY THING

The film industry was going through one of its quiet periods, which happened from time to time, but at least these downturns gave me time to catch up with the real life which inevitably got sidetracked with all my travelling around the world.

In a casual conversation, my cousin Brian repeated a conversation he once shared with my dad, whom he had talked into telling of his experiences in the First World War. Strangely this was something I had never asked Dad for or even thought about; my memory of Dad was of his reluctance to talk about the war – his war. Now it was too late to ask questions and I realised that much had been lost between father and son. While I was trapped in the navy Brian had got to know Alf on a different level, even managing to get Dad to discuss his experiences during the 1914–18 war. Brian passed this on to me many years later, long after Dad had died. Sadly I was too young to show an interest in Dad's wartime experiences then. There was one account in particular which caught my interest. Quote: 'Alf struck an officer!'

As you might imagine, this captured my full attention as it was a most unlikely thing for Dad to do, although thinking about this later I would admit that he was not one to hold back with his opinions if he felt it was necessary. Even so, my memory of Dad was of a quiet, gentle soul, so now I had to find out if there could be some truth in this.

The story of life in the trenches is now well known from personal accounts of the conflict, and the passing of time makes it more difficult to prove them as true or false. It would seem that Alf was put on a charge for this so-called assault, which if true then he could have been executed for striking an officer. There again, the officer involved may have been a casualty – or not. Either way, it would seem that the incident remained lost in the fog of war, somewhere in the trenches of northern France. Of course, one could argue that Brian had exaggerated the story, though I would doubt that as there was no reason for him to do so, or perhaps the situation was not as serious as the picture Alf had painted. However, there is an interesting postscript to this tale.

Obviously Alf was a rebel, which Simon discovered later when he acquired a copy of Alf's service record. Before the war he had been a porter descended from a line of Suffolk stablemen and carriage makers, so it was no surprise that he would

Mum and Dad on the occasion of their fiftieth wedding anniversary on 18 December 1971.

end up as a horse driver in the Royal Field Artillery, galloping the guns into position before he eventually became a gunner.

Simon recently visited the National Archives at Kew while researching a personal project on HMS *Britannic*, the wreck of which he now owns. While in Kew he decided to look up Alf's army service record, which confirmed that Dad was often in trouble one way or another: late on parade; arguing with officers; leaving the stables without permission; improper language to an NCO; again late on parade ... It goes on and on, but although he was court-martialled in October 1916 for 'using threatening language to his superior officer', apparently for mistreating a horse, and for which he received forty-two days' Field Punishment No. 1 – handcuffed and chained to a gun carriage wheel for two hours a day – there is no record of Alf actually striking an officer.

Interestingly enough, recently seeing the film *War Horse* this brought back some of the stories Alf passed on to Brian. Another story Brian recounted was of a practice that became known as the 'third light' – an interesting example of what it was like in those muddy trenches. While waiting on orders to go over the top, the soldiers would keep their heads down, out of sight of enemy snipers. The stand-off would continue into the night, with the occasional flare and sporadic gunfire reminding both sides they were still there, even though they were unable to see each other. In the black of night the soldiers would stand around quietly chatting; one might light a cigarette, and a German sniper hiding in the dark would take note of the position. Should a second soldier take a light from the same match, the sniper would take aim; if a third soldier took a light he was shot. This action became known as the 'third light'.

With all this information coming from a cousin, I had to ask myself why Dad never told me about his wartime experiences, which in all probability was because

I never asked him. Although these amazing stories came as a surprise, this next account tells more of the man I knew and respected.

It is necessary to remember what it was like in those dark days when people lived from week to week with few luxuries, where the so-called working classes were given their pay packets to take home on a Friday for families to buy their necessary provisions. One Friday night Alf arrived home without his wages, claiming that he had lost the money. Lil was very angry and accused him of losing it at the White City dog track, which Dad strongly denied, saying he had not been anywhere near the place. Lil, however, was having none of this nonsense – not a word of it – and let him know exactly what she thought about this matter. It was some weeks later while she was out shopping that Lil was approached by a troubled woman, the wife of Alf's workmate, who thanked her for Alf's gesture of helping them in their hour of need. The tearful lady explained that they had lost their twins and did not have enough money to pay for the funeral expenses; it would seem that Dad gave his wages to his friend without a word to Lil.

This was a gesture I did recognise and was familiar with, and hence my need to record it. Dad's generosity and compassion to an equal was the man I knew, the man I would always remember him as. This still begs the question of why all these wonderful stories came from a third party. I took comfort in deciding that Dad just 'switched off' and was reluctant to talk about his wartime experiences, while his son is proud to recall this small piece of lost family history. Even so, the credit goes to Brian, who managed to squeeze these revelations out of Dad; otherwise another piece of family history would stay lost in the fog of time.

But now it is time to get back to my own private adventures in life ...

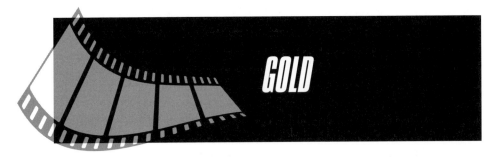

With film production remaining quiet in our unpredictable industry, I had time to consider writing an autobiography, should I ever get around to it. Later I would realise that this would be no easy task, particularly when trying to unravel the interesting from the boring, but that was a dilemma which I would face in my retirement now, as I struggle on, hoping to keep your interest.

Moving on, camera operating offers began to arrive with more consistency, including *Gold*, *The Hiding Place*, *Operation Daybreak* and *Shout at the Devil*, which would keep the wolves from the door and keep me busy for the next two years. *Gold* came as a happy reunion, with me working once again with Peter Hunt, who enjoyed the company of his trusted ally from *On Her Majesty's Secret Service*. However, this time Peter's cinematographer would be Osama Rawi, with whom I had worked before on *Alfie Darling*, a nonsense story made in the wake of the earlier and more successful Michael Caine film – we have all worked on films we would prefer to forget! Even so, I doubt I was of much help to Ossie, as my mind was constantly on personal matters with the issue of my divorce, not forgetting the friendly phantom of Cherry Trees, who kept reminding me that she was still around and sharing my pain.

The film, based on the novel *Goldmine* by Wilbur Smith, would star Roger Moore, whom I had last worked with back on *The Saint* in 1966. Roger was an actor who made the camera operator's job so much easier. He was a complete performer in every sense of the word and also enjoyed a wonderful sense of humour. Later you will see how I became his prized victim.

Gold would turn out to be one of the most hazardous films which I would work on as a camera operator. It was a trial for any camera crew to film deep underground in a goldmine where conditions were near impossible to cope with. During our filming I spent time down in the lowest part of the mine with the second-unit director, John Glen, having agreed to change places with John's cameraman, Jimmy Devis, who suffered from claustrophobia. Jimmy missed a wonderful visual moment as the cage slowly descended to the bottom of the mineshaft, passing countless black miners on many levels on the way down, the lights on their protective helmets mixed with the perpetual dust, creating a strange unforgettable image.

Leaving the mass drilling behind, we moved to a different form of transport in the shape and size of a coffin, which would take us to an even lower level where the new seams were being worked. Travelling in this Heath Robinson apparatus, quite apart from the ever-present danger of rock falls, it was necessary to lie completely flat to prevent our heads scraping on the rocks inches above. When we arrived at our destination a new atmosphere greeted us – it was a surprisingly large, cooler area where the mine took on a totally different character, with only the occasional lonely miner drilling to find a new seam in this extraordinary subterranean world. Although this was interesting and tested my curiosity, I will admit that the journey to the lowest point was something I could happily do without. Now it was time to return to our 'coffin' and start the long journey back to ground level, with both John and I grateful for our safe arrival back at the surface, where the sweet taste of fresh air greeted us.

One particularly dangerous scene which comes to mind was with Roger Moore and Simon Sabela struggling up to their necks in uncontrolled surging water as part of a mine flooding sequence, where Simon's character is eventually killed. They were not alone in the water, and the camera crew had to help steady me against the constant surging water as I battled to keep a grip on my handheld camera while capturing the chilling moment of the mine flooding.

Everything about this sequence was at best extremely uncomfortable, and the camera and everyone involved remained soaked to the skin throughout a long day's difficult filming. There was more to come: when completing the sequence in the so-called controlled conditions of Pinewood Studios the actors constantly disappeared from sight in the surging water. Nor was there room for any doubles or stand-ins; all were excluded from these tight spaces, with only my giant grip Jim Kane and camera assistant Ron Drinkwater helping me to stand against the pressure of the oncoming tide.

Another scary moment shared with Roger Moore and Susannah York was the scene in a small light aeroplane which could hold only four people – including the pilot. The scene was of the two actors flying back to the mine after hearing of the flooding disaster on the television, both of them sitting in the back seat while I sat up front next to the pilot, filming them. With no room for the director, the actors had to direct their own performances.

So now came a genuine drama with the aircraft itself. The plane was supposed to pass through a deep, narrow gorge with the cliff face close to both sides challenging the pilot's expertise in manoeuvring the plane, tilting the wings if necessary – it really was that close! Looking through the camera, my concentration was focused entirely on Roger and Susannah's performances, watching them carefully as I had been instructed by the director. I would say that they were not at their best with all these aerobatics going on around, which was not surprising as I could feel the swaying movement of the plane while I struggled with the camera under the black cloth which I used to prevent any light creeping through the eyepiece and fogging the film. Happily we survived the ordeal.

In the film, Rod Slater (Roger Moore), the manager of the Sonderditch goldmine, discovers a plan to drill into an underground lake with the intention of flooding the mine so that members of a criminal syndicate can make a killing by rigging the price of gold on the international market. Co-starring with Roger was Susannah York, the veteran American actor Ray Milland, Bradford Dillman, John Gielgud and Simon Sabela, not forgetting hundreds of very brave black miners.

THE HIDING PLACE

It would seem that I inherited the problem of my bad memory from my mother Lil, so that important events and accounts are lost, while painful experiences such as *The Hiding Place* would remain as a constant reminder of our tragic past.

What came from the post-war years were the many stories of the Jewish families and their loved ones who suffered under the German occupation. One particular account which captured the public's interest was the story of the young Dutch girl Anne Frank, a teenager who lived with her family in Amsterdam during the war. Sadly Anne would not survive the ordeal, dying in the Belsen concentration camp in 1945. However, she would become famous for the diary she had kept, which was first published in 1947.

There was another true story of a Dutch Christian family who secretly sheltered Jewish refugees in their home above their father's workshop. Casper Ten Boom and his

Unit picture outside the concentration camp during filming of *The Hiding Place* in 1974. The camera crew are to the right, including Danny Shelmerdine (clappers), Ron Drinkwater (focus), Michael Reed (cinematographer) and me.

daughters Corrie and Betsie were devoted Christians who were appalled with all that was happening around them under the German occupation and decided to build a false brick wall in their home, behind which they could hide Jewish families from Nazi persecution. The wall was created little by little by gathering up old bricks scattered around the city and smuggling them into their home in order to build the hiding place. Eventually they were discovered in February 1944, with Betsie and Corrie sent to the Ravensbrück concentration camp where Betsie died in December 1944. Corrie was accidentally released two weeks later due to a fortunate clerical error!

It was Corrie's 1971 book which encouraged the Billy Graham Organisation to finance the making of the film, a backer that might suggest a strong religious bias. However *The Hiding Place* was not weighed down that way but was more concerned with the personal issues of Corrie and her family's commitment to their faith in risking their lives for others.

This true story benefited from having a wonderful director in James Collier, a quiet, gentle human being who set out to capture the atmosphere of Ravensbrück as he recreated the past darkness which had existed in those menacing days. He was helped in no small measure with the careful selection of Michael Reed as his cinematographer, making this the perfect team.

One scene in particular would leave even the most hardened film crew saddened as Betsie lay dying on a wooden bedstead, where her only comfort came from

With director James Collier in a snow-covered concentration camp. James was one of my favourite directors, full of compassion in the moment of others' suffering.

Corrie nursing her with a little help from another prisoner as the director recreated Betsie's death, summoning a chilling and unforgettable atmosphere that would affect the entire unit. Words alone could not do justice to this scene.

Watching this director working with his actors, it seemed to me that James Collier came from the same school of directors as José Quintero, a director who harmonised his actors to his very own excellence. In return, the director would be rewarded with memorable performances from his actors, allowing this spectator looking through the camera to appreciate the art of good directing. With the Collier method it seemed that every person in my frame – and here I include the crowd artistes in the background who were given their own special part to play – responded well to the director's wonderful skills. This was no 'Cut – over here, boys!' director; James quietly strived for perfection with the screen performances and the feel and timing of the camera movement matched the mood. He was a true, honest director with whom I was privileged to work and learn from – shades of Roman Polanski.

Julie Harris (Betsie) and Jeannette Clift (Corrie) both gave extraordinary performances, as was recognised in all of the reviews, while Michael Reed's photography captured the camp's chilling atmosphere with his clever 'painting'. Oddly enough, this project took place when my own marital problems were coming to an end. Even so it was a timely reminder that my troubles were of little consequence compared to those of the Ten Boom sisters, as no doubt was true for many others.

It was Corrie's account which later influenced me to visit the Auschwitz-Birkenau concentration camp in Poland with Suzy, perhaps a necessary reminder of the cruelty suffered from other so-called human beings. With time moving on I was now ready for the next chapter of my professional life, and another sad story of Nazi persecution.

OPERATION DAYBREAK

The tragedy of war inevitably brings out the best and worst in the human race, times when we are reminded of the evils lurking round the corner. Opportunity once again came my way, working for Lewis Gilbert on his next 'exciting' adventure, *Operation Daybreak* – it is an expression I choose carefully with regard to Lewis. I had no idea how this project came about, as the last time we had worked together I was a clapper boy on *A Cry from the Streets*, the film on which Lewis had given Harry Gillam his break as cinematographer – which inevitably brings to mind a flashback ...

As a camera assistant – the lowest form of life in the camera department – I quickly learned that it takes time to make helpful contacts with the camera fraternity, but it is a necessary part of the journey when keeping an eye open for future employment. The lonely individual should be aware of the saying 'if the face doesn't fit', which could make it harder to establish those connections within the already established camera crews of the day. Keeping that in mind, *A Cry from the Streets* would set me a challenge to overcome all that nonsense and make sure that Harry would remember me on his debut as cinematographer and keep me in mind when any other films were offered in the future. My performance as Harry's camera assistant was faultless to the end, but as filming neared completion there was still no sign from the cinematographer that we would ever work together again; it would seem all my efforts were in vain.

Prague, 1975: On location with Lewis Gilbert during the filming of *Operation Daybreak*.

Filming the final battle sequences of *Operation Daybreak* at the cathedral of Saints Cyril and Methodius in Prague. I'm still smiling, so this must have been taken before the result of the Arsenal v. QPR game was known!

With the end of filming and the usual celebrations over we walked to our cars while chatting, with me believing that this would be the ideal time for Harry to make an offer of his next film. It never happened. After shaking hands we went our separate ways, but all was not lost. As I was getting into my car a shout suddenly came from Harry, now some distance away, calling me over to him. With great expectation I hurried to the cinematographer, certain of what he was about to say.

'Alec, if you hear of a film going, mention my name!'

I stood there, gobsmacked, totally lost for words. Then came take two with the shaking-of-hands bit, which Harry was fond of, before he drove away, never to be seen again. This experience would come as a timely reminder that my chances of moving up the ladder would not come easily, no matter how hard I tried to impress. One learns from experience on many levels.

Now, many years later, I would set out to impress my director, the same Lewis Gilbert. This time, however, I would be Lewis's camera operator on *Operation*

Daybreak, the true story of the assassination of the SS General Reinhard Heydrich, Himmler's deputy during the war. *Operation Daybreak* would also be an interesting reminder of what our lives would have been like had things worked out differently.

In recent years Lewis had worked with French cinematographers, which would continue with Henri Decae – a pleasant gentleman with a generous moustache and with whom I also enjoyed working. At the same time, I was at a loss to see how I came into this Anglo-French connection. Perhaps Lewis thought it would be to his advantage in having an English-speaking camera operator and my name had fallen out of the hat.

Working with Lewis Gilbert, you could be sure that life was never dull. One of the many memories we shared over the years was our filming of a battle scene in the centre of Prague, which involved a hundred extras dressed as German soldiers. The scene could only be filmed on a Saturday, when the police could seal off all the roads around the cathedral of Saints Cyril and Methodius – the same church where the Czech partisans were hiding after Heydrich's assassination, where the drama had finally played out fifty years earlier.

The not-so-comfortable filming of the crypt sequences, where the besieged Czechoslovakian paratroopers eventually commit suicide.

With our German army preparing to storm the building with tanks, machine guns and fire engines, the watching public witnessed the elimination of the partisans trapped inside the church ... except that on this particular Saturday there would be a distraction for our director, whose mind appeared to be elsewhere. What would an Englishman like Lewis Gilbert find so distracting in Prague on this particular Saturday afternoon?

Lewis's beloved football team Arsenal was playing an important match against my team Queen's Park Rangers, with the game being broadcast live on the BBC's overseas service. Due to the poor reception, our heads were glued to Lewis's small portable radio; with five minutes still left in the game the first assistant director arrived to inform Lewis that everything was ready on the set. With that I excused myself and moved away before being hauled back by Lewis grabbing my arm, insisting that I suffer the remaining moments of his pleasure. Arsenal won the battle, whereby I lost a sizeable bet, so making it necessary for Lewis to relish the moment until the final whistle confirmed that we could now get on with the job in hand, leaving me a broken man both in cash and humiliation. Worse still was that I would never hear the end of it from Lewis!

Filming at the train station in Prague – supposedly Berlin – we had to film Adolf Hitler, played by George Sewell, waiting to greet Heydrich, played by Anton Diffring. The plan was for the engine to stop on its prearranged mark so that the carriage came to a halt opposite the Führer. With the scene fully rehearsed, the engine driver backed the train to a reasonable distance from the platform, preparing to enter the station on cue so that Heydrich would step off the train, saluting Hitler in the customary Nazi fashion.

For reasons known only to the engine driver, he decided to change the scene as it had been rehearsed, by passing his mark and stopping a considerable distance down the platform. However, Anton recognised the driver's error and smoothly moved along the platform towards Hitler. Through the camera I had Hitler on the left of frame wearing his brown coat with swastika armband clearly featured on his left sleeve; as Heydrich approached, the two Nazis came together, only for Heydrich to continue walking straight past his Führer without a second glance and straight past my camera. Anton later claimed that he never recognised Hitler standing there with his toothbrush moustache and dressed in full Nazi uniform – another silly moment we look back on, sharing a quiet smile with each other.

More important was that I had won Lewis Gilbert's favour with this new relationship developing, where we would soon be working together with a secret agent 007, which would continue long into the future – unlike my efforts with Harry Gillam.

SHOUT AT THE DEVIL

As a camera operator mindful of the need for cooperation to improve the composition in the camera frame, it is necessary to build up relationships with the actors, so making the job easier. However, much depends on their attitude to this, especially with their changing moods where performance was more important. Tact and diplomacy usually paid off; grovelling could be resorted to when all else failed.

One of the many irritations which actors have to live with usually come with early morning calls, perhaps for make-up after having had little sleep – let's face it, actors are human beings, after all. Whatever their problems, a good camera operator quickly learns to recognise any signs which could leave an actor in a less-than-cooperative frame of mind, making the humble operator's life difficult – actors' personal problems are sometimes of little help to the poor soul looking through the camera.

With Michael Reed, lining up a shot on *Shout at the Devil* in the Transkei (1975). The director's viewfinder is a converted parallax viewfinder from an old BNC camera.

Preparing to shoot Roger Moore's point of view while being carried on a stretcher. In the background with hands on hip is clapper loader Danny Shelmerdine (not sure if that's a hat or his hairstyle) and Frank Ernst (first assistant director) holding the loudhailer.

I hasten to add that this daily challenge would never be a problem working with Roger Moore, whom I recognised as the total professional, but now it was time to enjoy the Lee Marvin experience which would test Peter Hunt's patience to the full on *Shout at the Devil*.

Based on another novel by Wilbur Smith, Roger's character, Sebastian Oldsmith, was described as a respectable Englishman looking for adventure, while Lee played Colonel Flynn Patrick O'Flynn, an Irish rogue who just happened to have a beautiful daughter Rosa, played by Barbara Parkin. You are aware of my thoughts on Roger Moore, so now let me share my praise of the late Lee Marvin, a down-to-earth actor, a star with few hang-ups – apart from one big problem.

It was no secret that Lee liked his drink; one morning his unscheduled early departure for one of the filming locations gave our anxious director Peter Hunt much reason for concern. However, it would seem that Lee had been unable to sleep and decided to leave early rather than wait for his usual call. When Peter heard of the actor's early departure it was understandable that he became anxious and worried about the state in which we would find Lee on our arrival, but on this occasion it was a false alarm and the colourful picture I recall was of finding Lee sitting on the dry red earth, with the local villagers sitting around him enjoying the white man's antics. Lee was as sober as a judge, although more than likely he would have had a couple of cans on the way to the location! With a clear-headed Lee ready for work, Peter was elated, at the same time privately admitting that he could never be sure what would be a good or bad day with our star.

With all of this unpredictability the producer, Michael Klinger, and director came to terms with this very delicate situation, in the end deciding that Peter with his usual tact should be the one to handle any setbacks which might occur as there would be little to gain in upsetting the actor. Even so there were times when Peter had to accept the inevitable, such as one memorable scene when, with time fast running out and the light fading quickly, work had to be postponed until the following morning.

The scripted action was simple. Roger Moore, the expectant father, paces up and down while waiting on the first cries of a newborn baby being delivered; Lee would also pace up and down with fatherly concern for his daughter. Unfortunately, when Lee arrived on the set the next morning he could barely stand, let alone walk! He had been on a bender the previous evening and was in no condition to perform on camera, which came on a day when the actor was in every scene on the call sheet; it was certainly not good news. Head-scratching time – what to do?

What do you mean, 'RUN!'?

A kindly helping hand from Roger Moore, which would have been even more appreciated if he hadn't been the one who pushed me into the water in the first place!

Filming Lee Marvin's close-up for the life raft sequences in the large tank at the Mediterranean Film Studios on Malta. This is the only European filming tank that has a south-facing natural horizon with the real sea, giving the camera operator a far greater degree of movement.

Mindful that some directors automatically ignore alternative suggestions put to them from those in their close team, I might have hesitated in offering a suggestion. My normal hesitation came with the thought that some directors allow their egos to get in the way of the problem, but this was never the case with Peter Hunt, who had previously taken me to one side when I was reluctant to speak up about any thoughts I had, worried that they would intrude on the director's territory.

'Alec, if you have an idea to make a scene interesting, tell me. If I like it I may use it!'

Of course, I understand this can be thorny territory to tread on with some directors, but in my experience difficult directors have been in the minority. I am not suggesting that directing by committee is desirable – absolutely not. Even so, the camera operator, remembering Ernie Day's professional relationship with Ken Annakin, is very much a part of the director's team.

In the dreadful silence and with no sign of any other ideas I reluctantly – *very* reluctantly – offered a suggestion to Peter. With Roger's immaculate costume partly consisting of highly polished brown shoes, contrasting with Lee's grubby clothes with dirty worn-out boots turned up at the toes – a scruffy bugger – I could follow Roger's shoes with the camera as he paced up and down, timed to the off-screen dialogue, eventually taking the camera over to Lee's unsightly boots where, if necessary, the rest of the scene could be filmed on the actors' faces when Lee sobered up. It was not much to offer but Peter agreed this was all we could hope for in Lee's present condition.

'ACTION!'

More in hope than expectation, Roger's polished shoes walked to and fro with the camera staying with his every move as the scene covered the required dialogue. With the eventual arrival of Lee's footwear into shot, through the camera it suddenly seemed as if Lee's boots were starting to tip backwards, heading out of frame. He had passed out!

'CUT!'

Lee Marvin was a likeable man who had little control over his alcohol intake, which at times could be embarrassing for all to witness. One scene on board the fictional German battleship *Blücher* would leave all the cast waiting around while Lee could barely stand, yet somehow that did not matter as we all loved him. You took Lee as you found him.

Lewis Gilbert is a true professional in every sense of the word, a director with whom I had the pleasure to work on four films, a man who contributed much to a relaxed atmosphere on the set, so when he asked if I would join him on a trip to Japan my 'Yes please' came long before the director had finished extending his kind invitation.

Seven Nights in Japan was a story of love in unusual circumstances, with an attempted assassination of a British prince played by Michael York, because of his love for Japanese girl Hidemi Aoki.

Japan would be a new experience for me. I had heard rumours suggesting that Japanese people ate raw fish with rice at every opportunity – a bizarre combination should this be true. To be honest, I have absolutely no idea where this silly idea came from, unless it was a strange person who will remain nameless winding me up. Even so the thought of it would quickly cool my earlier enthusiasm for the trip. What would also be unhelpful was the idea associate producer Bill Cartlidge had in mind for the catering, introducing the crew to a Japanese supermarket which, as you would expect did not go down well; with all this nonsense I settled for the occasional Kobe steak, which would probably have made a minuscule dent in Bill's monetary plans.

Once again Henri Decae was the director's chosen cinematographer, although I later suspected that Lewis was less enthusiastic about that decision. Little things were starting to bother him and were clearly noticeable as Lewis sat near the camera – my domain – where I take note of all that goes on.

Hearing of my forthcoming Japanese trip the headmaster of Simon's school had asked a favour of me: if possible, could I contact a university lecturer, an old colleague of his now living in Tokyo, just to say 'Hello'? When we eventually arrived in the capital city towards the end of our Japanese location I duly contacted the university, passing on the headmaster's message and being more than grateful that the don's English was good enough to understand me and say that he would be in touch with Simon's headmaster about our meeting. With this in mind I thought it appropriate to invite the professor with his wife to join me for dinner at our very smart hotel, believing that this would impress him, and he accepted.

So that we could recognise each other, we arranged to meet outside the hotel. A small gentleman stepped from a chauffeured limousine where I – 5 feet 5 inches tall

Seven Nights in Japan (1975) and another photo for the album.

in shoes – looked down on this kindly old gentleman. Evidently the academic was well-known and respected by all the locals, who eagerly gathered around him as he turned to me, smiling politely and bowing. Meanwhile his wife, a sweet old lady, emerged from the car in full kimono dress, also bowing her head and remained that way, standing a little behind him. What to do, methinks?

Unsure what to do next but at the same time certain that I did not want to offend these beautiful people with their traditions, in my unease I held out my hand, half bowing half nodding, Del-Boy style, hoping that he would at least appreciate the gesture. Regaining control, I then led the professor to the restaurant, with his wife insisting on keeping her distance behind; I slowed down, encouraging the dear lady to join us, but that didn't work and she preferred to keep her distance from the two men. I was surprised that this tradition still existed in modern Japan, but again this could have been a custom the older generation preferred to observe. The evening passed slowly – very slowly – the conversation was difficult with embarrassing long pauses. In the end I doubt that I did Simon any favours at all, but this was a new country to visit and a new experience to see the diverse locations in Kyoto and Tokyo.

With filming soon to end, Lewis quietly called me to one side from the unit, waving a cable from Cubby Broccoli inviting him to direct the next James Bond film. I was delighted for Lewis as it had been almost ten years since he had directed *You Only Live Twice*, and was even more delighted when he asked if I would join him on *The Spy Who Loved Me*, confirming that our professional relationship was strong and would continue on his next two films.

With my puffed-up ego working overtime I decided that operating the camera was probably the most rewarding position in the camera department, where, detached from all the politics around me, I could at least 'hide' under my black cloth, a place where at times it would seem as if the actors were performing just for me. No doubt this assertion would appear strange if not ridiculous to some, so let me underline this by telling of an Ernie Day operating experience when he was on *Lawrence of Arabia*.

The scene Ernie described was a Peter O'Toole monologue, with the camera focused entirely on the actor. To assist the performance, David Lean required the camera to track slowly forward into a close up, the timing of the movement synchronised to the actor's performance – a simple shot on the face of it. After one rehearsal for timing, Ernie and grip were both ready.

'ACTION!'

The camera moved slowly forward as rehearsed, the tracking precisely timed before coming to a stop as rehearsed at the end of O'Toole's long dialogue. The actor then slowly stood up, again as rehearsed, but the camera did not follow him as planned. Ernie Day, my hero and probably the best camera operator of all time, admitted that he had been 'hypnotised' by O'Toole's performance, which was obviously a compliment to the actor's technique even if not apparently appreciated by Mr O'Toole, who would leave Ernie with unprintable thoughts on this matter.

You may remember that Ken Annakin had asked Harry Waxman to use Ernie Day as his operator on *Swiss Family Robinson* – the director's confidence in his camera operator was important to him. However, it would seem that even Ernie had his failings, so at least I could console myself when remembering how I let down Harry Waxman. Like Ernie, I am a human being after all.

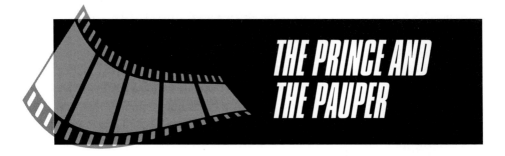

THE PRINCE AND THE PAUPER

Four long months would pass before my planned assignment with 007 was due to begin, a brief meeting with Eon's production office suggested that I should make myself available from mid-August onwards. With my constant travelling around the world, staying at home would make a welcome change, particularly with the tidying up of family issues. Cherry Trees with its resident ghost was now sold and past history so a temporary move back to Croxley Road would be necessary while I hunted for a new family home – perhaps in London?

However, things would not work out as planned when a phone call from production manager Basil Keys asked me to meet him at Pinewood Studios about a film called *Crossed Swords*, an adaptation of Mark Twain's *The Prince and the*

Lining up the village scene in which Oliver Reed is put in the stocks and pelted with rotten fruit. From Left to right: Jack Cardiff (leaning against the table), Richard Fleischer looking through his viewfinder, while I look on, with Suzy standing next to me, to control the Hungarian extras.

A photographic compilation of Frank Elliott's sense of
humour on *The Prince and the Pauper*. When working in
front of the camera as 'Second Guard' Frank took the stage
name of Tyrone Cassidy.

Discussing a set-up with director Richard Fleischer.

Even the grip had an opinion.

No wonder I'm losing my hair ...

Pauper, which was also the eventual title of the film. This would be my second film with that story background, the first having been with Paul Beeson in 1961 during his Disney period. This time, though, our filming would take place in Budapest, Hungary. Although I had no intention, wish or desire to spend the next three months away, my curiosity allowed me to meet Basil and a lengthy discussion followed, but only with Basil's assurance that I could leave the film if *The Spy Who Loved Me* came forward. With this agreed I accepted his generous offer.

If truth be told, the only reason I found *Crossed Swords* remotely interesting was the cinematographer Jack Cardiff, whom I had never met before but whose name alone went before him as a respected 'painter of light'; suddenly there was now an opportunity to work with the grand master himself.

Among the many films credited to Jack Cardiff were *Black Narcissus*, for which he won an Oscar, *The Magic Box*, *The Red Shoes*, *A Matter of Life and Death*, *The African Queen* and *Scott of the Antarctic*, all classics lit by the man with whom I would now be working. Perhaps it was Jack's CV to which I succumbed, but now with this sudden chance I would hope to learn much from working with the great man himself, let alone the many interesting conversations we would share together.

Filming began at Pinewood Studios before we moved on to Budapest, where we would meet up with a party of professional Hungarian technicians all waiting on our arrival. My only problem with foreign locations was the inevitable challenge of language and communication, where – if past experience had taught me anything – it was helpful, indeed necessary, to have a good relationship with the first assistant director in my work. However, with the Hungarian first assistant constantly busy with British assistant director Nigel Wooll's problems, his assistant could work alongside me as my interpreter.

Szemes Zsuzsanna's English was perfect; an assistant director who would understand the camera operator's problems. 'Just call me Suzy!' would be the answer to the pronunciation problem with which I struggled; how could either of us visualise what those few words would eventually lead to – a relationship neither of us could possibly imagine!

MY 'MATE' OLLIE

By working with Jack Cardiff I would meet and work with his regular crew for the first time: Frank Elliott, his camera assistant, and Miki Thomas (clappers). Both were generous in their support to me, though I remained cautious of Frank's reputation as a 'character'. I would soon find out why he had this reputation when a series of events led to my initiation into 'Club Oliver', which inevitably got me into all sorts of trouble.

Oliver Reed – 'Ollie' to his friends – with whom I had previously worked on *The Hunting Party* was, for all his faults, a very good actor, and glad I am to tell that Ollie and I shared a good working relationship. But of course that came at a price. Oliver's well-known off-screen drinking exploits were no help to him or his reputation, which would increase one morning when he did not turn up for work; Ollie had been arrested for fighting, which you could be sure was alcohol related.

At another party celebrating Mark Lester's eighteenth birthday, Oliver arrived late to the gathering with a young lady on his arm – a prostitute – his present to Mark on reaching manhood! As you might imagine, Ollie's 'gift' did not go down well with the invited guests, and it was also embarrassing for the young ladies in the cast who were present at the celebrations.

Soon it would time for my own initiation into 'Club Oliver'! This happened when I was 'summoned' to attend Oliver's birthday party, who insisted that the camera crew should join him, along with other invited guests. Knowing well of Oliver's past exploits on *The Hunting Party*, there was little chance that I would be interested in Ollie's merrymaking, but I then made the silly mistake of asking Frank to phone Oliver and apologise for me: 'Tell him I cannot make it – make up some excuse ...'

Frank duly obliged: 'Ollie, Alec bottled out and doesn't want to come!'

It will come as no surprise that Frank's pathetic plea on my behalf would be rejected out of hand, so for the sake of Oliver's cooperation I succumbed to the inevitable, which I still suffer in nightmares.

The dinner was held at one of Budapest's finest restaurants, the Hundred-Year-Old Restaurant, where Ollie had invited a dozen hand-picked guests who, on demand, would be required to celebrate anything that entered his head. This began by toasting every member of his family, absent friends, everyone at the table and that chap over there in the corner who smiled. Ollie was heading for one glorious 'mis-'ap!'

Here I should explain that I cannot drink more than a half-pint of lager – and would prefer a shandy. However, Ollie was not having any shandy nonsense that night, bellowing: 'We toast with wine – bull's blood!' – deadly poison for any non-drinker. It was a hot, sticky summer night and a musician was walking around the garden playing a violin – the perfect setting for Ollie's celebrations. Desperately in need of salvation from what lay ahead a cunning plan came to mind. Hoping that this would save me, I carefully positioned myself with my back to the bushes with Frank sitting opposite and our host seated at the head of the table. My confidence slowly returned with the knowledge that my ingenious survival plan was in place, thanks to the seating arrangements.

The evening began with a sober verse of 'Happy Birthday' with Ollie insisting every toast should be downed in one go, with the guests obediently accepting Oliver's ruling. To start the proceedings his first toast was to his mum, with the guests conforming by downing the 'poison'. Although I went through the motions, instead I cunningly tipped the glass over my shoulder, polluting the sad, ill-fated shrubbery behind. I managed to get away with this clever deception for three or four toasts when Judas sitting opposite noted my ability to stay clear-headed and decided to watch me on the next round of drinks.

Frank would not have long to wait. With hindsight, if I had acted with a hint of inebriation then I might have got away with this clever deception; sadly, the thought escaped me and Frank whispered to Oliver what I was up to. Now closely watched by my host the inevitable happened and I was soon pissed out my mind and totally incapable of doing anything in that condition, leaving my previously sober reputation now hanging in rags!

The rest of the celebration is a hazy blur, apart from the vague memory of Ollie and Frank dragging me back to the hotel, covered in chocolate with the scuffs on the tips of my shoes providing the evidence; I was in a terrible mess. Seeing my condition on entering the hotel lobby, the guests asked what had happened; Frank completed the evening's entertainment by telling everyone that I had been in a fight! Apparently the double act carried me to my room and put me to bed. I remember little of this but at least I was now a fully paid up member of 'Club Oliver', where I could expect to be left alone and in peace.

Should any consolation come from all this nonsense it would be that Ollie and I ended up good pals; the sacrifice made was worth the pain suffered and from now on I would enjoy Ollie's unending cooperation throughout what would be a difficult film for a camera operator. Although Ollie's drinking exploits would leave a sad mark on his standing as an actor, I always believed that his performances came from the heart – possibly from personal experiences.

With filming soon to end, it was no longer possible to hide my relationship with Suzy, which had become personal. I knew that I would miss her when I returned to the UK but I still had my appointment to keep with 007 and now it was time to say goodbye. However, fate had other plans for me, even when my replacement arrived to take over for the last two weeks of filming ...

THE SPY WHO LOVED ME

Before returning from Budapest, I had been asked to suggest a few names as my replacement. Unfortunately the selected camera operator did not get on with the director, Richard Fleischer, so he would return to the UK once a replacement could be found. Once again the Budapest production office called me at Pinewood, asking me to recommend another replacement.

Coincidence? I'm not sure about that, but *The Spy Who Loved Me* had gone back two weeks, which I had only discovered on my return to England. Now the sudden delay on *Spy* left me hanging around with little to do. When I explained the problem of *Crossed Swords* to the Bond production manager, David Middlemas, he quickly got the message and gave me his blessing to go – if only to get me out of his busy office. The next morning I was on my way back to Hungary.

October 1976 and back on location in Egypt for *The Spy Who Loved Me. Left to Right:* Alec Mills (camera operator), Doug Milsome (focus puller), Danny Shelmerdine (clapper loader) and Claude Renoir (cinematographer).

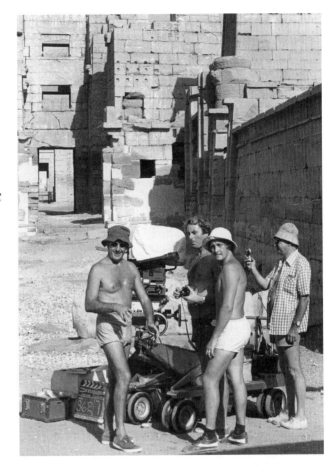

With my return to Budapest, the first thing to do was to speak to the departing camera operator, who was realistic about the situation; in truth he was happy to go home. Returning to the set I was welcomed back, and assumed that few knew the real reason for my sudden return, even if it was obvious to Suzy. Making the most of that final week, we decided that she should apply for a visa to visit England for the Christmas celebrations, but even this would not come easily, with Suzy's application coming from a communist country. Yet another setback ...

Sure enough, back home a knock on the door confronted me with two very tall gentlemen.

'Mr Mills? Mr Alexander Mills?' they enquired.

Inspector Plod and his silent companion looked down at me with great suspicion, introducing themselves as Scotland Yard detectives. There was no alternative but to let them in to Lil's home, where the two ice-cold law enforcers started asking personal questions: where would Suzy be staying ... sleeping ...? questions that frightened the life out of Lily – what on earth had her son been up to?

I casually mentioned that I was a friend of agent 007 but they remained unimpressed and the joke died. Two hours would pass before the grilling came to an end, with the law enforcers persuaded that all was well in this household – a true and honest Brit helped in no small way by Lil bribing them with the traditional cuppa to help lighten their suspicions towards me. All that remained now was for the Passport Office to issue that all-important visa to the British Consulate in Budapest; with all this bureaucracy we decided that Suzy should apply for the necessary document straight away, four months before it was required.

Meanwhile, back at Pinewood, my suspicions that Lewis had not been happy with Henri Decae were confirmed with a change of cinematographer, although his preference would remain for a French cameraman. This time it would be Claude Renoir, the grandson of the famous impressionist artist; he fitted in well with his pleasant personality.

This time 007 was tracking Britain's enemies to Abu Simbel, Luxor and Karnak, not forgetting the pyramids of Giza, the usual preferred Egyptian filming locations which eventually end in the torture of Cairo's stifling summer heat, where endless sandstorms made filming difficult to cope with. The Luxor location would inevitably bring the grumblings of poor catering which eventually reached the ear of Cubby Broccoli, who just happened to know where he could get his hands on an unlimited supply of spaghetti, which our friendly producer cooked and served himself – a rare treat, to be sure, of which I unashamedly took advantage of by approaching our illustrious chef with plate in hand.

'Please, sir, can I have more?'

'More? MORE?' Cubby bellowed back, appreciating the Dickens moment. Wiping his hands on his spattered apron, he happily refilled my plate ... a wonderful man, not only for his cooking.

Another location involved our filming on board a nuclear submarine at the Faslane Naval Base on the shores of Gare Loch in Scotland. Lewis suddenly came up with the idea of filming head-on a torpedo being loaded into the tube, and to meet with the director's 'wishes' (I choose the word carefully as I suspect that Roger Moore was really behind this) I would be required to ease myself backwards into the heavily greased confines of the tube, pulling my handheld camera with accessories along with me while in the receding background Lewis and Roger stood grinning, their echoing voices in the chamber asking, 'Can you swim, Alec?' Roger was pointing his finger, indicating that he was close to the firing button but this was no time for accidents or one of Roger's practical jokes, although no doubt he would have enjoyed the vision of me travelling through the water hanging on to the nose of the torpedo which was now sliding straight towards me. In the black, claustrophobic silence with the nose of the torpedo only inches from the lens I finally yelled 'CUT! I can't swim!'

At the end of any 007 location the comfort of Pinewood's sound stages would always be a welcome sight as we returned to more familiar surroundings. Even so a Bond script guarantees no let-up for artistes or crew as the action continues in the confines of the studio. On a stage we allegedly enjoy the benefit of more controlled filming conditions, but there was one occasion when I was reminded of a similar situation in *Gold*, except that instead of Simon Sabela this time Roger would enjoy the more attractive company of Barbara Bach, in the guise of Major Anya Amasova, a.k.a. Russian Agent Triple-X, his gorgeous adversary.

We were filming a flooding sequence where our two heroes were trying to escape certain death from the villain's lair, Atlantis, when a sudden powerful surge of water became too much for Barbara to handle. As she was washed away from Roger's outstretched wet hands he tried to catch her, but this time 007 failed. Looking through the camera, a new hero became aware of the situation and I managed to grab her outstretched arm before she sailed on past my camera. My reward came with a kiss ... as I smiled smugly back at 007!

A Bond film would not be the same without the usual team from the Ministry: an irritated 'M' played by Bernard Lee or the frustrated genius of Major Boothroyd – a.k.a. 'Q' – played by Desmond Llewelyn, and of course the delightful Miss Moneypenny (Lois Maxwell), who forever keeps alive her dream of romance with James.

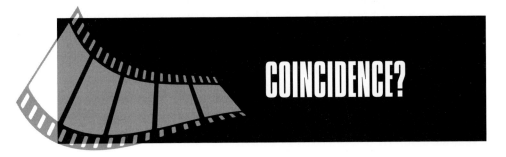

COINCIDENCE?

With everything that happened throughout my career I am not sure that I really believe that it all was just 'coincidence' – which is possibly a convenient word used to cover up the reality – so was this next event meant to be? Many questions remain unanswered in life and time alone will tell ...

With time moving on I waited on news of Suzy's trip to England which, it would seem, was not going to happen. My one consolation was that my daily adventures with 007 were keeping me occupied. Although my thoughts were not completely with Budapest, people on the set knew about and were interested in Suzy's arrival; in particular, there was a gentleman going by the name of Fred, a unit driver who had kindly offered to meet Suzy at Heathrow should she manage to get there. Everyone was being very kind to me.

With the Christmas holiday fast approaching and still no news from the embassy in Budapest, Suzy chased the officials every day with little gain. It would seem that confirmation was required from London before the documents could be issued and now, well into December and both embassies closing down for Christmas, the planned holiday appeared doomed to fail; it would take a miracle for this to happen now.

Enter Fred, the miracle man – a gentleman I hardly knew – who came onto the stage to see me.

'Any news with Suzy?' he enquired.

Many people are employed on films and one rarely gets to know them all by name as was the case with this Fred, but for some strange or wonderful reason he was kind enough to take an interest in our situation. Out of courtesy I explained the situation which Suzy found herself in and he listened patiently to the story, then turned back as he left.

'I'll make a phone call.'

He smiled and off he went about his business while I smiled too, wondering who this clown was. Obviously I didn't take the gentleman seriously, thinking it unlikely that this kindly person would have any influence over government administration. Even so, Fred was kind and sympathetic to my cause, where by now I had accepted that Christmas would be celebrated in Croxley Road. However, it turned out that Fred's fiancée worked in the visa office in London and he had asked her to check out the situation and see if Suzy's visa had been granted, and if it had, then why it had not been forwarded to Budapest.

Apparently it was still in the out tray; undaunted by all of the red tape, the lady somehow managed to get the visa transferred to the British embassy in Budapest, where it was quickly passed on to the applicant. By now Suzy had given up all hope of news ever coming from the embassy, which had closed down for the holiday. Even so, the 'miracle' continued on its way when a kind lady at the embassy who was aware of the situation phoned Suzy with the news. On receiving confirmation that the visa had been approved, she hurried to the embassy to collect the precious document, where again our 'luck' held with Suzy managing to get a ticket to fly to London, when normally at that time of the year the airlines would have been full.

Take what you will from all this, but if this situation had been written into a script it would probably be considered ridiculous, stupid or absurd – at best most unlikely. Yet this really happened, but again anything can happen in the world of James Bond. I realise, of course, that all this reads like fiction while others will see it as just coincidence, but, whatever label they choose, and in spite of all the red tape of government administration, Suzy and I would celebrate the holiday together – and all because of a gentleman going by the name of Fred.

To bring this extraordinary account to a close, I would not meet Fred again after the holiday or for the rest of the film, so I would never get the opportunity to thank him for his help, although I am sure we will meet again in the future, in another place at another time. Some may ask if this person ever existed or if it could all just be in my imagination. All I can say is that there is no denying this really happened. What's more, in the future I would pay much more attention to these so-called 'coincidences'.

A close friend and colleague, John Alcott, and his wife Sue loaned us their flat over the Christmas break in Chelsea, so Croxley Road would no longer be required.

Dear Mr Cardiff,
Recently I enjoyed your film The Magic Box which as a camera assistant I was of course interested in your contribution with the photography. Soon I hope to continue my career as a camera assistant when completing my national service in the navy, possibly to meet and work with you one day. Should you have need of a camera assistant … (blah … blah …blah … ending with my insufficient Carlton Hill credits.)
Yours sincerely …

That was the general gist and part of an impertinent letter addressed to Jack Cardiff now many years past; I imagine it is probably not unlike those sent by today's students, so I can understand their passion and why they need to do this.

Although I cannot recall the exact wording, I confess that the letter was rather cheeky in its day, addressed to 2 Soho Square, London – then the ACT Union office – in the hope that it would be forwarded to the cinematographer. I never received a reply from Mr Cardiff or even something to say that the letter had been passed on or not; however, all was not lost when my wish to work with the great man himself would eventually be realised on *The Prince and the Pauper*.

A year later I would once again be working with Jack, this time on *Death on the Nile*, which was directed by John Guillermin, whom I had first worked with many years earlier on *Guns at Batasi*; his cinematographer at that time was Douglas Slocombe. Filming at Pinewood Studios and Salisbury Plain in the early days of

Hello to Alec what a worker you are! Enjoyed working with you. Bette Davis

On *Death on the Nile* Bette Davis and I shared a great respect for each other – it works better that way!

CinemaScope, two focus pullers were required on the camera crew on *Guns at Batasi*, with Jimmy Devis claiming the camera assistant's role while I would be relegated to working the anamorphic element, which was fine by me as this gave me more time to watch the director at work from the sidelines.

When John Guillermin came under my discreet observation, I remember the first impressions that I had of his forceful directing manner, his endless energy matching his aggressive approach to filming, his skill in handling actors with his positive directing. Another opportunity now came my way to learn from this animated director, particularly of his handling of the many star 'names' in Agatha Christie's *Death on the Nile*. However, this time Jack Cardiff would be the cinematographer with me as his camera operator. I never dared to ask Jack if he received my letter, but with my good fortune of working with the great man I could add yet another fine-looking credit to my ever-growing CV.

Death on the Nile would enjoy an international cast including Peter Ustinov, Mia Farrow, David Niven, Bette Davis, Angela Lansbury, George Kennedy, Simon MacCorkindale, Maggie Smith, Jack Warden, Sam Wanamaker, Olivia Hussey, John Finch, Lois Chiles and Jane Birkin, with I.S. Johar as the captain of the Nile boat *Karnak* which featured in the story. The names alone would make this an interesting experience where in all probability more than half the budget was spent on the actors' contracts alone, but what did come as a surprise from this amazing cast was that in the background there lurked a quiet conspiracy in the shadows throughout our filming, where unseen scheming proved that even film stars are human beings after all.

As this cold atmosphere on the set slowly built, I felt uncomfortable about all of the nonsense going on; after all, I am the director's camera operator – his ally. However, tight-lipped actors trying not to be overheard held whispered conversations near the apparent refuge of the camera – where I exist – resentful of the director. I unintentionally found myself listening in to a conversation between David Niven and Peter Ustinov.

'When Bette gets here she'll sort him out!'

A nod in response confirmed that our director was not popular with several members of the cast.

From this I assumed that the conversation was about John's aggressive style and directing manner, which it would seem was not appreciated by everyone. I wondered if this could be a deliberate strategy on John's part to establish exactly who was running the show with all these 'names' around. I remembered it as being John's style when directing *Guns at Batasi*, with which I had been impressed. Even so, I doubt that many in the *Nile* cast would have chosen to discuss this issue with John, preferring instead to wait on David's prediction for Bette Davis to 'sort him out'! Miss Davis, of course, had a reputation for standing no nonsense from anyone, although in my humble opinion I admired John's energetic style of directing, even if it was not to everyone's taste.

John would set an equally high standard on himself, and his relationship with his crew which would be challenging too, starting with our filming in Cairo. With the help of Egyptian porters we climbed to the top of the Great Pyramid at Giza, carrying the heavy camera equipment needed for a short scene with Simon MacCorkindale, Mia Farrow and Lois Chiles. It was a hot, oppressive Egyptian summer as we slowly climbed to the summit in the heat of the day, the perspiring actors with their make-up running and a frustrated crew with an impatient director. A dreadful atmosphere was slowly building, all of which would be unhelpful to good relations. The director now set a challenge for the construction manager John Paterson, who would be required to build a tracking platform overnight which would allow the camera with me operating it to 'float' over the pyramid's surface – the construction manager achieved the eighth wonder of the world for so little gain.

All this unnecessary aggravation was reminiscent of filming in Australia with its stifling heat, where it had been necessary to tread carefully with Harry Waxman and remain alert to his ever-changing moods. It would seem that John was having the same problem and it would only be a matter of time before he too exploded.

Travelling down the Nile in the steamer *Karnak*, we stopped off to film at various well-known tourist sites, including Cairo, Aswan and Luxor – all atmospheric locations carefully selected for this film of the Agatha Christie novel where Hercule Poirot (Peter Ustinov) sets out to catch the murderer. It was around this time that Bette Davis finally arrived to join the cast on board *Karnak*. The 'queen' of Hollywood would now make her grand entrance. As she arrived on board all of the artistes eagerly gathered around Miss Davis, introducing themselves to this Hollywood icon – a little phoney, I thought at the time – with the director playing his part by offering his hand, in what could easily be a scene from our script.

```
             John Guillermin
Welcome, Bet!

A pause, with the new
arrival curiously studying
the director

             Bette Davis
                (Aloof)
My name is Bette, or Miss
Davis!
```

Filming Mia Farrow on the river steamer *Karnak*, with director John Guillermin. Standing behind me, making sure I don't fall into the Nile, is my long-time grip Chunky Huse.

With those few words the lady immediately slotted into the character which David and Peter had portrayed. To their joy, John had been put in his place, though in the end it would not work out quite as they had predicted.

Unperturbed with all this, John kept to the script in keeping Christie's game of suspicion alive. One particular scene would require a point-of-view shot of one of the suspects running up a long, narrow stone staircase, with the echoing footsteps adding to the drama; it sounds easy but almost impossible to film with a handheld camera – Steadicam had yet to be invented. The problem would be resolved with John suggesting I should sit on Frank Elliott's shoulders, operating the camera while he ran up the narrow staircase. Although Frank was a strong lad I was not too keen on this idea; even if it did work, my effort operating the camera would look dreadful and, should he trip, I would find myself tumbling back to the bottom – a long way down. Nevertheless the director insisted, so we tried. Frank staged this impossible act twice, for which he gets much of the credit.

With no let up coming from the scorching overhead sun and temperatures rising, John was clearly unhappy with everything that was going on around him, the disturbing signs of his frustration now making it necessary for everyone to keep their heads down or, better still, stay clear of his eye line altogether. The lucky ones could discreetly melt into the background – out of sight, out of mind – but the camera crew, always in the front line, had nowhere to hide.

There came an occasion when Frank and I were sitting on the camera dolly, quietly taking note of all this nonsense going on around us; filming that day had not gone well for John, who needed to vent his frustration on someone – anyone would do. Unfortunately it happened that I was nearest to him on this occasion, so today's target would be Alec Mills. However, even the director's trusted ally was not about to take any disrespect from this very rude man, nor would I allow myself to become John's whipping boy!

After all this time I cannot remember what John's problem was, but something or someone triggered off his latest outburst, allowing him to let off steam. With the director launching his verbal abuse directly at me it required an immediate response. John's rudeness was offensive and totally unacceptable; what is more, he was completely wrong, so it was necessary to sort this out there and then. Jumping off the camera dolly, I hurried to confront this arrogant, rude-mannered man face to face. Rude words – very rude words – were exchanged; my dad would have been proud of me! John was clearly out of order and well he knew it, which in the aftermath would leave a pointless sulking atmosphere through to the end of filming.

Most of the actors appeared uneasy with John, with the possible exception of Mia Farrow, who had also worked with him on *Guns at Batasi*; the no-nonsense Bette Davis was also quite unruffled. John seemed content to live with the consequences of this dreadful atmosphere which he alone had created. Thinking about it later,

I believe John deliberately set out to make it clear to his heavyweight cast and crew that he was the one directing the film, not them. I just happened to be in the way at the wrong time.

Although my confrontation with John came out the blue, let me say that I was not proud of my reaction to his rudeness. I am a mild-mannered person so it would take a great deal for me to react in this way, particularly to a director. However, one can only take so much unwarranted, unnecessary disrespect before one reacts. This regrettable incident was over and forgotten in minutes – at least by me – but sometimes there was as much drama behind the camera as there was in front of it.

After a period of sulking, John returned to his usual unpredictable self, his eye line now carefully avoiding me, leaving an uncomfortable relationship between us through to the end of filming. This unpleasant incident would come back to haunt me in the distant future.

As for Bette Davis's reputation of standing no nonsense from anyone, in the end there would be no question of her 'sorting John out', as David Niven had confidently predicted. That would never happen. As for myself, I found Bette – sorry, Miss Davis – to be polite and really quite charming, if a little scary!

Looking back on Agatha Christie's plot of murder with bizarre relationships, the growing sense of conspiracy, the whodunnit atmosphere and, of course, the real-life loathing with the anti-John plot – this is where I would have been among the suspects, had the murder really happened.

In spite of it all, John achieved his goal both on screen and off, creating a wonderful film. Be that as it may, I doubted that John would ever want to work with me again.

Two interesting years had passed since I had last had the pleasure of working with James Bond and Lewis Gilbert. This time, however, the UK's tax regime meant that, with the exception of the model unit Moonraker, the unit would be based in Paris, away from Eon Production's natural home at Pinewood Studios.

Oh dear ... Paris: the Moulin Rouge and the Folies Bergère, Toulouse-Lautrec and Oswald Morris – names and places which would bring back the youthful fire in me, where the hallowed universities of my further education could now be revisited.

Many years had passed since last I visited this beautiful city filming *Father Brown*, then a young man seriously interested in the female form, if not quite the same as that portrayed by Lautrec. Perhaps I would revisit the Folies and give myself more time to study ...

Apart from Lewis Gilbert and Roger Moore, it was also another opportunity to work with Lois Chiles, who was confirmed as the new Bond girl while *Death on the Nile* was still in production, so even before shooting began I was familiar with the location, director and leading cast.

Working in this exciting city would be to experience the civilised working conditions of the French film industry, where filming started at midday, after lunch, and continued non-stop through to 7.30 in the evening, with snacks and drinks available on the stage throughout the day – a total of seven-and-a-half hours; so what could be wrong with that? Although this timing may not be to everyone's preference, it is worth considering the benefits that came with this arrangement, such as getting up later in the morning, missing the early Parisian rat race traffic, cheerfully avoiding the same problem going home in the evening and giving everyone time to eat out or see a film without the worries of having to get up early the next morning. Paris for the Brits was simply heaven. The production also gained from the momentum of filming not being broken by taking lunch. Frogs and Limeys united, all were happy to go along with this very sensible

Filming at Vaux-Le-Vicomte with Jean Tournier, Corinne Cléry and Roger Moore. (© 1979 Danjaq, LLC and United Artists Corporation. All rights reserved)

arrangement, except when filming exteriors, when we would revert to normal daylight working hours.

I enjoyed eight wonderful months filming *Moonraker*, which began with my own pre-production filming of Rio de Janeiro's famous carnival, a spectacle one could only fully appreciate by being there. I had a mixed camera crew of both English and French technicians as our filming extended over three incredible days and nights, with the constant movement of floats in procession and attendants in costumes keeping the excitement alive.

When the festival was over we were invited to join a gathering of press and documentary camera crews who by tradition are all invited to the 'hookers' ball', a grand evening where the prostitutes of Rio take time off from work. Later we would return with the main unit to complete the carnival sequence with the principal artistes, where 007 would enjoy a cable car ride and several punch-ups with his old adversary Jaws, played by Richard Kiel, whose audience popularity in *The Spy Who Loved Me* persuaded the producers to bring him back, making Richard the only Bond henchman ever to appear in two films.

Our location filming in Venice would also bring an invitation card from Roger Moore, inviting Suzy – now my wife – and me to join him in celebrating his fiftieth birthday at a party with friends, where by chance I found myself sitting at the dinner table opposite the American film director Herbert Ross.

One of my many on-screen fights with Roger Moore. This time 007 makes his point.

Flashback: This account comes from 1972, while I was working on one of my earliest films for Stanley O'Toole, *The Last of Sheila*. The director was Herbert Ross, Ernie Day was the cinematographer and I was now confirmed as Ernie's camera operator.

It was during the first week of filming on a millionaire's yacht off the coast of Nice; a sudden change in the weather conditions moved from glorious sunshine to a heavy overcast mist, with the horizon slowly merging into grey mass. Unhappy with the situation, Ernie explained the obvious matching problem to Ross, who, for reasons known only to himself, urged Ernie to put a white net in front of the lens. Once again Ernie politely made his view known to the director, pointing out that, with the existing conditions and now adding the net, the rushes would look awful. Even so, Ross insisted and Ernie reluctantly complied with the director's wishes, if only to make the point.

Looking through the camera everything looked dire with hardly any shape at all, which I quietly whispered to Ernie if only to back up his comments to Ross.

'I know, I know,' he snapped back; understandably Ernie was unhappy with all this and the obvious result.

When the rushes were viewed the next day they were as bad as Ernie had predicted, but what happened next could not be foreseen – it was nothing short of a total disgrace. Although I was not a party to the post mortem on the rushes it would seem that Ernie was made accountable for this, in spite of his protestations to Ross which had been completely ignored. Ernie was subsequently removed from the film with another cinematographer brought out from the UK, while in the meantime Ross suggested that I should take over lighting until the replacement arrived. Angry at the injustice of everything that had happened, I refused, explaining to Stanley, the producer, that the fault lay not with Ernie but with Ross himself, who obviously had a different agenda and issues with Ernie photographing the film in the first place. I immediately resigned my position.

In past years, when cinematographers were unhappy with photographic conditions, the clapper boy would chalk on the clapper board 'Shot Under Protest', which would clearly be seen at rushes the next day. I wondered whether, if we'd done this, it would have changed the situation and put the blame where it should have been laid in the first place, but with the questionable politics of the situation, I seriously doubt it.

With filming suspended for the day I sat alone on the beach in a state of total disbelief at all that had happened so quickly. My wonderful world was now suddenly falling apart with Ernie moving away from the scene as quickly as possible while I returned to the Hotel Westminster where the unit was based to reflect on this disgraceful decision. This disbelief continued when I called my wife Lesley to tell her about the situation, but before I explained the real story she said that she had already heard that I had been 'sacked' and was coming home. Of course this was not true, but it was interesting, if not suspicious, how quickly the industry grapevine had moved into action.

The next day, Gerry Turpin arrived to take over from Ernie, along with his camera operator Derek Browne, leaving me to become even more cynical about the cutthroat side of this beautiful industry. Like Ernie, I quickly departed from the scene, but this personal experience would not be lost on me – a reminder that others would always be waiting in the shadows, particularly when the face doesn't fit!

To bring this sad flashback to a close, which all began at Roger Moore's birthday party, Ross carefully studied me across the table, his stare somehow recognising me although still unsure where we had met before. Finally came the moment of truth.

'Alec, have we worked together in the past?'

Knowing the situation, Suzy tightly squeezed my hand, reminding me where we were, so making it necessary for me to bite my lip and say no, though clearly – dearly – I wanted to tell him what I really thought of him face to face. My dad would have approved of that, considering how he spoke to his officers in the trenches; it would seem that we share the same genetic fundamentals in the Mills family.

Back to *Moonraker* ...

Lewis now had a new cinematographer, Jean Tournier, whom I had also worked with before on a French film called *Allez France* when the unit were on location in London; I was Jean's camera assistant. This change of cinematographer came about when Claude Renoir, Lewis's first preference, was unavailable because an eye accident forced him to withdraw from the film. At a private meeting called by Cubby and Lewis to discuss the situation, I was invited to suggest any names who might be considered for the position. I just happened to mention Jean Tournier's name, explaining that I had worked with him and recommended they see some of his work, in particular *The Train* with Burt Lancaster, even though the film had been shot in black and white. Although I was not party to the final decision, they loved Jean's work, and rightly so, leaving me quietly pleased with my recommendation. We became good friends and for many years we regularly exchanged Christmas cards until they suddenly stopped in 2004; Jean had passed away.

To be honest, I was hoping they would bring in an English cinematographer, which would have given me the opportunity to suggest Michael Reed, not because Michael was a friend but more for his highly praised work on *On Her Majesty's Secret Service* from both sides of the Atlantic. This was not to be, as Lewis continued to favour the idea of a French cinematographer, which perhaps made sense with *Moonraker* based in Paris.

Even though I was filming out of the country, other responsibilities across the Channel meant that I was never far from home. Before moving to Paris the new Guild of British Camera Technicians, better known as the GBCT, had been formed. After I had passed some fairly innocuous comments at the first general meeting I was invited to become their first chairman. It soon became clear that some producers were not in favour of this new organisation and they became vocal in their opposition, accusing the guild of being a trade union in disguise, which of course was not true. However, with an untainted guild arriving on the scene, we needed articles for the new magazine; with this in mind the editor, Kevin Kavanagh, suggested that while in Paris I should interview Cubby Broccoli, the legendary producer who deserves much more credit from me than has been offered so far. Even so, this awkward question would need to be asked.

'After years working with British cinematographers, why did you decide to use a French cameraman?'

I admit it was with some hesitation that I put this improper question to Cubby, who sensed my unease; after all, here I was generously employed by Cubby and

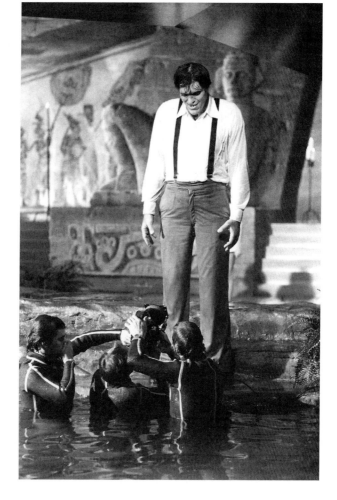

The huge, if dripping wet, 7-foot 2-inch frame of Richard Kiel towers over the camera crew on a stage in Paris while filming on *Moonraker*. After surviving the sinking of Stromberg's *Atlantis* in *The Spy Who Loved Me*, Richard is the only Bond villain to return in a later film, even if he did end up as a good guy. (© 1979 Danjaq, LLC and United Artists Corporation. All rights reserved)

working in Paris, so why was I rocking the boat? A long pause followed with Cubby thinking about this carefully, eyeballing me before taking a puff on his Montecristo cigar, slowly releasing the smoke, followed with another long pause, leaving his nervous camera operator waiting on the expected terse reply.

'Alec, if the director wants a French cinematographer ... British or Chinese cameraman, he can have him. The chemistry of those two on the set is very important for me ...' A pause came with an afterthought. 'It's vital for any film!'

It happened that Cubby's answer was already working for me personally, with Lewis inviting me to be his camera operator in France, so I quickly moved on.

Having read Cubby's interesting autobiography *When the Snow Melts*, it would seem to me that the producer appeared to be quite cynical about all of his secret agents in one way or another. After the parting of the ways with Sean Connery, George Lazenby proved to be an unworthy 007 while even Roger Moore received the tiniest little dig from this great producer, although in Roger's case you would need a magnifying glass to spot it; they really were great pals. Timothy Dalton's two Bond films were not enough to pass judgement with the Broccoli pen, but from all I have witnessed in my twenty years of service with three secret agents, I would suggest that Cubby's relationship with Roger was closer than with any of his other 007 agents. A part of Roger surely died when hearing of Cubby's sad passing.

The only downside of living in Paris was the expense, as I had rented a small apartment in the 16th Arrondissement. To compensate for this, a generous *per diem* occasionally allowed me to hop on a plane back to England for the weekend, following Lewis's example. Most weekends we shared a car to Charles de Gaulle airport, where on one occasion we arrived late and found ourselves at the back of a very long queue.

'Alec, stay close to me!' Lewis whispered in my ear.

Bewildered, I looked on as Lewis, the master of deception, slowly inched his way past the other passengers in the queue, occasionally striking up a conversation with some to cover up his outrageous behaviour, which he did with surprising ease, at the same time towing along his embarrassed camera operator until we soon found ourselves nearing the front of the queue. It would seem this was a pastime which Lewis particularly enjoyed – never once was he challenged by others in the queue. As for me, it was the first and last time I would go through this embarrassing ruse, preferring to stay at the back and watch Lewis weave his way through the crowd.

Although *Moonraker* was filmed outside the UK, the usual Ministry officials were still around, if just a little longer in the tooth. Bernard Lee once again played M; Desmond Llewelyn reprised his role as Q, with the delightful Lois Maxwell continuing as the ever-reliable Miss Moneypenny. Michael Lonsdale would be cast in the obligatory role of the Bond villain, while Bond girl Lois Chiles was Dr Holly Goodhead, joining 007 on his mission into space, where I floated around, trying to keep hold of my handheld camera!

It was time to move up the ladder and start thinking in terms of lighting, which of course is easier said than done unless a friendly producer or director is prepared to give you that big break. Of course it might never happen, but either way it would be a difficult decision to make, leaving behind the glamorous world of James Bond, trying instead to find employment on even the smallest of B movies as a cinematographer. Should the dice fall the wrong way it would be easy to fall into the trap of giving up, becoming yet another cynical failure in the history books.

Perhaps an agent would help with the transition, but with few realistic lighting credits to your name his job would be made much more difficult. Perhaps a necessary sacrifice would need to be made on my eventual journey into the unknown; should I decide to go ahead with this self-promotion, considering my limited lighting experience from the odd crumb put my way, I should at least present myself to my preferred gaffer as someone full of confidence, hoping to disguise any potential weaknesses that I might have had.

The gaffer, of course, is the chief electrician, who in all probability would understand my passion to start lighting while at the same time he would be aware of my lack of experience on such matters, which could be a problem for him with his cynical team of sparks if I failed to impress. Of course he would be helpful with suggestions – perhaps too helpful – which could cause offence if not followed, or could even divert me from my own thoughts or ideas. I'm weak ... obviously I was not ready to move up yet!

Watching different cinematographers go about lighting over the years and their techniques, their preferred gaffers usually got to know enough about their boss's preferences even to pre-light a set, making his life less arduous under the perennial issues of an over-ambitious call sheet. Jack Cardiff's gaffer would not find his task easy as they prepared for the cinematographer's arrival on the set; only then would Jack start his private 'painting', possibly making the pre-light null and void. Jack Cardiff was very much a spur-of-the-moment cinematographer, his approach to lighting a personal expression likened to an artist mixing colours in his painting, inspired by his extraordinary imagination. A little poetic, you think? Well, perhaps, but in Jack Cardiff's case I believe this to be true. One could argue that this is the same of all cinematographers but again I would disagree: the phrase 'That'll do' would never spring to mind for Jack Cardiff.

In the many discussions we shared together, the artist/cinematographer spoke of his early days visiting art galleries, studying the painters' style, light source, contrast, even the use of backlighting. In his retirement Jack also took to painting, so perhaps one day a 'Cardiff' will be as famous as the artists he so admired. It was on Jack's advice that I visited the Rembrandt Museum in Amsterdam.

'Alec, stand back and look carefully at the paintings and take time with what you see.'

Needless to say, I did, although to be honest I gained little from the experience as my taste lay more with the art of Turner and Constable.

Yet among all the compliments, I hold in admiration this cinematographer's bold approach to lighting. Notwithstanding my limited understanding of the subject at that time, there were times when Jack Cardiff surprised me, when he would occasionally turn to use one of his own mix of filters which he carried with him in a little case, or possibly add the odd filter to a light – similar to an artist mixing paints. From behind the camera I silently questioned the boldness of Jack's dangerous insight, or his incredible courage where I could only sit and wonder if I was witnessing a disaster in the making. But there was little chance of that happening with Jack Cardiff, who was simply 'painting' his canvas on the set, the final result giving much in which to delight.

One story Jack told me was when he was watching the rushes with the director sitting next to him. After a while, the director whispered, 'Jack, it looks rather dark to me!'

'Yes, that's right,' came the cinematographer's whispered reply, 'but, you see, that's how I see this scene.'

There was no further comment from the director. To be honest, even this nonentity was sometimes surprised by Jack's boldness, but at least I knew enough not to question it.

The only reason I mention this story is that Jack Cardiff was way ahead of his time when it came to creating more and more beautiful images on our screens. Damn it, I wish I had his courage, his boldness to do the things he saw in his mind's eye! Even so I believe that my experience of working with the master would help my experimental moments in my own 'painting', while always keeping in mind that without the authority of the master's back-up it could well end up in my being sacked!

As Jack Cardiff's camera operator I would inevitably postpone any ideas I had of moving up to lighting. My plan now was to observe Jack, a cinematographer who broke the so-called rules of cinematography – at least the rules I had come to know by way of my mentor Harry Waxman. Playing it safe was not in Jack's vocabulary, whereas Harry would always respect the rules; I was still not sure where I stood with these different opinions. Under Harry's wing I obeyed the rules but with Jack this could easily have cut short my career.

With this in mind I decided I would learn more from working with Jack on his next film *Avalanche Express*, where I would meet up with Lee Marvin a second time. A quick hug would cement our respect for each other, while at the same time I knew there would be occasions when our leading man might not be in the best state of health. I was wrong in this assumption as Lee appeared to be a totally different person from *Shout at the Devil*.

This should have left our director with few problems to be concerned with, but Mark Robson was himself in very poor health at the time, working from his very cold air-conditioned Winnebago while outside Munich was going through an unrelenting heat wave. With Mark's confinement it was sometimes necessary for me to visit him in his trailer to check on the director's requirements from the camera's point of view, before returning to the stifling heat where my glasses quickly steamed up. Only when everything was ready would the director come out to direct the action, before quickly returning to his chilly mobile home once it was in the can.

Unfortunately it would seem that *Avalanche Express* was plagued with illness as Robert Shaw, our other lead actor, was also unwell during the filming, which only added more problems for our ailing director; even so Mark managed to struggle on through to the end of filming, helped by the love of his kindly wife, who nursed him throughout. It would not be a surprise to learn that both Mark and Robert sadly passed on shortly after filming was completed.

Unfortunately *Avalanche Express* was a disappointing film, coming from a poor script about a Russian general played by Robert Shaw who is defecting to the West with the help of CIA agent Harry Wargrave (Lee Marvin). The supporting actors were Maximilian Schell, Horst Buchholz and Mike Connors, with Linda Evans in the female lead. Although the plot deepens, the film offered little to keep an audience's interest; the critics would not be fooled, either, voicing their opinions accordingly, but at least this was another opportunity for me to watch the grand master of lighting at work.

By contrast, *The Awakening* would be an interesting horror script based on Egyptian mythology, although no doubt historians would find the story disappointing – more than likely inaccurate or impossible. On the other hand, a simpleton like me would prefer to enjoy the idea of believing that it could all be true – films are meant to entertain, after all. The story was of an archaeologist (Charlton Heston) who goes in search of the tomb of a past evil Egyptian queen, Kara. When he opens the vault the queen's cursed spirit escapes from the tomb, acquiring residence in the womb of Heston's pregnant wife, where the dead queen is now free to possess his unborn child.

Once again, the subject would take us to the favoured tourist locations in Egypt, Luxor and the river Nile, ending up in the Valley of the Kings. This was a period when films often used Egyptian mythology as backgrounds to the story, which inevitably meant using the same locations and background – occasionally virtually identical shots. Even so, for all the effort, I was not sure the film really achieved the hopes of the producers or its director Mike Newell, for whom I had much respect.

This would be the last film where I would have the privilege of operating the camera for Jack Cardiff OBE, BSC. Jack will rightly be remembered as one of the great British cinematographers of the age; with his passing I considered myself privileged to have worked with this wonderful, imaginative cinematographer, though the question remains, did I learn anything from the master? In humility I believe that I did, though probably not enough to be more experimental with my own 'painting', unlike Jack Cardiff who would never back away from a challenge.

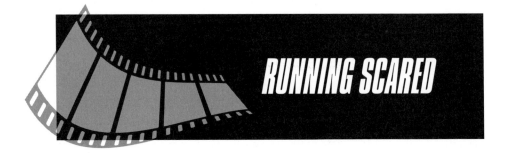

RUNNING SCARED

Flashback: The importance of being Ernest, or Ernie Day. Ernie was at his peak as first-choice camera operator to both David Lean and Ken Annakin. However, Ernie was also popular with actresses as he quietly charmed them with his pleasing personality when in need of their cooperation – a technique I would note and gladly follow.

I wondered if this first-choice label could be the reason why Ernie held back from becoming a cinematographer for so long. Sadly I would never learn the answer to that question but in 1971 the time finally arrived for Ernie to move up with a call from the actor David Hemmings, who was to write and direct his first film with Ernie as his chosen cinematographer. It was a shrewd choice by David, knowing that Ernie's calm composure and diplomatic skills with actors would steer him through the frightening pressures to which a new director would be exposed.

With *Running Scared* keeping Ernie busy with the lighting he would need a camera operator 'who he could work with' – Ernie's words! Although there were many established camera operators available at the time, for reasons known only to him he chose to offer the position to this relatively new camera operator still struggling for recognition. Of course I had worked with Ernie before on *Swiss Family Robinson* and other films where we had shared a good working relationship in Harry Waxman's team, but I had no idea or reason to believe that I would be Ernie's choice as camera operator. The offer was of course eagerly accepted before he had time to change his mind.

It was some weeks later at a more appropriate time that I asked Ernie about his thoughts on this matter, reminding him that I was still fairly new to camera operating while there were many more experienced operators available at the time. Ernie carefully – deliberately – measured his reply, hoping not to offend.

'I need a camera operator who would be a help to me rather than someone with a strong personality!'

At the time I thought this an interesting reply if not quite the compliment for which I was looking, leaving me to draw on my own conclusions ... then deciding that it would not be to my advantage to pursue the matter further. In effect, Ernie was indicating that he wanted a camera operator he could oversee on the film; he would get the set-ups the way he wanted them, believing that this would have caused offence to a more experienced camera operator. I fitted the bill nicely; Ernie knew that there was little chance of a personality clash with Alec Mills, though on the other hand being intimidated by Ernie Day was no bad thing as I would learn from the master and would gladly follow his technique throughout my operating career.

As an aside, camera operators in the UK are usually involved in lining up the sequence with the directors when getting the set-up. I did this, and I make no apology for that, but this usually works with the cinematographer's support, his nod of approval confirming that I had not overstepped the mark by making it impossible for him to position his lights or creating unnecessary time constraints. I sometimes wonder if this is why American cinematographers get the set-ups with the director, leaving the camera operator just to operate the camera.

Understandably, David cast actors whom he had been comfortable with in the past: Maxine Audley, Georgia Brown, Gayle Hunnicutt, Edward Underdown and

Robert Powell, all happily contributing to David's debut as director, who in turn shared his opportunity with Ernie Day. Both director and cinematographer were confident in their new roles with David's wise choice and Ernie's technical expertise paying dividends with the photography.

Running Scared was an attention-grabbing subject filmed in the Midlands, which I struggle to recall accurately to this day. I vaguely remember that it was the story of a student who commits suicide while his friend (played by Robert Powell) looks on, having promised not to interfere, before later falling in love with his dead friend's sister – a strange theme that enjoyed a noticeable Michelangelo Antonioni influence hovering in the background under David's direction, a devoted admirer of the Italian director. Even so I would hesitate to claim that the film did well at the box office.

Possibly more important, even if I did not know it at the time, was the additional bonus of working with the producer Stanley O'Toole, who in the future would play an important role in the development of my own career both as a cinematographer and director, which is how it works when contacts become friends.

VISIT TO A CHIEF'S SON

The day my schooling came to an end was the start of my real education, when I started to learn about people and their strange customs. My tutor was the cinema which would inevitably become my addiction, while not forgetting the role of television documentaries. My filming education came from a mixture of both; I would learn to respect my colleagues who work in documentary films where danger often dwells – a word I choose carefully when recalling filming on *Visit to a Chief's Son*.

Visit was my third film with Ernie, having also worked together on *Made* for director John Mackenzie, with Carol White and the folk rock singer Roy Harper. This time we would be on location in Africa, filming a simple story of a white boy's friendship with the son of a Masai chief – hardly exciting material for a film, you would think, and you would be right, but at least this experience would leave me with a few interesting tales to tell on a cold winter's night back home.

Filming in Kenya meant living under canvas – safari time – where a hippopotamus suddenly burst to the surface with the sole intention of annihilating my focus puller Doug Milsome and me when we dared to get too close while filming her new offspring, which our tracker conveniently forgot to mention as we silently paddled down an unnamed river. Suddenly it was time to abandon ship and run like hell, dragging the camera equipment with us into a thicket, not sure what awaited us there! This would be a normal daily routine with our filming, never knowing where the next hazard would come from. Sitting around the campfire at night we would then relive our daily exploits, with the odd exaggeration of the close calls we had shared, which you could be sure would quickly be added to the growing list of narrow escapes. I don't ever recall sleeping in a tent as a boy scout. In Kenya a camp bearer outside would make sure that any unwelcome nocturnal visitors did not enter our tents while we were asleep.

Nor was the realism only behind the camera. One scene in the script called for the young Masai boy, played by Jesse Kinaru, to be circumcised in a tribal custom proclaiming that the boy had now become a man – a warrior! It happened that our Masai boy was due for this procedure, which by tradition takes place at the first light of dawn. In his wisdom our kindly director Lamont Johnson suggested we should film the moment at the boy's real ceremony rather than as a staged scene. However, to do this we would need permission from the witchdoctor who would be performing this delicate operation. It seemed that the old man was happy with this; his only proviso was that the ceremony should not be disturbed by our filming. With the deal done and palms crossed one felt as if the old man had worked with film people before.

We arrived at the location in the early hours and well before the first signs of light had appeared on the horizon; it was a cold, early morning with a tranquil atmosphere as the Masai community slept peacefully in their huts. In preparation for the delicate operation the young boy had been put into a cold running stream for an hour or so to freeze his genitalia, and it was in this quiet, serene setting that Lamont whispered his instructions to me: 'Alec, get as close as you can with the camera without disturbing the old man or the proceedings ... be careful not to upset him!'

With the ritual only minutes away, Doug and I crawled slowly to our approved position, staying low, hoping not to be too obvious or disturbing. Without the luxury of lights or fast stock Ernie could only hope that we had enough exposure to record the ceremony on film. At this point an eerie silence took over the proceedings, a cold, gentle breeze passed by without a murmur from anyone as we waited on dawn. Still no one spoke as the ageing witchdoctor worked himself up into a state of excitement, and yet another chill passed as we waited on Ernie's borderline exposure before we got the thumbs-up, which finally came, with the director signalling the good news to me. Show time!

Testicles frozen, the boy came out of the water on cue, accompanied by the grinding noise of my handheld Arri IIC camera, which from a distance was not too disruptive for the old man. We had to get this right – there was no question of a take two with this scene. Checking back with the director to see if we had enough footage to establish the master scene as planned, it seemed that he was happy. However, Ernie gave the famous 'get closer' signal, which was not in the draft that the director had given me. Doug and I crawled closer, knowing that the nearer we moved to the operation the more likely the noise of the camera would be heard, but again this appeared to be no problem for the witchdoctor. With our confidence growing, we felt we could do almost anything.

'Get closer ...'

More waving instructions came from my hero, who was now way back in the distant background. However, this time our intrusion came at the time when the witchdoctor was just sharpening his knife for the big cut, which was too much for the old man to accept. He turned towards me, looking directly into the camera – which of course no actor would do – his painted face no longer hiding his frustration. This time I had gone too far! Waving his knife in my direction, he made it clear that he was not pleased with this close intrusion. Doug and I froze and remained still as another cold breeze passed, though more than likely this was our nerves rattling. One thing was certain: I would not look back for any more instructions from our spineless colleagues in the distance.

I am pleased to tell that Doug and I survived the ordeal without any spells being cast on our bodily parts, with everything remaining intact. However, it was at this point when I decided that I would not make a good documentary cameraman.

Visit to a Chief's Son starred Richard Mulligan as a scientist studying the ways of the Masai people, while his son (John Philip Hogdon) becomes friendly with a young Masai boy (Jesse Kinaru). Johnny Sekka played an educated Masai who had a problem with Mulligan's attitude towards the tribe but sadly this mixture of feature-documentary entertainment was in the end a disappointing letdown. It was an interesting experience, if dangerous at times, but offered little for an audience to appreciate the ways of the Masai people, either film or documentary-wise. But at least Ernie enjoyed good reviews for his fine work.

As part of the filming we were presented with an opportunity to film a total eclipse of the sun on 30 June 1973, with a gathering of scientists and photographers from around the world joining us for the occasion. Sadly our efforts were not used in the finished film.

My next film with Ernie would find me back in Budapest, operating the camera for the Oscar-winning director Franklin J. Schaffner, who won the award for *Patton*, the story of the legendary American general of the Second World War. It happened that Ernie had worked with the director before as his camera operator on *Nicholas and Alexandra* and he was in a position to caution me as to what might happen with our honoured leader, suggesting I might experience the same problem he had had with him.

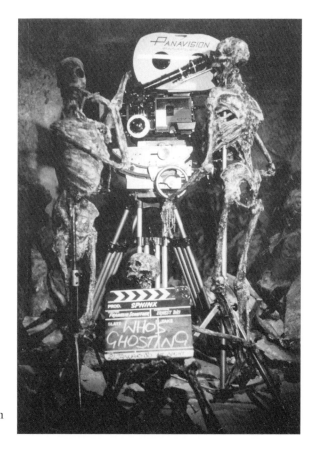

Sphinx (1980) – Elliott's masterpiece, giving new meaning to the expression 'skeleton film crew'!

With Ernie's forewarning, I prepared myself for my meeting with Mr Schaffner by carefully researching his films with questions which I might ask about *The Boys from Brazil*, *Papillon* or *Nicholas and Alexandra* (the list goes on), hoping at least that this would impress the director. Sadly I never got the opportunity.

The first week of filming was not easy; communication of any kind with the director was almost impossible as he quietly sat in his chair, preferring to ignore me, the stern look on his face permanently imprinted, warning off any contact – just as Ernie had predicted. The director's expression gave little away apart from the occasional rub of the chin as his cold stare surveyed all that went on around. Try as hard as I might, my efforts to win him over would be in vain – a hopeless situation for any camera operator. When the director joined me up on the camera crane I thought this would be the ideal time to break the ice, but again my attempts failed miserably and it would seem that Mr Schaffner was more interested in the activities going on below us than having a chat with me. Apart from telling me of his requirements, the director hardly spoke to me. With little sign of any communication between us the first week passed very slowly ...

So came the start of the second week, when the real Franklin Schaffner appeared on the set: different, polite, well mannered and fun.

'Good morning, Alec, and how are you this fine day?'

Ernie's accurate description of the director was now confirmed; it would seem that I had passed the director's assessment of me as Franklin apparently was not one to stand fools gladly and needed to establish where the weaknesses lay in his crew. With the director's soft tone I felt more comfortable, knowing that I had passed his examination and from now on I would enjoy a close relationship with the boss, a humorist who played his part in the Anglo-American sense of humour which he enjoyed sharing with Frank Elliott.

With our filming completed in Budapest we moved to Egypt, filming the customary tourist locations of Cairo, the Valley of Kings and Luxor. We were filming at a time when the hotels were usually full up with tourists; as a result, the unit's accommodations would be split up, with Frank and me finding ourselves billeted on a houseboat which normally cruised up and down the Nile, bringing back memories of the John Guillermin experience on *Death on the Nile* – this time without the associated hassle.

The boat was pleasant enough if a little cramped, but generally everything worked out surprisingly well; I would even admit to enjoying the experience. Others preferred accommodation elsewhere, but for Frank and me the boat would make a pleasant change, just as it would for our historical researcher working on the film. He was a kindly gentleman who pored over his reference books with little interest in all that went on around – a typical boffin both in manner and appearance – the perfect candidate to suffer Frank's wicked sense of humour. Sitting in the lounge one evening, Frank started speaking to me in a whispered tone, which I assumed

1 Located on the Brazilian–Argentine border, the famous Iguazu Falls provided an ideal location for the climax of the speedboat chase along the Iguazu River before Bond unexpectedly escapes with a cunningly concealed hang glider.

2 Filming from Sugarloaf Mountain in Rio de Janeiro, before Bond and Holly Goodhead have their next encounter with Jaws. The exteriors were filmed in Rio, with the sequences inside the cable car filmed in the more controlled environment of the studio.

3 Sharing a joke with cinematographer Jean Tournier in the woods near Vaux-le-Vicomte, just before we set the dogs on Corinne Cléry.

4–6 Pre-production sequences for *Moonraker* were filmed over three days during the Rio Carnival in February 1978. The biggest carnival in the world provided a particularly colourful and noisy sequence for the film.

7 Yours truly in Rio with my long time friend and camera assistant Frank Elliott.

8–10 The impressive space station set built for *Moonraker*, this time not at Pinewood but on one of the stages at the Éclair Studios, Épinay-sur-Seine, to the north of Paris. At the time production designer Ken Adam's sets were allegedly the largest ever built in France.

11 With Albert 'Cubby' Broccoli while filming *Octopussy*. A native New Yorker, Cubby began making films in the UK in the early 1950s and produced close to fifty films using British technicians. In 1989 Cubby was the first winner of BAFTA's Britannia Award for Excellence in Film; in 2011 they announced that the award would be renamed the Albert R. Broccoli Britannia Award for Worldwide Contribution to Filmed Entertainment. (© 1983 Danjaq, LLC and United Artists Corporation. All rights reserved)

Opposite top: 12 Camera crew group photograph taken while filming on *The Living Daylights* near Ouarzazate in Morocco. *Left to Right:* Frank Elliott (focus puller), Hassan (Moroccan camera department assistant), Alec Mills, Roy Wealleans (camera truck driver, kneeling with clapperboard), Mike Frift (camera operator), Simon Mills (clapper loader) and Chunky Huse (grip).

Opposite bottom: 13 Ouarzazate Airport in November 1986. The Lockheed C-130 Hercules was provided by the Royal Moroccan Air Force, courtesy of King Hassan II of Morocco, who was always keen to welcome filmmakers to his country.

14 With my son Simon at Ouarzazate Airport. In spite of the fact that we were filming in the Moroccan desert, the altitude combined with the northerly wind blowing off the Atlas Mountains had most of the unit shivering for much of the filming.

15 Q's workshop on 11 December 1986 at Pinewood Studios during the royal visit by the Prince and Princess of Wales. While special effects supervisor John Richardson speaks with Prince Charles in the foreground, Princess Diana admires my very distinguished nose. (© 1987 Danjaq, LLC and United Artists Corporation. All rights reserved)

16 A rushed lunch on *Licence to Kill* (1988) with Frank Elliott (focus puller) and John Tythe (gaffer). Even in the supposedly controlled conditions of a studio film set you sometimes had to grab a quick bite whenever you could.

17 The *Licence to Kill* camera crew while filming on location in Acapulco. *Left to Right:* Mexican camera assistant, Simon Mills (clapper loader), Alec Mills, Mike Frift, Chunky Huse and Frank Elliott. The white-painted Villa Arabesque in the bright Mexican sunlight caused a number of lighting headaches when composing the individual shots.

18 Filming on a tracking vehicle at Key West on *Licence to Kill*, as the villain tries to make his pre-title sequence escape. *Left to Right:* Alec Mills, Frank Elliott, Chunky Huse, John Tythe, Keith Hamshere and Mike Frift.

19 Filming outside Krest's warehouse at Key West. The weather looks lovely but the average relative summer humidity of about 75 per cent left the film unit totally drained by the end of the day.

20 *Octopussy at Thirty* – the Bondstars summer barbecue at Pinewood Studios on 7 July 2013. *Left to Right:* Colin Miller (sound editor), John Grover (editor), Alec Mills (camera operator), Tony Waye (assistant director), Paul Weston (stunt supervisor), Maud Adams (Octopussy), Elaine Shreyeck (continuity), Kristina Wayborn (Magda), Alan Tomkins (art director) and Peter Lamont (production designer).

21 Signing autographs at Gareth Owen's annual Bondstars summer barbecue at Pinewood Studios, where the fans have a chance to meet the artistes and crews who make the films.

22 Perhaps I was a gladiator in an earlier life. Filming in an amphitheatre near Naples while working as Jack Cardiff's second-unit cameraman on *The Last Days of Pompeii* (1983).

23 I am being introduced by director Bill Faure (pointing at me) to the Zulu king, Goodwill Zwelithini kaBhekuzulu, the eighth monarch of the Zulus. I was told to bow low.

24 Leon Lissek coming off worse this time around. Next to him is Bruce Redman, the Australian assistant director.

25 On location in Portugal. Me, Chunky Huse (grip), Deborah Moore (Roger's daughter), Frank Elliott (focus puller) and John Maskall (camera operator) ... all in love with Debs!

26 *Christopher Columbus: The Discovery* (1992). On location in the US Virgin Islands, director John Glen looks as if he's thinking of taking up piracy.

27 Lining up on an Arri III while filming *Aces: Iron Eagle III* in Arizona (1992). My expression seems to reflect my own feelings about this particular film, with John Glen's sunglasses and military cap probably disguising a similar look on his face.

28 With Miki Thomas on yet another trip to Egypt, this time on *The Awakening* (1980). Filming included the customary tourist locations in Cairo, on the Nile and at Luxor. Another thing that never changed were the number of flies!

29 On location in an amphitheatre in Cornwall while filming *On the Third Day* (1983). Mike Frift is now my camera operator, with Frank Elliott standing above me. Jack Coggins (the gaffer, with cigarette in mouth) keeps a wary eye on me as I play with my brand new light meter. The film was written, produced and directed by Stanley O'Toole, who also gave me a screen credit of associate producer on the film, even though I still don't know exactly what it meant.

30 Filming in the allegedly more controlled conditions of the big tank at the Mediterranean Film Studios on Malta. The actual boat floated on metal drums but was a full-size replica of the one used in the Virgin Islands. Here you can clearly see the artificial horizon between the tank and the sea, but once the water is stirred up the join becomes almost invisible.

31 Working on
The Saint in 1966.
This was my first
television series as
camera operator
after Mike Reed
gave me my break.
It was also my
first experience
working with
Roger Moore, who
also directed this
episode.

32 Thank you,
Richard, but
you should be
on your knees,
you fool. Who
do you think you
are – the director?
(*The Prince and the
Pauper*.)

Another shot of the usual suspects beside the Great Sphinx at Giza. Director Franklin Schaffner in his black jacket stands over my shoulder, with cinematographer Ernie Day standing to the right. Miki Thomas (clappers) and Frank Elliott (focus) stand to the left in the back row, with Chunky Huse (grip) once again front and centre in the front row.

was so as not to disturb the expert as he bent over his reference books near us, just close enough to hear what Frank was saying: 'She came to my room after everyone went to bed!'

For a moment I thought Frank was serious before suddenly realising what he was up to, so now I had to respond to this untimely conversation. With my curiosity awakened to see where he was heading, Frank continued to reel him in. Needless to say, the researcher's interest in his book changed, and he was soon eavesdropping as the discussion continued and no more pages would be turned over until we went to bed!

Sphinx was an archaeological adventure film and during our filming in the Valley of Kings the production was given permission to film a scene inside Tutankhamen's tomb. Such a thing was unheard of at the time, with some of the more superstitious unit members jokingly regarding it as tempting fate, deciding that, like Lord Carnarvon, those who entered the king's chamber would surely die. I will leave it there, not wanting to tempt the outcome in any way ...

Inevitably, our location filming would end in Cairo, where our work enjoyed the picture-postcard backgrounds of the Pyramids and Sphinx at Giza, providing an interesting visual atmosphere even if adding little to the story. However, the critics, weary of the number of films based around Ancient Egypt which all appeared to come out at the same time, would not be fooled with their reviews. Perhaps it was time for them to turn their talents to ridicule, unless it really was the curse of King Tut getting his revenge for our disturbing his rest. Lesley-Anne Down, Frank Langella and John Gielgud survived the experience and tried to get something from this very thin script involving murder, forgery and the black market, but generally I would agree with the critics.

You win some, you lose some!

EYE OF THE NEEDLE

There are times when you recall strange things happening. One such time was when the heavy rain beating down on my window woke me; the dark skies outside produced a strange reflection of my face mirrored in the glass, giving an appearance of tears falling down my cheeks – a weird moment that I remember to this day. Perhaps my distant thoughts were of my constant travelling around the world which had excited me in the past, but now with age moving on I was not so sure that this enthusiasm existed any more.

With all the merry-go-round of foreign travel around the world, *Eye of the Needle* would make a pleasant change with our wartime story being filmed on the rugged island of Mull, the perfect setting for the film version of Ken Follett's novel *Storm Island*, allowing Alan Hume's fine 'painting' to capture the island's bleak isolation.

It had been many years since I had last worked with Alan. I had first been his focus puller in 1964 on *Carry on Cleo* – possibly my favourite of the Carry On films – before operating for him thirteen years later on Peter Hunt's *Gulliver's Travels*, so I looked forward to working with him again. There was more to Alan Hume than met the eye; without doubt he was one of the most pleasant cinematographers with whom one could possibly work. My recollection of Alan is of his wonderful sense of humour and his daily struggle in trying to control his laughing on the set with the clowning around of the Carry On gang. Alan practically cried with laughter until the tears ran down his cheeks as he tried to compose himself; I would be in good company here.

Mull, one of the largest islands of the Inner Hebrides, could easily be described as an open door to nature's weather. Cold, rainy and windy followed by more rain, the

Gulliver's Travels, directed by Peter Hunt; my first film operating for Alan Hume. While I operated a close shot on Richard Harris with an old Arri IIC and 9.8mm Kinoptic lens, the animated Lilliputians would be added in post-production. My grip helping to steady the camera is Colin Manning.

sun appeared to deny the island's existence that year, which in a strange way helped the dramatic setting to the story, where our filming rarely stopped in the ever-changing conditions – a problem which would test any cinematographer's patience to the full, just as it did for Alan. Any thoughts he had of lighting continuity would quickly go out of the window, though in the end this would prove to be a bonus for this interesting wartime story.

Working with home-grown and international cinematographers over the years one gets an insight into their individual inner strengths. It could be their technical expertise, personal temperament or just that he was a very nice guy with bundles of energy. Alan Hume was blessed with all of these qualities. Recalling the films we shared together over the years, including *Third Man on the Mountain*, *Kidnapped*, *Wombling Free* (one to forget), *Shout at the Devil*, *The Spy Who Loved Me*, *Carry on Cleo*, *Gulliver's Travels*, *For Your Eyes Only*, *Octopussy*, *Eye of the Needle* and *Return of the Jedi*, I can now claim to understand him well; the label I would place on Alan Hume would read, 'the director's ideal cinematographer'.

It may seem strange and perhaps difficult to explain, but after this preamble of Alan and his temperament I found myself questioning my own personality, which struck a chord with a memory from my early years back in my Carlton Hill Studio days.

Filming part of the
Allies' phantom
army discovered by
the Nazi spy on *Eye
of the Needle* (1980).
Director Richard
Marquand sitting
with back to camera
and focus puller Mike
Frift.

Who was it who said
that the film business
was glamorous?

Richard Marquand and me in the boat, while Alan Hume stands on the pontoon with Roger Simons (first assistant director) wondering if the light will ever change.

Flashback: Leaving school as a cheeky 14-year-old I suddenly found myself lacking confidence in my new adult surroundings. Meeting famous names would leave me nervous about joining in conversations, preferring to remain silent for fear of being labelled 'that cocky little bugger!' Unlike Alan, I felt uncomfortable as I struggled to establish my own personality with people, which perhaps was down to my own insecurity, even though I needed them as friends – my future contacts. Clearly this was my Achilles heel until I met up with Harry Waxman, who quickly sorted out that problem. In time this lack of self-confidence would pass as my self-belief started to assert itself. Perhaps someone smiled at something I said, setting off the self-confidence that had lain dormant, igniting the necessary spark that would help my career to move forward and for me to become accepted as one of the team. Although this was from the distant past I still had doubts that I would ever match Alan's reputation; his personality made this an impossible mountain for anyone to climb.

Eye of the Needle was an interesting story which caught the flavour of war time. The main character was a fictional German spy codenamed the 'Needle', played by Donald Sutherland, who attempts to escape from Britain in 1944 with stolen plans of the Allies' D-Day landings. While waiting to be picked up by a U-boat off the

Hanging over a cliff on the island of Mull. In spite of Alan Hume's apparent concern, Chunky Huse (my grip) always made sure that I was securely tied off in situations like this.

The evil spy discovered. Lining up a scene with Christopher Cazenove and Donald Sutherland. Also in the picture are Eddie Stacey (stunt arranger), Angela Allen (continuity) and director Richard Marquand.

The obligatory location still taken on Mull. Director Richard Marquand stands at left with Donald Sutherland crouching to the left of the camera. The camera crew included Mike Frift (focus) and Simon Hume (clappers), with Chunky Huse (grip) taking pride of place (again) in front of the camera.

The Eye of the Needle camera crew. From left to right: Simon Hume (clappers), Mike Frift (focus puller), Alan Hume (cinematographer), me (behind camera), Richard Marquand (director) and Valerie Booth (continuity).

coast of Scotland his stolen fishing boat is wrecked in a storm and he is washed up on a small island.

Christopher Cazenove played a crippled and frustrated ex-RAF fighter pilot living on the island with his wife Kate Nelligan. Unaware that the man is a spy, they take him into their home, where the frustrated wife adds a little sexual flavour to the wartime mystery and where the spy takes advantage of Kate Nelligan's problem with her husband's crippled condition. Be that as it may, the Needle still has an appointment to keep with the U-boat and tries to escape from the island in a small rowing boat, though by now the wife has discovered who he really is, bringing the dramatic ending to the story when she sabotages the radio and shoots him as he rows away from the shore.

Masterfully directed by Richard Marquand, the film brought back wartime memories I well remember, with posters on walls warning that spies were among us as the director skilfully recreated the atmosphere.

As was usual with Alan Hume, *Eye of the Needle* had barely started filming before his next film was already being discussed, with a call from the director John Glen offering ...

John Glen, an editor of repute on the Bond films, had proved his directing ability on the second units of *On Her Majesty's Secret Service*, *The Spy Who Loved Me* and *Moonraker*. Recognising John's talent, Cubby Broccoli now promoted him to direct the first unit on the twelfth film in the James Bond franchise, *For Your Eyes Only*.

Reading between the lines in John's autobiography – *For My Eyes Only* – I can only imagine the agony of waiting for the written confirmation to arrive in the post, the sleepless nights pacing up and down as he prepared to take the next step into celebrity which would surely come with this new role. It was an exciting time for John, who deserved this opportunity; you probably remember that Cubby Broccoli did exactly the same for Peter Hunt with *On Her Majesty's Secret Service*, where, if the truth be told, it was Peter and John who were responsible for the slick editing that contributed much to the success of the early Bond films.

With John now at the helm it would not be a surprise to learn that Alan Hume would be his choice of cinematographer. Both had enjoyed a successful relationship in the past and were responsible for one of the best – if not *the* best – Bond opening sequences, with 007 skiing off the top of Mount Asgard on Baffin Island and a parachute opening out into a Union Jack. When this was screened at the Odeon Leicester Square the packed audience exploded into proud cheers and applause: an emotional moment, with tears falling from British eyes. However, *For Your Eyes Only* would be no easy task for John following 007's spectacular journey into space on *Moonraker*, even though others thought that this mission had been a little far-fetched even for a Bond assignment. Possibly it was, even so *Moonraker* would prove to be a spectacular journey guaranteeing financial success, which of course is what 007 is all about.

It would be good to be back on planet Earth after my trip into space on *Moonraker*, and I continued to suffer Roger Moore's misbehaviour as the willing, long-suffering stooge to his never-ending sense of humour.

Prior to the main unit beginning filming I travelled to Lincolnshire with John to film the establishing sequences of the British spy trawler *St Georges* – it was supposed to be in the Ionian Sea but we made do with Grimsby – where the

On location in Corfu with Alan Hume (cinematographer, partially hidden), Chunky Huse (grip), Simon Hume (clapper loader) and Stefan Kalipha, who plays the Cuban assassin Hector Gonzales, shortly before he murders the Havelocks. (© 1981 Danjaq, LLC and United Artists Corporation. All rights reserved)

director's choice was for the camera to sit more or less on the surface, suggesting a periscope viewpoint. With my past experience of filming in the North Sea I was not sure this would work, knowing all too well that salt water and handheld cameras just do not mix. Even so, what we managed to achieve in the constant swell was not as bad as I had feared – also considering that I cannot swim. *For Your Eyes Only* was off to a good start.

First-unit filming with the principal actors would begin with 007 shadowing his adversary to Cortina d'Ampezzo in Italy, where I would also enjoy the pleasures of my favourite climate and the nightlife atmosphere of this very popular skiing resort. With the first-unit filming in Cortina completed we moved to our next location on Corfu, leaving the second unit behind to complete the filming of more of Willy Bogner's incredible skiing and bobsleigh sequences with stunt doubles. By contrast, Corfu was where we mixed with dedicated sun worshippers on their holiday, who – all of the same mind – are prepared to suffer the pain of gaining golden suntans if only to impress their neighbours back home. Filming on location, we meet many people, usually local residents who are interested in the filming taking place and ask the same questions about the stars. In return they are happy to share their gossip and tales of their famous holiday resort. Tourists generally remain indifferent to our labours with some even resenting our presence by turning away, preferring instead to work on their suntans.

Our location was the mountain of Metéora, which would be difficult to climb, the slippery surface making it impossible even for James Bond. At its peak was a monastery housing the monks, isolated from the outside world, with all their needs or anything else the religious order required pulled to the top in a basket, keeping them safely inaccessible in their sanctuary. The gossip from our curious locals was of young boys who occasionally made trips up in the basket, though of more concern to the production were the monks' attempts to disrupt our filming by hanging out their washing and making loud noises. In the end we got most of what we needed, with a few additional sequences being filmed once we were back at Pinewood.

Some of the cleverer sequences we filmed in the studio involved matching our dry-for-wet shots with the wider angle sequences that had been filmed by the underwater unit in the Bahamas. Underwater filming is difficult enough at the best of times and can only be carried out by properly qualified technicians, but some of Alan's supposedly 'underwater' sequences with the principal actors were little short of miraculous. On a stage it was simple enough to film close ups on the principal actors' faces, filming at high speed through a water tank (with the occasional air bubbles for added effect) while a hidden fan blew through the actors' hair. The effect was totally convincing – another simple camera technique seemingly forgotten in this CGI age.

The tried-and-tested Bond formula would continue to please, with the customary beautiful girls, the latest gadgets for 007's teasing of Q and Miss Moneypenny's eternal flirting with James. This time, however, M would be conspicuous by his absence, with Bernard Lee having died in January 1981 before we were scheduled to film his scenes at Pinewood. Rather than re-cast the part the producers felt that it would be more appropriate for the rewritten script to have M on sabbatical with the distraught Minister of Defence played by Geoffrey Keen, whose hair seemed to get greyer with every 007 assignment, filling in. Topol now joined the cast as Bond's unlikely ally with Julian Glover as a convincing baddie, while Carole Bouquet would take the lead female role with the very pretty professional ice-skating champion Lynn-Holly Johnson adding to the interest.

Alan Hume had now reached the peak of his career so it would not be a surprise to learn that his next film had already been arranged with director Richard Marquand, with whom we had previously worked on *Eye of the Needle*. Alan would be the cinematographer on what at the time was supposed to be the final episode in George Lucas's *Star Wars* film series, with me tagging along…

Whatever occupation we follow as a career, either by choice or opportunity, our lives become routine, at times making it difficult to understand others with their unseen problems. The film industry is no different; in our work we meet many interesting people, actors and technicians alike, who possibly have different opinions to our own.

On the other hand, others have temperaments which need to be handled more carefully otherwise you could never be sure of the final outcome. Some remain biased with their own opinions and make it clear that there can be no further discussion on the matter, which usually fits their character. We all recognise these sad people with their depressing attitude to life, but that is their problem so we get on with the job. As human beings we have the right to different opinions which others may find difficult to accept and certainly not easy to write about. Even so, one's honesty remains, whatever the outcome; but 'if the face doesn't fit' is a problem which we all experience from time to time – we might need to handle a situation more carefully.

'Revenge of the Jedi' was the original title on the script, although this would change before filming began at Elstree Studios, the English home of the *Star Wars* movies at the time. This decision came from the producer George Lucas, who decided that the word 'revenge' was not a Jedi concept and would send the wrong message to young people. *Return of the Jedi* was to be the last instalment of the original trilogy created by George Lucas, with Harrison Ford, Mark Hamill and Carrie Fisher continuing in their established roles, as would Alec Guinness as Ben 'Obi-Wan' Kenobi.

Having enjoyed the two previous *Star Wars* films I looked forward to working on this final episode, and to be part of the experience. Episode VI (the prequel trilogy had yet to be made) had a fun atmosphere on the set, where the randy dwarfs competed for individual stardom. Although I use the word 'randy' with tongue in cheek, this observation comes from their adventurous ways; should an attractive lady pass through the stage she would quickly draw the magnetic attention of our small friends, their stature not holding them back!

This lively feeling on set every day is how I would prefer to remember my time on *Return of the Jedi*, with enjoyment had by all and a daily routine which would make my Ewok experience one to remember; in the end, though, I would be left with a feeling of bitterness and resentment due to the behaviour of a fellow human being.

Return of the Jedi was the last film in the series and would finally expose the face behind the mask of Darth Vader, the villain, who was finally unmasked by his son, Luke Skywalker. Secrecy surrounded the production to such an extent that few people had a complete script, and even those complete scripts were carefully numbered to avoid them being copied and passed on to the press – my number was 021. However, another dark mask was hiding in the shadows, where possibly the original title word 'revenge' would be more appropriate. I would now learn the hard lesson of when or when not to have an opinion which differed to those in higher authority – let alone expressing it!

Filming had barely started in January 1982 when the nameless one decided that he had seen something in the rushes that he did not like. I should explain that his concern had nothing to do with my work – that I clearly remember. What I also remember is that his comment was not particularly important; as the Americans say, 'hardly a big deal'! To be fair to the gentleman, though, it was his right to have an opinion and to express it, but it was also my right to disagree with his point of view, which I did, politely – a big mistake! Perhaps it was because camera operators only operate the camera in America, leaving the cinematographer to discuss the rushes with the director, but here in the UK the director and camera

With Richard
Marquand,
George Lucas
(looking through
the camera) and
Mike Frift (focus
puller) at Elstree
Studios on *Return
of the Jedi* (1980),
with an evil Sith
Lord peering over
my shoulder. He
wasn't the only
one ... (© & ™
Lucasfilm Ltd. All
rights reserved.
Used under
authorisation)

operator probably work far more closely together. If this were not the case then I
would have been guilty of breaking the so-called unwritten rule of minding your
own bloody business, Alec!

Later on, George Lucas came in to see the rushes with the director; after the
screening both were happy with everything they had seen on the screen with no
further comment about the concerns of the other person. You would have thought
that this would have been it, but sadly this was not the end of the story. After
that the nameless one would not speak to me again throughout our filming in the
studio, preferring instead to look the other way and totally ignore me. In hindsight
this should have been a clue as to what would come.

With our filming going well and the constant banter on the set, the unit began to think about flying on to America for the six weeks of location filming at Yuma in Arizona, followed by Crescent City in California. It was at this point that strange things started to happen which gave me reason for concern, though somehow I could not put my finger on the problem. Even so, something was definitely wrong and there was a sudden change in attitude directed towards me personally, particularly from the production office, which was surprising since we had had no problems with communication regarding my work in the studio. My suspicion that something was wrong would be confirmed when the production manager, with whom I had worked in the past and enjoyed a good relationship, was noticeably avoiding eye contact with me, sometimes turning to look the other way. Strange ... this was not the friendly colleague I knew and respected, so obviously something was wrong. I mentioned this to Alan, who thought it was just my imagination, even so the concerns persisted and refused to go away. I would soon be proved right.

To bring this sad account to a close, all I wanted was for someone to give me an honest explanation as to why the camera operator on the film was the only member of the camera crew not to go to the USA, which could only leave me with the inescapable conclusion that a real-life Darth Vader here on planet Earth was seeking his revenge on me, now sadly leaving me with a legacy of bitterness towards this wonderful Jedi experience. What irritates me to this day, even in retirement, is how an adult can be so immature in turning a nothing issue into a personal vendetta for no real reason at all. I can only think that this gentleman was hurt by my honest comment – a sad creature, to be sure – though no doubt we all meet up with this sort of person at certain times in our lives.

If my comments appear sour, let me emphasise that I really enjoyed working on *Jedi*; everything about the experience was truly amazing, apart from my one moment of apparent madness when it seems that I had the audacity to politely disagree with a man in high office. However, I must also be completely honest with all that happened and say that to my knowledge no one spoke up to challenge this childish decision that the camera operator would not go to America; others would need to live with that judgement. Am I bitter after all this time? You bet I am!

Recently I read somewhere online that Alan also had a falling out with the same person with whom I had the problem, which was apparently due to the poor treatment of the director Richard Marquand; after that Alan was allegedly transferred to another unit while Alec Mills took over as cinematographer. I do not know where this came from but obviously it was untrue as that idiot had got rid of me earlier on. The film business is a tough world to survive in.

There would be one more interesting postscript to this account, which was not surprising. I would later be told that the same person had been given 'other responsibilities' on the film, possibly due to the harm he caused Alan, though I doubt he would have any conscience about all the damage he created for us both.

Thinking later about this unpleasant incident I was reminded of my dad, who 'impolitely' dared to share his opinion with an army officer about his mistreatment of a horse on the Western Front. It would seem that we definitely share the same DNA so I will now dry my eyes and make an effort to put this sad experience behind me ...

On the other hand, something positive would come from all this foolishness. Now more than ever I felt this would be the time to move up the ladder and start thinking in terms of lighting, come what may. Politics such as this finally forced me to take the decision which I should have made earlier, and underlined the direction in which my future really lay.

On his return to the UK Alan offered me his next film, *The Hunchback of Notre Dame*. Although still smarting from the injustice of the *Jedi* experience, I decided not to bring the issue up and let sleeping dogs lie. What would be the point now, anyway?

Alan had much sympathy about what had happened to me on *Jedi*, but it seemed that in all innocence I had not recognised the danger signals in the situation which I had created for myself.

The few offers of work as cinematographer which I had been given so far had come in small doses – crumbs put my way as I was probably the cheapest cameraman around and desperate to try out my new light meters. One of the promised crumbs was a small television film for Stanley O'Toole called *Island of Adventure*, a pilot for a proposed Enid Blyton television series which in the end was not picked up by a broadcaster. Other promised work never came through, leaving me concerned at the pattern now forming around me after my *Jedi* experience. Then again, perhaps I was just feeling sorry for myself.

Then, out the blue, *Biddy* arrived to put a smile back on my face. While I would never know how this came about, I sensed that my life was changing in this transition period. The director Christine Edzard and her producer husband Richard Goodwin, with whom I had worked on *Death on the Nile*, had phoned to offer me a pleasant little film to photograph, restoring my faith in human nature, knowing that this time I would be working with genuine people. However, what came as a surprise – and disappointment – was that Christine suggested that the camera should be kept locked off when filming. Of course this is the director's right, especially as the director has a particular understanding of the subject matter, but I thought it a shame, as camera movement creates atmosphere, adding mood to a scene. I mentioned this to Christine, who politely listened to a second opinion before sticking with her original judgement on the matter, which of course I respected, this time without any negative repercussions.

Either way, working with the charming Christine, I found *Biddy* to be a very enjoyable experience. The story was of a prim and proper housemaid, methodical in everything she did and sure to see that everything was put away and placed neatly folded in the right place. That sets the scene for the delightful Biddy and her relationship with the family's children.

While I was working with this very interesting director who allowed me the freedom of expression with my contribution, matters were complicated by a call from Ireland to film a test for Lewis Gilbert on a film which he would soon direct. Christine's kindness towards me made it impossible for me to accept the job. If I had taken Lewis's offer, then possibly my career as cinematographer would have taken off much earlier, as Lewis's film *Educating Rita* was so successful.

With my confidence steadily growing, I was then offered a second unit as cinematographer on *The Last Days of Pompeii*, providing me with yet another opportunity to work under the baton of the maestro himself, Jack Cardiff, who was well aware of my dream to move forward.

Here I am reminded of a night sequence by the water's edge that would take time to get right if it was meet with Jack's approval. What was of no help to me or my nerves was the producer, who constantly walked up and down, making sure I noticed that he was looking at his watch. With the authority of my mentor behind me, I never wavered and refused to give in to this over-the-top intimidation. There were other snippets hardly worth a mention, but these short experiences would play an important part in strengthening my self-belief as I moved slowly towards my goal.

So to get to the point of all this waffle: the question remains – why did I agree to accept Alan's kind offer to operate the camera on *The Hunchback of Notre Dame?* If truth be told, I gave in to Alan's persuasive powers because I believed that I had little chance of being offered a film as a cinematographer – at least that is what I held to at the time. However, chance had not abandoned me altogether, and the moment arrived while we were testing camera equipment for *Hunchback.*

It was a timely call from Stanley O'Toole, offering me a small film to photograph, *On the Third Day* – a personal project for the producer which he would write, produce and direct himself; he was quick to point out that he had little money to splash around in his tight budget. Stanley's offer came at a crucial point in my career after giving in to Alan's tempting offer, though both would help to erase the sad memory of my *Jedi* experience which, as you can see, still lingered in the background. With Stanley financing the film himself it was clear that there would be little money to play with, but as far as I was concerned currency would not be an issue for me. Nor would the Herb Ross incident with Ernie Day – which I believed Stanley should have smoothed over – concern me any longer. All that now faded with time and memory; nothing would stand in my way with this big break!

NEGOTIATING SALARY

Working with Stanley O'Toole over the years, it was inevitable that we would get to know each other's strengths and weakness, particularly when it came to discussing my salary. Stanley always had the advantage in these encounters, knowing I had no agent at that time to protect my interests. Wearing his producer's hat, crying over his 'very tight budget', he kept the 'negotiations' simple by not looking me in the face when announcing any figure he had in mind, knowing well that I might start laughing before he rejoined the real world where I exist. However, I would be prepared for these encounters where any discussions of my salary over the years would become a joke, which I suspect we both enjoyed anyway.

It happened that during our ongoing negotiations for *On the Third Day* Prime Minister Margaret Thatcher was speaking on the radio about the situation in the Falkland Islands. At the time we were driving around Cornwall looking for suitable locations but Stanley's attention appeared to be tuned more into the radio with the constant updates about the military situation. With all the distraction going on in the South Atlantic this had to be the ideal if not fortuitous time for him casually to remind me for the umpteenth time of the small budget he had in mind, particularly with regard to the subject of my salary, before quickly returning to the radio for updates from Maggie on the conflict, cutting off any further thoughts I had about discussing the matter. Stanley would always pick the moment of where and when would be ideal to discuss this issue. The latest news from the Falklands on the radio provided the perfect time for my driver to plan his strategy.

I played along with his little game, trying to keep a straight face as I watched Stanley agonise as he waited on my deliberately delayed response to his ridiculous figure, at the same time knowing that I had already made up my mind, but this

would come in my own time. Eventually, to put him out of his misery, I told Stanley
as a friend that I would photograph the film free of charge, so now we could both
concentrate on the job in hand. My relieved driver turned to me with a broad smile
on his face. Stanley had won the battle this time but the fact is that my sacrifice
was necessary, if only to gain that all-important screen credit of cinematographer.

The filming in Cornwall would take four weeks to complete, with the constant
friendly banter between us continuing to grow. Stanley directed his first film while I
photographed my second, at the same time keeping my technical camera-operating
eye open for him just in case he ran into any potential problems with editing
or other unforeseen issues, just as Ernie Day had done for David Hemmings on
Running Scared. However, like Ernie, I would only intervene should it be necessary.

While I could not be sure if Stanley's film – a horror suspense story about a man
who breaks into an old headmaster's family home to reveal himself as his unknown
illegitimate son – would ever reach the cinema or television screens, it would not be
the issue for me. We all have our dreams and Stanley was now fulfilling his, while
at the same time pointing my career forward in the right direction; I hoped that our
partnership would continue long into the distant future.

Letting my thoughts run riot, I also dreamed one day of directing a film. I am
not alone in this ambitious idea, where as an experienced camera operator over

Negotiating my salary with Stanley O'Toole: 'You agreed the deal, Alec, I can't change
it now!'

many years I worked with directors who at times I believed had little or no idea of how to get the best from a scene with the use of the camera, and – dare I say – with the actors too. However, to balance this I would learn from directors who had great imagination and the courage to put their ideas on the screen. Truly this is not conceit on my part as there are many directors with camera department pedigrees: Freddie Francis, Guy Green, Jack Cardiff, Ronald Neame and Denis Lewiston, to name but a few – all cinematographers of repute and with a great deal of experience. Equally, editors also proved their worth behind the camera and were more than capable as directors, but at this time any thoughts I had of directing were just a pipe dream; I was doubtful that I would ever get the opportunity or responsibility of such high office.

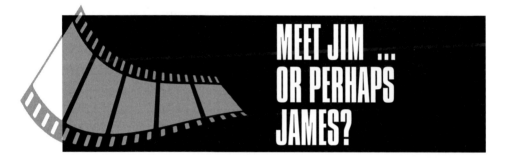

MEET JIM ... OR PERHAPS JAMES?

Working with Stanley O'Toole would leave me wondering where I stood in this unusual relationship: at times I felt genuine friendship towards me, while on another day he would wear his stern producer's hat, keeping me at a distance. Recognising the danger signals, I would then back off until he came back from whatever strange mood he was in.

With the day's schedule successfully completed I would be rewarded with an invitation to have dinner with his family while discussing the next day's call sheet; my ever-present camera assistant Frank Elliott with his amusing charm would fit in well with the fun and games of the O'Toole household.

One night, with the meal over, Riki O'Toole, Stanley's wife at the time, suggested that we might like to join them in a session with their Ouija board – an occasional pastime which the family apparently enjoyed. Although I admitted to being uncomfortable with this, I still agreed to watch the proceedings. I was reminded of a film scene as the lights were dimmed for atmosphere as we sat around a small table, waiting for 'someone' to join us. Minutes passed ... nothing ... total silence ... You could hear a pin drop. No one spoke as we waited on a contact from the other side. What a waste of time, I thought to myself with all this nonsense.

Suddenly we were joined by a visitor from the 'other side'; James – or perhaps Jim – now made his presence known to us. We all looked at each other, silently enquiring if anyone knew a James, but apparently none of the participants recognised any person of that name who had passed over. Still not sure about any of this stuff, I whispered to the group, hoping the spirit couldn't hear me.

'I know a Jim ... but he's not dead yet!'

There is no way now or in the future that I would ever want to communicate with anyone on the other side as I had no idea how to handle this situation. Even so, the other participants urged me to reply. Hoping not to offend James – or Jim – or any other poor souls who had passed over and were listening in to this ridiculous conversation, I hesitated to use the word 'dead' under any circumstances. Everyone was patiently waiting on my response, and I was still not sure if I wanted a chat with this silly Ouija board that was staring at me. Urged on by my silent partners, though, and looking directly at the board – as if it was Jim – I decided to go for it.

'Well, I know someone called Jim but he's not ... mortem yet!'

That comment suddenly had everyone laughing hysterically, as doubtless was Jim and his mates in the hereafter, all enjoying a good laugh at my expense. It quickly brought the night's entertainment to a close for me. Never again would I glance into the strange world of the afterlife in this way.

Apart from that, Stanley's little film would be a rewarding experience, where for the most part I was given the artistic freedom to help his dream come true. However, a happy experience does not necessarily mean a successful one, although no doubt there were some consolations for Stanley with all the freebies from his hand-picked crew, which I doubt cost him a fortune anyway.

Back home following my debut as cinematographer with Christine and now Stanley, still no offers came my way. Once again my thoughts turned to other camera operators who had the same burning ambition, waiting for that one opportunity which might never arrive. Perhaps like me they had their partners encouraging them not to weaken and stay firm, but soon another year had passed me by. Another year older, another year wasted ...

OCTOPUSSY: MY PRIVATE REVOLUTION

Time was fast moving on, but it seemed that offers as a cinematographer were still too few and far between for me to consider the change as permanent. Was it time for a rethink? In spite of all my positive intentions it was inevitable that mind games would start tormenting me, making me question whether I was doing the right thing; with Suzy's encouragement, I held out for as long as possible, my patience being tested to the full.

Inevitably the ugly face of temptation arrived, with this particular devil wearing Alan Hume's hat, tempting me to take up the handles again. Alan had phoned, casually mentioning his next film with John Glen: *Octopussy*.

'John was wondering if you would be interested, Alec?'

Alan knew how serious I was about moving up to lighting – we had discussed this many times – but even so he thought I should at least consider the offer, which did not take me long. I remained firm.

'Please thank John for his consideration but I have to turn down the offer. Give my best to 007!'

Happy with my resolve, if saddened at my decision, I could not foresee John and Alan ganging up to talk me out of my so-called retirement from operating the camera. It was only on John's insistence that I agreed to meet them at the Black Horse pub in Fulmer village for lunch, hoping that I might at least get a second or third unit as cinematographer.

We were going through the usual pleasantries of going back down memory lane – as you do – reminding ourselves of the good times shared together, when John decided that he had softened me up enough to say: 'Alec, do this for me and I promise you will not regret it!'

Kind words – bold words – which strangely I remembered hearing from another smooth-talking director whose promises came to nothing, so how could I take John seriously with that statement?

I am a weak man and easily manipulated. With the shared enthusiasm of both John and Alan my Achilles heel gave way. *Octopussy* would be my fifth James Bond film as camera operator and, if I am totally honest, I will also admit that I was a little relieved with the sudden opportunity to replenish a fast-dwindling bank balance.

Octopussy would be my second experience of working in India, which had previously given me the impression of a country in no hurry to move forward, a place where tourists bask in golden, dusty sunsets viewed from the balcony of their luxury hotel – possibly with an iced gin and tonic close to hand. In truth, when you look behind what the tourists see, there are people living in poor conditions, where 'holy' cows stroll through the streets depositing faeces everywhere and where the divide between rich and poor appeared to be enormous. Would I ever forget the discomfort of seeing that young woman feeding her little baby in the thicket?

All of this was a world away from the Bond locations in Udaipur, including the Monsoon Palace, the Lake Palace and Jag Mandir. Putting conscience aside, *Octopussy* would bring back many wonderful images of my youth as a devoted fan of the *Hotspur* comic. There again I also enjoyed W.E. Johns's *Biggles* series, with his far-flung colonial adventures – a childhood hero. Now, under John Glen's baton, *Octopussy* would recreate all those wonderful memories, inspired with Alan's wonderful photography and where we would share many interesting experiences. One I remember in particular was when I played 007, holding my trusty handheld Arri IIC while in a tuk-tuk being chased by the baddies who were firing at me – they missed!

A stroke of good fortune would find me and Suzy moving into the Palace Hotel. This opportunity came about when a room had suddenly become vacant and with no one else in any hurry to move in and knowing full well that this chance would probably never happen again we took up the offer, quickly killing off all of my principles about poverty. The five-star hotel, where the stars of the film would normally reside, was a different world, but although you might read this as my good fortune there would also be the downside that it allowed Roger Moore to carry on tormenting me with his endless wicked sense of humour, even when we were off duty.

Let me offer a short insight into Roger Moore's quick wit, though possibly it will be more amusing if the explanation reads as script.

On our return from foreign parts we filmed a short sequence with James Bond outside Sotheby's, the auctioneers in Mayfair, requiring only the director, camera crew and make-up. After completing our filming, we drove to Peterborough to join up with the rest of the unit, who had gone ahead with the production vehicles in preparation for the train sequences being filmed on the Nene Valley Railway. Arriving late, I just had time to grab a quick meal, collect a call sheet and retire to my room. Here I should explain my preference was sleeping nude. Exhausted, I knew that I would sleep well …

It was in the early hours when I suddenly 'sensed' someone creeping into my bed – could I be dreaming? In a state of semi-consciousness I turned to look at the figure, now comfortably in bed and covered by the sheet, with only her blonde hair visible. Believing that my luck had changed I gently pulled the sheet back to unmask the fair maiden, only to find that she … was a HE!

Panic now took over very quickly. Waking from the shock, I jumped out of bed, shouting at him as my outrage slowly woke the man from his deep slumber; seemingly lost and still half-asleep he looked around the room before finally sliding out on the other side of the bed. There I stood, hands crossed over private parts, while he stood confused and on the other side of the bed wearing his shorts and vest. He looked around the room as he listened to my verbal onslaught, still not sure where he was or whether he had made a mistake – a big mistake – but for me this was no laughing matter, even if it did seem more like a scene from a Laurel and Hardy script:

Bedroom. Night

Alec
(Shaking … shouting)

Who are you? What the hell are you doing in my
room?

Blonde Man
(Sleepily … politely … looking around)

This is … my room … Who are you?

Alec
(Still shaking)

Get out, you f***ing idiot, etc., etc.

(I did go on a bit)

> Still not wide awake, the zombie turned and
> slowly walked out of the room without another
> word spoken, leaving me in a state of shock
> from this terrible nightmare experience. I
> hurried to the door to find that the lock
> didn't work; a chair under the handle would
> suffice until morning, I hoped that I might
> get some sleep.
>
> Fade out, next morning, cut to …
>
> Int. Breakfast Room. Day
> A table for three, Elaine Schreyeck
> (continuity), Roger Moore (the enemy);
> a tired Alec arrives to join them for
> breakfast, Roger in the process of telling
> Elaine a story going around the unit.

Roger

> Apparently this lorry driver sleepwalks when
> he gets involved with heavy drinking with his
> mates!

Alec
(Cutting in)

> That was me, Roger; this man came into my
> room in the early hours … of … the … morn …
> ing …
>
> Suddenly realising I had just made the
> unbelievably charitable mistake of providing
> Roger Moore – of all people – with ammunition

for his deadly wit, which of course would
happen now and too late to do anything about
it.

                          Elaine
Was he tight, Alec? (As in DRUNK)

                          Roger
The first time, Elaine, only the first time!

007 was now placed on my death list!

It was not just Roger Moore who could exploit the humour in a particular situation. Another of our UK filming locations included RAF Northolt, doubling as a South American airbase for the title sequence where 007 would make his customary escape, this time in a small Acrostar jet which I recall was to have originally featured in an earlier *Moonraker* sequence.

The art department had been working at Northolt for a couple of weeks prior to the main unit's arrival, building and dressing the set, which happened to include dozens of palm trees along one of the perimeter roads. These were visible from outside the base and so the inhabitants of Ruislip, unaware of what was going on, became naturally curious and questions were asked about the sudden appearance of these trees. I do not know exactly how the story got out – it was probably one of the sparks – but by the time we arrived at Northolt representatives of the local Ruislip press were eagerly monitoring the airbase entrance in expectation of the imminent arrival of hundreds of Argentine prisoners of war from the Falklands, having been told that the palm trees had been put up 'to help make them feel more at home'!

It just goes to prove that you should never believe everything that you hear on a film set.

HOT TARGET

Time was fast running out, with few signs of any more work being offered to me as a cinematographer. Even so, offers as a camera operator would still be politely turned away, with me explaining to the caller of my decision to move up to lighting. In the meantime I prayed for Divine intervention.

Then one day an old colleague from the past telephoned; Denis Lewiston had been the camera operator on the second unit of *Blow-Up* and had gone on to achieve status as a cinematographer after working his way through the traditional ranks of the camera department. Like others before him, Denis had a burning ambition to direct a film and the opportunity had come his way with an original story, co-written by Denis with Gerry O'Hara. The screenplay was originally titled *Restless* but would eventually be released with the title *Hot Target*.

Denis's call was to ask if I would be interested in photographing and operating on the film, which would be filmed on location in New Zealand. I hesitated to answer this totally unexpected invitation, knowing well his odd sense of humour from past times and wondering if he was being serious. Either way, I did not want Denis to have second thoughts due to my hesitation, so I decided to play along with his kind offer – just in case it was real.

For an inexperienced cinematographer *Hot Target* would offer an unusual challenge, with one of the sets being coloured completely black – though I wasn't sure black was even a colour. In any event, Denis would send photographs from a magazine to show me what he meant and to which I could refer in order to reproduce the look on screen. At this point anxiety took over in the conversation as I tried to hide my concerns at Denis's challenge. Ideas like this usually come from past experiences stored away in the personal memory bank; one day they could be useful. This is how it was with Denis, whose idea of the black set came from renting an apartment in America owned by a gentleman whose choice of furnishings was black, prompting him to revisit the experience in *Hot Target*.

Flying to Auckland with insane images in my head, my thoughts were focused entirely on Denis's favoured black set, but now it was too late to talk him out of it. I could only hope that the actors were not the same colour wearing dark suits! The more I thought about the problem the worse it seemed to get, reasoning that you cannot put more light on a subject just because it is black – an interesting challenge for a beginner.

I gave my undivided attention to *Hot Target* as my confidence grew by the day. I was grateful for Denis's help in collecting another valuable credit as cinematographer. It must be said that the combination of lighting and camera operating did not work for me; my concentration was now more with my lighting. Combining the two positions slowed down Denis's plans with his tight schedule, let alone the complications of the dreaded black set that was on the horizon. We both realised that it would take time to get right – not a good situation for a new cinematographer.

Denis never questioned my speed at any time, for which I was grateful, though no doubt this was of concern to him with the ambitious schedule. However, he did suggest that he would be happy to operate the camera as well as direct, giving time for me to concentrate more on my lighting. Although I admit to having pangs of conscience about this, I gratefully accepted Denis's generous offer; he had been a fine camera operator in his own right and was now making this gesture to ease my pain.

I am pleased to say that *Hot Target* finished on schedule and in the end my worries with the dreaded black set would not materialise. What did come from the exercise was the realisation that I would never be happy at the thought of combining the two positions of lighting cameraman and camera operator on a film – a dual role which later would sadly become the norm for many. As a result of this decision I would subsequently lose a number of films offered to me, but I would cling stubbornly to the principle that life was too short to let my artistic contribution suffer just to accommodate an accountant's balance sheet.

Of course there are others who will disagree with this, suggesting I am old fashioned or that they prefer doing both jobs themselves, which again I consider to be a mistake for many reasons. With age fast creeping up and students eagerly waiting in the wings for their big opportunity, I doubt that today's cinematographers will have a change of heart about this situation.

While I am in this controversial mood I would also say that I believe that camera assistants who have risen through the ranks on the studio floor and under a professional technician's guidance probably make better camera operators than film-school students who are taught to operate the camera as well as light. Okay, perhaps I am old fashioned, for which I will not apologise, but there is much more to operating the camera than just looking through an eyepiece and keeping the actors in the frame.

SHAKA ZULU

Moving up the ladder would not come easily, nor would knowing that others would gain from any operating work I politely turned away, as those important contacts built up over the years gradually began to disappear. However, with *Biddy*, *On the Third Day* and now *Hot Target* added to the CV there could be no turning back.

Unfortunately, my move came at a time when the British film industry was experiencing another of its periodic slumps in film production. At times I wondered if Divine intervention was trying to tell me something, or possibly testing my courage in holding out. Although the odd titbit here and there would help my

Filming Senzangakhona's wedding on *Shaka Zulu* (1984). I wasn't sure what was happening in the madness of it all, but somehow you came to accept it. The man with the red and white cap in the background is 'Biza', a white Zulu who grew up with Zulus and spoke the language like a native. He was our cultural expert, interpreter and later assistant director.

staying power it would not be enough to meet the demanding requirements of the British Society of Cinematographers, and I was hoping that one day I might win the right to add that valued BSC credit after my name.

One thing that would help to address the problem would be an agent. If the word was to spread that 'Alec Mills, director of cinematography' was now available to the film world then possibly the dream would continue, provided that someone out there was willing to take a chance with me. Dreams or not, an agency soon called to say that they would like to represent me, which was strange when I had not spoken with anyone about this before – coincidence again? This would allow my puffed-up ego to exaggerate the importance of my three modest credits, with fingers crossed my man would be in a position to spread the word of my availability.

Although I was not expecting to be drowned in offers, the gentleman soon called back.

'Alec, would you be interested working on a film in South Africa, and by the way does the name Shaka mean anything to you?'

No, was the simple answer to the second question. Shaka meant little or nothing to me, but when researching Shaka's history it would seem way back in the 1820s

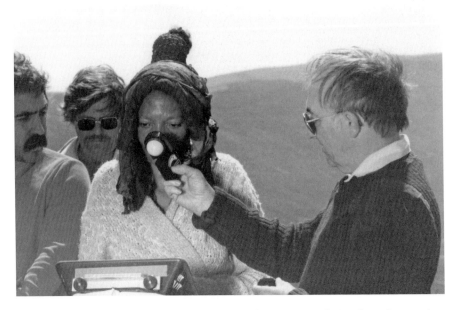

August 1984, Dundee, South Africa. Preparing for a scene with Nandi as she wanders in the wilderness with her illegitimate son, Shaka, and her daughter, Nunko, cast out from the Zulu tribe.

the name alone spread fear among the Zulu nation. Suddenly I realised this could now be an exciting opportunity to work on a production that would help my career to move forward; at the same time I knew that it would require a big sacrifice from me to be working abroad. My heartbeat started to race as I tried to control the excitement of an agent showing an interest in me, while also knowing I would need to keep calm and play it down as if I was swimming in offers; obviously he knew differently – let's face it, we are all actors playing our part in a scene.

'It's a film/television series to be filmed in South Africa about a Zulu king – Shaka Zulu ...' Then there came an interminable pause when I thought we had been cut off before he decided to carry on. '... to be filmed in Zululand ...' Another long pause, still no response from me. Finally, with hesitation in his voice, he dropped the bombshell: 'It will take a year to film!'

With that comment my heartbeat quickly returned to normal, knowing well I had no intention, wish or desire to leave my family behind for a year. My hesitation in answering his question was obvious to the caller who now realised that no cameraman could possibly be interested in leaving home for such a long time. Thanking him for his interest, I declined.

Thinking about this hasty decision later, I understood that as a new cinematographer looking for recognition I would need more lighting experience

The white men raising the British flag in Zululand. Edward Fox, playing Lieutenant Francis Farewell, is saluting in the foreground as Robert Powell, playing Dr Henry Fynn, looks on.

The entrance to Shaka's capital, Bulawayo.

with more credits, which would surely come after a project like *Shaka Zulu*. If past experience had taught me anything, it was that opportunities like this do not come often, so perhaps this offer should not be rejected out of hand so easily. After discussing it with Suzy a suggestion was put to the production: I would be prepared to do six months filming on *Shaka Zulu*, with both parties keeping open an option with the second stage of filming. This idea was put to the director William Faure, who agreed and quickly became 'Bill'.

While I had now won my first film/television series as cinematographer, it meant the sacrifice of being abroad for a long time – out of sight and out of mind – possibly delaying any success or recognition here in the UK, which was always important to me. But if this was the only way forward then so be it: anything ... anything to move my career forward.

Within days a large package arrived from Johannesburg containing fifteen scripts. Settling down to read each episode it soon became clear that I was involved with something big – possibly even spectacular. *Shaka Zulu* would hand me a photographic experience which would stay long in my memory throughout my entire career as a cinematographer, from which I would learn much with its many unforeseen challenges, not least with my first encounter of filming black actors – Nubian black! The scripts were written by an American, Joshua Sinclair, who had obviously researched the Zulu history in painstaking detail.

Shaka's capital, Bulawayo. We were shooting with over 2,000 Zulu warriors for days.

Flying to Johannesburg would bring the sudden reality of the *Shaka* experience and the usual worries now started playing with my mind. Whether in heaven or hell, the legendary Zulu king would take his toll on me with the excitement of it all as my mood turned to one of anxiety as I started to think about the challenge ahead. The long flight gave me time to reflect on my apparent insanity, so that soon I had convinced myself that I had just made the biggest mistake of my life. Should there be anything of any comfort it was that I had managed to arrange for Frank Elliott, my trusted camera assistant, to join me later.

Following my meeting in Johannesburg with Bill Faure, our talented young director, I flew on to Durban; from there it was a dusty three-hour trip by truck, sitting next to a nervous Zulu driver as suspicious of me as I was of him as we drove deep into the heart of Zululand. By now I had reached the lowest point of my depression. Finally we arrived at our destination of Eshowe, where the British had been besieged for two months during the Zulu War in 1879. Now it was too late to change my mind.

Here I finally came face to face with the Zulus *en masse*, where I would learn more of their traditions and past violent history as portrayed in our thirteen scripts. Finally came my meeting with the towering muscular giant himself – Shaka Zulu, who appeared in the guise of actor Henry Cele.

To be honest, I could easily believe this man to be the real Shaka. He carefully studied me with his piercing eyes with not the slightest glimmer of a smile or welcome towards me. Was this to be Henry's portrayal of Shaka's classic Zulu greeting? Whoever this Shaka was, he would obviously be in charge throughout our filming – with no arguments coming from me. Later I would read that this was Henry's way of keeping in character both on and off the set until filming ended – a true method actor. No doubt this would have met with the approval of the ghost of Shaka himself, who was probably looking down on all this. Henry would keep that way throughout our filming, even though it would make my work difficult, particularly when in need of his cooperation with my lighting of him.

Eshowe was a township shared by the black and white communities, where the white population enjoyed a comfortable existence in their agreeable homes; Zulu accommodation appeared to be less so as they preferred to retain their inherited tribal traditions. For all that, rarely did I sense any hostility between the two communities, though when reading the faces one felt that a degree of resentment still lurked silently in the background. Even so, the problem of racial segregation appeared to be less evident in Eshowe, where everything remained relatively quiet – at least on the surface – though this could not be said of the other regions. It would not be easy for a wanderer passing that way to describe Eshowe; it would probably be called a 'hick town' – a short stop-over. It immediately brought back memories of my small guest room in that drab hotel somewhere in the outback of South Australia, but it was just about habitable enough and this nomad gratefully accepted it.

Shaka meeting the white men (the 'swallows') for the first time. Henry Cele wears his traditional Zulu crown; his prime minister is on his left.

Most of the South African crew shared rented houses in the surrounding area, which I would also have preferred but at least I had a room to myself at the hotel, which had been taken over by the production company as a base for the wardrobe, make-up, camera and sound departments. Everyone shared its basic facilities where every day hordes of Zulus would camp outside, waiting to be called to the set.

Already I was asking myself if I could survive six days, let alone six months! There was absolutely no chance that I would be interested in the second phase of the schedule, but then something strange happened which would make everything work out for me. Coincidence yet again?

Unknown to me, David Bracknell, our first assistant director, had phoned Suzy back in England asking her if she would be his second assistant. David was completely unaware that Suzy was my wife. Until she mentioned it, I had known nothing about it. The excitement of Suzy joining the production would take away all of the doubts that I had about working on the production. Added to that, Tony Busbridge, a British ex-pat living in Johannesburg, would join me as my camera operator; with Frank arriving shortly this would complete the professional crew forming around me and suddenly the situation was looking a lot healthier.

The first six months passed relatively trouble-free. Building relationships with our Zulu friends would take time but things gradually progressed with a daily improvement as the Zulu suspicions towards the whites slowly eased. One thing

A nice crane shot of the Zulus carrying the newly built boat *Chaka* to the sea. This is the boat that will take the whites and the Zulu representatives back to Cape Town to meet the British governor.

that helped to capture their interest was Frank's 'magical powers': in reality party tricks he played on his children, though even Frank would need a willing hand for his 'miracles' to happen – me! With the Zulus suitably impressed with Frank's magic they demanded to see more of his supernatural powers, which helped with the building of good relationships between the two cultures.

Bill Faure's filming education came from studying at the London Film School, where he had found it impossible to let go of Shaka's life, passionate about the legend of the Zulu king which told the story of the warrior's existence from his birth as the bastard child of Nandi, his mother, to Prince Senzangakona, the father whose treatment of Nandi would eventually turn Shaka to violence. Our ten episodes, after the original fifteen scripts had been reworked by the American partners, would cover Shaka's entire life, from before he became king of the Zulus and his confrontation with the British Empire, finally ending in his murder and the dramatic burning of his corpse – my grand cinematic finale! The scripts were carefully researched and based on historical fact, setting the scene by starting the story in 1882 with Queen Victoria meeting Cetshwayo, then the leader of the Zulu Empire, and deciding to restore him to power with Britain not getting involved in Zulu politics. The story then goes back in time to tell of the many interesting accounts of Shaka's early life and his struggle through his young years as a boy, ending in his tyrannical government over the whole Zulu nation, which came by fear or force – not unlike Hitler, in many ways. *Shaka Zulu* is the true story of the Zulus' past violent history; like a Shakespearian drama it is full of intrigue – king against king, Zulu against Zulu, tribe against tribe, blacks against whites.

Mythology and witchcraft also played its part in our telling of Shaka's incredible story – similar to Polanski's *Tragedy of Macbeth* – but in Africa superstition and legend remain as important to this day as it was then. On one occasion a green mamba snake wriggled its way through the film unit and the Zulu camera-car driver was convinced it was the spirit of Shaka making his presence felt. Whether or not he was showing his pleasure or displeasure with our efforts was not recorded.

At another location somewhere in a remote corner of Zululand, an old lady emerged from her hut to watch the filming. Explaining that we were recording Shaka's life history she pondered a moment before saying, 'Had we a Shaka today our lot would be a happier one since only he could bring the Zulus together as a powerful nation.' Of course that is what Shaka did in his lifetime. Today, Shaka is still the Zulus' champion, comparable with other empire builders such as Napoleon, Alexander the Great and Julius Caesar. In terms of African history Shaka was all of these to his people.

Henry Cele, our all-powerful Zulu king would be a dangerous and intimidating Shaka to deal with. Should he look directly at you with his piercing eyes and threatening stare you would feel extremely uncomfortable. The truth is, I could never be sure exactly where I stood in our conversations, though in reality Henry was a quiet soul, a gentleman and a wonderful actor. The main problem I had with my lighting of Henry was his smooth matte-black skin, which needed grease applied to it to lift it to a more reflective texture. This worked well, but with a white face close to Henry's very dark skin the balance was difficult to control when the actors moved around, which occasionally showed in the production's final grading where it had not been possible for me to be present.

My only real frustration came with the lighting equipment used in the confines of the interior straw hut sequences, due to the ever-present danger of overheating in the small confines, which would cause a fire. I finally settled for the log-fire effect, which worked well in the smoky atmosphere; possibly a few extra tungsten lights in the hut sequences would have been useful, which I missed out on due to my lack of experience in matters of quantity, but even so I was pleased with the final outcome. For night exteriors with Zulu love in the air I used 3M material as the moon, which I had carried with me after reading the script, while a stormy night sequence required dramatic lightning flashes overlaid with the sound of thunder suggesting an evil presence.

Generally things worked out well, creating the right working atmosphere, though there were times when we found ourselves in hostile situations. This came as a result of violent intimidation directed towards our Zulu friends when we unintentionally strayed onto the so-called 'white' territory bordering the black region. Now for the first time we came face-to-face with the reality of racial segregation – apartheid.

A white camera crew working with black Zulus could not possibly be accepted by some of the white locals, whose pointed finger-wagging and threats warned us away from 'their' territory. A verbal confrontation escalated to the waving of sticks and stones being thrown in our direction as menaces directed at the crew now forced us 'nigger lovers' to move on. The situation eventually became far too dangerous to continue with our filming; with little chance of any further discussion, we were forced to take the obvious hint.

Living in a civilised country such as ours it is easy to forget that these situations do exist as we turn a blind eye to others' internal problems. Now for the first time we would experience hate on both sides, which would inevitably affect our efforts in the filming, although Frank's magic would help in no small way to heal the rift.

With the first six-month option completed without too many problems, it was time for our three-week break, with the Brits starting back to the UK to celebrate Christmas at home. My previous concerns about working on the second phase would not materialise, and by now I was totally committed to filming Shaka's life. With Suzy on the production too it was not hard to make the decision to return to Zululand.

On our return to Eshowe it was clear that the earlier friendly atmosphere was now missing, and there was a far less welcoming mood compared to the earlier

Edward Fox and Robert Powell heading for their boat. By this time in the story the whites had gone native.

enthusiasm enjoyed by our overpowering Zulu army. I spoke with Bill Faure about this – he understood the Zulu mentality, their ever-changing moods. It would seem that they had become bored with the project. The director tried hard to recapture the Zulus' earlier enthusiasm, helped in no small way with Frank's 'magic powers', the atmosphere steadily improved by the day. However, one could never lose the feeling of resentment with apartheid lurking in the background.

Although this black and white community coexisted well enough, sadly the simmering background to all this meant that we never really knew where it would all end. The thought of just 'existing' in the hotel for another six months did not help Suzy or me feel more comfortable, especially when it appeared to be overrun as a permanent Zulu encampment, having an unsettling effect on us both. Never knowing if things might take a turn for the worse, we finally decided to move into a small rented bungalow away from the madness of it all.

Amid all the struggles and not helped with the eternal heat and dust of Natal, *Shaka Zulu* dragged on and on. With our challenging scripts we felt as if the production would never end as the schedule kept slipping back with time wasted filming second-unit material. Discussing this problem with the director, I recommended my old friend Jimmy Devis as an established second-unit director/cameraman who could help with this problem; Jim would join the unit for the next six weeks to help get us back on schedule.

On the beach with Edward Fox, at the start of a long journey for the whites back to Cape Town.

SABC Television also became concerned with the slow progress of our filming, which, as you would expect, did not come easily with thousands of spear-carrying Zulus, all frustrated at the silly games which the whites enjoyed playing.

Fourteen long months would eventually pass before *Shaka Zulu* finally came to an end, and now it was time to bid farewell to our Zulu friends. I was grateful for the experience in understanding how the Zulus had inherited their sadistic past from Shaka, but more important to me was the technical knowledge I had gained from the challenges which I had had to solve with my own photographic struggles. I now look back on the production with much satisfaction after seeing the final result on the screen.

All good things eventually come to an end. SABC celebrated the moment with the traditional end of picture party with a wonderful atmosphere as everyone relaxed at the end of a long challenging series. With all pressure off, it was time to unwind before flying home. As Frank and I were both teetotal there was little chance we would wake up the next morning with a hangover. Our priority was to be on time at Durban airport before Bill Faure decided he needed more covering material.

Frank being Frank, with an equally greedy Alec, it was difficult to refuse the waiters' offerings as they kept refilling our plates with their sweet delights. Coming to the end of the merrymaking, I found myself feeling very tired ... slowly drifting ... which was the only way I could describe my fast-changing condition. At first I put it down to over-tiredness with the heat and body relaxing. I went along with this self-delusional dream. Now with the celebrations over we walked out to my car, where the fresh air had a sudden, unexpected impact on my condition.

I vaguely remember struggling to get 'up' into the driver's seat, where everything seemed distorted ... unreal. My manner had changed; apparently I was rude, complaining that the car's wheels were too big for a vehicle of this size, which was confirmed when I looked out the window to see Frank apparently looking up at me, wondering what the hell I was going on about as he climbed up next to me. Looking in the rearview mirror I noticed someone sitting in the backseat.

'Throw him out,' I said angrily. 'Who the hell is he, anyway?'

By now Frank was thinking I had lost my mind, explaining that there was no one there, but to humour me he checked anyway. Satisfied all was well, I drove slowly back to my apartment, and by now the car wheels had stopped growing, although the car now seemed to be 'floating' above ground – a weird car, I thought to myself. Dropping Frank at his flat, I drove slowly back to my bungalow in this strange dream-like state. Once inside, feeling thirsty, I turned to the refrigerator but was unable to reach the door, even with my curiously long arms. Still none of this bothered me as I happily relaxed in this strange dreamlike state before falling into a deep sleep in the chair.

The next morning I woke feeling very fragile. I would later learn that Frank had been through a state of mind similar to the one that I had experienced, though in

The launch of the boat *Chaka* (possibly Shaka's real name), with me laying down the law! And to think I used to dislike the navy pigs!

his case more delayed. Before starting out to the airport we shared our goodbyes with Bill Faure, who then revealed all about our condition. It would seem that the delicious cakes which we had greedily consumed were generously laced with cannabis seeds to get the party going – shades of Antonioni again? They had never considered that anyone would eat as many as we did. It would seem that our greed was responsible for our state of mind, resulting in an interesting experience one never forgets – or would want to repeat!

It was time to return to our own civilisation, England, this peaceful isle. Insanity awaited our return when we learned that, due to the apartheid situation, the transmission of South African television productions was now banned in the UK. *Shaka Zulu* would be one of the casualties, so the question now was whether

I can't remember what the joke was about. Knowing Frank, it was probably at my expense, but obviously Robert Powell and Edward Fox enjoyed it.

anyone would ever see the series here in the UK. Would the viewers be interested to learn of Shaka's story on television, or – more importantly – would any producers see the results of my photographic efforts? Worse still, there was even a possibility that the Brits working on the film could be blacklisted by the ACTT – our own very political left-wing trade union at that time – for working in South Africa at all, but fortunately that problem would be resolved before getting tangled up in the courts.

Edward Fox, Robert Powell, Trevor Howard, Fiona Fullerton, Christopher Lee, Roy Dotrice, Gordon Jackson, Kenneth Griffith and Dudu Mkhize all happily contributed their talents to the screen version of E.A. Ritter's 1955 novel *Shaka Zulu*, where our fourteen long months of filming would hold faithfully to the detailed script, retaining the atmosphere of the period. An interesting American article of the time wrote that *Shaka Zulu* was the most repeatedly screened mini-series ever shown on syndicated television in the United States, with the series achieving cult status. By 1992 it had been seen by over 350 million viewers, dislodging John Marshall's *The Hunters* (1962) and later *The Gods Must Be Crazy* (1981) with its follow-ups as the prime shaper of American perceptions of African tribal history.

I settled for that, though it does seem strange that, to my knowledge, *Shaka Zulu* was never broadcast here in the UK, which no doubt was inspired by the boycott. If it was shown, then I missed it. Even so, I was pleased with the American reviews – you win some, you lose some!

Fourteen long months working in a foreign country – out of sight and out of mind – had not been an easy decision to make. However, should the gamble pay off, which it did with *Shaka* receiving excellent reviews in America, then perhaps the sacrifice was worthwhile.

On my return to London I would learn that I was not the only cameraman with this problem; others before had in their frustration at the shortage of opportunities also looked abroad in order to fulfil their ambitions. I happened to be discussing this problem with Ronnie Maasz, a colleague who at the time was enjoying a successful reputation filming overseas, but that was not the life for me, and at least I could now take comfort from my three little films; with *Shaka Zulu* added to that all-important CV there could be no turning back now.

My optimism grew as my good fortune continued, my L-plates could now be removed, with Stanley O'Toole offering me his latest film with the Oscar-winning director Franklin Schaffner. It would seem that after helping Stanley to make his debut as director one good turn deserved another, but this time there would be

Filming *Lionheart* near Budapest in 1986. Frank Elliott is on the crane, with Franklin Schaffner standing behind me.

On location in Budapest at the famous Fishermen's Bastion. The hooded figure on the horse is Eric Stoltz, the lead character in the film; holding his reins in the foreground is Dexter Fletcher and on my right is Sammi Davis.

no haggling over my salary in Stanley's car – I now had an agent to deal with that problem.

Even so, I still had my concerns with the director's reaction to me photographing his film. The last time we worked together I had been Franklin's camera operator on *Sphinx*, where I suffered a week of filming before he decided whether or not he could trust me. However, my reservations were dispelled by the director's generous support towards me; apparently Franklin had also enjoyed the *Shaka* series in America.

Once again our filming would take place on foreign soil, this time in Hungary and Portugal, but sadly there is little of interest to record of *Lionheart*, a simple story of orphans travelling across Europe who are captured by the wicked Black Prince, who then trades the children off as slaves until a young knight on his way to the Crusades decides to sort out this nasty problem. Eric Stoltz, Nicola Cowper, Dexter Fletcher and Deborah Moore set out to protect the orphans, while Gabriel Byrne would prefer to sell them off as slaves to interested parties.

Franklin tried hard to get something from this thin script, which to some extent he succeeded doing, but with the story handed him there was little else anyone

Setting up a crane shot while the Hungarian assistant director Gábor Váradi calls out the instructions.

On location in Hungary, near Visegrad. Franklin Schaffner stands in the foreground on the right, Eric Stoltz is in the hooded cape, Nicola Cowper on the horse and Dexter Fletcher is leftmost in the picture. I am on the ladder next to the camera.

Setting up a scene on location in Portugal where the abducted children have been tied up.

could do, even an Oscar-winner. If truth be told, it was a slow uninspiring tale, making it difficult to be complimentary with the director's efforts and in the end it offered little in the way of entertainment. Roger Moore's daughter Deborah made a convincing debut in the film. Dad would no doubt be proud of her sword-fighting skills, although you could be sure he would make his tongue-in-cheek humorous comments on Deborah's effort.

The film received mixed reviews, most of which I remember as being ordinary at best, but at least this was another credit added to my CV, even if it was of little consolation to the poor director, who always carries the can. Nevertheless, an interesting plus came from a 'lesson-learned' on our arrival at one early morning location. The set was covered in a low-lying fog, but our tight schedule meant we had to film something, come what may. When I saw the rushes I could not have been more pleased with the mood created by the fog – a cold early morning with a dramatic mist adding to the tragedy of the scene. Although my director was impressed with my work, I wisely decided to share the credit with an outside influence.

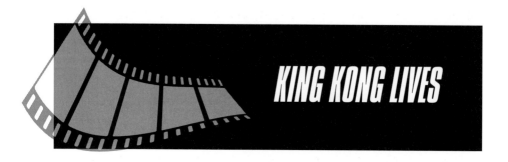

KING KONG LIVES

I am a romantic who believes that life works in mysterious ways. Usually when strange things happen without reason or explanation we pass them off as coincidence and they are soon forgotten; thinking about this next event, I wondered if it was strangely connected with something which had happened earlier. Does any of this make sense, or am I sounding like some strange weirdo? It gets worse when I ask myself as a free spirit if our lives are planned for us, no matter what profession we choose, but we are left few clues as to how life will play out. We all experience good and bad times, some of which we may well answer for in time – possibly I will go to hell – so why do I write all this nonsense?

My career would eventually move forward in a strange way, but not before an unlikely sequence of events occurred, where an important decision would be made about my future, finally bringing about the traditional fairy-tale ending. It was early one morning, far too early to wake up, but the damn phone kept on ringing. It was the beginning of a set of circumstances that would lead to everything I could possibly wish for or even have dreamed of. The phone call was a short conversation with a strange unnamed voice interested in my availability, and would I be interested in a film in America? If so then someone would call back later with all the details. Still in my sleepy state, I said yes, though my questions would remain unanswered as he quickly rang off.

Okay, this had to be a set-up – a friend disguising his voice, I was foolishly going along with his weird sense of humour. I had smiled when asked about my availability but I was tired and the joke had gone too far and I went back to bed. Later it occurred to me that this might not be a silly prank after all and that someone really had put my name forward for a film. Then some hours later the promised call came, this time from a different voice with instructions to collect my ticket at Heathrow and fly directly to Wilmington, North Carolina; a driver would meet me at the airport. That was it ...

Even as I flew across the Atlantic it was still unclear why I had been asked to replace the cinematographer Peter MacDonald on a film. All I knew was that the production was entering its second week of filming and Peter had abruptly been rushed to hospital with appendicitis. Now suddenly here I was, flying to America with many questions still unanswered. My unease came not from any lack of confidence in my ability or the fact that I would be working with a strange American crew, but the fact was I knew nothing about the production or the director.

The penny finally dropped when the unit car driver casually mentioned the name of the director of *King Kong Lives* – John Guillermin – which suddenly began to explain all of the evident secrecy. It would seem that John had asked for me as Peter's replacement. My mind now started to play games with me – would John remember our war of words on *Death on the Nile* after all this time? Of course he would, so was he taking this opportunity to settle an old score and sack me? I would soon find out.

With my childish overactive mind stirring up this sudden insecurity I was left with persistent thoughts of flying back to the UK on the next available plane. My

Standing beside King Kong's huge animatronic hand, it is strange to think that the King Kong miniature from the original 1933 film was only 18 inches tall!

fears were working overtime as I was taken to the set where filming was in progress with a temporary cinematographer. An assistant director led me to meet John, who at the time was sitting in his director's chair with a severe look on his face. His eyes were fixed on my approach.

'Alec. Good to see you; sit down!'

A good start, I thought. We chatted away for fifteen minutes or so without any signs of my early departure back to the UK as my confidence slowly began to return. After a short conversation the assistant director called John back to the set. Was that it? I asked myself.

Not quite ... After a few steps John stopped, turning back to me with a penetrating look on his face. Now came the moment of truth: 'Alec, I seem to recall you have a temper.'

'Not me, John,' I shamelessly replied. 'You're confusing me with someone else!'

He looked at me, his eyes narrowed ... suspicious ... not really sure as he considered my reply. Finally, he smiled – perhaps more a smirk, I thought – before turning back to his set. John had seen through my obvious fib, but perhaps it was enough to confuse him.

Overnight I read the script to bring myself up to date for the next morning when I would be introduced to a giant ape going by the name of King Kong. Knowing of John's capabilities as a director, of which I earlier admitted being an admirer, I doubt that he would have seen this script as anything worthwhile. Nor, indeed, would the followers of the giant ape, all of them believing that King Kong was now past history. It would seem that everyone thought so, apart from the producer Dino De Laurentiis, even when these opinions were echoed in the press. More importantly, John and I worked well together – it would seem that our past flare-up was now forgotten.

Although I had my private concerns about John, I would certainly benefit from this latest opportunity of working with him in Wilmington, where I also enjoyed typical American hospitality with a self-drive car and a condominium on the North Carolina beach. As always with Americans I was made to feel welcome at all times, which helped to repair the Anglo-American relationship damaged after my *Star Wars* experience. However, even with all the courtesy shown to me I doubted that America was where I would choose to work permanently. My reason in mentioning this was that I now had an agent in Los Angeles who promised the earth should I move to the USA. Privately I knew this was not for me as my family back home would always take precedence.

Wilmington Studios could not be compared to Pinewood in size although it was still large enough to service other productions of a similar scale to *King Kong*, and it happened that Ken Adam was also there, working on *Crimes of the Heart*. Ken, of course, was the brilliant production designer who set the high standards on the earlier James Bond films; over the years we would get to know each other well on

The Spy Who Loved Me and *Moonraker*, where more often than not he would stay close to my camera, making sure that I saw every inch of his beautiful and very expensive sets through the camera lens.

Hearing that I was working on the next stage, Ken came over to see me. I assumed that his interest lay more with the gigantic ape lying powerless on an operating table, but not so. It would seem that Ken had received a phone call from Tom Pevsner, Eon Productions' associate producer back at Pinewood Studios, about the new James Bond film. Apparently Cubby Broccoli had phoned Ken to ask his opinion about the possibility of me photographing the new 007 film!

I laughed, 'Yes, yes, pull the other one, Ken!' What else could I think?

Ken kept a straight face, convinced that I could be in with a chance. With the sudden realisation that he might be telling the truth, the other sounds on the stage suddenly became strangely muted and I switched off from the ape altogether. Still unsure what to make of Ken's message, the dream I had once considered with little expectation that it would ever happen was suddenly on the verge of becoming reality. Over the years I had enjoyed every moment working with James Bond – five films as camera operator – but never did I consider myself as a potential 007 cinematographer. The adrenalin started to flow and Ken gave me a reassuring smile and said he had told Tom that I would do well. As he left, his parting words suggested that I could get a call that night.

Our sleeping giant.

So came the longest night *ever!* Silently I rehearsed my reply to the call, should it come, pleased of course, excited certainly, but not over-excited as I tried to remain professional. The phone was working but still no call came and with Suzy not around to calm my anxiety it was past midnight and well into the early hours before I finally fell asleep.

The next day I kept the news to myself, just in case the call did not come. The longest night would be followed by the longest day as I struggled through the day's schedule. Ken dropped by to see if I had heard anything, though more likely it was to see if Cubby had taken his advice, but with no call from Pinewood it was back to concentrating on the saga of *King Kong*.

Returning to my apartment, I checked the phone, but still no messages, and I told myself that it was now too late back home for any news. It was long past midnight when the sweet purring sound of the instrument finally summoned me to pick up the receiver; it was Tom, confirming the offer to photograph the new James Bond film!

This was an emotional moment for me, where all my prepared thoughts and responses to Tom's call suddenly came to nothing. I was lost for words; this had to be the most exciting time since I came into the film industry in 1946. Not surprisingly, I quickly accepted Cubby's Broccoli's generous invitation, punching the air as I thanked Tom. At least he cannot see the tears in my eyes even as I type this ...

With all this going on in my head I barely slept that night, but at least it seemed that the plan was finally coming together – if a little late! Obviously this opportunity had come my way because Alan Hume was unavailable, but with other prominent cinematographers no doubt phoning their agents to remind them of their availability, the odds on me would have been long. I would even have betted against myself, but my particular dream had become reality: Alec Mills had finally been recognised as a cinematographer and would photograph *The Living Daylights*!

Lying awake that night, unable to sleep, I was reminded of John Glen's promise to me in the Black Horse, asking me to come out of my so-called 'retirement' to operate the camera on *Octopussy*. His words still clearly echoed in my head: 'Alec, do this for me and I promise you will not regret it!'

At the time, it never occurred to me that John was serious with this comment, but with Alan committed to another film John could now honour that pledge, which would leave me forever grateful to him.

We all need a little help and luck at times. Both came my way in abundance, although if I am really honest I still believe that fate played its hand in this. Now of course I could not get back to England quickly enough.

After receiving all the congratulations handed out on the *King Kong* set it was necessary to keep a level head and concentrate on the job in hand; with four weeks still to go, this was no time for cock-ups – sorry, mistakes! John Guillermin smiled and gave his best wishes, which again left me wondering who had put my name forward to go to Wilmington in the first place. Obviously it could only have been John himself, his conscience perhaps righting a wrong? Whether or not my trip to America was luck or predetermined, it was still another small part of Alec Mills's imaginary journey.

Whatever one chooses to believe, there had been too many 'coincidences' in my life even before this bizarre series of events which, you may remember, all started with a strange phone call from America. Then I asked myself if all this nonsense was in my imagination and just one of my own daft fantasies. The answer was simple. I would stick with my daydreams where anything is possible with secret agent 007!

As age fast crept up, I realised that I had inherited a bad memory. It would seem that I had worked with John Glen before without realising it. This came to light when reading John's autobiography *For My Eyes Only*, where I discovered that John was the sound editor on *A Cry from the Streets*, the same film on which I first met Lewis Gilbert and Peter Hunt, but as a busy clapper boy I would hardly have noticed such things. Many years and films would pass before we all met up with James Bond, where I had been the camera operator for Peter while filming *On Her Majesty's Secret Service*, later working with John in the bowels of a goldmine as second-unit cameraman on *Gold*. The last piece of our professional relationship finally slotted into place when John invited me to be his cinematographer on *The Living Daylights*, and the tree which I had struggled to climb finally bore fruit.

There was also a new James Bond. Timothy Dalton inherited the coveted role from Roger Moore, although, as it had for Alan and me, the opportunity had come his way by *force majeure* after Pierce Brosnan was forced to turn down the role – much to his reported annoyance – due to a previous commitment to the NBC television series *Remington Steele*. Tim is a fine actor and arrived on the scene bringing a harder-edged approach to the secret agent, reminiscent of the earlier Sean Connery era. However, when a new face replaces an established actor biased supporters take sides, making their opinions known about who they think is the best Bond – if not always fairly. Generally the public are inclined to favour the predecessor, which in this case was of course Roger Moore.

You can be sure that similar comparisons would be made between cinematographers, with Alan Hume and Alec Mills being judged in the same way. Alan was a hard act to follow, a fine cinematographer with a great deal of experience, but this would be my sixth mission with 007 so I had little reason to feel uncomfortable in such friendly surroundings. But – there is always a 'but' in my case – conscious of the self-inflicted pressure that I put on myself, I was also aware that the first day would be important – very important – as the contract had yet to arrive in the post.

Photographic tests were as helpful to me as they were for Timothy Dalton, who was working in the shadow of his predecessor. Timothy's camera-friendly test was a normal procedure on Bond films to see how the new secret agent comes across on the screen photographically. It happened that Tim's test would be shot on a kitchen set where a vicious fight takes place using the heavy cooking utensils to hand for one glorious Bond punch-up, and we also shot a more sensitive sequence written twenty years earlier from *On Her Majesty's Secret Service*.

Filming in Pinewood guarantees that the cinematographer enjoys the best facilities and projection that one could ask for, leaving little room for excuses should my efforts fail to impress. James Bond should look magnificent, unassailable, particularly with Cubby Broccoli and John Glen scrutinising the results in Theatre 7. It seemed that both were pleased with everything on the screen. Taking me aside, Cubby said, 'Looks great, Alec!' Even so, the pressure would stay with me for some time.

John Glen had proved his credentials as Cubby's choice of director when working on earlier Bond films as editor and then second-unit director. Having directed the last three Bond films, he was also well aware of the daily routine on a film set. Directors and cinematographers are both aware of the rules regarding schedules and budgets, to which I would be no exception, but there are occasions when the cinematographer needs to make an adjustment to his lighting after a rehearsal, which would probably take a couple of minutes to correct. John's face would drop as anticipated as he heaved a sigh: 'A couple of minutes?'

His sigh suggested his frustration at my request, with which I would learn to live. John was not serious, of course, but at the same time it was a convenient reminder that I should not make a habit of this. Our lives are full of strategies and politics, and I would learn to handle these tricky situations without offending anyone. Even so, the mental demands I placed on myself would eat away inside me during the filming. I could not remember such pressure before, even on *Shaka Zulu*. However, I would quickly adjust to others' problems, trusting that they would do the same for me.

The established 007 formula continued to please, this time with locations in Gibraltar, Austria and Morocco, where the customary action scenes would involve the camera crews working in dangerous situations alongside the stuntmen.

Cameras are always positioned for maximum dramatic effect to capture that spectacular moment, which usually works well, but should anything go wrong it could leave both stuntmen and camera crews seriously injured. Fatalities are rare, although not unknown. I had my own close call at Ouarzazate airport.

One particular scene demanded my concentration to be fixed on what was happening in front of camera, so I was paying little attention to what was going on behind. In this case it was a Moroccan Air Force C130 Hercules aircraft which was fast closing on me. With the noise of the engines competing with the smoke and battle raging in front of the camera, I was unwittingly backing into the aircraft's path. Apparently the pilot was trying to attract John's attention to what was happening but, wearing ear defenders, I could not hear John's warning as the battle raged on. The outcome remained in the balance until suddenly I found myself being pulled back from the closing propellers – a close call with my thanks going to John, who pulled me to safety.

With the exterior filming completed, we returned to Pinewood Studios, where the most expensive sets awaited our arrival and where the cinematographer could

On location in October 1986 with Timothy Dalton and director John Glen, while filming some of the earlier night sequences outside the Musikverein Concert Hall in Vienna for *The Living Daylights*. (© 1987 Danjaq, LLC and United Artists Corporation. All rights reserved)

now enjoy complete control over his work. The major sequences included all of the location interiors as well as Bond's fight with bad guy Necros (Andreas Wisniewski), which perfectly matched the exteriors filmed halfway around the world in Morocco and over the American desert. Another clever sleight of hand was to use reflections of children dressed as adults in the window of the Prater Park café set to give the impression of greater space.

During the filming we had an official visit by Prince Charles and Princess Diana, who came on the set where we were filming the sequences in Q's workshop. Apparently both enjoyed their walk-about as flashbulbs captured every moment of the royal visit, during which the couple generously posed for a photograph of Diana breaking a sugar-glass bottle over Charles's head. I was fortunate to be introduced in the line-up, if a little disappointed they didn't ask for my autograph. I could not help but smile when Charles first spoke to John, saying, 'And what do you do?'

With so much happening on *The Living Daylights* I was very pleased with the end result, where the established 007 formula continued to wow the audiences, guaranteeing success at the box office. However, in keeping with the 'all change at the top' policy, this time a new James Bond would be joined by a new and younger Miss Moneypenny, played by the attractive Caroline Bliss. Agent 007 would still cast his eye over a beautiful girl, this time a Czech cellist played by Maryam d'Abo, while the usual regulars from the Ministry were still around, with M, now played by Robert Brown, and Q keeping up their disdain for the secret agent, which of course is what we all expect and enjoy.

I was grateful for my sixth mission with 007, but especially grateful to John who had given me an opportunity I thought was lost. I had found myself back home in a team that I had wrongly believed had already disappeared forever.

From a cinematographer's point of view, work on films or on a television series is much the same, except that television budgets and schedules tend to be tighter and we probably work longer hours in the day – ten or twelve would not be unusual.

The main television series on which I worked as a cinematographer were *Press Gang*, for which the writer Stephen Moffat won a BAFTA award for Best Children's Programme, *The Dirty Dozen*, *About Face*, *Seekers* and *Soldier Soldier*. Maureen

On location in Zagreb, Yugoslavia in 1988 while filming *The Dirty Dozen* television mini-series, a spin-off of the successful 1967 movie.

Waiting for the sun to come out from behind a cloud.

Lipman's *About Face* was probably my favourite, with the actress appearing as a different character in each episode, which reminds me of an amusing tale ...

For one episode Maureen was dressed and made up to look like a filthy old hag living on the streets of London – 'The Bag Lady'! An early morning call was planned, with our filming scheduled to take place during London's rush hour, where we would find our unrecognisable actress – dirty, scruffy, in full tattered garb – pushing her way through London's unsuspecting West End crowds as they hurried past her on their way to work. With our camera hidden inside a telephone maintenance tent, we could now record every reaction on a long zoom lens. Of course no one recognised Maureen, this scruffy old hag cadging 'dosh for a cuppa', nor would she get any sympathy from a distrustful public desperately trying to avoid her as they hurried on by.

With little success from the fleeing public, Maureen eventually arrived outside the theatre where she also happened to be performing in a play during the evening. Unscripted, Maureen decided to go inside in her rags to 'scrounge' a couple of free tickets, but was speedily cast back into the street, protesting to the doorman who she really was. The moment was sadly lost to the camera in the passing crowd. Maureen is a delightful lady to work with but also a talented actress blessed with a wonderful sense of humour.

Filming on location in Northumberland for *Come Snow, Come Blow* (1993); Gary Love and Robson Green teamed up again after working on *Soldier Soldier*, with Gary directing and Robson producing. The cast included Rodney Bewes, Denise Welch (another *Soldier Soldier* veteran) and her husband, Tim Healy.

The same could be said of the *Soldier Soldier* series, where we were working with a team of actors who performed together on a regular daily basis. Two of the series were filmed on Cyprus and in Münster, Germany, where the producer Annie Tricklebank would always be around in support of the cause. I enjoyed working with this lady, and the whole team of actors who made this an interesting experience.

Now the only reason I mention this subject is that television inevitably brings together a mix of the various people with whom we need to deal in our working lives. Some have strange personalities while others are difficult to reach out to or even describe, which brings to mind *The Dirty Dozen*, a television series filmed in Yugoslavia. This would not be a pleasant experience for anyone, and my one consolation from this episode would be my happy return to England to prepare for my next film, my seventh assignment with 007 ... our grand finale?

The fairy tale continued; perhaps 'Licence to Thrill' would a be more appropriate title when it comes to describing my life with James Bond. In twenty years of service with the secret agent I would learn to accept his various guises, which for me would change on three occasions.

Whatever mask 007 chose to wear I would always remember the fights we shared together and the bruises suffered, even when taking on the challenge of a Japanese swordsman. There were times when I played the villain in the fight, holding my handheld Arri IIC camera with the focus set on 007, then the same thing again in reverse, but this time filming the villain. The flexibility of the camera harness gave me the freedom to move around, adding realism to the fight. However, there were times when the so-called choreography did not go quite as planned, as my wife would testify when on one occasion I came home with a black eye because I became too ambitious with the camera and somehow got tangled up in the brawl. Needless to say, she refused to believe my explanation.

With these close ties soon to end, even though I did not realise it at the time, I would miss the many punch-ups which James and I shared together, so perhaps this is also my last opportunity to relive those past 007 moments with ageing colleagues, who agree that a little exaggeration is acceptable with old tales.

Reminiscing about the past would leave me with a great deal of satisfaction, and on reflection I was grateful for my own survival after the close calls we had shared together. Now as cinematographer, I could watch the punch-ups from a distance and in relative safety, with the camera-operating responsibilities now handed over to Michael Frift.

Licence to Kill, written with Timothy Dalton's more hard-edged depiction of the agent in mind, was a violent film about drugs, the seedy world of its manufacture, cartels and distribution. John Glen captured the atmosphere so that you could sense the mood and the smell of danger with the cover-ups and betrayal, yet for all John's efforts this was be his last mission with the secret agent, as it would be mine.

For tax reasons Eon Productions had been forced to leave Pinewood for sunnier climes. This time we would be based at Churubusco Studios in Mexico City with locations in Cancun, the Florida Keys, Key West, Mexicali and Acapulco, which would not only provide the usual combination of technical challenges but also one or two occurrences that were less easy to explain.

I was not in a position to recce a location in Acapulco where filming would be a challenge for any cinematographer. It was a beautiful luxurious home owned by a friend of Cubby Broccoli, and the interior of the property appeared to be built

Lining up the interior sequences for the Casino de Isthmus, in reality the Casino Español in Mexico City. Timothy Dalton (James Bond) and Carrie Lowell (Pam Bouvier) are seated at the blackjack table, with Talisa Soto (Lupe Lamora) ready to take their money. (© 1989 Danjaq, LLC and United Artists Corporation. All rights reserved)

entirely out of white marble, the complete reverse of the problem I had experienced with Denis Lewiston on *Hot Target*. The doors opened out onto the bay with Acapulco across the glistening water; there was a waterfall one could only dream of with a funicular down to the water line where a private motor boat waited to transport guests back to the mainland. I pinched myself; I was in heaven. However, although this privileged lifestyle was pleasing to the eye, for a cinematographer without the help of a generator there would be little chance of balancing the interior exposure to that of the spectacular view of the exterior. Although I was concerned by this, in the end 'Lady Luck' came to my rescue in the form of reflected light bouncing off the glossy marbled structure surrounding us – not perfect, but it would still be my saving grace. We never stop learning in the film industry and grateful cinematographers take advantage of any unexpected aids.

One of the more cultural locations used was Ernest Hemingway's old home in Key West, where M, played for the last time by Robert Brown, 'revokes' 007's licence to kill. I use that word as the original production title had been 'Licence Revoked', but due to American understandings of the word the title was eventually changed to *Licence to Kill* – another case of our two countries divided by a common language! As a result, Bond finds himself out on his own, determined to take revenge on the villain, played by Robert Davi, responsible for crippling his long-time friend and colleague Felix Leiter, played by David Hedison. Perhaps the most interesting location was at the Otomi Cultural Center at Temoaya, an amazing structure which could have been specially built for a Bond movie.

For its sheer mystery – if you believe in this sort of thing – special mention should made of the location near the town of La Rumorosa, where Arthur Wooster's second unit filmed parts of the climactic tanker chase sequence. Located near Mexicali on the American–Mexican border, a number of unexplained incidents took place. The road was already known to be dangerous due to the sharp bends and sheer drops. While you are always prepared for the occasional accident while filming stunts and action sequences, too many mishaps and strange occurrences – including spectral figures beside the vehicle compound at night – seemed to be happening to be called just coincidence. Added to that, no one could explain one image taken by the second-unit stills photographer George Whitear, of an explosion with what looked like skulls and faces in the flames, and the flaming fingers of what appeared to be an arm shooting down over a precipice. To add to this, a Mexican policeman later said that the explosion had been filmed on the exact spot where several nuns had been killed in a road accident a few years before.

All of the images for the film were achieved by separate units spread across the country, with Mexican camera crews working alongside the Brits on both the first and second units and the miracle of John Grover's slick editing once again ensuring that everything came together to complete the illusion. As ever, the film unit observed the life of both the rich and poor, and, while it was only a film to us, you were always aware of the government officer assigned to keep an eye on us. However, one thing is undeniable; through my twenty years of service with 007 I would experience the taste of a privileged life, mixing with the famous and visiting some of the most beautiful places one could possibly imagine. To balance this, I would also never forget some of the poverty-stricken locations visited with our filming, where the poorest struggled to survive and where strangers with cameras are looked on with great suspicion.

We finally completed filming in Mexico City in November 1988. At the time there was little to suggest that this would by my last outing with 007, but behind-the-scenes legal actions meant that it would be more than six years before another foot of film would turn on a Bond film. By then Cubby Broccoli had taken a backseat, placing Eon Productions in the capable hands of the next generation: Cubby's daughter Barbara and stepson Michael Wilson. When the franchise finally emerged from the legal mire there would be a new producer, a new Bond, a new director and a new cinematographer, which is how it should be ...

With change on the way, whether the older generation likes it or not, upheaval inevitably brings casualties to the elders of the filming community who sometimes find change difficult to cope with. It must be said that my twenty years of working for Cubby Broccoli and his delightful family was one of the happiest professional experiences of my filming career – genuine professional people whom I came to respect.

The only question now was, how long would it be before I also found myself struggling with the outgoing tide?

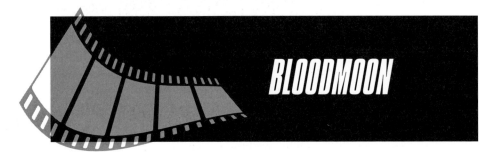

BLOODMOON

There is a strange uncertainty with the film industry whereby you can never be sure in which direction it is heading; exaggerated stories of doom and despondency rarely helping the situation. Then one day, out of the gloom, came a call from the National Film and Television School at Beaconsfield; Ernie Vincze, the head of cinematography, was asking if I would be interested teaching at the NFTS. Knowing little of the new technology which was beginning to overtake the camera department, not to mention the fact that age was fast creeping up on me, I carefully considered his tempting offer.

Bloodmoon (1989):
working on the
script and hoping
for a miracle to
happen. It didn't.

Beaconsfield had a lot to offer. Apart from finally bringing on the challenge of the complexities of the dreaded computer, which so far I had failed to come to terms with, this change in direction would help to keep me in touch with the younger generation of cinematographers who would soon join the army of the already unemployed as I prepared them for the uncertainty ahead. Then, as I contemplated my sudden interest in teaching and with little prospect of more films being offered to me, out of the blue came another call which would turn my career upside-down.

'G'day mate, do yer fancy coming darn-under to do a film for me?'
Stanley O'Toole's impression of an Australian accent was truly awful, as pathetic as my skills in conveying his portrayal to paper. But the surprising news was that Stanley was in Australia. The NFTS would have to be put on the back burner.

Stanley's plan was not quite as simple as he first thought, as it would seem that the Australian film technicians' union was unhappy with the idea of an English cinematographer coming over from the UK to film in Brisbane, explaining that they already had their own cinematographers available – which was a cheek, considering that Australian cinematographers were already working here in the UK.

At this stage my trip was put on hold, although I knew that my producer friend would not give up that easily. It turned out that my dependable supporter was actually setting up a series of small films for Australian television, where by chance he came upon a get-out clause in the union's ruling. The accent now quickly back to normal – back to business.

'Alec, would you consider directing a film for me?'

Hang on, did I hear that right? At first I assumed this was Stanley's weird sense of humour, certainly not a genuine offer, but apparently there was method in his madness as it was possible for the producer to bring in an overseas director if he wished. Past experience suggested that Stanley would get his way, but when he sensed my hesitation he quickly reminded me of my capabilities when I helped him during the filming of *On the Third Day* – but that was moons ago!

Within days a parcel arrived in the post, giving my first glimpse of the 'script' – if you could call it that. In fact, *Bloodmoon* was absolute rubbish but, as bad as it was, Village Roadshow had accepted it. If I am honest, *Bloodmoon* with its low budget and lower artistic merit was something of an exploitation film for which Australia was particularly known at this time; one critic had even coined the

'Our Father, who art in Heaven ...' how did I get into this awful mess?

phrase 'Ozploitation' film'. Needless to say, I passed on my thoughts to Stanley, if a little more diplomatically.

'Alec, I know it's crap, so rework the storyline and make it more acceptable!'

As usual with the producer the discussion quickly ended with the phone being put down.

Stanley had thrown down the gauntlet, challenging me to improve on all of the garbage that lay before me. It was now time to learn new skills and face up to the predicament of making sense out of this ridiculous script, at the same time keeping the original story. Unfortunately the truth was that the changes required to improve this absurd storyline would require a professional scriptwriter who no doubt would have preferred to start by tearing up the old script and starting over. As that was not about to happen, all I could do was buckle down and try to develop the storyline into something I believed would be enough – just – to make it acceptable to Stanley.

Let me say I was not proud of my input or the changes made – I am not a scriptwriter. Even so, Stanley accepted all of them; my one consolation from all this nonsense was that I had been given an opportunity which would probably never be repeated – to direct a small film.

Flying to Brisbane, relaxing in the luxury of first-class travel, my thoughts were in sympathy with my new colleagues – those unfortunate directors on whom I had poured such scorn from time to time. With this script I could expect to be voted in as chairman of their exclusive club. Returning to my senses, I put all negative thoughts aside and went back to working on the script. I had no real anxieties with directing, especially as I had a cast of young unknowns with no particular names of repute to worry me, although it would be easy to understand their concerns with this preposterous story.

With my arrival at the studio it would seem that Stanley was still struggling with one scene in the script where a teacher was having an affair with one of the students. The actress pencilled in for the part had promised Stanley that she would have no problem with nudity, but even so he had reservations and would need confirmation before casting her. The solution was simple; as director, I should see the actress walking up and down naked to check that she had a good figure – 'perks for the director' he had assured me. Well, someone had to do it, but even so I insisted that another lady from the production office should be present. Satisfied that the actress had the required 'merits' on which Stanley insisted, needless to say she got the part.

To make the story work with my very tight schedule it was necessary to plan every single scene and shot in advance as there would be no time for the luxury of filming additional sequences to salvage this pathetic script. With the help of my enthusiastic Australian crew my thorough preparation paid off, leaving little chance of being hesitant with any decisions made. Even more important, I would

He did it! The director identifies Leon Lissek as the murderer while filming *Bloodmoon* in Australia.

also be seen as positive in my judgement by both cast and crew. In all humility, after many years of working on films decisiveness would not be a problem for me; my one satisfaction would be in knowing I was capable of doing the job.

The cinematographer John Stokes, a local Brisbane cameraman, remained faithful to the cause, as did Stanley, who kept his promise in allowing me a free hand to get on with the job without interference, which was much appreciated. So now it was all down to the director working with a cast of young actors, many of whom had never worked on a film before but were still keen to work with a director who had never directed before – it was surely a prescription for a disaster in the making.

Directing would be a wonderful experience, and I enjoyed taking on the challenges which all directors must face up to. Even more pleasing for the accountants, *Bloodmoon* completed filming on schedule, after which I was given a week with the editor to complete my own rough-cut – a new experience where I could employ John Glen's fast cutting techniques in the hope that it would help to disguise the paper-thin storyline.

Flying back to the UK, I continued the editing in my head, trying to mask the weaknesses in the story before the press carried out its death sentence on the sad director who in the end always gets the blame. I consoled myself knowing that *Bloodmoon* would never hit the headlines, nor would I be surprised by the predictable reviews. The critics would not be fooled, echoing my own thoughts, and I also recognised the hidden message of friends and colleagues who preferred to hide quietly behind a polite understanding. Even so, my conscience was clear; *Bloodmoon* had been a professional exercise, which Stanley appreciated.

Back home it was suddenly time to have second thoughts about my attitude to directors with poor scripts; should I be more sympathetic to their cause? Although these issues remain a concern for any director, there is still no reason to accept the 'that'll do' attitude which has always bothered me. This issue would not concern me now I had experienced a director's suffering, but at least it now gives me the right to have an opinion.

Settling down to assess the past weeks in Australia, I relived every moment – every scene with the extra cuts that I would have made had time permitted. I was still proud of what I had achieved on *Bloodmoon*. Most of the reviews had been pretty negative, but for me it had been a useful exercise in coming to understand what directors face up to; even if they hate the script they still get on with it, knowing that others like me would eagerly grab the opportunity should it come their way, even if it was not particularly helpful to their CV.

Try as hard as one may, there is little one can do with a poor script where at the end of the day only the accountant feels satisfied with the day's schedule being completed, which is probably why Stanley called me again, offering another film in the series. At least I could now allow myself a moment of satisfaction, believing that I had done a reasonable job on *Bloodmoon*. However, this self-assurance would quickly pass when I read my next script, *Dead Sleep*, with its own undoubted frustrations to come.

As before, the schedule gave little time to discuss any of the actors' concerns with the script, which I most certainly shared. Even so Stanley believed we could still come in on time, which was more important to him. I cleared my head, putting all this negative thinking behind me. Flying to Brisbane fully preoccupied in the new script – which, true to form, was little better than the last – in my head I could already hear Stanley's standard reply to the many questions I had: 'Do the best with what you have!'

Knowing all too well that in the end I would submit to the inevitable, when I arrived at the studio I was confronted with a disturbing change in studio policy; instead of the previous freedom given to me on *Bloodmoon*, all this had gone. Even more worrying was that the friendly atmosphere had changed, with unseen problems suddenly emerging in the preproduction battles from which Stanley had previously shielded me. However, the customary scheduling problems remained, and I felt they would not be made any easier when, with a wry grin on his face, Stanley said, 'Alec, you will have an American actress to deal with this time!'

Linda Blair arrived from Hollywood to complicate matters, the pretty eye-catching star moving smoothly into the production office to meet Stanley and her director. I had prepared myself for the moment; my plan was to be polite and courteous to our American celebrity – to stay British! At the same time I could not help thinking about the Bette Davis scene on her arrival in Egypt on *Death on the Nile*, promising myself I would not go over the top with the welcoming fawning which usually happens with a star's arrival; I would leave that false titbit exclusively to Stanley.

In my experience, actors enjoy the luxury of being made a fuss of, which was fine with me – there's no biz like showbiz – but looking ahead at the tight schedule and other problems which would come my way with this script, a star would be of little help to a director. Let's face it, I could hardly say to an actress like Linda what Stanley said to me: 'That's the script, now get on with it!'

My fears would soon be tested when prior to filming I spent time rehearsing scenes with the actors in the screening theatre. In part this introduces the actors to each other while at the same time it would give me the opportunity to listen to questions they might have about their lines; I was sure that there would be plenty with this script!

When Linda and the Australian actress went through a reading, for reasons known only to Linda she appeared to misunderstand the interpretation by placing a little humour into the scene, possibly assuming the other actress would echo her reading. The Australian actress was a little bemused and I quietly explained that the scene was not humorous and even if there was a hint of humour in the dialogue it should not be played that way. So now came my first challenge, which in all likelihood would need a touch of the José Quintero technique to sort out; already I was being tested and we were only just getting to know each other.

Linda was hurt and politely protested at my opinion but, while I respectfully listened to her feelings on this matter, I would not move from my opinion, believing that the scene should be played without any suggestion of humour. Sitting quietly in the background of the screening theatre Stanley decided to join in the conversation, politely confirming my own counselling: 'Linda, the scene may have hints of humour in the dialogue but it's not necessary to play it that way.'

I believe I passed my test there and then, giving Linda little ammunition for complaints should there be any in the future. To be fair to Linda, I found her to

Linda Blair probably felt the same way as I did, although my expression was more of shame with what was going on in front of camera. *Dead Sleep* (1990).

be cooperative and extremely professional throughout our association. For Stanley it was also useful for him to see how I handled our leading lady, and in the end the relationship worked well. Linda's claim to fame came from *The Exorcist*, where she had played the little girl who is possessed by the Devil, but it would seem that in this case I was not to be cast as the Devil incarnate. Linda was efficient and supportive to the cause, with everything going as planned. Like Linda, one should ask questions about the poor script disease which flourished at that time but from which no one really gained.

To a certain extent *Dead Sleep* was an interesting tale loosely based on a true story, of a doctor who induces sleep in patients, using drugs to keep them in that condition; while they are under the influence of an anaesthetic the patients are then given electric shocks to control their ailment, with few being cured of the problem and others getting worse, with one committing suicide. The reviews varied, with one even praising the film based on personal experiences (!) while others were less charitable, but with scripts of that calibre, what did they expect?

Before I returned to the UK Stanley invited me to dinner at the local Irish club in Brisbane where they were celebrating Saint Patrick's day. I would guess that there were 200 Irishmen and women sitting around the room enjoying imported Guinness, which as the evening progressed helped to speed up their hatred of 'the bloody English'! Taking note of this I decided to keep a low profile, wisely joining in the laughter.

Late into the night's entertainment with the help of the plentiful 'black stuff', the local custom would require one guest from each table to stand up and tell a joke, which more often than not would be to the detriment of the 'bloody English', before sitting down to a great ovation. Watching the comedians taking their turns, Stanley leaned over to me.

'So what joke are you going to tell, Alec?'

I laughed; he was kidding ... surely? Unfortunately Stanley was serious and suddenly it was time to start worrying. Although I whispered my protestations, explaining that I did not know any jokes and also reminding him that I was English, Stanley insisted that it was my obligation as guest to represent our table. I was already dead ...

'Table 31!' the MC shouted.

The office wall on *Dead Sleep* shows my detailed notes and shot lists in the forlorn hope of trying to finish on time and on budget. I'm getting greyer every day.

Unsure of the outcome, reluctantly – very reluctantly – I stood up, nervously glancing around the hall covered in green decorations with Irish tricolours as the inebriated audience waited in full expectation of my 'funny story' where it was again time to turn the screw on the 'bloody English'.

'There was an Englishman, a Scotsman and an Irishman ...'

TOO LATE – already too late! I had the joke the wrong way round: the fall guy to these silly stories is usually the last nationality mentioned. Even so, I carried on, hoping that no one would be offended with this terrible outrage – it was a fun evening after all, only a joke, surely? With a reasonable Irish accent I would probably have got away with this badly timed story but I am not big on accents and did not fancy my chances of survival.

I ploughed on, hoping my Irish friends, like Stanley, would laugh at my weird sense of humour considering that every joke so far had been dedicated to the abuse of the 'bloody English'. With a fading voice I managed to grind out the punch line, which of course died with my audience, except for one mistaken young man who attempted to applaud before realising his mistake when reminded by friends that I was an Englishman. Sitting down to a cold atmosphere of mumbling and coughing – obvious disapproval – Stanley decided it was probably time to leave. 'Preferably to the airport,' I whispered.

Dead Sleep was a valuable experience, if only to confirm the problems which directors face when dealing with high-profile film stars and how much I envied the likes of David Lean, Roman Polanski and others of that ilk who could pick and choose their subjects.

As for the film itself, I would try to rise above the critical outcome which would surely follow.

A CHANGING INDUSTRY

Who am I to write of directors who are good or bad or of relationships with unpredictable actors?

From clapper boy to camera assistant, camera operator to cinematographer, over the years I enjoyed working with directors whom I respected and believed worthy of that title, directors from whom I could learn while others I considered better skilled at managing schedules rather than actors. Now I can admit to being very much in the second division, but at the same time I am grateful for the experience with all of the nonsense I served up, and grateful for the knowledge which came from actors' concerns with how a scene should be played. When both parties held to opposing opinions, I would turn to the teachings of José Quintero – a director whom I admired and who would never consider such a script.

I also appreciated Stanley's gamble. He was a man who trusted me over the years and with whom I enjoyed a close and successful relationship, even when playing silly mind games in our salary negotiations, so it not only came as a surprise but also a disappointment to learn that he had decided to retire from the industry. Nor was I helped by the more disturbing thought that I too was knocking on a bit. Stanley had been a good friend and supporter over the years and would be sadly missed.

It was finally time for me to consider what was happening in those fast-changing times where the number of valued friends and colleagues was fast declining, lesser in number as age gave way to youth and the new generation waiting in the wings. The 'safe' industry of the older generation was no more but while some of my colleagues spoke in terms of retirement I still believed that I had more to offer.

Even so Margaret Thatcher's annihilation of the unions' closed shop policy had allowed the floodgates to open, with film schools and colleges now offering media courses. With the unions' powers now fast in decline, working hours slowly increased – ten- or twelve-hour days – and production companies knew full well that most would go along with their unreasonable demands. My refusal to operate the camera as well as light would also reduce the number of films offered to me in the future.

The technical winds of change were also starting to blow through the camera department as the age of high definition and digital cameras challenged my cosy world of film as the new technology made life difficult if not impossible for many elders of the camera department to come to terms with. It seemed like a foreign language to me but I could have few complaints after working for so long in my film world, both black and white and colour, where one appreciated the value of different film emulsions. The joys of filming were fast fading; I remembered the distant past and the glorious memories of my interview at Carlton Hill Studios. That now produced an attack of conscience or perhaps even guilt as I had not appreciated Lil's endeavours on my behalf; trips down memory lane would not help to right any perceived wrongs.

While I was in this down-in-the-dumps state Suzy noticed that many of my past adventures were missing from the script, somehow lost in the fog of my appalling memory – a family legacy not helping body and mind to stay fully engaged with this late challenge. I decided to salvage a few fading memories both good and bad, and now hand them over to the dreaded computer before this author completely faded to black ...

With Suzy's encouragement, I considered a possible working title: 'A Life in Films' ... 'Thanks for the Memories' ... 'Trips Down Memory Lane' ... 'That Reminds Me' ... 'I Am What I Am' ... 'Fate and Me' ... and others, but with fading reminiscences my story could only end as a series of flashbacks. Unfortunately a fellow pensioner, one Lewis Gilbert, had recently published his autobiography as *All My Flashbacks*, so I decided to hold off from picking a title until my story was finished and more carefully thought out, finally settling with 'I Am What I Am', which seemed appropriate – until I was told by my publisher that the title had already been used by the actor John Barrowman for his autobiography!

In this wonderful film world where we live and breathe we all have interesting tales to tell, not only for the reader but also the family who knew so little of my past adventures. You would imagine that this mental exercise would be easy, with so much material, but the first day ended in disappointment, with time wasted staring at a blank computer screen while other thoughts kept interfering, sidetracking any memories that suddenly came to mind. It would have been easier to switch off the computer and stumble into a depression, but when I was in a more positive frame of mind I would quickly rush to my notepad if a flashback suddenly came out of the blue, scribbling it down before that too disappeared. Progress would be painfully slow as I tried to recall old stories worth telling ...

The background to all this gobbledygook was that another year had passed since a film had come my way; the technical evolution of the industry was slowly taking its toll on my generation. I knew that I should be taking this computer thing more seriously, but then again, perhaps that damn phone would ring one more time.

It did!

My prayers would be answered with a call from John Glen, taking away the pain of doubt eating away inside. He asked me to join him along with Christopher Columbus and his followers in their quest to find the new world, travelling to far away places including Spain and the US Virgin Islands before our journey's end on Malta.

Heading this memorable cast was the French actor Georges Corraface as Columbus with Catherine Zeta-Jones keeping the female interest alive. Tom Selleck and Rachel Ward as the Spanish king and queen would help to draw in the public, but none of these names would come bigger than Marlon Brando as Tomás de Torquemada, the Grand Inquisitor of the Spanish Church. *Christopher Columbus* was more than just a list of well-known names or faces; the film offered a catalogue of stories for those like me who share an interest in the politics of filmmaking. From day one a cocktail of hate simmered beneath the surface; there's no biz like show biz!

It would seem that Marlon Brando had a total dislike of the Salkind family, the producers of the film. We assumed that the feeling was mutual as the producers did not appear to like Brando either, resulting in a sense of loathing which quietly lingered on the set. This intense dislike of each other came from a previous encounter back in 1977 on *Superman*, when Brando reportedly sued the Salkinds for $50 million, but with Ridley Scott's rival film *1492: Conquest of Paradise* in production at the same time, the Salkinds needed a big name that would help to sell their version of the story to Warner Bros. Marlon Brando was certainly a big name and according to the press was paid $5 million for his part in the film. Sadly this undercurrent would persist throughout our filming where Brando's antagonistic relationship with the producers remained unwavering, which in turn reflected in the atmosphere on the set, playing out to its inevitable conclusion of making relationships difficult to build on. It was necessary to tread carefully – very carefully.

Adding to this delicate situation, it would seem that our star also had a problem with memory retention, for which I have much sympathy these days. However, in Brando's case it was to be a dilemma for an actor of such standing. To help him overcome this problem a tiny unseen hearing aid was discreetly concealed in his ear while in another room close to the set his personal assistant would support the actor by reading out his lines at the appropriate time. Brando would then deliver them on camera, the arrangement working well. Problem solved!

Even so this uncomfortable atmosphere remained on the set as Brando eyeballed everyone around him, the stare in his piercing eyes making sure that neither Alexander nor Ilya Salkind were on set while he was performing. To be fair to the producers they tried to stay clear of the actor, hoping not to upset him any more than was necessary.

As for myself I survived with Mr Brando, who politely listened to any concerns I had with my lighting of him; after all it was in his interest to help me make him look good. I realised, of course, that I could be sacked if he thought differently, but apparently my attempt to obtain Brando's cooperation worked well, and produced the occasional smile in my direction, suggesting he liked me. For my part I found the actor to be professional and very cooperative; even so, I thought it best not to get too close.

With the Brando magnetism working on camera one felt a certain respect from those in close attendance. He certainly had my admiration with all of the successful films in which he had starred, but I also had high regard for John Glen's handling of this extraordinary situation, which was sensitive and understanding – extremely professional. With my usual practice of watching all of this nonsense going on behind the scenes, I could not help but notice the other actors' facial expressions, their bewilderment at it all. I could only imagine how they felt with all this attention focused on Marlon Brando, but life goes on ...

We humbler members of the crew had problems of our own, when we learned while filming in the Virgin Islands that our salaries had not been paid for the past six weeks! The problem was that we were soon flying to Malta to complete the final scenes in the large studio tank at the Mediterranean Film Studios, at which point the inevitable unit meeting was called to sort out this worrying situation. The initial reaction had been to stop filming until all the back pay had been settled, but after a lengthy discussion it was agreed to give the company time to sort out the problem, with the proviso that from then on our salaries would be paid one week in advance. At a unit meeting I pleaded with Hugh Whittaker, the Panavision representative from London, who it would appear was having similar problems, not to remove the film gates from the Panaflexes, which would have rendered the cameras useless.

The producers' promise to fly the money to Malta ensured that we kept filming, although two rolls of exposed film still disappeared mysteriously one night from the camera room; we suspected that the 'thief' was the owner of the hotel who had apparently got wind of the situation and had decided to keep the rushes as security of payment – obviously he had worked with film people before.

The situation was finally resolved when a chartered aircraft arrived with two attractive ladies carrying suitcases full of US dollars, resulting in a long queue outside the accountant's office in the hotel as everyone collected their honest reward; I was near the head of the queue, closely followed by Catherine Zeta-Jones. To complete the story, the two missing rolls of film turned up – obviously the hotel got their money too!

What started as an unpleasant situation would end as an amusing incident, where in all innocence I would be the victim of our assistant director Brian Cook and his wicked sense of humour, with me making a complete fool of myself. With our pockets full of dollars now came the inevitable problem of security, with everyone sensibly putting their sudden wealth into their hotel safety deposit boxes. With filming soon to end I happened to be talking with Brian in the hotel lobby about the past financial crisis. As we chatted, Brian's attention was drawn towards the hotel's security room, studying two suspicious-looking characters in their dark suits and trademark glasses.

'It's the Mafia,' my well-informed friend confirmed.

Being the honest fool that I am, I believed Brian's theory – why wouldn't I, with rumours already going around that the local Mob were aware of the cash being held at the hotel? In hindsight the rumour had probably been started by Brian. Remembering my earlier experience while working in Italy on *The Roman Spring of Mrs Stone*, and having no intention of allowing the Maltese Mafia to get their hands on my hard-earned cash, I decided to withdraw my cash from the hotel safe. I had led a sheltered life before meeting Brian. Hurrying to my room, I wrapped the dollars into small packs cut from plastic bags courtesy of the hotel and secured them around my waist, with a smaller amount tucked into my socks for added precaution. Confident that all was now well, for the last two days of filming I went to work dressed this way, totally convinced of Brian's sincerity, and told no one of the measures that I had taken to foil the Mafioso, or why I was walking with a strange gait with the occasional sound of rustling plastic coming from my torso. Of course there was no Mafia, but at least I could share this moment of insanity with friends later, as I do here in these flashbacks.

'CUT!'

As a footnote, none of the Columbus epics produced with such high hopes to coincide with the five-hundredth anniversary of the discovery of America would prove to be a box office hit. The distributors had seemingly misjudged the public's interest in the anniversary, but while our film won the all-important race to be released first, both *Christopher Columbus: The Discovery* and Ridley Scott's *1492: Conquest of Paradise* failed to recoup anything like their reported $45 million budgets. On the other hand, *Carry on Columbus*, with its minuscule budget and filmed in only five weeks at Frensham Ponds and Pinewood Studios, would in all probability break even.

ACES: IRON EAGLE III

Winter was fast approaching, bringing the usual shorter daylight hours. The Christmas of 1991 would soon arrive with the film industry entering its annual hibernation period, so the last thing I was expecting was a phone call from America with John Glen inviting me to join him on a new film in Tucson, Arizona. I hardly had the time to answer John's question before Suzy, listening-in to this 'private' conversation, decided she would join me on the trip. How could I say no?

While the film *Iron Eagle III* passes quickly from memory, the name Tucson and its association with the famous Western films of the past would quickly capture

John Glen lining up a high-angle shot. These days manned cranes are increasingly rare, with remotely operated camera heads having become the norm.

my imagination, knowing that this would make a fitting end to this personal account of my life and career. Filming would start after the Christmas festivities were over and the production manager greeted us at the airport with a broad smile on his face.

'Alec, welcome to America where Christmas celebrations are shorter than in the UK!'

Hello America, I thought to myself, recognising that the tone in his voice suggested that he was not particularly smitten with English technicians or it seemed our way of life. Possibly the poison still lingered in me after my *Jedi* experience, which unfortunately would continue throughout our filming.

With John spending Christmas in Los Angeles, there would be little point in hanging around town where the unit was based, so – short holiday or not – we hired a car and drove 200 miles north where Suzy and I enjoyed Christmas in Arizona. Our journey started with a gentle climb towards the mountains as we headed for the Grand Canyon National Park, where we had our first sighting of a light dusting of snow as we passed through Phoenix. The snowfall steadily increased as the road climbed higher towards the sky. Finally we arrived at the canyon, by which time the conditions had turned into a blinding snowstorm.

We quickly found our hotel before moving into tourist mode; with only two days to view the canyon in all its glory – truly an unforgettable experience – our short

An unusual
snap taken
just as a
Japanese Zero
makes a low
pass while
filming in
Arizona.

stay would be spent taking pictures of the surrounding magnificence from every possible angle and enjoying our first visit to an IMAX cinema.

Before Suzy returned to the UK we had time to visit Tombstone – cowboy country! To be honest, this would be the highlight of my trip to the States, where film aficionados and historians remember Tombstone as the town where the ghosts of the famous gunfight at the O.K. Corral reside in the cemetery and where gullible tourists like me are reminded of Wyatt Earp and Doc Holliday's confrontation with the Clanton gang – now embarrassingly portrayed by a team of stuntmen trying to recreate the moment while demonstrating how bad they can be at acting. Strolling down Main Street, we passed the saloon bar, the brothel (now closed), the Bird Cage Theatre and the old barbershop, not forgetting the shabby hotel or legendary Crystal Palace saloon. Sadly, the sounds of gunshots in the background were missing, as were the sounds of a badly tuned honky-tonk piano coming from the saloon bar ... youthful images coming to mind as I wandered down memory lane of Hollywood's history of the Wild West. A visit to the outlaws buried in the notorious Boot Hill Cemetery was interesting, and there I paid my respects to the villains whose past had contributed much to the entertainment of my young years – R.I.P., lads!

I would love to go on reminiscing about past cowboy history but memories soon turn to sadness – perhaps dwelling on past history is not such a good idea, after all. Even so I enjoyed the experience of filming in Arizona, which sadly would end in disappointment with *Iron Eagle III* receiving mixed reviews at best, as usual due to a poor script and stereotyped characters – possibly one sequel too many? Yep, best to leave it there, I reckon.

Louis Gossett Jr, Paul Freeman, Horst Bucholz and Christopher Cazenove were the names hanging around town on *Iron Eagle III*, while the producer's actress wife Rachel McLish would take the female lead. Christopher and I had worked together before on *Eye of the Needle*, and the film also provided another chance to work with my old friend Mitch Ryan, a fellow survivor from the awful *Hunting Party* experience in Almería.

Had *Iron Eagle III* been my last contribution to the world of cinema then Tombstone, with all its flashbacks to my younger days – I am a dreamer, after all – would have been the perfect location to end my career. However, there was one more episode still to come, leaving me grateful for one last picture before my retirement – a word never to be mentioned in my script ...

COINCIDENCE ... AGAIN?

Returning to the UK with little expectation of any more films being offered, my intention was to relax at cliff-top house, near Saunton Sands in north Devon – our home by the sea and the perfect setting to consider the aspects of my life which so far were little more than scribbled notes. I was busy at the time so I had jotted them down, planning to fill in the detail later. This would not happen yet: my reliable old friend 'coincidence' reappeared, resulting in a strange sequence of events which led to the unexpected offer of a television series.

It all began with a phone call from Jimmy Devis, who mentioned that Al Burgess, a colleague from the past, had also bought a house in nearby Croyde, where it would seem we were now neighbours. I phoned Al, suggesting we meet up for a drink at the local inn, but he was busy setting up a television series on which he was the associate producer so it would be more convenient if I saw him later that day.

The 'coincidence' I refer to came after my call to Al; apparently his cinematographer Norman Langley phoned withdrawing from the production, *Moving Story*. Of course doubting voices will say that this was just a coincidence or just plain lucky that I called Al at that time. Perhaps it was; on the other hand, it would be easy to say I was lucky enough to be in Devon in the right place at the right time, over 200 miles from our usual home in Buckinghamshire. I would also doubt that my name would have been in the frame to take over from Norman when Al first started looking for a replacement.

I realise this question of fate or destiny – call it what you will – is difficult for many to accept, but what they see as nonsense somehow works for me. As a young man I too was an unbeliever in such things and quickly passed them off as coincidence; later in life I would have reason to think more about all the incidents which occurred at key moments without reason or explanation. In any event, I suddenly now found myself working on another television series...

Moving Story, written by Jack Rosenthal, told the story of a group of removal men led by Warren Clarke who played the character Bamber, so-called because he was a mine of useless information and was not slow to bore his colleagues with his knowledge. It was a nice enough series which eventually ran for a couple of seasons, but as it continued I realised I could no longer ignore the fact that the energy which had served me well in the past was noticeably on the decline. In all likelihood this was the moment when I first accepted the possibility of my retirement. There – I had finally admitted it.

With *Moving Story* soon to end, the intention was to retire in the promised land of Devon, but again that would not happen. John Glen had other ideas in his personal script, which obviously differed to mine ...

THE POINT MEN

Settling down in the calm of retirement, I was mindful not to record any past experiences, both at work and in private, in a way which might be seen as exaggerated. Over the top they are not, although I will admit to taking a little licence here and there to keep the reader's interest, at the same time quietly acknowledging my personal beliefs. To some the experiences will appear strange, or even laughable to others. I understand that, but my life could never be dull working in an environment with such exciting people around me, actors and technicians alike, who all played their part in my interesting journey through life.

This brings to mind an interesting lady I first met while we were filming in Budapest, an extraordinary spiritualist going by name of Mari Deseõ. I sat there spellbound, listening to this lady's broken English, taking in everything she said. It was a casual, friendly conversation and not preaching in any way; nor was I brainwashed, but what she did say would leave me with ideas which would change my life in an extraordinary way. I would not recognise the effect of this conversation until later, when a series of coincidences would now make me remember that past experience, which is where I leave this issue ...

In humility, I can say that I enjoyed a successful career even if I was lucky to survive my personal disaster on *House of Secrets*, which I still have every reason to believe was a lesson I had to experience if only to succeed in the end. Sadly Harry Waxman and Guy Green were no longer around to help me achieve my goals, both having moved on to pastures new, but writing of my past experiences would help me in the transition from an exciting working environment to the slow unimaginable boredom of retirement, where it would be easy to switch off and disappear into emptiness. The computer also helped in no small way but only with the help and expertise of my wife, whose hair became greyer by the day as I tested her technical patience.

I was in this frame of mind when out of the blue Ernie Vincze called again to remind me of the teaching post offered at the NFTS, which I assumed was now long forgotten. I knew this would interest me and would be something I would enjoy, but again it seemed as though that particular scene was not yet written in the Alec Mills script. John Glen was once again on the phone to complicate matters with the offer of a film in Luxembourg. I would have hated to let John down even though the teaching activities at Beaconsfield would be less demanding, but the drug of another film would be too much to resist.

It happened that the timing of *The Point Men* would not clash with the new school term, allowing me the opportunity to team up with John for what would be the last time. The question of my fitness remained quietly in the background but it would be impossible to say, 'No thank you, John!' In spite of my physical health and mental tiredness *The Point Men* would be another addition to my CV, although at my time of life that now seemed less important.

So now I found myself wondering how the new intake of film students would handle the challenges which John and I had faced over the years. With quality giving way to impossible schedules, they would quickly learn the weight of responsibility and what it is like to be in the firing line, and many would not survive. However, these silly worries would quickly disappear when I had a light meter back in my hand.

With the inevitable low budget and predictable tight schedule, *The Point Men* would set a challenge for both director and cinematographer, with no time for photographic tests with our lead actor Christopher Lambert, who was still working on another production. The evening before filming began I was 'summoned' to meet and have dinner with Christopher, producer Silvio Muraglia and John Glen with his wife Janine. I prepared myself for an evening of social conversation with the usual banter of getting to know each other in a pleasant setting; it would turn out to be more than that.

Aware that I had had no time for photographic tests, Christopher, like many actors, was clear in his views as to how he would like to be photographed and look on the screen. It became apparent why this dinner had been arranged when the social chatter suddenly disappeared with all concentration now focused on Christopher and me, while the others look on silently.

Listening to Christopher's concerns it was necessary to point out that, with his other commitment, we had had no time to do any photographic tests, which was even more complicated by the fact that he was in the first scene in the morning.

'Oh, don't worry about that, Alec, you'll get all the time you need,' came Christopher's timely reply.

I took a deep breath, sighed and sat back in the chair, turning to look directly at John, who in turn looked towards Silvio, whose lips curled in acceptance of 'Christopher's law', clearly understanding the implication of the actor's comment. If nothing else at least I could expect fewer 'How long, Alec?' questions from John; nor would I be so concerned with John's maxim, 'Will it put more bums on seats?' My mate Chris was on the case now!

I enjoyed working with Christopher and gave him all the necessary attention without hurting John's directing time. As a result, Christopher was happy in how he looked on screen, as was John, who also had to deal with the other ridiculous political issues that directors have to put up with. It was at times like this that one appreciated the luxury of working for Cubby Broccoli.

The Point Men would not be an easy film for John, who suffered constant interference from the producers which stood in the way of common sense, as usual underlined with their ridiculous schedules testing the director's ability to make it all work. Yes, I am being repetitive, for which I will not apologise. That was the state of the film industry at that time. I also know that this will be my last opportunity to make the point.

On a brighter note, I still had enough energy to cope with all of the demands the director would put on me, which as it happens worked for us both. At the same time I knew that it really was time for 'The End' frame to appear as I now struggle to remember other missing flashbacks in my career.

REFLECTIONS

Throughout my life, from schoolboy to pensioner, even in the lost years in the navy, somehow things have always worked out for the best, one way or another, although not necessarily without pain or anxiety. Still, you instinctively know when it is time to fade out.

The phone finally stopped ringing, the silence suggesting that my services would no longer be required; the show was over with the safety curtain slowly coming down. The final scene would read 'Coming to terms with retirement', which of course is easier said than done.

It would be easy to use terms such as retirement and just put the blame on my physical concerns, but in reality it was time to wind down and quietly reflect on a fast-changing film industry with which I was now out of step. To help with this problem I spent many hours reading autobiographies of old friends and colleagues: Freddie Young, Christopher Challis, Oswald Morris and Jack Cardiff, talented cinematographers of my era who in their refreshing honesty never claimed their work was faultless – an example that I would choose to follow with my own small effort.

Many lessons would also be learned from working with talented directors of my generation; would I ever forget Guy Green's kindness to me when I needed his compassion due to my negligence? We all make mistakes and that error was unforgivable, but not with Guy Green. Working with honest people such as Guy would inevitably influence my own attitude to others, whether good or bad, which probably saved my career. In all humility, I can say that the verdict on my career is one of reasonable satisfaction – possibly eight out of ten, which was pretty good considering I never attained such approval at school – helped in no small way by the contribution of cinematographers who in their day demonstrated their art as 'painters of light'; my appreciation goes to all of these fine gentlemen. Even so, there would always be a guardian angel helping me in my long journey, but only when writing this memoir did I realise who it was.

My choice will surprise many when I name Harry Waxman BSC as my minder here on planet Earth. Perhaps this is fanciful imagination – I am a dreamer, after all, but I still ask myself why Harry and I, total opposites in so many ways, were strangely tied together. Perhaps it was the cinematographer's patience in his teachings, his unhurried manner, knowing I would struggle to understand the technical expertise which he slowly drilled into me. Now I can recognise my earlier immature attitude from my schooldays; I could not have progressed further without the patience, the authority, of a Harry Waxman to point me in the right direction. Harry's strict guiding influence would make my life easier so that I could simply follow the guv's strict set of rules, at the same time promising myself not to forget my nightmare experience when filming *House of Secrets* – Harry would make sure of that. It is necessary I should record this in my writing of the cinematographer who would always be my champion. I know others might disagree and I listen to their accounts of Harry, which more often than not are about his temperament rather than his talent. There was much more to Harry Waxman, which others prefer to forget.

Jack Cardiff! What could one say about a grand master of lighting, a 'cinematographer extraordinaire' widely praised by many as the true painter of light. Whatever label we choose to give him, it would be necessary to work alongside such an artist to understand his individual talent, to watch him and take notes, then take more notes and sit back and admire the person behind it all. The films and conversations we shared together would be crucial in my own transition to cinematographer.

By contrast, Gilbert Taylor's quiet personality was the total opposite of Harry Waxman's, and I never forgot his demonstration of the Schüfftan process while we were filming Polanski's *Macbeth*. An opportunity later came my way to demonstrate this process to the students at the NFTS in the hope that one day they would also be in a position to use the technique. No doubt there are other special effects that are now sadly lost to memory with the passing of time, which is a shame when you consider how those trail-blazing cameramen led the way with their pioneering ideas. I hope future historians will keep this in mind with their writings in this CGI age.

Michael Reed was just as important to me as Harry Waxman; both men moved my career forward at different stages and took time to understand this young fool, which I would recognise and appreciate later. Michael must also take the credit for keeping my career on course with his patience towards a characterless clapper boy desperately in need of recognition as an adult. I will forever be grateful to Michael for his understanding and management, and I would never forget that it was Mike who gave me my break as camera operator on *The Saint*, starting me on my long journey to fulfilment. Michael Reed is my Saint!

SUMMING UP

The problem I had writing about personal experiences was that it would inevitably involve others who may perhaps remember incidents differently to me – I might enjoy a film but my wife might not necessarily share the same experience. I assume this happens to all who take on the curse of writing about their own lives. Now I find myself reading and re-reading what I have written, over and over again, hoping not to offend the others involved in my story. All I can say is that what you have read is as accurate and honest an account as it could be – at least from my point of view – from my early school years where my mother was responsible for turning a dull life into an exciting occupation, to the beginning of a career which would eventually become an obsession.

It was not my intention just to write my life story or to offer a collection of anecdotes which over the years would put a smile on friendly faces – at least for those who are still around who shared those same moments. It was only under pressure from my family that I sentenced myself to years of torture trying to recall important events of my life, including the good and not-so-good times. This would not be enough to explain who I was 'inside', or why I would be prepared to share and discuss private emotions openly. In fact, I did not want to forget how all this happened to me so I hope you will understand why it was occasionally necessary for me to repeat myself. That is a bad habit, for which I apologise, but I offer no apology for my passion to explain everything as seen through this writer's eyes, even if it is a little laboured at times. We all have our secrets which others would not understand, sometimes leaving us open to ridicule, but at my time of life I no longer really care what others think. I am what I am, comfortable with my years of existence here on planet Earth and happy with what came from my personal journey.

Should I be asked if I have regrets in life, the answer is yes, of course – we all do – but not with my work! Do I wish my youthful attitude to learning had been different? Yes, of course: one way or another I have paid for being academically wanting and feel uncomfortable in certain company. However, to balance this, I had the ability to play the piano reasonably well – at least, well enough to pass a junior exam at the Royal Academy of Music – which I am proud of while at the same time a little sad at not knowing what might have been achieved in the world of music if my preference had been in that direction. I was the in-between man and Lil's aspirations for me to be a musician failed miserably; an inspection of my too-small fingers would quickly put an end to that silly idea. Yet, with all the ups and downs of youthful enthusiasm, I would gain far more from my travels around the world, the wonderful experiences shared, something which cannot be taught in any school. I have no regrets in this personal flashback, which I consider an honest appraisal of Alec Mills, the man and his journey.

In all this I forgot to mention the BSC and GBCT accolades, even serving as vice president of the British Society of Cinematographers for seven years – something I could never have considered or even thought possible with my wasted youth. I had no idea what I would do in the workplace when I finished school, nor would I care in which direction life pointed me, feeling that the problem would take care of itself. Even so, it is necessary to ask myself how I came to deserve all of this good fortune freely handed to me. I can only put it down to working in the ranks of British camera technicians, with the great cinematographers of my time who allowed me to play the fool in their personal scripts.

It was important that I did not leave out the account of my family before the war: a personal history of those not so good old days when life was not easy for my parents or the proud working-class families who struggled to scrape a position in life. Possibly a few forgotten chestnuts still remain to be written, which perhaps are better saved for another time in another place. However, I will enjoy living off these past reminiscences, which I hope will be replayed time and again with old mates at the local watering hole as we retell the same old stories as if they were new. I should also apologise to my family, who continue to suffer these accounts, having heard them all before many times; they smile politely at a silly old fool holding on to past memories, reluctant to let them go. It hurts when they have the disrespect to correct my account if I get the story wrong – it really is sad getting old ...

This background will not deter the students at the NFTS, where wannabe cinematographers will inevitably discover that this film industry could also become their obsession, where sacrifices would be made to move on and move up. Many of them will wait quietly in the wings for their opportunity. That is how it was for me, and I was feeling down in the dumps when another film was suddenly offered to me in South Africa, again about Shaka Zulu.

The offer came from the director Joshua Sinclair who wrote the original series. In conversations over the phone I could not be sure if Joshua had directed a film before and I suspected that his know-how was limited, even so, the director appeared positive in his suggestions and said that I should wait to hear from him.

Joshua's offer came while I was filming the television series *Soldier Soldier*; we would stay in contact over many months as the film went through the usual preparation period; everything appeared to be going well for the director, who claimed Roger Moore would be playing the lead role in the film. Hearing this, I foolishly mentioned my relationship with Roger.

With time passing, the film kept going back and doubts now started to creep in but, to the director's credit, he kept me informed about the obvious lack of progress. Finally Joshua arrived in England to film tests with his Italian leading lady, suggesting that all was well. I was asked to organise the shoot, camera crew and stage space, with the lighting and camera equipment all generously supplied free of charge by Samuelson Film Service through the old pals' network. The only item not free was film stock; Samuelsons would have nothing to do with that nonsense, so I took care of that problem myself, if only to keep Joshua's show – and mine – on the road, and would worry about collecting the money later.

Roger never came to England for the test. By now he was past believing Joshua about the situation in which the film appeared to be, finally pulling out altogether. However, after all this time, I continued to go along with the director's requests, though privately admitting this was more in hope than expectation that the film would ever take off.

Later Joshua casually mentioned that he was having financial problems and needed to sell some of his valued paintings to pay the bills; I also had the impression that his house could be in danger of going the same way, yet even with all of these mounting problems the call finally came to travel to South Africa to prepare filming. My agent still had reservations with all this; only with guarantees of return flights and accommodation would I be allowed to travel to Johannesburg.

After all the hassle it was good to finally get going. My enthusiastic director greeted my arrival with the news that Roger was still interested in the film, even though privately Roger had told me he had pulled out. Nevertheless, Joshua remained as determined and positive as ever, saying, 'Roger is still on the show – phone him, tell him you are here and all is well!' With that appeal I became more concerned than ever, not for the film or that I would be abusing my relationship with Roger, but suddenly realising that I was getting involved in matters which did not concern me and were well above my pay grade, and even that I was being used. Reluctantly, I tried – and failed!

Undeterred by this setback, Joshua decided that we should travel to the Transkei where a large boat was already under construction and where we would meet up with the talented production designer Hans Nel, who designed the original *Shaka Zulu* series. My hopes started to soar again when I saw what Hans had achieved so far; the set looked truly magnificent! All my negative thoughts now quickly began to diminish, though somehow they would not go away completely. Now came the whispers in the background that Hans had no money to finish building the sets, alarm bells started ringing again, this time louder than ever.

We were looking at the wall, having a pee, when Joshua casually mentioned a call he had received on his mobile; his solicitor was advising that more money was necessary to keep the film on track, which I assumed would mean Joshua selling more of his treasured paintings. He paused before turning to speak, his thoughts elsewhere ... fortunately he'd finished peeing! This was the first time I had seen genuine concern on the director's face, leaving me to assume that the money had not been in place from the beginning, with Joshua alone financing the pre-production period in the hope that all would be well in the end. Sadly this did not happen and I returned to England out of pocket with yet another hard lesson learned, as others have also learned before and after me. We all become addicts to the drug of making films – I was no different.

The never-say-die Joshua, just like many others, was the total film addict who remained confident all would be well in the end. In a way it did turn out well – if not for me. Later I learned that Joshua directed the film *Shaka Zulu: The Citadel* in Italy with Henry Cele once again playing the title role; this time the critics would be far less enthusiastic.

I still hope one day to meet up with Joshua, if only to hear the full story – he owes me that. I bear no resentment to the man, whom I liked very much. He may have been naive about films and their financing, but again I could see much of myself in Joshua as he gambled to get his story off the ground.

Following the collapse of the film, I travelled north to Newcastle to film *The Rag Nymph*, a mini-series made by Tyne Tees Television as part of their Catherine Cookson series. Frank Elliott, my ever-loyal camera assistant, joined me but sadly this would be the last time we would work together; other issues would change his life and our long-standing friendship.

Pinewood Studios was the venue where the BSC celebrated 'Operators' Night', an occasion in the calendar when camera crews get together and pat ourselves on the back, handing out awards to deserving technicians during an evening of celebration and high spirits. Frank was much quieter that night; his cheerful personality was noticeably missing, which was very unusual for him. With the evening drawing to a close he took me aside from all the revelry to tell me that he had been diagnosed with Parkinson's disease and that his working days would soon be over. The atmosphere suddenly chilled, not unlike a scene from a script: '*An uncomfortable atmosphere takes over the scene with muted sounds of high spirits carrying on in the distant background*'. Frank's worst moment would read like that.

He spoke quietly of his concerns for the future as he tried to come to turns with the situation while I encouraged him to carry on and not worry, although I sensed that Frank was not really listening to me. My friend had many colleagues in the film industry who enjoyed his irrepressible sense of humour – his company. Frank has recently passed away; he was a king in the eyes of the Zulus, my ever-loyal friend and camera assistant for twenty-five years.

THE PHANTOM RETURNS

Working in the film industry we experience both good and bad times and have many interesting stories to tell, but what still remains unresolved is the unfinished account of the Cherry Trees apparition, where you may remember the friendly spirit who happily shared our beautiful cottage in Bledlow Ridge, now many years past. Every word written in that account was an accurate description as told to Lesley and me, finally ending with my own personal 'experience' of the spirit.

Clearly, over time, stories of this nature change or become exaggerated, conveniently giving others something to smile about as they silently retain their biased scepticism. However, while others would prefer to keep their silence on such matters and offer no opinion, I would ask them not to dismiss out of hand this postscript which recently came to light purely by 'accident'.

Driving one day through Bledlow Ridge with Suzy I pointed out Cherry Trees to her, explaining the alterations that had been made over the years, the most noticeable being the beautiful thatch which had been replaced with tiles, taking away the original attraction of cottage – at least for me – and removing its previous character. Seeing the current owner cutting the lawn, we walked down the drive to speak with him, explaining that I was a previous owner of the property now thirty years past and curious to see the other changes made. Of course the crucial question I needed to ask was the issue of the Cherry Trees ghost, which would be difficult to bring up. I silently smiled to the friendly phantom, which probably recognised me walking down the drive – okay, maybe that was wishful thinking ...

After chatting for a while, the owner kindly invited us inside to see the changes they had made; the furnishings were now modern, which I thought took away the essential atmosphere Cherry Trees had previously enjoyed – to each his own, I thought to myself, still with no suggestion of any unseen company. Trying hard not to be too direct with the question that desperately needed to be asked, I finally managed to get it out, if with some hesitation: 'Do you get any unusual visitors from time to time?' – a direct reference to the past history passed on to Lesley.

The man paused and looked at me carefully. Then to my delight without hesitation came his reply: 'Yes ... yes we do,' he smiled.

He went on to explain that he had once seen the spirit out of the corner of his eye, as his wife had, so fulfilling the legend of the friendly apparition who visits the cottage should it enjoy a happy environment, which you will remember was the condition the gardener had explained to Mrs Metcalf many years earlier. When the owner's elderly mother had been staying at the cottage, she had also experienced the presence of a knocking noise in a separate room, only to find there was no one there, which matched my own experience of the spirit moving around the cottage with the creaking beams above me as I tried to hold a conversation with her. No longer would I believe that I was mad.

Another interesting account came from the owner's wife, who had been experiencing pain with a slipped disc and found it necessary to lie flat on the floor for relief. As she lay there, she sensed 'someone' behind her head, but in her condition she was unable to turn to see who it was, and she heard a woman's voice saying, 'Don't worry, it will be all right!' A few weeks later the lady had an operation on her back to repair the disc – after which she has been fine!

Of course, you will draw your own conclusions from all this 'rubbish', which may well be that I should be put in a home, but I would answer that by asking you to open your minds to all this. Strange things happen in life which may draw our interest while others will see it as nonsense. With so many questions in life which cannot be easily be explained away, I tend to favour curiosity. I include those things in this autobiography, hoping that it might at least open up new frontiers for others like me with opinions about life after life.

On a personal note, I will finish with a story from my retirement, which has brought with it the inevitable chores of domestic responsibility while Suzy is still working. When I was standing one day in the queue at the local supermarket the cashier, who obviously knew the customer in front of me, politely asked the ageing gentleman if he was enjoying his retirement. I carefully tuned in to this interesting question, knowing the same could be asked of me. After a long pause, followed with a thoughtful sigh, I sensed his dementia in his short confused reply, as the man finally confessed to missing his workmates.

'No, not really ...'

Head down, he slowly walked away.

Of course I now recognise those same words, and I miss my friends as well as my occupation, but now it was time for me to walk away with my dreams fulfilled. Now I wonder where my next living form will take me – possibly more images to think about?

Sweet dreams, believers!

FILMOGRAPHY

Clapper/Loader

Year	Title	Director	Cameraman
1947	*Eyes That Kill*	Richard M. Grey	Ray Densham
1948	*The Monkey's Paw*	Norman Lee	Bryan Langley
1949	*Vengeance is Mine*	Alan Cullimore	James Wilson
1954	*The Golden Link*	Charles Saunders	Harry Waxman
1954	*Fabian of the Yard*	Anthony Beauchamp & Edward Thompson	Hilton Craig
1954	*Father Brown*	Robert Hamer	Harry Waxman
1954	*The Sleeping Tiger*	Joseph Losey	Harry Waxman
1955	*They Can't Hang Me*	Val Guest	Stanley Pavey
1955	*Mozart's Don Giovanni*	Paul Czinner	Stanley Onions
1956	*The Battle of the River Plate*	Michael Powell & Emeric Pressburger	Christopher Challis
1956	*Moby Dick* (Second Unit)	John Huston	Oswald Morris

Focus Puller

Year	Title	Director	Cameraman
1955	*Contraband Spain*	Lawrence Huntington	Harry Waxman
1956	*Lost*	Guy Green	Harry Waxman
1956	*House of Secrets*	Guy Green	Harry Waxman
1957	*Robbery under Arms*	Jack Lee	Harry Waxman
1957	*High Tide at Noon*	Philip Leacock	Eric Cross
1958	*A Cry from the Streets*	Lewis Gilbert	Harry Gillam
1958	*The Gypsy and the Gentleman*	Joseph Losey	Jack Hildyard

1959	*Third Man on the Mountain*	Ken Annakin	Harry Waxman
1960	*Swiss Family Robinson*	Ken Annakin	Harry Waxman
1960	*Kidnapped*	Robert Stevenson	Paul Beeson
1961	*The Roman Spring of Mrs Stone*	José Quintero	Harry Waxman
1961	*Greyfriars Bobby*	Don Chaffey	Paul Beeson
1961	*Nearly a Nasty Accident*	Don Chaffey	Paul Beeson
1962	*In Search of the Castaways*	Robert Stevenson	Paul Beeson
1962	*Tarzan in India*	John Guillermin	Paul Beeson
1962	*The Prince and the Pauper*	Don Chaffey	Paul Beeson
1963	*Three Lives of Thomasina*	Don Chaffey	Paul Beeson
1964	*Doctor Syn, Alias the Scarecrow*	James Neilson	Paul Beeson
1964	*The Moon-Spinners*	James Neilson	Paul Beeson
1964	*Carry on Cleo*	Gerald Thomas	Alan Hume
1966	*The Fighting Prince of Donegal*	Michael O'Herlihy	Arthur Ibbetson
1966	*Eye of the Devil*	J. Lee Thompson	Erwin Hillier
1966	*Blow-Up*	Michelangelo Antonioni	Carlo Di Palma

Camera Operator

Year	Title	Director	Cameraman
1966–68	*The Saint* (TV series)	Various	Michael Reed
1968	*Where Eagles Dare* (Second Unit)	Brian G. Hutton	Arthur Ibbetson
1969	*The Valley of Gwangi*	James O'Connolly	Erwin Hillier
1968	*Chitty Chitty Bang Bang* (Second Unit)	Ken Hughes	Michael Reed
1969	*Guns in the Heather*	Robert Butler	Michael Reed
1969	*On Her Majesty's Secret Service*	Peter Hunt	Michael Reed
1969	*Two a Penny*	James F. Collier	Michael Reed
1970	*The Private Life of Sherlock Holmes* (Second Unit)	Billy Wilder	Chris Challis
1970	*The McKenzie Break*	Lamont Johnson	Michael Reed
1971	*The Tragedy of Macbeth*	Roman Polanski	Gilbert Taylor
1971	*The Hunting Party*	Don Medford	Cecilio Paniagua
1972	*Running Scared*	David Hemmings	Ernest Day
1972	*Made*	John MacKenzie	Ernest Day
1974	*Diamonds on Wheels*	Jerome Courtland	Michael Reed
1974	*Gold*	Peter Hunt	Ousama Rawi
1974	*Visit to a Chief's Son*	Lamont Johnson	Ernest Day

1975	*The Hiding Place*	James Collier	Michael Reed
1975	*Operation Daybreak*	Lewis Gilbert	Henri Decae
1976	*Alfie Darling*	Ken Hughes	Ousama Rawi
1976	*Shout at the Devil*	Peter Hunt	Michael Reed
1976	*Seven Nights in Japan*	Lewis Gilbert	Henri Decae
1977	*Gulliver's Travels*	Peter Hunt	Alan Hume
1977	*Wombling Free*	Lionel Jeffries	Alan Hume
1977	*The Prince and the Pauper*	Richard Fleischer	Jack Cardiff
1977	*The Spy Who Loved Me*	Lewis Gilbert	Claude Renoir
1978	*Death on the Nile*	John Guillermin	Jack Cardiff
1979	*Moonraker*	Lewis Gilbert	Jean Tournier
1979	*Avalanche Express*	Mark Robson	Jack Cardiff
1980	*There Goes the Bride*	Terry Marcel	James Devis
1980	*The Awakening*	Mike Newell	Jack Cardiff
1981	*Sphinx*	Franklin Schaffner	Ernest Day
1981	*For Your Eyes Only*	John Glen	Alan Hume
1981	*Eye of the Needle*	Richard Marquand	Alan Hume
1983	*Octopussy*	John Glen	Alan Hume
1983	*Star Wars: Episode VI – Return of the Jedi*	Richard Marquand	Alan Hume

Director of Photography

Year	Title	Director
1982	*Island of Adventure*	Anthony Squire
1983	*Biddy*	Christine Edzard
1983	*Space Riders*	Joe Massot
1983	*On the Third Day*	Stanley O'Toole
1984	*The Last Days of Pompeii* (Second Unit)	Peter Hunt
1985	*Hot Target*	Denis Lewiston
1986	*Shaka Zulu* (TV series)	William C. Faure
1986	*King Kong Lives*	John Guillermin
1987	*The Living Daylights*	John Glen
1987	*Lionheart*	Franklin Schaffner
1988	*The Dirty Dozen* (TV series)	Various
1989	*Licence to Kill*	John Glen
1989	*About Face* (TV series)	John Henderson
1989–90	*Press Gang* (TV series)	Various
1992	*Seekers* (TV series)	Peter Barber-Fleming

250

1992	*Aces: Iron Eagle III*	John Glen
1992	*Christopher Columbus: The Discovery*	John Glen
1993–96	*Soldier, Soldier* (TV series)	Various
1993	*Come Snow, Come Blow*	Gary Love
1995	*Moving Story* (TV series)	Various
1997	*The Rag Nymph*	David Wheatley
2001	*The Point Men*	John Glen

Director

Year	Title	Cameraman
1990	*Bloodmoon*	John Stokes
1992	*Dead Sleep*	John Stokes

ACKNOWLEDGEMENTS

My sincere thanks go to many who would not understand how they contributed much to my exciting life and occupation; I am forever indebted to them all.

Where else would I start but with the camera department, and the talented cinematographers who guided me on my path, including Harry Waxman, Michael Reed, Jack Cardiff and Alan Hume. And not forgetting the foot soldiers without whom no camera department can properly function; I would like to thank all of the camera crews who have worked with me over the years, in particular Frank Elliott, Michael Frift and Chunky Huse.

To name but a few, the directors who most influenced me include James Collier, Peter Hunt, Roman Polanski and José Quintero, while not forgetting Lewis Gilbert (a wonderful director if also a sadly misguided Arsenal supporter) and John Glen, who both did so much to keep me in the Bond family. Special thanks are also due to Cubby Broccoli, Barbara Broccoli, Michael Wilson and, last but certainly not least, Sir Roger Moore, who so willingly provided the foreword to this book. Perhaps it was to make up for all the evil jokes he pulled on me over the years we worked together?

On the publishing side, my particular thanks go to Stephanie Wenborn, Meg Simmonds and Rosie Moutrie at Eon Productions' Piccadilly office for their kind assistance with MGM in obtaining the permissions for the Bond photographs contained within the book, and also to Christopher Holm and Sarah Garcia at Lucasfilm. Thanks are also due to Mark Beynon and Christine McMorris, my editors at The History Press, for helping to guide me through the publication process, and also to Gareth Owen and my son Simon for reading and correcting the original manuscript – so if it's right then I will take the credit and if it's wrong he can take the blame! I appreciate all their help in allowing my story to hang around a little longer.

Above all, my wife Suzy, who puts up with my silliness in old age, my offspring, Simon and Belinda, who I adore so much, and the many friends and colleagues whose names I easily forget these days, but who all played their part in my story.

My thanks to you all …

INDEX

ROADS TO RENEWAL

MICHIGAN STATE EMERGENCY WELFARE RELIEF COMMISSION
& STATE CIVIL WORKS ADMINISTRATION

Bottom row: Louis M. Nims, Commissioner;
Charles H. Bender, Chairman; W. J. Norton, Commissioner

Top row: Ernest Brooks, Secretary; Fred R. Johnson, Administrator;
William Haber, Assistant Administrator.

ROADS TO RENEWAL

THE REPORT OF ACTIVITIES AND ACCOMPLISHMENTS
OF THE CIVIL WORKS ADMINISTRATION IN MICHIGAN,
NOVEMBER 1933–MARCH 1934

with an Introduction and Afterword by **James R. Anderson**

Michigan State University Press | *East Lansing*

♾ The paper used in this publication meets the minimum requirements
of ANSI/NISO Z39.48-1992 (R 1997) (Permanence of Paper).

Michigan State University Press
East Lansing, Michigan 48823-5245

LIBRARY OF CONGRESS CATALOGING-IN-PUBLICATION DATA
Names: Anderson, James R., editor.
Title: Roads to renewal : the report of activities and accomplishments of
the civil works administration in Michigan (November 1933–March 1934) /
with an introduction and afterword by James R. Anderson.
Description: First Edition. | East Lansing : Michigan State University Press, 2020.
Identifiers: LCCN 2020004708 | ISBN 9781611863789 (paperback)
| ISBN 9781609176532 | ISBN 9781628954135 | ISBN 9781628964141
Subjects: LCSH: United States. Federal Civil Works Administration for Michigan.
| Public works—Michigan—History. | Public service employment—Michigan—History.
| United States. Federal Civil Works Administration.
| Public service employment—United States—History.
Classification: LCC HD3890.M52 .R63 2020 | DDC 362.5/94840977409043—dc23
LC record available at https://lccn.loc.gov/2020004708

Book and cover design by Charlie Sharp, Sharp Des!gns, East Lansing, Michigan
Cover illustration is a merger of two photos: Left: Old Rapid River Bridge, Kalkaska,
Michigan; right: New Rapid River Bridge, Kalkaska, Michigan, built under the CWA
program.

Michigan State University Press is a member of the Green Press Initiative and is
committed to developing and encouraging ecologically responsible publishing
practices. For more information about the Green Press Initiative and the use of
recycled paper in book publishing, please visit www.greenpressinitiative.org.

Visit Michigan State University Press at *www.msupress.org*

Contents

Tables and Charts

Tables

Charts

Introduction

James R. Anderson

Late last November, Detroit was electrified by the launching of the CWA program. Almost overnight, thousands of men were put to work and carloads of tools and equipment were rushed to project locations.

—*Detroit News*, April 6, 1934

There are three main themes in the historic, but little-known document introduced by this interpretive essay. For the first theme, the report presents a remarkable, almost unique case history of how extreme unemployment, destitution, and despair in Michigan were directly addressed and significantly reduced by direct federal employment through the creation of the Civil Works Administration (CWA). The CWA was a short-term but decisive, highly innovative, and influential federal program of work relief established by the Franklin D. Roosevelt administration at the depths of the Great Depression in November 1933. It was designed to confront the national unemployment crisis directly and swiftly, because approaching winter would compound existing misery.

A second and parallel theme is the astounding and determined degree of close governmental coordination that extended from the federal level, especially the executive branch, to the county, city, and village level of Michigan—from Washington, D.C., to Copper Harbor at the tip of the Keweenaw Peninsula, almost 1200 miles away. The third theme grows directly out of the second: how swiftly the largest single employment program in Michigan's entire history was implemented.

How New Deal Investment and Michigan Governments Brought Recovery and Hope out of Depression Peril

The harshest blows of the Great Depression struck in late 1932 and through October 1933. Few can imagine, and even fewer are still alive to remember, the extraordinary economic and political misery endured by the people and state of Michigan during this time. The American production economy had been cut in half: gross national product, one of the most widely known and cited of economic indicators, plummeted to around 50 percent of 1929 levels, and industrial production, a primary source of jobs and prosperity, also declined more than 50 percent.[1]

Bank failures multiplied with deepening effects. Across the United States, thousands of banks shut their doors and locked out depositors. The banking system was paralyzed and mostly closed down from late 1932 to March 4, 1933. This explains the significance of the creation of the CWA and its impact on Michigan, as documented in this volume.

Michigan experienced savage triple blows of extreme levels of industrial unemployment, a statewide bank shutdown by order of the governor, and the exceptionally harsh winter of 1933–34. With governmental cooperation inspired and sometimes ordered by the CWA, some 165,000 unemployed, destitute, and malnourished people of Michigan were given productive employment on 12,000 varied public projects in less than four months, a dizzying speed for any institution, governmental or otherwise, in any era of history. The CWA compiled similar records of achievement in other states. We focus on the Michigan CWA report, examining how the governments, people, and economy of Michigan, with significant investment by the CWA of the federal government, confronted and coped with economic despair, destitution, and hopelessness at the Depression depths of 1932 and 1933. By the time the CWA was combined with the Federal Emergency Relief Administration (FERA) in April 1934, Michigan had begun to emerge from the wreckage of the Depression and was on a solid road to recovery, economically and in terms of morale.

The road to recovery was comprised of thousands of projects, including many actual roads. The projects were selected and administered at the county, city, and sometimes state levels, with labor and materials financed by the federal government. The CWA launched this recovery which we can justifiably call the Second Hundred Days, comprising the period from November 1933 through March 1934. It can be compared with the more famous (first) Hundred Days of the Roosevelt administration, from March through June 1933, when some sixteen landmark legislative acts were passed and signed into law. The

Michigan CWA report, reprinted in this volume, documents the process and projects that put people back to work and launched the recovery, after the stabilization focus of the First Hundred Days.[2]

.   .   .

There are ample volumes that recount or summarize the impact of the Great Depression on the people and economy of the United States. There are few book-length publications that recount and recreate the misery of the Great Depression in Michigan. There are none that document, with both quantitative precision and subdued but real passion, a substantial revival of Michigan's vital economic signs in barely one hundred days. Acting with urgent swiftness and a high degree of coordination, the county, city, and state governments of Michigan, in concert with the federal government, demonstrated that democratic governments could address and take decisive actions to begin healing economic desperation. The subtext of this report is therefore the theme of how the people of Michigan and the United States chose democracy over dictatorship as the road to renewal, unlike Germany and Japan.

The only state-level document known to report on this renewal of economic democracy is *Civil Works Administration in the State of Michigan, November 17, 1933–March 31, 1934: A Report of Activities and Accomplishments*. It was published by the Michigan State Emergency Welfare Relief Commission, designated under federal authority as the State Civil Works Administration Board. This definitive report, so far as I know, never circulated outside the state, county, and federal agencies directly involved, although copies were distributed to a few state libraries, such as the State Library of Michigan and Michigan State College.[3] The report was filed with the Federal Civil Works Administration, and copies were distributed to selected State of Michigan departments and counties. It is not even clear that it was distributed to all or most of the counties. This document is foundational and magisterial in reporting the economic rebirth of Michigan. These are words rarely applied to reports of government agencies, especially at the state or local level, and they are chosen with care. With this publication, we make the CWA report available to a wider public, including government officials, legislators, teachers and scholars, and general readers with interest in this deeply troubled, and yet inspiring, time in our history.

.   .   .

Why not leave coverage of this painful subject to the general national histories of the Depression and New Deal era? Michigan experienced the misery of the Great Depression with distinctive and unwelcome severity, a distinction it would gladly have yielded to others. Unlike any other state, with the possible exception of New York, Michigan suffered a triple paralysis, briefly characterized earlier and well recognized in the CWA report, instead of the more widespread pattern of agricultural and industrial crisis, combined with severe but not complete bank closings.

First, Michigan's manufacturing sector, led by the nationally and internationally vital automobile industry, suffered horrific declines in industrial production and employment. In the bellwether automobile industry, for example, total domestic vehicle production plummeted from 5,337,000 in 1929 to 1,332,000 in 1932, a catastrophic and unprecedented decline of 75 percent. During the same period, the wholesale value of vehicle sales dropped 78 percent, compounding the already crushing effect of production declines.[4] In a time when being jobless could soon mean hunger or even homelessness, unemployment in Michigan reached levels more extreme than most other states. This fact is indicated and to some extent borne out by the definitive unemployment data of the 1930 census, which showed the early impact of the stock market crash of 1929, but gave only a hint of the unfolding catastrophe, which would take another three years to fully manifest.

Michigan's place as a leading industrial state can be seen in the acute differential between unemployment rates in Michigan and the United States as a whole. Michigan's unemployment rate in 1930, at 8.2 percent, was 64 percent higher than the national rate of 5 percent. This distressing differential would continue through late 1932 and early 1933, haunting major industrial cities like Detroit. Detroit approached unemployment levels nearing 50 percent. In mining areas of the central and western Upper Peninsula of Michigan, nearly 80 percent of miners lost their jobs, decimating whole communities.[5]

Second, Michigan's banking structure almost completely collapsed by late 1932 and early 1933, adding a banking stroke to an industrial heart attack for Michigan's already desperate economic situation. Some two hundred banks were already closed in Michigan in early 1933, and Detroit functioned with only six banks, of which the two largest were extremely unstable. Governor William Comstock feared that mounting withdrawals threatened total collapse of the banking system and declared a full Michigan bank holiday on February 11, 1933. He extended it indefinitely a week later, with allowance for limited withdrawals. The Michigan banking system was entirely shut down from then on until after March 4, 1933, the day Franklin D. Roosevelt was inaugurated, thus compounding Michigan's Depression destitution. No state had more reason than Michigan to be fearful; none had more reason to listen closely when Roosevelt declared in his inaugural address that "the only thing we have to fear is fear itself."

Third, Michigan's industrial and financial misery was further compounded by the weather. The harsh winter of 1933–34 presented substantial parts of the state with snow up to five feet deep and frost up to six feet deep in ground that usually had to be shoveled and excavated for CWA projects. Shovel handles often broke in frozen earth; however, the alternative was broken timetables or even lost projects and the jobs they provided.

Destitution and hardship were so extreme that they often break through the clear and dispassionate language of the CWA report.

Against the backdrop of the bitter harshness of the Great Depression, this interpretive essay highlights the purpose, structure, and almost entirely positive impact of the work and programs of the CWA in Michigan. The essay thus has a dual purpose. First, it provides the reader an overview of the contents of the report, closely aligned with the actual text. Second, it is intended to highlight the report's specific and proven resources for those who ponder the problem of investing in productive jobs in times of economic hardship and desperation.

From Prosperity to Depression: Background of the Civil Works Administration

In the half century between the end of the Civil War and its entry into World War I, the United States moved from the condition of a nation exhausted and almost broken to an industrial dynamo, envied by European nations that once scorned it. Its manufacturing strength grew rapidly behind the double shield of high peacetime domestic investment and protective tariffs. It was also substantially fed by the opening of western lands and continuous large-scale immigration.

The industrial growth during this time was unrelenting though at times uneven, and was drastically disrupted by the economic hardship and unemployment of the Panic of 1893. In September, the American Federation of Labor, under the leadership of Samuel Gompers, addressed the jobs crisis in its "Certain Fundamental Truths" resolution. It called upon the New York City government, as well as the New York governor and U.S. president, to make "appropriations for immediate relief and public employment." The resolution further declared "that as food obtained by work is more enjoyable than food obtained, even as a right, without work, we ask the city authorities to provide ways and means for the commencement and continuance of public works, and the employment of the new unemployed directly and not by contract."[6] Neither the resolution nor the idea of work relief was taken up at the time. The idea of directly linking relief with productive work lay dormant and mostly unneeded for forty years, as the United States prospered and grew without major depressions, until Franklin D. Roosevelt was inaugurated as president and Harry Hopkins joined his administration.

Two Decades of Industrial Growth

Sustained and even accelerated industrial investment and capital formation powered re-covery from the Panic of 1893. Unhindered by excess imports, foreign trade deficits, and accumulated foreign debt for anything but railroad investment, the American industrial economy grew rapidly from the late 1890s until 1921, with brief recessionary interruptions in 1907 and 1921. American manufacturing employment enjoyed its fastest growth during this time, under two progressive Republican presidents, Theodore Roosevelt and William Howard Taft, and a sometimes progressive Democratic president, Woodrow Wilson. Manufacturing jobs doubled in the first two decades of the new century and established American industrial preeminence, the permanent foundation of all military preeminence.[7] Notably, the fastest and most sustainable manufacturing employment growth took place in peacetime, not during World War I, and perhaps surprisingly, not during the 1920s up to the crash of 1929. By focusing our attention on productive employment, especially in the manufacturing sector, we will more fully understand underlying weakness in the American economy of the 1920s, and we also gain valuable insight into why the Axis powers made the fatal error of underestimating American industry on the eve of World War II.

World War I

Once the United States entered World War I, manufacturing industry provided both a bedrock of production strength and a decisive material and logistical shift in the balance of power between the Allied and Central Powers. It would again be decisive in World War II. On April 6, 1917, the New York Times published a memorable landmark of U.S. industrial strength and employment when it reported the U.S. declaration of war in a rare eight-column triple banner headline. The headline read as follows: "House, at 3:12 A.M., Votes for War, 373 to 50; $3,000,000,000 Asked for Army of 1,000,000; Nation's Gigantic Resources Mobilized." The sub-headline is striking and revealing: "32,000 Plants Offered; No Nation Ever Had Such Enormous Resources for Waging War." The lead paragraph of the article fully and forcefully expanded the headline: "Actual and potential resources which, all told, probably never have been equaled by those of any other nation in the history of the world, are brought into the great war under the American flag." The New York Times specifically celebrated American "industrial resources incomparably the greatest in the world, already mobilized for public service."[8] No finer, more accurate tribute could have been written to the manufacturing dynamo that the United States had created in the decades leading to World War I. This high praise from the New York Times reminds discerning readers of its tradition going back to the Civil War of celebrating industry in times of military peril and triumph, but being frequently critical of the protective tariffs that nurtured the industrial economy in peacetime. American industrial investment after the Civil War both created American industrial supremacy and allowed incomparable industrial resources to be accumulated before World War I. Equally important, American industrial growth and resources provided the essential foundation for the expansive growth of the middle class through the 1920s.

The Crash Decade

The three presidential administrations from 1921 through early 1933 were Republican, resembling in duration only the Republican domination of the presidency between 1900 and 1912. The three presidents—Warren G. Harding, Calvin Coolidge, and Herbert Hoover—took a much more restrictive view of the proper role of the federal government in the economy than did their predecessor progressive republicans, Theodore Roosevelt and Taft. Harding, Coolidge, and Hoover nonetheless took an expansive view of subsidizing business indirectly through tax cuts and through support of Federal Reserve Board policies of generous and eventually lethal credit expansion. Economists often call this a tight fiscal policy coupled with support of expansive monetary policy. The three presidents focused primarily on tax cuts mostly benefitting capital and the wealthy and least supportive to incomes of wage earners and the middle class. The one major cluster of exceptions to this policy was Republican initiatives and support for the troubled farm sector, suffering from the debt burden assumed for expansion during World War I.

Republican credit policy was rooted in determination to give all possible leeway and support to the financial sector and its patron saints, the investment bankers of Wall Street. Progressive reform lawyer Louis Brandeis, appointed to the United States Supreme Court by President Wilson in 1916, described this powerful interest group as the "Financial Oligarchy."[9] The stated and substantially achieved goals of these three administrations were to minimize regulation of the financial economy and indirectly boost employment and production through tax cuts. These achievements contributed to elevation of the stock market, at least through September 1929. From 1924 through 1929, the Dow Jones Industrial Average of stocks, then and now a popular index of stock values, set record highs. From 1927 through early September 1929, the index more than doubled, rising from 156.41 at the end of January 1927, to 381.17 in September 1929,[10] far exceeding the real growth of the production economy during the same period. Other stock market measures showed similar patterns of more than doubling during the comparable period.

The Republican romance with the financial sector proved to be the fatal attraction of the 1920s, a love affair which ultimately proved catastrophic. The steady growth of the stock market, which far outstripped the growth of the production sector of the economy after 1927, was considered by the three presidential administrations to be fundamentally healthy, defining a new era of perpetual prosperity, instead of being a distorted, out of control credit and debt bubble.

The consequences were cataclysmic. Alan Greenspan, past chair of the Federal Reserve Board, provided the clearest explanation and criticism of the operation and consequences of excessive credit expansion:

> When business in the United States underwent a mild contraction in 1927, the Federal Reserve created more paper reserves in the hope of forestalling any possible bank reserve shortage. *The excess credit which the Fed pumped into the economy spilled over into the stock market- triggering a fantastic speculative boom.* Belatedly, Federal Reserve officials attempted to sop up the excess reserves and finally succeeded in braking the boom. But it was too late: by 1929 the speculative imbalances had become so overwhelming that the attempt precipitated a sharp retrenching and a consequent demoralizing of business confidence. As a result, the American economy collapsed . . . The world economies plunged into the Great Depression of the 1930's.[11]

With the exception of the beginnings of a federal highway construction program and Hoover's initiation of the Hoover Dam on the Colorado River, a project that would be completed during the early New Deal of the Roosevelt administration,[12] there were no notable infrastructure or other major federal investments such as occurred during the World War I mobilization, and relief programs were regarded as state and local responsibilities.

In a discussion of American productive growth and decline, to speak of the "Roaring Twenties" is a misnomer, even if we stopped our discussion with the financial blue skies of the stock market in the summer of 1929. Although often used by historians, the phrase belies the fact that they focus primarily on the financial asset inflation reflected by the stock market rather than on the significant weaknesses and vulnerabilities of the underlying production economy. After the steady industrial growth from 1895 to 1920, the production economy as a whole was ready for consolidation, especially after the intense production spurt of World War I.

The important point to keep in mind here is that at any given time there are two economies operating side by side, a financial economy and a production economy. When the economic system is running in a healthy and sustainable way, the two economic sectors function in a dynamic balance with each other. In a healthy economy, the banker and the industrialist work productively in tacit, sometimes explicit, tandem, with limited regulation and assistance from the federal and state governments. But if the financial sector is favored over the productive industrial sector, serious, even lethal, distortions occur.

In the 1920s, somewhat surprisingly, industrial employment was essentially stagnant, even before the stock market bubble burst. In the Harding-Coolidge-early Hoover era, the industrial economy, as opposed to the financial economy, first weakened, then wobbled, and then spurted briefly, and by late 1929 essentially returned to the level of 1920. From 1920 through 1929, manufacturing employment in the industrial economy managed a miniscule growth of 46,000 jobs, from 11,013,000 in 1920 to 11,059,000 in 1929, hardly a roar, offset by rapid growth in construction employment, which more than doubled from 1,582,000 to 3,340,000.[13] The federal government did little to provide or stimulate manufacturing employment through this period.

We can draw a useful contrast between the Harding, Coolidge, and Hoover administrations on the one hand, and the Theodore Roosevelt and Taft administrations, on the other. The 1920s Republican presidents effectively favored finance over industry, while Roosevelt and Taft both favored regulated industry over finance. Roosevelt and Taft achieved a more stable and sustainable result, with the manufacturing economy enjoying vigorous growth, laying the essential foundation for World War I weapons and munitions production.

More than the Gains of the 1920s Were Destroyed

In the twelve years of Republican presidents,1921–33, the building and the bursting of the financial asset bubble returned per capita gross national product back to 1906 levels. The inflation of the 1920s stock market bubble brought real per capita gross domestic product, a measure of family and personal prosperity, to $6899 per capita in 1929 before its lethal crash to the Depression low of $4777 in 1933, a plunge of more than 30 percent and below the level of 1906.[14] The parasitic stock market roar ended up erasing almost one-third of American productive prosperity, achieved over a quarter century by the American economy.

Other standard measures of business and financial activity fared as badly or worse in the between late 1929 and 1933. In this grim period, manufacturing employment plummeted 33.6 percent from 11,059,000 at its 1929 peak to 7,348,000 in 1932. This appalling level was only slightly above the 7,278,000 manufacturing job level of 1905, the first year of President Theodore Roosevelt's second term in office. In other words, the manufacturing job gains of a twenty-six year period were wiped out with the stock market collapse.

Construction employment fared even worse, cratering 66.6 percent, declining from 3,340,000 in 1929 to a 1933 low of 1,114,000 in 1933. Construction employment dropped below 1900 levels, although how far is unknown because the historical statistics series we utilize began at 1900.[15] We can state, however, that all the construction employment gains of the early twentieth century disappeared after the crash.

Other measures of business, finance and earnings, little known and rarely publicized, also show that the crash and Depression destroyed far more than the economic gains of the 1920s. Agricultural and manufacturing employment were comparable, ranging between 10.4 million and 11 million. Income derived from agriculture declined 66.6 percent, from its modest 1925 peak of $9.05 billion, already below 1920 levels, to $3.04 billion in 1932, a catastrophe in itself. But a far worse long-term income measure quickly emerged: Farm income in 1932 had fallen to a level virtually identical with the 1900 farm income level of $3.034 billion, mining income fell below 1907 levels, and construction income fell to 1901 levels. Almost a third of a century of income gains in vital agricultural and industrial sectors vaporized when the 1929 bubble burst.[16]

Maybe the most revealing measure of economic damage, and one of the most rarely referenced, is the Census Bureau concept of net capital formation, drawing on data developed by Simon Kuznets, which cratered from an annual average of $4,711 millions during the 1924–33 decade and spanned the crash, to $1,239 millions annually during the Depression decade of 1929–38.[17] Capital formation, simply stated, is the process of converting savings into investment in tangible assets. According to the classic Kuznets study, net capital formation in the American economy during the Depression decade had collapsed below the $1309 million annual average of the 1879–88 decade, the worst in a half century.

Rising from the Wreckage: The New Deal, 1933–34

The economic destruction facing the New Deal was therefore deeper and more damaging than the incoming administration even realized. Stabilizing and reviving the stricken economy thus represented an achievement far more difficult and substantial than initially recognized. Roosevelt's call for a New Deal for the American people reawakened the 1893 labor resolution "Certain Fundamental Truths," mentioned earlier. In advocating direct federal and governmental employment in place of relief payments, it brought forward an idea which had lain dormant for more than three decades.

Roosevelt was inaugurated as president on March 4, 1933. At this time, the American and world economies were paralyzed. Not only were 25 percent of non–farm working Americans without jobs, but the national banking system had, for all practical purposes, ceased to function. Some 80 percent of U.S. banks were shut down.[18] In the days before his inauguration, the president-elect was urged by many prominent political figures, including Walter Lippmann, to declare a full national emergency and to confront the Depression by decree, meaning executive orders without specific congressional debate or authorization. These calls, often couched in the evasive language of American euphemism, amounted to appeals for Roosevelt to assume dictatorial powers.[19] He refused.

The only good news for Roosevelt was that the magnitude of the catastrophe gave him the political support, both congressional and popular, to override the longstanding oligarchic axiom that financial privilege should be disturbed, taxed, or regulated as little as politically possible. One of Roosevelt's first major actions was to declare a formal bank holiday, in order to reform and reorganize the banking system. He then appointed Harry Hopkins as the administrator of FERA, to throw a lifeline to the 25 percent of the American workforce without jobs, food, and hope.

The Pivotal Contribution of Harry Hopkins

Where and how does Harry Hopkins fit in this drama? Hopkins assumed important responsibilities for Roosevelt at both the state and federal levels from 1931 until Roosevelt's sudden death on April 12, 1945. Roosevelt, as governor of New York in 1931–32, created the New York Temporary Emergency Relief Administration (TERA) to create jobs for unemployed workers. He appointed Hopkins as the director of TERA in October 1931. They both were committed to programs of work relief and to treating the unemployed as workers with skills rather than as dependents on doles, thus upholding the workers' dignity and morale as much as possible.

On May 19, 1933, Roosevelt appointed Hopkins to take charge of federal unemployment relief efforts as administrator of the newly created FERA. On his first day at work in the as yet unorganized and chaotic FERA office, Hopkins disbursed over $5 million in grants to states that had submitted proper applications for unemployment relief. This swift action, which would become a pattern for Hopkins through his FERA and CWA service, earned him a front-page picture in the next morning's *Washington Post*, with the caption "Money Flies."[20]

Creation of the Civil Works Administration

What happened next constituted one of the most dramatic highlights of American peacetime economic history. Six months into the Roosevelt administration, Hopkins, President Roosevelt, and his top advisers sensed momentum stalling. The economy was still weak, with employment growth feeble, and manufacturing production, particularly in the automotive sector, crucial for Michigan, was flagging again after some recovery in early 1933.

Crucially, Hopkins was convinced that emergency money relief—the unemployment compensation of its time—was not clearly focused enough to jump-start new hiring for the American economy. The relief payments and programs sponsored by state and local governments and by charitable groups, such as the ones in Michigan, were mitigating some starvation and homelessness by direct relief payments, but they did not directly create jobs. Further, the limited funds for these programs, both public and private, had been expended steadily through 1931 and 1932 as the Depression deepened, and were nearly exhausted by late 1933, four years after the crash of 1929. Meanwhile, national and state Republican leaders, still following the Hoover model despite his landslide defeat, were advocating strict economy and austerity.[21] Most unemployed people on relief were still malnourished.[22] Hopkins further realized that too many of the Public Works Administration projects being administered by Harold Ickes were only slowly putting workers on the jobs and would not provide paychecks until after the winter of 1933–34.

Impatient and visionary, Hopkins knew that drastic action was needed and needed quickly. Faced with a palpably slow recovery and the knowledge that Roosevelt would not support any program without support from organized labor, Hopkins deployed the vision of the American Federation of Labor's 1893 "Certain Fundamental Truths" resolution. in a successful effort to enlist Roosevelt's support for a program of direct federal employment. He persuaded Roosevelt to create the CWA, which brought to life the idea of fast relief through direct federal employment for productive work.

On Thursday, November 9, 1933, at the urging of Hopkins and other administration officials, Roosevelt issued Executive Order 6420-B, creating the CWA, under the FERA, with Hopkins as its director. Its stated purpose was "to provide regular work on public works at regular wages for unemployed persons able and willing to work." It had a three-fold mission: to generate quick, short-term job growth through productive employment; to get money circulating fast through the economy; and to begin a recovery in the industrial sector by using public infrastructure investments, thereby stimulating investment and hiring in the industrial sector.[23] Crucially, it did not follow the traditional, much slower, and less certain financial pathway of funneling money into and through banks, hoping they would make loans to businesses and further hoping businesses would hire additional workers.

One week later Hopkins presented his plan for direct federal employment to a hopeful but apprehensive nation and put it immediately into action. By involving states, counties, cities, and other local governments, Hopkins and the network of government agencies under the CWA, put 4 million Americans, skilled and unskilled, to work on some 180,000 projects, in the next four months. Hopkins and Roosevelt in effect organized a full-scale jobs mobilization under federal sponsorship and with primary federal funding. There is no comparable peacetime economic program or achievement in Michigan or United States history. The Michigan CWA report commented that it was "appropriately described as the greatest welfare undertaking ever known to the world."

How was so much achieved with such incredible speed? And how were 4 million jobs created across the United States in four months, 165,000 of them in Michigan? Most of these jobs were created and paychecks issued within barely sixty days. The key to answering the question of speed of implementation is that the CWA formally and authoritatively joined federal and state Depression relief structures and transformed them into work relief structures instead of ordinary welfare relief structures.

The CWA in Michigan

In its regular session earlier in 1933, the Michigan Legislature had created the Michigan State Emergency Welfare Relief Commission. A commission of three members appointed by Governor Comstock was given statutory responsibility over "the distribution of the state and Federal funds used for the relief of destitution or unemployment within any and all parts of the state." "Any and all" was quickly operationally defined and interpreted to mean cities, villages, and especially the eighty-three counties of the state. A comprehensive framework was already in place in Michigan and elsewhere across the country when the CWA came into existence in November.

It was immediately after the presidential executive order of November 9 that Hopkins announced that under the CWA, state relief organizations would be repurposed and named as "state civil works administrations." The Michigan Emergency Welfare Relief Commission was changed into the Michigan Civil Works Administration. With a stroke of the pen and federal funding, its purpose changed from subsistence relief transfer payments to productive employment at reasonable wages.

The critical key to understanding the swiftness with which 165,000 workers were employed on 12,000 different projects is the pivotal role of the county relief structures. On November 13, under Hopkin's direct orders, which were conveyed through Fred R. Johnson, then State Relief administrator, all the existing county relief commissions in Michigan—and all other states—were designated as local CWA administrations. This created a direct conduit for project selection, funding, and general administration between the federal government and the local levels. The creation of county-level CWA administrations proved to be a stroke of administrative genius for executing the federal goal of 4 million jobs in four months.

The impact of the county-level CWA administrations is described with enthusiastic candor in the concluding chapter of the report. It explains:

> The CWA venture was hastily conceived and hastily executed. The latter was possible because the substance of the President's order was substantially "put men to work," and the governing rules were in essence, *"Pick a project, hire men, and start to work."* The approval of projects was therefore virtually the only possible source of delay (aside from a dearth of tools); and since the spirit of the CWA readily caught on, *all obstacles were surmounted with surprising facility.*[24]

As we look more deeply at the all-important question of how the CWA achieved so much with such incredible speed, we find structural and administrative answers. When we consider the overall structure of American government, the structural answer emerges quickly in one word: *counties*. On first reading of the CWA report we find an almost diffident description of how an existing state and national structure of county-level relief organizations were transformed into CWA work relief hiring agencies. It is tempting to pass over this lightly, on the assumption that federal funding energized the county bodies. Funding is always important, but if a program is to create 165,000 productive jobs in a few weeks, a truly gigantic and well-focused project planning and allocation structure and process must have been substantially in place by November 1933, before the dollars could reach the projects and workers. As detailed earlier, the basic structure and procedures were already in place in Michigan and the rest of the country's more than 3,000 counties, and their related relief structures and expertise. The CWA Michigan Report takes frequent notice of their vital role.

Paramount Role of Counties in CWA Structure

The proof of this becomes clear when we examine this report both minutely and comprehensively: we find that the word *county* is used 188 times in a report of 153 pages and 25 photographs. Sometimes the word has a simple use, as in "in each county." But the use of the word *county* is so varied and extensive that it reveals by repetition the vital role of counties in the CWA process and projects. Consider the following illustrative list of usages, in chapter order, which is short of being comprehensive by 176 citations:

- "County Sanatorium improvements"
- "Wayne County Places and Cities"
- "Such as county road commissions"
- "existing county relief commissions"
- "state and county road authorities"
- "83 County School Commissioners"
- "by County Administrators"
- "in the hands of the county authorities"
- "approved by the County Administration"
- "other municipalities of the county"
- "cleaning of county drains"
- "Ingham County CWA float in parade"

This list provides a quantitative illustration of the central importance of counties in the entire CWA structure and administration.

Impediments and Hurdles

The CWA in Michigan and other states worked against impediments and hurdles that in some eras and settings might have proven to be impassible barriers. But the severity and gravity of the Depression muted for years to come the political opposition of those who advocated and often implemented austerity or "strict economy" as the proper cure for the Great Depression. Most potentially strong opposition had been voted out of all key levels of elective office in the 1932 elections. In Michigan and elsewhere the general political mood was a call for action against the roots and ugly fruits of destitution and the Depression. In Michigan, the 1932 election resulted in a Democratic governor and replaced overwhelming Republican dominance of the House of Representatives and Senate with narrow Democratic majorities.[25]

The CWA report emphasizes its own achievement by skillfully weaving into its overall account descriptions, often vivid ones, of the hurdles it faced and overcame in putting Michigan back to work. Harsh weather, shortages of tools, and shortages of some materials, were the most frequent obstacles to keeping workers working and completing projects. Project selection could be mostly completed irrespective of weather. The report speaks directly and simply on this issue: "CWA operations were carried on under the most adverse weather conditions." The exceptionally harsh weather slowed the hiring of workers, and project completion, but never completely halted it, despite the winter of 1933–34 being one of the most severe in several decades. The report referred to it as "unusually severe weather conditions" and "extremely cold weather." In particular, the report discusses in several places the construction problems created in northern Michigan, especially the Upper Peninsula, by snow three to five feet deep, and by frost that penetrated the ground to depths up to six feet.

Second, a "dearth of tools" was one of the most unusual impediments ever to arise on a peacetime civil works project, as well as one of the first significant indicators that the desperate need for productive work was significantly relieved by the swift implementation of CWA programs. The tool shortage was altogether a creation of the determination, quantity, and range of CWA construction undertakings, and it amounts to a peacetime equivalent of frequent side effects of wartime mobilization. The report notes with satisfaction that each county administrator, once notified of his CWA employee quota, had to place tools and materials on the job forthwith. This "resulted in the placing of great numbers of rush orders with dealers."

The report further notes that "The shovel market in Detroit, for example, was completely depleted, and tool delivery in Ingham County was delayed as long as two weeks at times. Even manufacturers were unable to meet demands within required time limits." These were not spot shortages; shortages were widespread across Michigan, as well as the United States, in the early weeks of CWA projects because of the enormous demand for construction equipment and tools generated by the tens of thousands of projects throughout Michigan and across the nation, and the report refers frequently to them.

Third, further evidence of the economic recovery is seen in the widespread shortages of materials other than tools. Shortages of materials and supplies are a frequent drumbeat in the CWA report. For example, materials and supplies were "extremely scarce" in Ingham County and were accompanied by manufacturers' backups and delivery delays. Work was frequently held up, and men were forced to remain idle. The speed and magnitude of the peak employment of over 165,000 workers—which was reached in almost 60 days from the national launching of the CWA—on 12,000 projects in four months, stands as a permanent tribute to administrative determination and worker zeal in project completion.

The Immense and Tangible Results

The CWA made an immense contribution to the survival and recovery of U.S. democracy from the depths of the Great Depression. Chapter 5 of the report, titled simply "Projects Executed," documents the projects undertaken and completed in Michigan. The report describes the range and types of projects in matter-of-fact prose, often eloquent without intention. We should remind ourselves that almost every one of these projects was actively sought and often campaigned for by the communities and counties involved, from Alger to Wayne, from Iron Mountain to Detroit. The report emphasizes project eligibility criteria and is understandably silent on the local prioritization of projects and on the campaigns for project selection. Project prioritization at the local level, as well as local support for particular project, were outside the scope of CWA concern, as long as basic project criteria were being met.

The simplest evidence of the scope and achievement of the CWA in Michigan is the fact that chapter 5, "Projects Executed," and its companion chapter 8, "CWA in Detroit and Wayne County," comprises nearly sixty pages in the original report. When chapter 7, "FERA Activities," is included, seventy-five pages of the report, nearly one-half of the volume, is dedicated to project descriptions. The report thus documents the Michigan portion of a peacetime public investment in tangible capital assets of permanent value without precedent or matching successor for a four-month period in American and world history. It deserves to be called the Second Hundred Days, although the peak levels of employment and project advancement were achieved in under one hundred days.

Chapters 5 and 8 offer a survey of the wide range of projects undertaken and completed by the CWA. By far most of the projects were locally administered and were subject to the jurisdiction of the civil works administrators of the respective counties and other local authorities. In the report's own words, "The following tabulation indicates a few of the more common types of work:"

CONSTRUCTED	IMPROVED
Roads	Drains
Sewers	Schools
Breakwaters	Roads
Bridges	Parks
Retaining Walls	Playgrounds
Drains	Publicly owned utilities
Public Buildings	Sewers
Sidewalks	Sidewalks
	Public Buildings
	Water supply

The report then describes twenty-one specific and varied projects in detail, by type, place, and scope. The group includes only a small sample of locally administered projects, taken from thirteen general classifications of local projects carried on within Michigan. Other common types of projects included surveys and services required by local public departments, such as police, fire, health, schools and libraries, and even zoos.

Chapter 5 also summarizes another major category of projects: those administered directly by the state. This category included numerous projects supervised directly by particular state departments or authorities. They ranged from state aeronautics projects to vocational schools.

Employers Vote with Their Payrolls

The effects of all the CWA projects were electrifying. They found deep emotional, economic, and political resonance across the entire state, and virtually the entire population. The hopeful public mood created by the legislation of Roosevelt's First Hundred Days was revived and amplified, a point demonstrable in the employment and production statistics cited earlier. Almost 100,000 Michigan relief cases were closed due to CWA projects. Hence our characterization of the CWA period as The Second Hundred Days. Employers began to take hope and rebuild private payrolls, especially in manufacturing. The emphasis with the CWA was on speed: project approval, payment of wages, and payments to vendors. An advantage of this short-lived but well-focused work relief blitzkrieg, not fully realized at the time, was that its swift and decisive administration explicitly discouraged execution delays and minimized opportunities for corruption and construction of political and bureaucratic fiefdoms. Direct and swift federal expenditure to hungry wage earners and industry became high octane fuel for restarting the American economic engine.

Most important, the public began to take hope, and started looking to the future, public morale rising notably "at the most critical period in the history of Detroit." Public letters, newspaper articles and endorsements, and the overwhelming demand for CWA projects all evidenced the hopeful shift in the public mood. In March 1932 the Communist Party had drawn 30,000 attendees to its Detroit rally; in March 1934, as the CWA program drew to a conclusion, a similar party rally drew about 100 persons. The corroborating verdict of the 1934 elections will be discussed later.

The effect on citizen morale was positive and almost incalculable. At a time when many other nations at the time, notably Germany and Japan, were taken down the path of dictatorship and war by their elites, the CWA was a remarkable institution history because it gave Americans a constructive, democratic, and peaceful pathway to economic recovery, and the American political and financial elite gave almost full assent. Its effects on workers, families, businesses, communities, and a full spectrum of governmental institutions and activities were almost entirely beneficial. As the report states, "The improvement in morale, both among CWA workers and citizens in general, was as remarkable as it was urgently needed."

Conclusion

The two concluding paragraphs of the CWA Report of Activities and Accomplishments in Michigan merit direct and full quotation. The administrators of the report richly deserve to be heard in their own words:

> Both the physical assets and the alleviation of unemployment distress, which were brought to the State of Michigan through the CWA program, were of extreme value. On the one hand, the state is richer by $45,000,000.00 worth of needed public improvements, which stand as worthy monuments to a bleak, dark period in American life when organized planning triumphed over seemingly insurmountable obstacles. More important, 167,000 needy persons were employed on an equitable basis and thus enabled to earn $36,000,000.00. The

significance of the latter as a medium of eased welfare burden, improved business, and—most important—enhanced morale, independence, and self-respect, is not readily overestimated.

The judgment must prevail that the CWA enjoyed the wide public favor with which it was endowed in Michigan because it definitely and satisfactorily alleviated a critical condition.

Afterword

When the struggling public, expert peers, and President Roosevelt all agreed on the immense and lasting contribution of the CWA, we should take careful notice. Let's briefly examine two specific developments, one economic and one political, after the conclusion of the CWA at the end of March, 1934. Going forward, the CWA became the Public Works Administration and the Works Progress Administration, continuing the momentum and morale of the CWA up to the outbreak of World War II, when direct war mobilization provided millions of jobs, but for purposes of combat and destruction

Manufacturing Jobs Surpass 1929

When Roosevelt and Hopkins took up their jobs in March 1933, American manufacturing employment had dropped to 1906 levels, a loss of nearly a quarter century of U.S. industrial job gains in just three years. But the twenty-six years of manufacturing job losses were almost entirely recovered in the four years of Roosevelt's first term, rising 41.8 percent from the abysmal 1932 levels, not seen since 1906, to 9,827,000 in 1936.[26] We should note that this growth, substantially fueled by the CWA projects, was by far the greatest four-year manufacturing job growth in American history to that time, and is comparable to the growth during the 1940–45 period of World War II. As Roosevelt completed the first year of his second term in 1937, manufacturing payrolls rose above their 1929 peak levels by year-end, reaching 10,794,000.

Endorsing jobs at the polls, the public verdict was overwhelmingly supportive of the Roosevelt focus on direct job creation, launched through the CWA, rather than money relief in the form of unemployment compensation. The Democrats won a landslide Congressional victory in 1934, and another landslide presidential and congressional victory in 1936. Both elections, as well as the fact that *American industry endorsed the CWA with its payroll growth*, are powerful and irrefutable testimony to the superior economic and political value of focusing Depression-era employment recovery on direct and swift job creation rather than on subsidizing unemployment.

But this remarkable achievement, especially considering the 1905 level of manufacturing employment at the low point of the Depression, was little noted and readily forgotten by critics of the New Deal, who in the late 1930s included foreign leaders Adolf Hitler and Hideki Tojo. In other words, the loss of twenty-eight years of manufacturing employment was more than recovered in barely five years.[27] The Democrats, often with labor support or acquiescence, later severed the New Deal bond of productive work with relief payments. Some commentators, critics, and scholars, more or less across the political spectrum, would say it was and remains a mistake to sever this bond and replace work relief with direct unemployment compensation.

The evaluation of the CWA by other governmental agencies at that time and later was also strongly favorable, to judge by the limited known publications. A key example is an important U.S. Army study, sometimes called the Lee report of 1934, which praised the economic mobilization as accomplishing in four months what the Army had needed almost two years to accomplish during World War I. The full text of this Army report is readily available in specialized documents on the New Deal.[28] It gave generous praise to both the administration and achievements of the CWA.

Photo Gallery

A valuable photo gallery included in the report provides visual witness to the work of the CWA. It comprises photos of typical CWA projects in Michigan, ranging from superb before and after photos of the rebuilding of the Old Rapid River Bridge in Kalkaska, to a Hippopotamus and African Bird Exhibit Building at the Detroit Zoological Gardens, to an Ingham County CWA float in the City of Lansing seventy-fifth anniversary celebration on May 18, 1934. The selection shows the immense variety of capital investment projects completed in the four months of intense activity by the CWA.

■ NOTES

Unless otherwise noted, the information and quotations in this introduction come from the report published in this volume.

1. United States Bureau of the Census, *Historical Statistics of the United States: Colonial Times to 1970*, republished as Ben J. Wattenberg, *The Statistical History of the United States: From Colonial Times to the Present*, (New York: Basic Books, 1976), p. 716. Hereafter cited as *SHUSCTP*.

2. Similar CWA summary documents exist for every state, although they are difficult to locate, even with skilled assistance from the staff of the National Archives.

3. Knowing that the document existed from research in the Franklin Delano Roosevelt Archives at

Hyde Park, New York, I first located a copy of this report in the Michigan State University Library and subsequently located draft and final versions of the report at the State Library of Michigan. I do not know if it was distributed to any city libraries. It almost certainly was distributed to at least a few governmental bodies of Wayne County, especially Detroit. The actual distribution of this report remains a prominent question.

4. *SHUSCTP*, p. 699 and passim. Also see David M. Kennedy, *Freedom from Fear: The American People in Depression and War, 1929–1945* (New York: Oxford University Press, 1999), ch. 6, esp. pp. 163–165.

5. Kennedy, *Freedom from Fear*, p. 87.

6. "'Certain Fundamental Truths': The AFL Protests Unemployment," History Matters: The U.S. Survey Course on the Web, http://historymatters.gmu.edu/d/5310.

7. The Census Bureau publishes annual manufacturing employment data starting with the year 1900. *SHUSCTP*, "Series D 127–141, Employees on Nonagricultural Payrolls, by Major Industry Divisions, 1900 to 1970," p. 137.

8. "House, at 3:12 A.M., Votes for War, 373 to 50; $3,000,000,000 Asked for Army of 1,000,000; Nation's Gigantic Resources Mobilized," *New York Times*, April 6, 1917, p. 1.

9. Louis D. Brandeis, *Other People's Money and How the Bankers Use It* (New York: St. Martin's Press, 1995), ch. 1, "Our Financial Oligarchy."

10. "Dow Jones History . . . 1920–1929," *The duCati Report* (blog), April 1, 2018, https://leduc998.wordpress.com/2008/05/15/dow-jones-history1920–1929.

11. Alan Greenspan, "Gold and Economic Freedom," *The Objectivist Newsletter*, 1966, reprinted in Ayn Rand, *Capitalism: The Unknown Ideal* (New York: New American Library, 1966). Emphasis added.

12. Kennedy, *Freedom from Fear*, p. 63.

13. United States Bureau of the Census, *Historical Statistics of the United States, 1789–1945* (Washington, D.C.: United States Bureau of the Census, 1949), "Series D 62–76, Industrial Distribution of Employed (NICB): 1900 to 1945," p.65. Hereafter cited as *HSUS, 1789–1945*.

14. The percentage of decline and the comparison year for the scope of decline are the important numbers here. See *Social Democracy for the 21ˢᵗ Century: A Realist Alternative to the Modern Left* (blog), http://socialdemocracy21stcentury.blogspot.com/2017. The source adjusted the original current dollar figures for the 1930s and early 1900s for intervening inflation to 1990 dollars.

15. *HSUS, 1789–1945*. Manufacturing and construction employment data, in somewhat different formats, are also provided in *SHUSCTP*, "Series D," pp. 144, 145, Series P 58–67, pp. 669–680.

16. HSUS, Series A 154–164. National Income—Realized Private Production Income by Industries (NICB): 1799 to 1938, p.14.

17. *HSUS, 1789–1945*, "Series A 198–207, Gross and Net National Product—Averages Per Year by Decades (Kuznets): 1869 to 1938," p. 15. We are here utilizing the Census Bureau and Kuznets definitions of both decade and net capital formation. In its Income: Series A, 101–207 Text Notes, the Census Bureau states (p. 8), "'Gross' capital formation [series A 199] includes producers'

durable goods whether for replacement or expansion, and 'net' capital formation [series A 200] includes only the output of *such goods representing expansion in the productive assets of the economy*" (emphasis added).

18. George Brown Tindall and David Emory Shi, *America: A Narrative History*, 8th ed. (New York: W.W. Norton and Co., 2010), p. 1083.

19. An extensive discussion of this issue, in the context of the climate of desperation in the United States and globally as the Depression passed its third anniversary, can be found in Jonathan Alter, *The Defining Moment: FDR's Hundred Days and the Triumph of Hope* (New York: Simon & Schuster, 2006).

20. George McJimsey, *Harry Hopkins* (Cambridge, MA: Harvard University Press, 1987), pp. 44–52.

21. Wilbur M. Brucker, "Inaugural Address," January 1, 1931. Wilber Brucker Collection, Library of Michigan, reprinted in Gleaves Whitney and Caroline Hoefferle, eds., *Messages of the Governors of Michigan*, vol.5, *1926–1941*. Mount Pleasant/East Lansing: Clark Historical Library/Michigan State University Press, 2003). Brucker called for "a sound program of strict and rigid economy in all governmental expenditures," and received strong Republican support for his sharply limited programs and tax policies (p. 104).

22. Kennedy, *Freedom from Fear*, p. 86. Vivid and still harrowing cases of hunger's widespread harm were described by Hopkins himself in his Depression-era book *Spending to Save* (New York: W. W. Norton and Co., 1936). One illustration is his description of child malnutrition on pages 50–51. Other illustrations are sprinkled throughout his book. Also see Kennedy, *Freedom from Fear*, ch. 6, "The Ordeal of the American People," esp. pp. 160–176.

23. "Civil Works Administration (CWA) (1933)," The Living New Deal, https://livingnewdeal.org/glossary/civil-works-administration-cwa-1933.

24. Emphasis added.

25. State of Michigan, *Michigan Official Directory and Legislative Manual* (Lansing: State of Michigan, 1933–34), pp. 266–269, 293–305, 306–317.

26. *SHUSCTP*, "Series D 127–141, Employees on Nonagricultural Payrolls, by Major Industry Divisions, 1900 to 1970," p. 137.

27. Ibid.

28. John C. R. Lee, Corps of Engineers, "The Federal Civil Works Administration," A Study Prepared for the Information of the War Department, ca. April 1934; unpublished typescript, from Harry Hopkins papers, reproduced in George McJimsey, ed., *Documentary History of the Franklin D. Roosevelt Presidency*, vol. 30, *FDR, Harry Hopkins, and the Civil Works Administration, Document 110* (Bethesda, MD: LexisNexis, 2006), pp. 562–585.

THE REPORT OF ACTIVITIES AND ACCOMPLISHMENTS OF THE CIVIL WORKS ADMINISTRATION IN MICHIGAN, NOVEMBER 1933–MARCH 1934

Foreword

The following pages are the record and report of the Civil Works Administration in Michigan during the winter of 1933–34. The document is, of course, not exhaustive. This is necessarily so, since a complete record of the unprecedented enterprise by which more than 165,000 persons in the state were enabled to earn wages aggregating about thirty-six million dollars in a period of 4½ months through work on about 12,000 projects of a public character, would be extensive indeed.

The first two chapters of this report comprise an introductory background. Succeeding chapters relate for the most part to detailed phases of the CWA itself.

Much of the material contained in Chapters V to VIII, inclusive, was prepared by the State officials, or the Michigan Emergency Relief Commission (and CWA) staff members, directly concerned with each project or activity discussed. These sections were edited prior to inclusion in the report in its present and final form.

CHAPTER I

Introduction

The pages of this chapter contain an introductory description of the State of Michigan. Attention is particularly centered upon those elements which had a direct or indirect bearing upon the CWA enterprise in the state.

Geography

Michigan, a north-central state, contains 57,980 square miles of area, which is 1.9% of the total area of the continental United States.[1] It ranks 22nd in area, among the states, and is the largest east of the Mississippi River except for Georgia.[2] the commonwealth is divided into an upper and lower peninsula, by the waters of the Great Lakes, the first named containing 29% of the total area of the state. Because the state is thus made up of two long and relatively narrow peninsulas, its farthermost points are great distances apart. The north and south dimension approximates 400 miles and the east and west length exceeds that distance appreciably. An idea of diagonal distances, moreover, may be gleaned from the fact that the westernmost tip of the upper peninsula is farther from

---

1. Michigan contains approximately 4% of the total population of the U.S.
2. The state ranks 7th in population.

Detroit than are Cedar Rapids, Iowa, St. Louis, Missouri, Ashville, North Carolina, Dover, Delaware, and Albany, New York.

Surface Geology

Being of glacial origin, the state has a slightly undulating surface made up of varying proportions of drift, sand, clay, gravel and boulders. Some areas of a rocky and mountainous character, in the Upper Peninsula, are an exception. About 25% of the state has been described as a deforested desert, by reason of barren soil and a short growing season. Over 10% is occupied by lakes and swamps, 50% of the area is in farms, ⅔ of which area is improved. Only 20% of the Upper Peninsula is in farms.

Climate

Considering the northerly location of the state, the climate of Michigan as a whole is moderate. The mean annual temperature of the state is 45°. This fact alone is, however, somewhat misleading because of the great temperature variations found in the northern and southern parts of the state at a given time. The ranges of the annual, January, and July mean temperatures are respectively 39°–49°, 19°–25°, and 65°–72°—the lower limit pertaining in each case to the northern part of the state. Since the northern section is subject to more extreme high temperatures than the southern section,[3] as evidenced by the incidence of the extreme high on record in a northerly location, it is apparent that a marked difference must exist in the extreme low temperatures of the northern and southern portions of the state.

Climatological records confirm this view. The range of extreme low temperatures extends from –15° to –49°. This marked difference between the extreme lows in different parts of the state is particularly noteworthy. It is not accounted for exclusively nor primarily by the north and south dimension of the state, but rather by the moderating influence of the Great Lakes. The prevailing winds being westerly, the western portion of the lower peninsula, particularly, enjoys moderated climate. The upper peninsula climate, where the prevailing winds are northwesterly, is on the other hand, but little affected by the lakes.

Except for the month of January, Michigan as a whole experienced the coldest winter in many years during the CWA period. The statement refers to average temperatures only;

---

3. The range of extreme high temperatures at various points in the state is 96°–108°.

in the Lansing area it is valid for a 20-year period. Eleven days of subzero weather were reported in the state during February alone.

The unusual severity of the winter in the state as a whole may be judged from the fact that the average temperatures during December, February, and March were respectively 1.3°, 7.5°, and 4.3° degrees below the respective normals of 25.1°, 20.0°, and 29.6°. The January average, however, exceeded the normal of 20.0° by 6.6°.

The effect of the severe winter upon the CWA is discussed in the final section of this chapter and at other points throughout the report.

Population

The population of Michigan is 4,842,325 persons according to the 1930 census. Certain subdivisions of the state contain residents as follows:

Detroit	1,568,662
Grand Rapids	168,592
Flint	156,492
Wayne County	1,888,946
State exclusive of Wayne Co.	2,953,379

Thirty-two percent of the population of the entire state is located in Detroit and 39% is located in Wayne County (including Detroit). The population density south of a line through the Saginaw Bay is more than four times that of the area north of such a line. The population center is thus located well towards the southern part of the state.

The division of population, as between urban and rural residents, is as follows:

	URBAN	RURAL
United States	56.2%	43.8%
"North"[4]	67.2	32.8
Michigan	68.2	31.8
Wayne County	75.1	24.9
Michigan exclusive of Wayne Co.	49.5	50.5

---

4. "North," as opposed to the "South" and "West," which are considered to comprise the remainder of the U.S.

Table I. Population, Nativity and Color Composition.

LOCALITY	NATIVE WHITE		FOREIGN WHITE		TOTAL WHITE		NEGRO		OTHER RACES	
	1920	1930	1920	1930	1920	1930	1920	1930	1920	1930
U.S.	76	77.8	13	10.9	89	88.7	9.9	9.7	1.1	1.7
Michigan	78.4	78.7	19.6	17.4	98.2	96.1	1.6	3.5	0.2	0.4
Detroit	66.7	66.4	29.1	25.5	95.8	91.9	4.1	7.7	0.1	0.4
Flint	81.6	82.5	16.5	13.4	98.1	95.9	1.9	3.7	—	0.4
Saginaw	80.6	80.1	18.7	13.8	99.3	93.8	0.5	3.5	0.2	2.7
River Rouge	74.6	67	23.9	20.3	98.5	87.3	1.5	12.4	—	0.3
Hamtramck	48.4	57	47.4	35.6	95.8	92.6	4.2	7.2	—	0.2
Ecorse	80.8	69.8	19	18.9	99.8	88.7	0.2	11.1	—	0.2

U.S. Census.

Michigan as a whole, it will be observed, conforms closely to the "North" but contains a larger urban population than the U.S. as a whole.

Certain aspects of the population composition are discussed under the heading next following.

Social and Racial Factors

A very large proportion of the settlers of Michigan came from New England and New York. Lesser numbers had been residents of Pennsylvania and other eastern states.

Some years ago an influx of foreign persons gave a marked foreign-born aspect to certain parts of the state. The data of Table I indicates that Michigan as a whole still has a high foreign-born population and that some communities have a remarkably large proportion of such residents.

More recently, the northward migration of large numbers of negroes has materially altered the character of some cities. The data of Table I bear on this point, also. While the percent represented by negroes, out of the entire population of the U.S. declined slightly in the 10-year period, it increased sharply in Michigan. Here the white population was greater by 27% in 1930, and the colored population greater by 182%. Much more startling changes, from the % viewpoint, occurred in Ecorse, River Rouge, and Saginaw.

Out of a colored population of 169,453 for the state, 71% resides in Detroit.[5] The negro population of the state increased by 109,371 persons from 1920 to 1930; 72% of this increment (or 79,228) occurred in Detroit.

---

5. 1930 Census.

Table II. Occupations of Gainfully Occupied Persons, 1930.

OCCUPATION	U.S.	MICHIGAN	DETROIT	FLINT	GRAND RAPIDS
Agriculture	21.4	12.8	0.3	0.5	0.7
Forestry & Fishing	0.5	0.7	—	—	—
Extraction of Minerals	2.0	1.1	0.1	—	0.1
Mfg.& Mech. Industries	28.9	40.8	48.5	58.3	41.6
Transportation & Communication	7.9	7.0	6.9	4.3	7.5
Trade	12.5	12.3	13.9	11.8	17.8
Public Service	1.8	1.8	2.4	1.7	1.6
Professional Service	6.7	6.4	6.2	5.9	7.9
Domestic & Personal Service	10.1	8.9	10.4	8.6	10.9
Clerical Occupations	8.2	8.2	11.3	8.9	11.8
Total	*100.0*	*100.0*	*100.0*	*100.0*	*100.0*

Figures represent % of total gainfully occupied persons, in each division). U.S. Census.

Occupations

Michigan is predominately a manufacturing state, as the data of Table II indicate. With the exception of a large manufacturing activity and a small farming activity, the occupations of the state parallel those of the country as a whole very closely.

Abundant resources in timber, iron, copper, and cheap water transportation are the likely factors which made Michigan the leading state in the manufacture of such products as automobiles, engines and waterwheels, threshing machines, and chemicals. Other products manufactured in very large volumes are furniture, foundry and machine shop products, and food preparations. The state is reported to contain over 8,000 manufacturing plants. Copper, iron ore, salt, and oil are prominent natural products.

More than half of all the products manufactured in the state are made in Detroit. The motor plants, foundries and machine shops, meat packing plants, and brass and bronze industries are centered here. The city is reported to contain upwards of 3,500 industries.[6]

The last U.S. Census reports 12.8% of all gainfully occupied persons in the state as engaged in agricultural pursuits. It further reports that 31.8% of all the people are rural residents. The percent of the population actually engaged in farming may be judged to lie somewhere between these limits. Farms represent half of the total assessed valuation in the state and exceed the capital in manufacturing plants by 100%.

Twelve percent of the total farming population of the state resides in the Upper

---

6. [Illegible.]

Peninsula. Seventy percent of the state's population (residing on 90% of the farms) is located within 140 miles of the southern state border.

Grain, beans, hay, fruit, beet sugar, and stock are produced. Market gardening is an extensive activity in the areas near Chicago and Detroit. Agriculture in certain parts of the state suffers by reason of poor soils and severe climates, as has been previously intimated.

The tourist and resort trade has in recent years assumed an increasing importance from the occupational and economic standpoint.

Financial

The citizens of Michigan, as individuals, probably do not ordinarily have financial difficulties more severe than those residing in other states. They, however, experienced particularly serious consequences when the entire banking system of the state ceased to function February 11th, 1933, by executive order of the Governor. An impending collapse of nearly the entire banking structure necessitated this action. The order to close affected 415 banks, having deposits of over $409,000,000.00, and five trust companies with deposits of about $58,500,000.00. So many of these financial institutions remained closed after the Federal government authorized the resumption of business by sound banks throughout the country that the citizens of the state were left in exceedingly bad financial circumstances. Over 90% of the banking resources in Detroit were involved, and about 55% of them remained frozen on August 1st. In some upstate communities the situation was even more acute. State funds in the amount of $8,000,000.00 remained impounded in August. On November 15th, 152 banks with frozen deposits of $64,380,737.00 were still closed, as were three trust companies.

The effect of the peculiar banking crisis in Michigan is discussed further in the final section of this chapter.

Significance of Characteristics Discussed Above

Each of the factors discussed above bears some direct or indirect influence upon the degree of need existing in the state for CWA aid or other assistance, or upon the actual conduct of the CWA activity.

The segregation of the basic factors from those which result from the action of basic factors is not easy. Beyond doubt, however, some of these characteristics influenced the past economic development of the state, and, in turn, its vulnerability to unemployment (and hence to the need for relief). The geography, surface character, and climate may be judged to have determined the original development of the state as to population composition and numbers and as to occupational (and industrial) endeavors. The character of the industries developed, may, in turn, be judged to have influenced changes in the character of the population, particularly with respect to foreign-born and colored residents, in recent years. As will be demonstrated in Chapter II, these types of residents have suffered disproportionate unemployment. This influence is confined to limited areas of the state, however.

The preponderant industrial character of the southern part of the state rendered it peculiarly sensitive to the economic disturbance. The specialized character of their industries was a further aggravating influence. The automobile centers (Detroit, Pontiac, Flint and Lansing), the furniture centers (Grand Rapids and Ionia), the paper mill centers (Kalamazoo and Monroe), the accessory city (Jackson), and the foundry and machine shop city (Muskegon) suffered early and severely. This is in harmony with subsequent data on unemployment in 1930, whereby Michigan is shown to have suffered more than the country as a whole and Detroit is shown to have suffered more than the state as a whole. A partial swing away from this condition is, however, suggested by the data of the following tabulation. The figures are index numbers indicating the relative resident family relief case loads in certain industrial counties in November, 1933, adjusted according to the respective populations. The state as a whole is taken as the base (1.00).

PLACE	CONTAINS CITY OF	INDEX NO.
State of Michigan		1.00
State exclusive of Wayne Co.		1.06
Wayne County	Detroit	0.91
Kent County	Grand Rapids	1.16
Genesee County	Flint	0.87
Oakland County	Pontiac	1.44
Saginaw County	Saginaw	0.56
Ingham County	Lansing	1.16
Jackson County	Jackson	1.31
Kalamazoo County	Kalamazoo	0.72
Calhoun County	Battle Creek	0.93
Muskegon County	Muskegon	1.28
Macomb County	Mt. Clemens	1.07
Monroe County	Monroe	0.38
Ionia County	Ionia	1.06

This development is reasonable, however, in view of the increasing effect of the adverse economic conditions upon the rural areas as the depression wore on. Agricultural pursuits became barren of reward toward the latter part. Poor yields and low prices brought rural residents to a low point on the resource scale in 1932 and '33. Similarly the copper and iron ore mining in the Upper Peninsula reached an approximate vanishing point, resulting in acute conditions of need in that area. The effect of these influences is reflected in the fact that as high as 63% of all the families in one northern county received relief in December, 1933.

Both unemployment and relief loads are discussed more fully in Chapter II.

Climate is perhaps the only factor discussed in this chapter which concretely and definitely influenced the actual conduct of the CWA activity itself. The range of climate, as heretofore mentioned, necessitated different types of endeavors in the northern and southern parts of the state. Work involving the pouring of concrete, for example, is either impracticable or substantially impossible (depending upon the particular job) in northern sections of the state in winter, but may well be undertaken in the southern areas. Some difficulty developed incident to making northern citizens understand that work had to be so selected as to warrant the anticipation of successful and efficient completion. Further, as will subsequently appear, the particularly vigorous weather of the past winter served to make more difficult of execution the work actually undertaken in all parts of the state, and thereby reduced somewhat the efficiency which might otherwise have been attained. Coats of snow as thick as five feet and frost lines as deep as six feet constituted definite obstacles.

Among the influences heretofore discussed, the financial situation in the state probably had the most direct bearing upon the <u>need</u> for the CWA program. The aggravating influence of this situation, as a factor contributing to destitution and the need for relief, is obvious. The continued impounding of the resources of a very large number of citizens naturally hastened the incidence of destitution in a great number of cases, and thereby accentuated the relief burden in the state. Similarly, the impounding of community welfare funds in the cities of Detroit, Flint, Grand Rapids, and Kalamazoo, definitely decreased the effect of private charity as an instrumentality for reducing the welfare burden borne by public funds.

Relief Situation Prior to the CWA Period

Unemployment

It is regrettable that satisfactory data upon unemployment prior to the CWA period are not available. It is therefore necessary to place reliance in statistics on employment in certain industries, in an incomplete unemployment registration report, and in the Federal census reports. Obviously none of these are adequate for reflecting the situation existing in the fall of 1933.

Extent of Unemployment

According to the 1930 census, unemployment (of persons able to work and desirous of working) existed as follows:

PLACE	NO. UNEMPLOYED	UNEMPLOYED AS % OF TOTAL POP.	UNEMPLOYED AS % OF GAINFULLY OCCUPIED PERSONS
United States	2,429,062	2.0	5.0
Michigan	157,812	3.3	8.2
Detroit	76,018	4.9	11.0
Grand Rapids	5,118	3.0	7.3

Flint	6,291	4.0	9.7
Wayne County	86,094	4.6	10.6
State, less Wayne County	71,718	2.4	6.4

Unemployment at that time was, therefore, more acute in Michigan than in the United States as a whole, and more acute in Detroit, Wayne County, and Flint, then in the state as a whole.

By January, 1931 the unemployed in Detroit had mounted to 253,568 or 14.2% of the total population.[1]

Turning, now, to employment, rather than unemployment: Statistics published by the Michigan Department of Labor and Industry for employment in industrial enterprise within the state show the monthly relation of numbers employed and the earnings of employees, by means of an index number referred to the base period 1923–26 (to which the index 100 is assigned). These are reproduced in Table III, and also upon the chart on page 18.

Some inference may be drawn from these facts, as to the extent to which unemployment became aggravated subsequent to the 1930 U.S. census. More especially, the table suggests the trend of unemployment, and its relative status in November, 1933. Apparently the bottom of industrial employment was touched in October 1932, and the minimum earnings occurred the preceding month. Considerable improvement had taken place prior to November, 1933, but it had not been fully sustained.

Table III. Michigan Industrial Employment Indices, 1923–1926 = 100.

| | EMPLOYMENT | | | | | EARNINGS | | | | |
	1930	1931	1932	1933	1934	1930	1931	1932	1933	1934
January	74.5	64.4	64.9	52.7	74.9	83.1	91.7	81.2	69.2	71.2
February	77	65.2	66.1	52.9	84.5	81	88.9	84	57.9	74.6
March	100.5	75.5	64.1	49.6	93.1	108.5	94.8	75	57.5	82.2
April	102.8	75.6	57.3	48.9	98.4	112.7	95.2	77.4	69	84.1
May	88.8	81.7	56.2	52		108.4	100.6	83.7	79.3	
June	83.3	77.6	56.4	60		101.5	91.4	76.7	83.9	
July	80.2	66.4	65.1	66.9		93	76.4	75.7	77.1	
August	75.3	63	59.4	71		86.3	80.1	65.3	75.4	
September	72	63.8	45.6	70.6		90	72.4	50.5	71.6	
October	70.5	51.9	40.9	66.1		91.3	94.1	63.3	69.2	
November	71.1	50.5	46.7	58.1		92.3	89.2	70.2	68.4	
December	71.9	55.8	50.5	64.4		84.9	85.7	67.4	66.6	
Year	*80.6*	*65.9*	*56.1*	*59.4*		*94.4*	*88.4*	*72.5*	*70.4*	

---

1. Special U.S. unemployment census, in 24 cities.

Industrial Employment in Michigan (Data of Table III plotted)

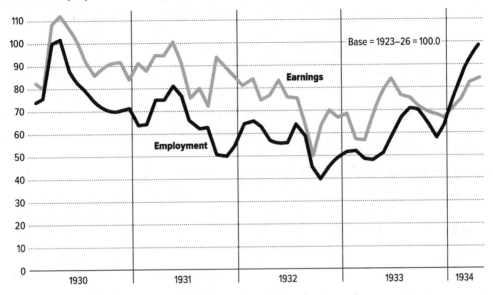

Automobile Production Shows Substantial Gain in 1933

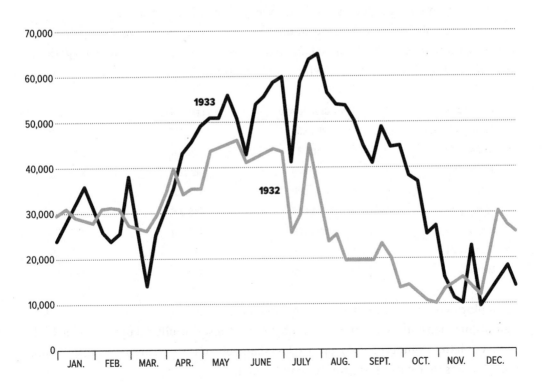

Because of the predominant place occupied by the automobile industry in the state, and because of its effect on allied industries, industrial employment parallels automobile production to a considerable extent. The latter is shown in the chart on page 19.

Registrations by the National Re-employment Service for the months September to November, 1933, totalled 74,802 in the state. The figure is obviously not indicative of the total unemployment in the state. This is explained by the fact that registration offices had not been opened in all counties, and by the further fact that the registration had not been completed in other counties. The total registration to March 31st was 285,953, in 73 out of the 83 counties of the state. Similar registration was performed in the remaining ten counties by the Michigan State Employment Service. The registration for the September–March period in these counties, which included the most populous areas in the state, numbered 308,420. The total registration by the two services, therefore, amounted to 594,373; but since some registrants secured employment before March 31st, the total registered persons seeking employment at one time numbered something less than 594,373.

in relation to the country as a whole, the employment situation was probably unfavorable in Michigan in the fall of 1933. According to U.S. Bureau of Labor Statistics, the % decline in employment and earnings in Michigan for October as compared with September (1933), for all the occupations covered by the reports, was exceeded in only 2 states. The October–November decline was similarly exceeded in only seven states.

That unemployment in the state at one time exceeded one half million persons is a safe conclusion. The Michigan State Emergency Welfare Relief Commission has gathered data, beginning January 3rd, 1934, which indicate as much. The figures are as follows:

WEEK ENDING	NO. UNEMPLOYED	CWA EMPLOYEES	TOTAL
January 13, 1934	354,603	166,499	521,102
January 20,	348,732	166,776	515,508
January 27,	340,424	165,254	505,678
February 3,	334,090	148,293	483,383
February 10,	281,648	148,916	430,564
February 17,	269,728	145,348	415,076
February 24,	271,414	139,375	410,789
March 3,	265,790	129,761	395,551

Unemployment of this extent—i.e., exceeding one half million persons—is particularly significant when compared with the number of persons gainfully occupied in 1930 in the state. The latter numbered 1,927,347. No less than 26% of the persons normally gainfully occupied was therefore at one time unemployed in the state.

Distribution of Unemployment

1930 census statistics emphasize the tendency of unemployment to victimize most severely the colored and foreign born, and to center in the larger urban areas. The former is indicated by the following tabulation, showing the unemployed, in that year, as a % of the total populations of the respective kinds (in the respective areas):

	MICHIGAN	DETROIT
Entire population	3.3%	4.9
Native white	2.6	3.5
Foreign white	5.0	6.5
All white	3.0	4.4
Negro	8.9	10.0

A more marked reduction in the % of gainfully occupied among the colored would also suggest a disproportionately large unemployment among that group. The following figures represent the gainfully occupied as a % of the total population for each group:

	MICHIGAN		DETROIT	
	1920	1930	1920	1930
Entire population	40.2	39.8	46.9	44.0
White	39.8	39.4	46.2	43.4
Colored	57.1	48.5	60.6	50.3

The above would appear to point out that negroes in both the entire state and in Detroit were much more severely affected by unemployment, than the white, in 1930. The statement applies only in a relative sense, as between 1920 and 1930.

The latter (i.e., the tendency of unemployment to strike cities most severely) is indicated by the following statistics, showing the % unemployed in 1930, in relation to the total population for each classification, in various types of areas:

Entire state.	3.3%
Incorporated places of 50,000 pop., and over.	4.4
Incorporated places of 10,000–50,000	2.9
Incorporated places of 2,500–10,000	2.5
Rural territory.	1.8

Conclusion

It would appear that unemployment in Michigan, while not at its peak in November, 1933, nevertheless exceeded one half million employable persons at that time, and that the condition was more severe in certain larger cities and among the foreign and colored residents, as well as in some northern counties.

Relief

The relief-granting authority and organizational set-up in Michigan is discussed in a succeeding chapter.

Amount of Relief Granted

The amount of relief granted is indicated by the charts on the following pages.[2] Assuming the average size of family as 4.6 persons it is apparent that approximately 17.5% of all families of the state received relief during November, 1933.

Much of the need for relief in Michigan has of course rested upon conditions which are common to the entire country. Yet it appears that some of the natural and economic characteristics of the state aggravated the burden. The distressing banking situation, the high foreign population content in some quarters, and the large numbers of economically unacclimated negroes in the automobile cities are weighty factors peculiar to the state.

Work Relief

Work relief as conducted prior to the CWA period was to a large extent locally administered. The state commission exercised very little supervision, and engineering was not stressed. All materials for work relief undertakings were locally financed,[3] and local bodies such as county road commissions, city engineering departments, park boards, etc., figured prominently in the actual conduct of the work.

It should be noted, further, that, pursuant to provision contained in the law creating

2. Attention is directed to the fact that the base of each chart does not represent zero. The vertical distances under the curves are therefore not proportional to the figures plotted.

3. Materials were financed out of state funds for certain projects carried out on property of the Federal government.

Families Receiving Public Unemployment Relief, Michigan, April, 1933–March, 1934

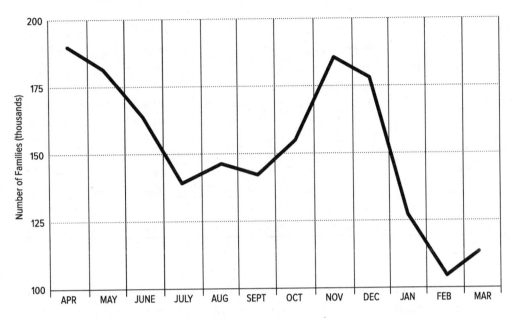

Obligations Incurred for Public Unemployment Relief, Michigan, April, 1933–March, 1934

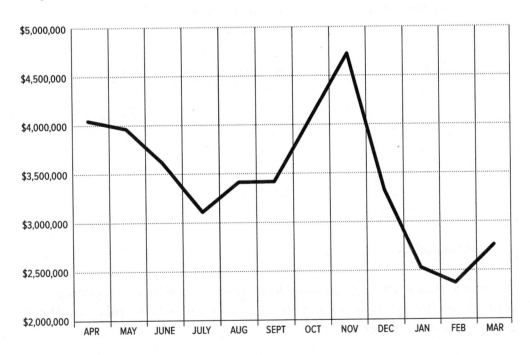

Table IV. 1933 Relief Expenditures from Public Funds in Michigan.

MONTH	LOCAL		STATE		FEDERAL		TOTAL AMOUNT ALL SOURCES
	AMOUNT	% OF TOTAL	AMOUNT	% OF TOTAL	AMOUNT	% OF TOTAL	
Quarter (Jan., Feb., Mar.)	$2,370,783.15	19.9	$80,579.03	0.8	$9,453,425.50	79.3	$11,904,787.68
April	409,116.39	10.1	21,381.39	0.5	3,637,482.15	89.4	4,067,979.93
May	294,671.68	7.4	31,406.66	0.8	3,661,970.39	91.87	3,988,048.73
June	196,421.40	5.4	39,192.55	1.1	3,401,361.20	93.5	3,636,975.15
July	147,019.85	4.7	32,104.47	1.0	2,945,542.54	94.3	3,124,666.86
August	181,439.15	5.3	992,166.29	29.0	2,254,460.38	65.7	3,428,065.82
September	292,752.17	8.5	1,010,908.26	29.45	2,126,580.34	62.1	3,430,240.77
October	206,664.98	5.1	1,007,033.14	24.8	2,839,668.35	70.1	4,053,366.47
November	179,211.98	3.8	1,011,476.73	21.2	3,569,340.51	75.0	4,760,029.22
December	139,048.21	4.2	983,011.74	29.76	2,202,687.00	66.12	3,324,746.95

the state relief commission, the State Highway Department prosecuted extensive road work upon a virtual work relief basis. The county road commissions operated under the same statutory provision. by far the greater part of all work relief labor was engaged upon road work.

As measured by the funds expended for relief for resident families, about one third of the relief granted in the six months immediately preceding the CWA period was distributed in the form of work relief. The exact proportion is as follows:

	PERCENT OF TOTAL RELIEF	
MONTH	DIRECT RELIEF	WORK RELIEF
May, 1933	69.4%	30.6%
June	69.9	30.1
July	65.4	34.6
August	61.6	38.4
September	61.8	38.2
October	64.6	35.4

Local Participation

The local, State, and Federal governments furnished relief funds in the respective proportions indicated by Table IV during 1933. The marked decrease in locally contributed funds, during the year, may be noted.

Concluding Statement

The foregoing discussion concerns the background of the CWA in Michigan; it presents the setting of the venture. The salient fact is that great need existed for assistance to destitute and near destitute people. The moderate improvement in employment attained before the fall of 1933 may also be noted. The greatly improved organizational and financial facilities for relief handling, brought about by the creation of Michigan State Emergency Welfare Relief Commission, is a further vital background factor touched upon in the next chapter.

Advent of the CWA: Organization

Pre-Existing Michigan Relief Organization

The Michigan Legislature at its regular session in 1933 enacted Public Act No. 201, whereby the Michigan State Emergency Welfare Relief Commission came into existence in July of that year.

This law set up a commission of three members appointed by the governor, whose primary duty it is to exercise general supervisory control over the distribution of the state and Federal funds used for the relief of destitution or unemployment within any and all parts of the state. The commission was granted powers sufficiently broad to convey complete control over the local relief-granting function. It was authorized to constitute a commission of three members in each county, with the approval of the governor, to exercise such powers as the (state) commission, with the approval of the governor, might prescribe. The sales tax act, passed by the Legislature at the same session, earmarked $12,000,000.00 annually for relief purposes.

Governor William A. Comstock appointed, as members of the commission, Mr. Charles H. Bender of Grand Rapids, chairman; Mr. William J. Norton of Detroit, and Mr. Earnest C. Brooks, Holland. The first meeting was held July 7th, 1933. The commission engaged Mr. Fred R. Johnson of Detroit as State Emergency Relief Administrator, and constituted local commissions in the various counties, as provided by the statute. Upon the resignation of

Mr. Earnest G. Brooks in September, 1933, Governor William A. Comstock appointed Mr. Louis M. Nims of Bay City as a member of the commission.

The above describes, briefly, the organizational set-up administering public relief in the state immediately prior to the inception of the CWA.

Creation of the CWA

When President Roosevelt created the Civil Works Administration—appropriately described as the greatest welfare undertaking ever known to the world—on November 8th, 1933, for the stated purpose of putting four million persons to work immediately at adequate wages, and designated Mr. Harry L. Hopkins to direct the enterprise, the latter immediately announced that existing state relief administrations would be named as state civil works administrations. Formal notice of such appointment and a statement of the attendant obligations were conveyed by the following telegram addressed to Mr. Charles Bender, chairman of the state commission, on November 10th:

> The State Emergency Welfare Relief Commission is hereby constituted the Civil Works Administration for the State of Michigan with yourself as chairman. It will be charged with responsibility for the execution of the civil works program in this state under the Federal Civil Works Administrator. The present Emergency Authorities in each county of your state is hereby constituted the Civil Works Administration for that county and will be charged with the responsibility for the execution of the civil works program in that county under the State Civil Works administration. Please telegraph formal acceptance of the foregoing on behalf of your state and local emergency relief administration and notify each local relief authority of their appointment. Detailed plans for putting civil works program into effect will be presented at meeting called in Washington on November 15.
>
> Harry L. Hopkins

The existing county relief commissions in Michigan were, in turn, designated as local CWA administrations, as the following communication sent out Nov. 13th indicates.

> To County Emergency Relief Commissions:
>
> Mr. Harry L. Hopkins, as Civil Works Administrator, has requested the State Emergency Welfare Relief Commission of Michigan to act as his representative in developing a new work program for Michigan. Our State Commission, in turn, is asking your county commission to similarly have charge of this development in your county. Your cooperation to this end is requested. Further information will be sent to you at a later date.

Very truly yours,
Fred R. Johnson
State Relief Administrator.

The state relief commission, consisting of the members above named, was therefore, responsible for the statewide direction of the CWA in Michigan, and the respective pre-existing county relief commissions were responsible for the local administration. In addition, Mr. Louis M. Nims, a member of the state commission, was designated to pass upon projects submitted for approval under the CWA program.

The State CWA organization consisted of five major divisions, viz: Purchasing, Payroll, Auditing, Correspondence, and Engineering-Projects. No major organizational changes occurred in the state during the CWA period. The Administrator, Mr. Fred R. Johnson, resigned effective May 1st, however, to return to his former post as Superintendent of the Michigan Children's Aid Society, the latter organization having "loaned" him to the State Commission. He was succeeded by Mr. William Haber, formerly Assistant Administrator.

The Launching of CWA Enterprise

T he Federal Government having determined to inaugurate the CWA and provide the funds, and having constituted the CWA authority in Michigan—it remained for the latter to put the program into effect in the state. Since the plan centered primarily about work upon local projects of a public character, the essence of the task in hand consisted of the selection of projects, the selection of employees, and the provision of necessary tools, equipment and materials.

Project Selection and Engineering

Work relief projects already under way in the state provided the first vehicle for absorbing the efforts of the new army of persons who became virtual employees of the Federal government. All such projects were transferred to the jurisdictions of the local civil works authorities, effective Nov. 20th, by wire of the state administrator under date of November 17th. These, together with road projects theretofore planned by state and county road authorities, comprised the principal activities engaged in during the first two or three weeks of the CWA period.

Nature of Permissible Projects

In addition to the requirement that projects undertaken must be of the kind ordinarily carried on by public authority (or with public aid) for the benefit of the general public, the state administration prescribed four tests as set forth in the following quotation:

> We are particularly concerned with the development of proper civilian work projects in your county. We desire to have you submit not only a list of projects on which your work relief people are engaged, but we also desire to have you prepare projects which will meet the following tests: First, they should be socially and economically desirable; Second, they should be the kind of projects that may be undertaken quickly; Third, it should be possible to terminate them reasonably quickly; Fourth, the proportionate cost for labor as compared with material should be high.

Any public project capable of meeting the foregoing tests was therefore eligible for CWA approval. Further, projects requiring considerable material expenditure were permissible when local authorities made substantial contributions for the necessary materials.

Engineering Organization

In order to have means of exercising supervision over projects, as contemplated by the Federal requirement that all projects prosecuted should first be approved by the State Commission, the latter created an organization charged with the duty of passing upon projects submitted for approval by local authorities, and with the further duties of carrying on a certain amount of project inspection and of rendering local authorities technical assistance.

As heretofore stated, this organization was headed by Commissioner Louis M. Nims, as CWA State Engineer. Mr. Nims surrounded himself with an office staff, and engaged six regional engineers to perform duties in their respective districts. The latter certified as to the intended purposes of proposed projects, examined each proposed project to ascertain the approximate correctness of accompanying estimates, inspected each project periodically during construction to determine whether good engineering practice was adhered to, enforced the rules and regulations promulgated by the State Commission, and rendered advice to local authorities when new projects were being proposed or considered. The assistance rendered local authorities was particularly valuable in those areas not having adequately qualified locally resident engineers, as in certain of the northern sections of the state. Wayne County, in which about one-third of all Michigan CWA work centered, was handled directly by the State Engineer and a staff of inspecting engineers located in Detroit.

Selection and Approval Procedure

Immediately upon announcement of the CWA program all public agencies interested in the work to be done, such as local engineering departments, school districts, county road commissions, and certain state authorities, began the preparation of proposed projects suitable to the demands of the CWA enterprise.

Before transmission to the State CWA engineering office, each proposed project was submitted to the respective county CWA authorities for approval. The local commissions were able not only to perform a certain amount of "weeding," but also, by virtue of familiarity with local conditions, to certify as to the intent of the projects. Their engineers, further, certified as to the reliability of figures and estimates filed.

Approval by the state project office was in each case conditioned upon conformity with the requirements of the CWA program. The quota of men allocated the respective counties was also considered. In many cases the approval of other state departments was a prerequisite to final approval by the CWA project office. For example, all airport work was approved by the state aeronautical director, and plans for involved construction work on school projects were approved by an office set up by the State Department of Public Instruction.

Proposals submitted to the state project office were promptly approved, if acceptable. An abundance of proposed projects of such character as to merit immediate approval was very early at hand. A notice of approval and a project number were sent the local authorities immediately in each case. Many of the initial project proposals submitted were inadequately prepared, due to the limitations of time. Within a month after the inception of the program, however, the procedure had been so perfected that definite information concerning the work under way and the money involved was at hand. Due to the fact that many projects were approved which later were discontinued, as worthier ones were instituted, it was found that the approval of projects on a quota basis was not possible. Consequently, it was necessary to continue to approve projects, and, as a result, Michigan approved about 25% over the actual amount of dollars involved in the CWA program.

Types of Projects Approved

While much of the initial CWA work was centered upon road projects, other undertakings considered more desirable were launched as soon as the necessary preparation and approval procedure could be completed. Sewerage, drainage, and sanitation work, for example, was commenced early and carried on during the entire period. In the belief that permanent monuments to CWA accomplishments were a proper objective to strive for, both repairs of existing buildings and the construction of new buildings were encouraged. Local contributions for material purchases were required by the state administration, as was completion by February 15th—a requirement attached to all projects. The popular response to the building repairs and construction proved excellent, and probably superior to that gained by any other type of project. Work of this type had the advantage of furnishing employment for a relatively large number of needy skilled laborers.

A number of the types of projects which received approval are mentioned in a succeeding chapter headed <u>Projects Executed</u>. Michigan CWA worked diligently in instituting desirable projects which would afford employment for all classes of workers, in accordance with the desires of the Federal Government. The Coast and Geodetic Survey project (which is further discussed in the above named chapter) was a very worthy undertaking from the engineering standpoint. The tax roll revision projects, carried on in the more populous areas, were particularly desirable in that they afforded employment for the white-collar man and technically trained engineer and, at the same time, afforded the local governments an opportunity to recover large sums of back taxes otherwise irrecoverable because of faulty descriptions.

City planning projects, aimed toward improvements to be effected by the respective municipalities in the future, and not necessarily under the CWA, represent a noteworthy type of CWA endeavor.

A necessary requirement in any program of this nature is that labor reservoirs be provided so that men may be transferred from completed projects to reservoir projects until such time as other worthier undertakings are instituted. Highway work was, in general, the largest labor reservoir, inasmuch as intermittent highway work involved no serious disadvantages. Airports were also included in this classification originally, but, as the program developed, airport work was commonly undertaken with the definite objective of completing a pre-determined amount of work.

Co-operation in Project Planning

Numerous states departments and institutions proposed projects to be supervised by themselves. Several such enterprises are discussed in a succeeding chapter. Further, such state authorities as the Departments of Public Instruction, Health, Building, Conservation, as well as others, rendered invaluable service by furnishing counsel and guidance to various county CWA commissions. In addition to assisting the counties in securing the greatest social and other benefits out of the opportunity at hand, these departments not infrequently also furnished supervision and materials, in order that desirable projects might be consummated.

Architects rendered the local and state administrations assistance by advising upon and drawing plans for structures proposed as CWA projects. To a large extent they were able to institute worthy projects and benefit themselves at the same time. Others, however, went too far in their enthusiasm, and aroused the hopes of local residents in connection with proposals which could not possibly be approved, because of the inability of the local authorities to provide materials or because of other insurmountable obstacles.

Percent Distribution of Project Types

The CWA enterprise in Michigan entailed about 12,000 projects upon which about $45,000,000.00 were expended. About $34,000,000.00, or 75% of the total, was expended before February 15th. The expenditure of the latter sum, upon about 6000 different undertakings, was distributed as follows:

1. City Streets 9%
2. Roads. 19%
3. Pest Control. 1%
4. Improvement to Public Land. 7%
5. Public Bldgs. & Equipment 7%
6. Parks & Playgrounds. 7%
7. Schools 17%
8. Utilities 5%
9. Waterways. 4%
10. Water supply 4%
11. Sanitation 13%
12. Admin; Prof; & Clerical 4%
13. Civil Works Service 3%

100%

Employee Allocation and Selection

Inasmuch as employee selection was for the greater part determined by rules emanating from the Federal CWA, this phase will be dealt with but briefly.

Quotas

The original quota granted Michigan numbered 161,000 persons. With the understanding that 40,000 of these were to be reserved for Federal projects, the state administration distributed a net quota of 121,000 among the counties of the state. In so doing, three quarters of this number was pro-rated according to the respective populations, while one quarter was pro-rated according to the respective relief case loads. An additional quota of 10,000 persons was granted November 27th, in order to permit adjustment of the quotas in certain northern and mining counties wherein those on work relief, prior to CWA, numbered two or three times the quota which could equitably be assigned such counties. A further quota of 30,000 persons, transferred from the unallocated balance of Federal projects, was received December 5th. At this time the total quota assigned for state and local projects stood at 160,750 persons.

The following tabulation shows the quotas distributed in Michigan at various times throughout the CWA period:

Nov. 17	121,000
Nov. 28	129,000
Dec. 9	157,503
Jan. 1	157,918
Jan. 29	144,375
Mar. 2	121,895
Mar. 9	109,210
Mar. 16	97,365

In distributing an additional quota of 8000 persons on Nov. 28th, the following counties were eliminated:

1. Those Counties where original quota on a 75/25% basis exceeded the number of men reported working as of November 1st.
2. Those Counties where original quota on a 75/25% basis was less than the number of men reported working as of November 1st by 100.
3. Those Counties when October family case load was less than the original quota.

Further, the remaining counties were treated as follows:

1. When percentage of persons on relief as compared with population exceeded 30%

(September figures and 1930 census), the allotment was made on a 75% basis of the number of men working November 1st over original quota.

2. When percentage of persons on relief as compared with population was less than 30% (September figures and 1930 census), the allotment was made on a 50% basis of the number of men working November 1st over original quota.

In distributing subsequent quotas, the commission was guided by circumstances and developments peculiar to the various counties of the state, rather than by fixed rules. The later quotas, however, involved only relatively minor adjustments in the proportions assigned each County out of the successive total quotas.

Sources of Employees

In conformity with the federal rule that the first fifty percent of the total state quota should be filled from the relief rolls before any other persons be hired, and preferably from the work relief rolls, 81,376 men from these sources were placed at work under CWA before December 1st; 63,891 were subsequently engaged through local offices of the National Re-employment service. The balance of a maximum employee total of 167,553, was engaged through certain state employment offices and recognized union locals.

The relationships between the State Employment and Federal Re-employment services, and the State CWA, insofar as placements were concerned, were outlined as follows by the latter:

1. The two services are not to function with respect to the local CWA until the latter submits a requisition for labor.
2. To permit of selection, the services will certify 25% more men than required for a given project.
3. The foreman or person in charge of a project, acting for the CWA, will select the labor from the list provided by either or both of the employment services.
4. Identification cards will be issued by the employment services.

Preferences

The preferences prescribed for employee selection were observed. As an example, approximately 10,000 of the men engaged through the National Re-employment service were veterans entitled to preference.

Distribution of Labor, by Types

No data is conveniently available as to the number of persons who performed work in the respective trades and occupations. Further, no data is at hand to show definitely the available labor, by types, at the beginning of the CWA enterprise. The registration statistics of the National Re-employment Service, for the months of September to November, inclusive, furnish a fair index of the latter, however. The distribution of this registration, by occupations, is indicated by the table on the following page.

Difficulties in Selection

Because of the attendant haste and because the CWA was planned to emphasize action and not investigation, some people who should not have been placed at work managed to get on the CWA rolls. When complaints were made and inquiries revealed the persons as not eligible under the Federal rules, they were discharged.

The tendency of all types of persons to register as skilled laborers, and notably as painters, is discussed in a subsequent chapter. Difficulties incident to determining an individual's status as skilled or unskilled are also discussed at a later point.

Tools and Materials

Tools

Under the original plans the procurement of tools was decentralized and the tools purchased or secured by loan were charged to each individual project. This procedure soon proved unsatisfactory. Thereupon a "Tool and Equipment Project" was constituted in each county, the state project (and engineering) office determining the amount of funds required and setting up the budgets. Thereafter all tools in the county were centrally procured under this master project, delivered to a central warehouse, inventoried, marked by stencils, tags, or burning, and assigned out to the various projects as requisitioned. In addition, local public works authorities, such as the county road commissions, etc., loaned a large amount of tools.

This reservoir of existing tools served to alleviate in part a distressing dearth of tools, which developed in the first weeks of the CWA period. The shovel market in Detroit, for example, was completely depleted, and tool delivery in Ingham County was delayed as long as two weeks at times. Even manufacturers were unable to meet demands within required time limits.

Table V. Distribution of Re-Employment Registration in Michigan. National Re-employment Service, Sept.–Nov., 1933.

INDUSTRIAL CLASSIFICATION	% OF TOTAL REGISTRATION	INDUSTRIAL CLASSIFICATION	% OF TOTAL REGISTRATION
Agriculture, forestry, fishing	22.8	Rubber products	0.3
Extraction of minerals	3.1	Textile industries	0.1
Building and construction (total)	—	Other textile mills	----
(a) Private	11.3	Tobacco manufacturers	----
(b) Public Works	0.1	Miscellaneous manufacturing	2.9
Civil works administration	—	Transportation and communication	6.8
Chemical and allied industries	1.1	Trade (wholesale-retail)	3.4
Clay, glass, and stone industries	1.1	Public utilities	1.4
Clothing industries	0.1	Professional service	1.5
Food and allied industries	2.3	Commercial service	1.8
Iron & steel prods., mach., and vehicle industries	18.9	Domestic and personal service	1.4
		Hotel and restaurants-institutions	1.0
Leather industries	0.4	Laundries and dry cleaning-industries	0.1
Lumber, furniture, and allied industries	6.6	Governmental service	2.7
Metal industries, except iron and steel	1.1	Miscellaneous unclassifiable services-industries	6.2
Paper and paper products	1.2		
Printing, publishing, and engraving	0.3	*Total*	*100.0*

The handling of, and accounting for, tools was in conformity with Federal regulations. Final inventories were made, which naturally showed some tools as lost. Affidavits covering the tools and equipment on hand at the time of the final inventory, and also the lost tools and equipment, were filed.

Materials

Necessary materials became exceptionally scarce during the first weeks of the CWA period. While the delay in delivery was not ordinarily of great length, nevertheless work was frequently held up and men were forced to remain idle.

The requirement of the State CWA that local authorities contribute materials, in substantial amounts, for certain projects and especially for building construction, has been mentioned heretofore.

It is estimated, on the basis of the most recent facts available, that the outlay for CWA materials in Michigan will, when the final accounting is complete, be found to approximate $8,500,000.00. This sum is equivalent to approximately 19% of the total CWA outlay in the state.

Projects Executed

F acts concerning a number of CWA undertakings prosecuted in Michigan are presented in the following series of resumés. Photos showing various types of work in
progress will be found at the end of this report.

Locally Administered Projects

By far the greater part of the CWA work in Michigan was centered upon projects which
were subject to the jurisdiction of the civil works administrators of the respective counties, and other local authorities. Since it is impracticable to give a full account of this
work, because of its nature and the circumstances attaching to it, the discussion of it is
confined to an enumeration of the most common types of undertakings and to a series of
sketches pertaining to typical projects selected at random from the file of (S-16) reports.

The following tabulation indicates a few of the more common types of work:

CONSTRUCTED	IMPROVED
Roads	Drains
Sewers	Schools
Breakwaters	Roads
Bridges	Parks

Retaining Walls

Drains

Public Buildings

Sidewalks

Playgrounds

Publicly owned utilities

Sewers

Sidewalks

Public Buildings

Water supply

Other very common types of work included improvements, surveys, and services required by numerous public departments, such as police, fire, health, schools, and libraries. The correction of nuisances and the improvement of sanitation also found wide favor.

The series of resumés which follow describe briefly the actual work done in each case, and include, in some instances, pertinent explanatory comments:

1. Water main replacement. 4800 ft. of 2" watermain on the County line Road in the village of New Baltimore afforded negligible fire protection to the area served. 3700 ft. of 4" cast iron pipe was laid in its stead, under CWA, at a depth of about 3 feet. Delays in the arrival of material shipments caused parts of the excavated trench to cave in, thus necessitating further work. 1100 ft. of pipe remained to be laid April 1st, when the project was rated as 60% completed. Total man-hours worked: 12,798.

2. Fill (for road). A fill 800 feet long was constructed across a mill pond at Hesperia, to an average depth of 8 feet and a maximum of 12 feet. Dirt was moved from a hill immediately to the north, where a cut 25 feet deep was made for the same road. Total length of road is ½ mile; shoulder width 36 feet. Surface graveled; one 15-inch culvert installed. Seventy-five percent completed under CWA; total man-hours worked, 13,980.

3. Flood protection (Grand River). The city of Grand Rapids has carried on a flood protection program since 1904, as available funds permitted. Some bad gaps remained to be closed, however. Therefore activities as follows were engaged in under CWA:

   a. A reinforced concrete retaining wall 418 feet in length was constructed near Bridge Street. 425 cu. yds. of concrete were required.

   b. 8143 cu. yds. of earth were removed from an embankment, at Wealthy Street, which constituted a flood menace. The dirt was deposited where additional flood protection embankments were required. An old railway trestle was removed incidentally.

   c. Deposits in the river channel, from 2 to 9 feet thick, and extending 300 feet out into the river, were removed in the vicinity of the Sewage Treatment Works and the Lake Shore Bridge. About 55,000 yards were thus excavated and deposited in a combined high level road and flood embankment.

The project was fully completed under CWA, and involved 207,494 man-hours of labor.

4. <u>Fish hatchery (enlarged)</u>. Two ponds were improved and three new ones constructed in the State Fish Hatchery in the city of Hastings. The existing ponds were cleaned out and levelled off. 1850 lineal feet of dykes were required in constructing the three new ponds; also 1528 lineal feet of drainage ditch. Other work included the installation of piping, feeding walks, raceways, boxes, and seepage walls. Project was 70% completed under CWA; man-hours of labor performed, 19,726.

5. <u>Sawmill project</u>. Pine, hemlock, and tamarack timber were cut and sawed up for lumber in Iron County on this project. Prior to April 1st, 3504 man-hours had been applied in logging and delivering to the sawmill 164,000 feet of timber and sawing 65,000 feet of same into planks and timbers for use on other CWA projects. This economical source of material proved very valuable.

6. <u>Record and book rehabilitation</u>. 556 man-hours were used on this project for the purpose of rehabilitating old records, for binding and mending books, and for revising and renovating card indexes, at Iron Mountain High School.

7. <u>Study of relief client food and housing</u>. 3453 man-hours of work in Kalamazoo County were sufficient to complete 60% of this project under CWA. The undertaking included the following:

    a. A compilation of statistics upon adequate minimum and balanced diets was made. Following analysis of same, a comprehensive report was prepared.

    b. The methods used by local merchants in handling groceries were studied, as were the prevailing prices of consumers' goods in the community.

    c. A housing survey directed primarily at residences occupied by relief clients in the city of Kalamazoo was carried on. Slum areas were catalogued and mapped. Houses not suitable for occupancy were listed, and an analysis of rent values was made.

8. <u>Platting of lands</u>. Under this project property already sold throughout Kent County in various parcels, but never platted for assessors' purposes, was reduced to assessor's plats. The original project called for the preparation of 148 plats containing 2619 lots. Seventy percent of the work was completed under CWA, through the application of 5515 man-hours of labor. Thirty-one plats were surveyed and recorded on drawings. Twenty-five of these drawings were transferred to tracings, and 205 tracings of existing recorder's plats were made.

9. <u>Survey of assessable real estate.</u> The purpose of this project, in the city of Lansing, was to lay the groundwork for the inauguration of a scientific plan of real property assessment. The work included the following:

    a. Block maps were made upon the basis of data contained in the original subdivision plats. Erroneous descriptions were corrected at the same time.

  b. Residence and business buildings were catalogued according to a standard classification. Area and cubic foot content, as well as structural type, etc., were recorded.

  c. Land value maps were prepared.

      While only 33% of the entire project was completed under CWA, some work was done on 20,000 out of the 30,000 parcels in the city. Man-hours totaled 8500.

10. <u>Rural road improvement.</u> Several existing rural roads in Isabella County were improved. The object was to grade, widen, drain, clear of brush, and fill low spots of all rural roads in the county needing these respective treatments. Bad corners also came in for attention. Work was accomplished as follows:

  a. Denver Twp: 1 mile graded and drained; 5000 cu. yds. dirt hauled for back filling.

  b. Chippewa Twp: ¾ mile graded and drained; 3000 cu. yds. filled around bridge.

  c. Coe and Lincoln Town Line: 6 miles drained and shoulders widened.

  d. Rolland and Broomfield Town Line: 2 miles brushed, graded, and drained.

  e. Deerfield and Broomfield Town Line: 2 miles drained and shoulders widened.

  f. Nottawa Twp: Hills cut down on 1 mile; 2000 cu. yds. deposited in low spots.

  g. Sherman Twp: Bad corner cut and rounded; 3000 cu. yds. of earth fill.

  h. Gilmore and Nottawa Town Line: 1½ miles graded, drained, and brushed; 5000 cu. yds. of earth fill.

  i. Union Twp: 2800 ft. of 15-inch tile installed for highway drainage.

      145,248 CWA man-hours sufficed to complete 65% of this entire project.

11. <u>Street car track removal and street paving</u>. Under this project an extensive length of street railway track, including some double tracks, was removed in Bay City. The street center was repaved to the extent of 22,312 square yards. The project absorbed 94,297 man-hours of CWA labor and reached 80% completion.

12. <u>County Sanatorium improvements.</u> 15,510 man-hours of labor were utilized in accomplishing necessary improvements at the Jackson County sanatorium. The following were included:

  a. All walls and ceilings of the hospital building were cleaned and painted, using 200 gallons of paint.

  b. The superstructure of an old building was removed. By constructing a roof over the basement, the latter was converted into a garage.

  c. The grounds were landscaped. This included the building of a parking lot, sidewalks, driveways, and paths, as well as trimming the ground surface and preparing beds for 1500 shrubs and 70 trees. 3000 cu. yds. of soil were moved, and 250 cu. yds. of cinders were screened and placed.

  d. A semi-rustic shelter building was erected.

    e. A concrete trench 200 feet in length, connecting the hospital building and the nurses' home, was constructed.

    f. The nurses' home was connected to the main heating plant.

    The project as proposed was 80% complete under CWA.

13. <u>School playground, etc</u>. Under this project, work was done at two schools in the city of South Haven. The Indiana Avenue School playground was graded and the playground equipment re-arranged. Old trees were removed, also. The entire interior of the Senior High School was cleaned and painted. 3507 man-hours of labor sufficed to complete the job 100%.

14. <u>Park and golf course construction.</u> The construction of a public park, 18-hole golf course, and club house was undertaken at Copper Harbor, Keweenaw County. An area of 165 acres was cleared, grubbed, and freed of debris; sand for traps was placed; two roads were constructed; and the building of a dam and a rustic log club house were commenced. The project was 50% completed under CWA.

15. <u>Park improvement.</u> A park owned by the city of Owosso and located a short distance north of the city was cleaned up and improved by needed construction. The following work was included:

    a. A covered shelter for picnic parties was constructed.

    b. 1600 feet of ditch was excavated and the banks stoned.

    c. Two small dams were built across a spring brook.

    d. Several flower beds and a large lily pool were made.

    e. Brick camp stoves were installed.

    f. One high bank and several lower banks were terraced.

    g. The park roads were graded and gravelled.

    7621 CWA man-hours brought the project to a stage of 75% completion.

16. <u>Athletic field construction.</u> The Traverse City High School athletic field was rebuilt under the CWA program. Cinders were removed from the quarter-mile running track, and replaced after laying a 2-inch coat of clay. The entire area inside of the track (i.e., football field, etc.) was covered with clay and with 3 inches of dirt, preparatory to sodding. A brick field-house 26 × 60, a brick ticket booth and gate entrance, and a concrete curb around both sides of the track were constructed. Existing bleachers were repaired and new ones built to accommodate 2500 spectators. The park fence was repaired and some new fences constructed.

    17,975 man-hours sufficed to complete 80% of the project, as originally planned, under CWA.

17. <u>Sewers and Sewage Plant.</u> A project in Grandville involved the extension of the sewer system and the construction of a sewage disposal plant consisting of a septic tank,

17,020 lineal feet of sewer ranging from 12 inch to 18 inch, and 1,038 feet ranging from 21 inch to 27 inch, were laid. Fifty-four manholes were planned. 122,260 man-hours brought the project to 93% completion (i.e., sewers 98% completed and plant 75% completed.)

18. <u>Drain and storm sewer improvement</u>. Drainage work was done in every township of Shiawassee County. The work included the grubbing of brush and roots from ditch banks and the perfecting of drainage grades by means of excavation from ditch sides and bottoms. 139 miles of drain were so treated. Further, 330 feet of tile drain were placed, mostly at a depth of from ten to twelve feet. 53,593 man-hours of CWA labor completed 60% of the project as planned.

19. <u>Storm sewer construction.</u> The so-called Silver Creek Drain storm sewer, connecting the systems of Grand Rapids and East Grand Rapids pursuant to court order, was constructed as a CWA project. It involved 16,951 cu. yds. of excavation and 3872 cu. yds. of backfill; 2222 feet of 8" by 5' sewer; 497' of 11" × 5¼' sewer; 118' of 24-inch tile; 96' of 12-inch tile; 82' of 8-inch tile; and 3 manholes. 82,296 man-hours of CWA labor completed 96% of the project.

20. <u>Reconstruction of community hall.</u> The existing community hall in Gladwin, 40' × 120', was razed, and replaced by a new building 60' × 120' with two-story front and new basement 20' × 120'. In addition to an auditorium (and gymnasium) 60' × 80' (with 60' × 5' balcony), the building provides showers and dressing rooms, two toilets, stage, kitchen, council chamber, American Legion room, and a library. 13,674 man-hours of CWA labor effected 95% completion of the project.

21. <u>School construction.</u> A four room school was partially constructed in Mount Pleasant under CWA 150 cu. yds. of concrete were placed in the substructure; 20,000 face bricks were laid in the walls; 3000 feet of roof trusses were placed; and incidentals, such as sewers, etc., were installed. 8016 CWA man-hours completed 50% of the necessary work.

Conclusion

The foregoing series of resumes indicates in some detail the character of the work performed upon a number of different local projects. The group does not include, of course, more than a small sample of locally administered projects. As the data of Chapter IV indicates, 13 general classifications of local projects were carried on in the state, and a vastly greater number of types would be in evidence if a more detailed classification were constituted.

The remainder of this chapter is devoted to a discussion of numerous projects not locally administered, but, rather, supervised by some particular state department or authority.

State Institutional Program

Numerous state institutions utilized CWA assistance for the purpose of consummating renovation and rehabilitation for which they had long had need, but which they could not effect out of their regular resources. The following list indicates the amount spent by each institution for materials and labor upon projects approved by CWA:

1.	Ypsilanti State Hospital	$84,485.63
2.	Traverse City State Hospital	18,206.69
3.	Western State Teachers' College	16,758.70
4.	Central State Teachers' College	18,007.63
5.	Kalamazoo State Hospital	23,798.36
6.	Michigan College of Mining and Technology	45,663.00
7.	Pontiac State Hospital	17,079.97
8.	State Public School	5,568.50
9.	Northern State Teachers' College	12,761.37
10.	Newberry State Hospital	25,297.96
11.	Michigan State Normal College	16,834.05
12.	Michigan State College	6,566.00
13.	Michigan School for the Deaf	624.50
14.	Michigan Soldiers' Home	10,180.90
15.	Michigan School for the Blind	2,457.10
16.	Michigan Home and Training School	1,438.55
17.	Michigan Farm Colony for Epileptics	4,352.00
18.	Michigan Employment Institute for the Blind	9,669.00
19.	Girls' Training School	6,667.30
20.	Boys' Vocational School	5,488.00
21.	State Sanatorium	9,254.63
22.	State Office Building	13,496.00
	TOTAL	*$354,655.00*

A considerable amount of materials was furnished by some of the above institutions, themselves.

Appreciable difficulty was encountered in securing sufficient materials to carry out the work involved in these projects. The fact that the material quota of each county was frequently absorbed by other undertakings in the county, resulted in inability of state institutions within such counties to obtain the full material quota called for by their projects as approved. It became necessary to discontinue some projects for lack of materials, since no further CWA nor State funds were available, and a few were never commenced.

Upon cessation of the CWA program many of these institutional projects were completed, and others were transferred to the Work Division program for completion. Unfortunately, still others remain uncompleted.

The work on this program was, in the main, well and efficiently performed. With few exceptions, the results were better than anticipated at the beginning of the program; in some instances the jobs were as well organized and efficiently operated as a well managed contract job. Limited efficiency prevailed on some occasions because work best suited to mechanical equipment was done with hand labor; but men were put to work and the spirit of the CWA was adhered to.

State Park Projects

At the time of the institution of the Civil Works program in Michigan, a vast amount of improvements urgently needed by the state park system had accumulated. For the most part these required much labor and little materials, and were, therefore, well suited to the needs of the CWA program.

Applications for project approval were made with the object of meeting the most urgent needs of the park system. The following tabulation indicates the location and magnitude of the work pursued:

COUNTY	STATE PARK	MAN HOURS	COST OF WORK DONE
Alcona	Harrisville	7,958	$5,718.45
Charlevoix	Youngs	264	2,068.38
Genesee	Bloomer #3	11,792	11,018.82
Gogebic	Gogebic	6,777	4,915.20
Huron	Huron	56,049	39,411.95
Leelanau	(D. H. Day North Port Pt. Lt. House site)	5,950	3,527.00
Livingston	Island Lake	2,359	1,393.75
Muskegon	Muskegon	51,837	31,197.58
Oakland	Bloomer #3	21,867	15,732.36
Schoolcraft	Indian Lake	12,655	8,992.52
Wexford	Wm. Mitchell	11,032	6,092.95
Total Man Hours		*190,007*	
Total Costs Reported			*$130,068.96*

The character of the work varied over a wide range. The usable area of certain parks near thickly populated areas was extended, to meet increasing use of those parks for camping and other purposes. This involved brushing, levelling, and filling. Sewers, park roads, and beaches were improved, and landscaping and erosion control work was effected. New sewage systems, wells, park buildings of various kinds,[1] boats, benches, and tables were constructed. Finally, buildings and equipment were treated with protective coats of paint.

Nearly all of the extensive state park improvements made possible by the CWA were of a permanent nature, and will prove of lasting benefit to patrons. Prominent benefits include closer proximity to a completely equipped park, improved sanitation, enhanced beauty, lessened fire hazard, safer driving, and greater opportunity for recreation and the general enjoyment of a park outing. Indeed, it is probable that some parks will remain open only because of CWA improvements. Other parks afford better facilities than would otherwise have been available for several years to come. It is clear that both patrons and the state benefit by this work.

State Library and Rural School Project

This project was organized January 3, 1934, with offices at 428 Tussing Building, Lansing, as a consolidation of two earlier projects. Its objectives were:

1. To give proper supervision over and criticism of plans for school buildings with special attention to an increase in library facilities.
2. To offer expert criticism, advice, and plans for landscaping school grounds in an effort to make school premises more attractive.
3. To answer the many legal questions involved in the proposed consolidation of rural school districts into township units where better buildings would be erected.

Competent personnel, including a director, assistant director, attorney, architect, landscape engineer, etc., was engaged to carry out duties entailed.

There are 6775 school districts in Michigan, distributed as follows:

> Primary rural districts 5526
> Graded districts 961
> Township units 167
> Rural agricultural 79

---

1. Such as bath house, group camp building, and tool and storage buildings.

3rd class city districts 39

2nd class city districts 2

1st class city districts 1

Total *6775*

A survey of the CWA school projects under way in Michigan was undertaken, and the following information obtained as of January 3, 1934.

CLASSIFICATION	NO. OF PROJECTS	AMOUNT
Cities over 50,000	8	$ 839,630.46
Cities from 10,000 to 50,000	79	467,351.96
Cities from 2,500 to 10,000	97	627,830.38
Villages	316	953,179.53
Rural Districts	2422	1,958,648.00
Totals	*2922*	*$4,846,640.33*

Seventy-one of those projects, involving structural charges in buildings, amounted to more than $5,000.00 each, and a total of $1,081,000.00.

Due to the neglect of school building repairs and improvements for the past three years, practically all districts were in need of some work. Nevertheless, only 43% of the districts in the state (i.e., 2922 out of 6775) submitted applications for approval of projects prior to February 15, 1934. Some district officers refused to apply, saying, "We will have to pay for this work done through the CWA." Others said, "Why apply? We will get nothing." Still others were too indifferent to apply. A few said, "Our school is good enough. We always carried water from the next farm; why ask for a well now?" In spite of these attitudes, however, 17% of the $34,000,000.00 expended before February 15th was devoted to school projects.

The project authorities above mentioned required the submission of plans and specifications, for approval, in all cases where structural changes to buildings were involved, in amounts exceeding $5,000.00. Such plans and specifications had to be prepared by a Registered Architect, in accordance with #8686, Compiled Laws of Michigan, 1929. Each of these projects had its own problem of adjustment to existing local conditions, and a satisfactory solution could be reached only after long and patient conferences with the respective Boards of Education, architect, citizens of the community, and staff members over the structural, educational, legal, and landscaping problems involved.

Preliminary plans and specifications for projects costing in excess of $5,000.00 and involving building charges were received subsequent to January 3rd in such numbers as to raise to total to 180 and the total dollars to $4,934,520.00. Final plans and specifications have been received from 42 of those projects and have been approved.

In connection with this state wide CWA work, a great effort was made to encourage the landscaping of school grounds, which are notorious for their barren appearance. Hundreds of landscape folders were sent out to school district officers, to commissioners of schools, to individual teachers, and to school patrons, urging that landscaping projects be requested from County CWA administrators. Free plans for all school grounds were offered and many were prepared in the CWA. School Projects office in Lansing. As a result one may frequently find a repaired, painted, redecorated, clean, sanitary school house standing in a landscape of pines, shrubs, and evergreens, presenting a pleasing appearance during the changing seasons of the year. The unused plans may well furnish a proper guide for school authorities themselves, for teachers, children, PTA organizations, and others interested in school landscaping to proceed on in the future to the end that more attractive school grounds will everywhere be found.

The project office, in addition to the interviews incident to the examination and criticism of preliminary plans, specifications, and final plans for 180 building projects under CWA scattered over the entire state, discharged the following duties:

1. Greatest number of Boards of Educations and Architects with plans interviewed in one day, 13.
2. Total number of architects furnishing plans, 40.
3. Rejected plans by 12 would-be architects.
4. Received and answered 305 letters.
5. Prepared 48 legal opinions pertaining to bonding, consolidations, and other school matters.
6. Revised details in school building code.
7. Prepared special landscape designs for 13 districts.
8. Furnished landscape material to 83 County School Commissioners.
9. Interviewed at their offices 12 County School Commissioners concerning landscape work.
10. Made 10 trips to individual schools desiring landscape service.
11. Landscape design applications under way, 50.
12. Made special trips to Bancroft, Laingsburg, Ionia, Charlotte, Flint, Pontiac, and Monroe, on details of problems submitted.
13. Contacted and advised with the following departments:
    - Department of Public Instruction
    - State Librarian

- Department of Agriculture
- State Highway Dept.
- State Treasurer
- Auditor General
- Securities Commission
- General CWA Office
- Ingham County CWA

14. Added library facilities to 55 school buildings.

15. Investigated 8 CWA complaints, some by personal visits.

16. Advised 20 Boards of Education concerning bonding.

17. Held 8 conferences with the State Department of Health on sanitary plans.

The project office service has been appreciated by County Administrators, by architects who have reciprocated with fine cooperation, and by the public, as evidenced by many letters on file.

The buildings desired at points scattered all over the state are listed in detail in the tabulation on the pages immediately following. (Certain buildings are now wholly or largely completed, as the notations Indicate). Most of these buildings are sorely needed to replace those destroyed by fire, such as at Casnovia, Wolverine, and Orangeville; by collapse as at Barryton; old, unsanitary and generally debilitated buildings as at Ionia; buildings needed for consolidation as at Olivet, West Branch, and Sunfield; and auditoriums for community centers as at Goodrich, Comstock, Wayland, and Ortonville.

The districts which submitted projects to the CWA now have new wells, new toilet facilities, new basements and library rooms, new floors, sound roofs, cleaned desks, repaired furnaces, rearranged windows (for unilateral lighting), clean and painted walls, tiled and graded school play grounds, new sidewalks, graveled drive ways, and in some cases even new school buildings, gymnasiums and auditoriums. Had school districts which needed new buildings been ready with plans and specifications in November much more buildings would have been done. More than 160 plans for such new buildings scattered over the entire state have been approved since January 1, 1934, and if a work program for unemployed men is necessary next fall, schools will be ready.

Airport Construction

The State Department of Aeronautics directed a part of the CWA program, whereby established airports were placed in first-class condition, and new airports were fairly well developed in many communities. The new fields augment those in existence for some years, the fields developed within the last two years by the State Department of Aeronautics, and the emergency fields established in our wooded areas by the Civilian Conservation Corps. Forty-one airport projects were approved during the CWA program, of which all but four were actually started, and a considerable amount of development work accomplished upon them. Of these projects, nine were existing airports on which distinctly necessary improvement work was accomplished. The remaining 32 fields were new. A total of $1,122,000.00 was approved for labor and material for airport work in the State, of which sum approximate $850,000.00 was actually expended. An estimated amount of approximately $300,000.00 in labor and materials was required for the purchase of materials and the payment of equipment rental. Since it is almost impossible to make an entirely complete usable airport by using only hand labor, it is absolutely essential that the final finish of the runways be done with equipment such as grader, scrappers, and tractor drawn floats. It is also quite essential that all these airports be properly seeded with a good grade of grass seed, and 100,000 lbs. of seed have been made available for delivery in the near future, through the FERA and Michigan State Emergency Welfare Relief Commission.

At the peak of the CWA program, over 5,000 men were employed on airport work in the state. The work accomplished generally consisted of rough grading and drainage work, removal of obstructions and hazards, and the erection of seven hangars. The construction of a greater number of hangars would have been highly desirable, as a hangar is a very essential part of any airport. Without a hangar, little if any interest in aviation will be shown on the part of local enthusiasts, as the depreciation of an airplane standing out of doors is almost prohibitive.

Considering the unusually severe weather conditions encountered during the CWA period, the accomplishments were satisfactory. The CWA was of very valuable assistance in furthering the work of the State Department of Aeronautics. Since the establishment of suitable airports in all communities is absolutely essential before the airplane will become a useful medium of transportation to a larger extent, the value of airport development as a permanent asset is apparent. Much local interest was displayed wherever a CWA airport project was underway, which may be regarded as tacit popular approval.

The tabulation on the pages immediately following indicates the approximate volume of work performed in the several cities, measured in dollars.

Extension of Control Surveys in Michigan (Geodetic Surveys)

For many years the Coast and Geodetic Survey has been building up a framework of Triangulation and First Order Leveling throughout the United States. This framework is marked on the ground by monuments so located that there are few points now in the

Table VI. Michigan Division of CWA School Projects. (State Department of Public Instruction). Report as of April 26, 1934.

CITY, VILLAGE, OR DISTRICT	COUNTY	TYPE OF PROJECT	ARCHITECT	COST
Alanson	Emmet	Aud. and class rooms	Mead	15,000
Alpena	Alpena	Gym and 12 class rooms	Gay	85,000
Arnold	Marquette	4 room building	Anderson	37,000
Atlanta	Montmorency	Com. Bldg. and 2 class rooms		21,000
Ashley	Gratiot	Aud. and gym.	Gay	12,000
Auburn Heights	Oakland	Gym. and 4 class rooms	Heenan	50,000
Augres	Arenac	Aud. and Gym.		17,000
Bancroft	Shiawassee	Gym. and 8 classrooms	Holmes	65,000
Bannister	Gratiot	Gym. and 8 classrooms	Homes	65,000
Barryton	Mecosta	Gym. and 10 classrooms	Holmes	81,000
Battle Creek Emmet No. 7	Calhoun	Community room 2 C.R.	Peterson	21,000
Battle Creek	Calhoun	Gym. and Field House	Chanel	31,000
Bay Port	Huron	Aud. and Gym.	Macomber	12,000
Bear Lake	Manistee	Aud. and Gym.	Wemhoff	8,500
Beaverton	Gladwin	Gym. and 4 class rooms	Holmes	25,000
Belmont No. 6 (Plainfield)	Kent	2 class rooms	Daverman	18,000
Benton Harbor	Berrien	Aud. and 7 rooms	Nowlen	46,000
Berrien Springs	Berrien	Remodeling 2 rooms		3,500
Big Rapids	Mecosta	Remodeling Aud. and Gym.	Batterson	44,000
Birmingham	Oakland	Remodeling Hill school	Price	41,000
Blanchard	Isabella	Gym. and Com. Room	Gay	15,000
Breckenridge	Gratiot	Aud. and Gym.	Francis	18,000
Bronson	Branch	Ag. Lab. and Shop	Wagner	6,500
Burnside	Lapeer	1 room school #6	State	4,000
Burr Oak	St. Joseph	Aud. Gym. 12 classrooms	Davenport	102,000
Burton Twp.	Genesee	Aud. Gym. 8 class rooms	Bacham	63,000
Burt, Lincoln #7	Osceola	1 room school #5	State	3,600
Capac	St. Clair	4 class rooms	Holmes	25,000
Casnovia	Muskegon	New 2 room school	Hertel	15,000
Cassopolis	Cass	Remodeling	Jones, N.R	2,000
Cedarville	Mackinac	Aud. and Gym.	Holmes	20,000
Centerville	St. Joseph	Vocational Bldg.	Hickok NR	1,800
Chalk Hills	Menominee	1 room school	Hubert	5,000
Charlevoix	Charlevoix	5 grade rooms	Worden	34,000
Cheboygen	Cheboygen	10 room building	Thompson	45,000
Clare	Clare	General Shop	Royzcki	2,000
Clayton	Lenawee	Aud. and Gym.	Kresbach	13,000
Colton	St. Joseph	Aud. and Gym.	Wagner	32,000
Comins	Oscoda	Community room	Gay	7,000
Comstock	Kalamazoo	Aud. and Gym	Batterson	31,000
Coopersville	Ottawa	10 room building	Holmes	42,000
Copemish	Manistee	Aud. and Gym	Weemhoff	8,500
Coral	Montcalm	Aud. and Gym	Black	8,000

DATE PREL. PLANS	DATE FINAL PLANS	PROGRESS AS OF APRIL 26/34	NOTES
2/16			
2/13			
3/29			One school burned Mar. 20; 3 buildings remain.
1/12			
2/23	3/20		
2/15			
			Discussed with Board
12/15	2/14	70 % completed	
12/15	2/25	80 % completed	
2/19			
2/2	3/16		
12/15	3/13		
1/18			
2/13			
1/15			
1/15			
2/15			
2/15	2/16	90 % completed	
1/15	1/31	80 % completed	
2/13			
2/15			
1/29			
1/24			
2/8			
1/23			School burned
2/15			
2/14			School Burned
2/25	3/15	Completed	
2/2			
1/31	2/6		
3/1			
2/19			
2/15			
12/14	1/27	Completed	
1/19			
2/13			
12/15	2/20	75% completed	
1/26			
1/5			$15,000 bonds voted
1/15	3/13		
2/23	3/26		

CITY, VILLAGE, OR DISTRICT	COUNTY	TYPE OF PROJECT	ARCHITECT	COST
Covington	Baraga	Gym. and 4 rooms	Hubert	77,000
Croswell	Sanilac	Gymnasium	Holmes	30,000
Crystal	Montcalm	Gymnasium	Gay	19,000
Crystal Falls	Iron	Garage	Hanson	20,000
Dearborn #8	Wayne	2 class rooms	Vicary	7,000
Dearborn	Wayne	4 room addition	Vicary	24,000
Dearborn #6	Wayne	2 class rooms	Vicary	15,000
Decatur	VanBuren	Heating plant		12,000
DeWitt	Clinton	8 room building	Munson	56,000
East Jordan	Charlevoix	4 room addition	Herrick	30,000
East Lansing Marble No. 8	Ingham	2 room building	Straight	18,000
East Tawas	Iosco	Aud. and Gym.	Bickel	24,000
Edenville	Midland	Aud. and Gym.	Holmes	20,000
Edwardsburg	Cass	Garage and M.T. room	Huffman NR	4,000
Elsie	Clinton	Gym. and Com. Bldg.	Gay	18,000
Elm Hall	Gratiot	2 room building	State	9,000
Erie #8	Monroe	4 room building	Stophlet	20,000
Evart	Osceola	Gymnasium Addition	Holmes	13,500
Fairplain #5	Berrien	4 room addition	Harper	11,000
Fairview	Oscoda	3 room addition	Gay	18,000
Farwell	Clare	Aud. and Gym.	Holmes	16,000
Forest Hill	Gratiot	3 room building	Holmes	20,000
Fountain	Mason	Gym. and Com. Building	Holmes	15,000
Freesoil	Mason	Gymnasium	Holmes	10,000
Gaines	Genesee	Auditorium	Zells	15,000
Galesburg	Kalamazoo	8 class rooms	Kingscott	50,000
Gaylord	Otsego	Gymnasium	Clark R.E.	11,800
Glen Arbor	Leelanau	Aud. and Gym.	Bauer	13,000
Goodrich	Genesee	Aud. and Gym.	Mackenzie	19,000
Gould City	Mackinac	New building	McGillis NR	20,000
Grand Rapids	Kent	4 room building	Hertel	35,000
Grant	Newaygo	Gymnasium	Sharp N.R.	15,000
Gregory	Livingston	New 4 room building	Holmes	16,000
Hadley	Lapeer	New bldg. -6 rooms	Gay	32,000
Hartland	Livingston	Aud. and 2 class rooms	Holmes	20,000
Hartwick	Osceola	1 room school #5	State	3,600
Hazlett Park	Ingham	Gym. and 4 class rooms	Munson	30,000
Hesperia	Newaygo	8 room building	Billingham	65,000
Hessel	Mackinac	3 room building	Holmes	15,000
Hillman	Montmorency	Aud. and 2 class rooms	Holmes	26,000
Holt	Ingham	Gymnasium	Holmes	12,500
Holton	Muskegon	New building	Straight	57,000
Honor	Benzie	Remodeling	Conklin NR	3,100
Hopkins	Allegan	Aud. and Gym.	Holmes	20,000
Houghton Lake	Roscommon	Aud. and Gym.	Holmes	19,000
Hoxeyville	Wexford	Remodeling	Sellers NR	11,000
Hudson	Lenawee	Gym. and 4 class rooms	Holmes	32,000

DATE PREL. PLANS	DATE FINAL PLANS	PROGRESS AS OF APRIL 26/34	NOTES
2/23			
1/15			
12/20	1/31	75% completed	
2/1	3/7		
1/24	1/31		
2/22			
2/6			
3/16			
2/13			
2/20			
2/15			
2/14			
1/15			
2/7			
1/11			
2/14			
2/28	3/20		
2/16	3/12		
2/19	2/26	80% completed	
2/19	3/9	80% completed	
1/15			
2/5	2/16		
12/30	3/9	20% completed	
1/5			
2/8			
2/16	3/12		
2/16			
2/6			
1/15			
2/28	3/23		(School burned)
12/15	3/20		(Report asked)
1/15		(March 20)	(Bond issue carried)
2/7			
1/8			Bond issue carried
2/14			
1/8			
2/2			
1/10			
12/15			
1/16			
1/5			
2/15			
1/30	2/15	90% completed	
12/15			
1/8			

CITY, VILLAGE, OR DISTRICT	COUNTY	TYPE OF PROJECT	ARCHITECT	COST
Husdonville	Ottawa	Aud. and Gym.	Weemhof	14,500
Hulbert	Chippewa	Remodeling	Cox NR	7,000
Ida	Monroe	Gymnasium	Stokes N.R.	8,000
Indian River	Cheboygan	New Building	Thompson	45,000
Ionia	Ionia	Aud. and Gymnaisum	Allen	80,000
Ithaca	Gratiot	Gymnasium	Cole	39,000
Kaleva	Manistee	Aud. and Gymnaisum	Weemhof	15,000
Kellogville	Kent	12 room building	Daverman	80,000
Kent #6 Fr. Paris	Kent	Library and Museum	Daverman	14,000
Kingsley	Grand Traverse	Aud. and Gym.	Bauer	17,000
Lake Leelanau	Leelanau	New Building	Worden	59,000
Lake	Clare	Aud. and Gymnasium	Holmes	15,000
Laingsburg	Shiawassee	New Building	Munson	65,000
Lansing #7	Ingham	2 room bldg. #14	State	16,000
Lansing	Ingham	J.H. 6 room addition	Black	50,000
Lambertville	Monroe	Aud. and Gymnasium	Langdon	16,000
Leland	Leelanau	Aud. and Gym.	Bauer	16,000
Leonard	Oakland	3 room building	Cole	20,000
Leonidas	St. Joseph	2 room building	Wagner	8,000
Leroy	Osceola	Aud. and Gymnasium	Lyndon	15,000
Lupton	Ogemaw	Gym. and 2 rooms	Munger	19,000
Manchester	Washtenaw	12 room building	Davenport	95,000
Manton	Wexford	Aud. and Gymnasium	Holmes	24,000
Manistee	Manistee	10 room building	Robinson	80,000
Marion	Osceola	11 rooms and gym.	Gay	76,000
Marine City	St. Clair	8 room addition to H.S.	Wyeth	33,000
Marlette	Sanilac	Aud. and Gym. 4R	Holmes	45,000
Martin	Allegan	Gym. and 2 rooms	Holmes	31,000
Mary Hawkins Scio #1 Fr.	Washtenaw	1 room school #11	State	3,500
Mass	Ontonagon	Gymnasium	Woodford NR	9,500
McBain	Missaukee	4 room addition	Gay	21,000
Mecosta	Mecosta	Aud. and Gymnasium	Holmes	27,000
Middleton	Gratiot	Gymnasium	Holmes	10,500
Mio	Oscoda	Aud. and Gymnaisum	Herbestriet NR	9,000
Merrill	Saginaw	10 room building	Cole	50,000
Mesick	Wexford	Garage	Nemmarch NR	5,000
Midland	Midland	1 room school	Dow	4,500
Milan	Monroe	New building	Holmes	30,000
Moline	Allegan	4 room building	McCarty	27,000
Montague	Muskegon	Garage		6,000
Mt. Pleasant	Isabella	4 room school	Holmes	14,000
Muir	Ionia	Aud. and Gym.	Gay	16,000
North Branch	Lapeer	Aud. and 3 rooms	Wyeth	36,000
Nestor	Roscommon	Gym. and rooms	Gay	18,000
N. Muskegon	Muskegon	7 room addition	Holmes	40,000
Olivet	Eaton	Gym. and 6 rooms	Sarvis	74,000
Onaway	Presque Isle	4 room addition	Holmes	18,000

DATE PREL. PLANS	DATE FINAL PLANS	PROGRESS AS OF APRIL 26/34	NOTES
1/20		80% completed	
2/1			
2/8			
2/15			
2/12			Bond issue of $20,000 carried.
2/13			
12/15	3/7		
1/18			
2/13			
2/16			
2/6			
12/15	2/15	60% completed	
1/16			
1/31			
2/27			
2/1			
1/11			Sch. burned in March.
3/9			Sch. burned in Feb.
2/1	3/15	70% completed	
1/31			
1/25			
1/20			
12/15	2/26	85% completed	
1/29			
1/31			
1/29			
2/10			
2/8			
1/31			
1/30			
2/15			
1/9			
1/26	2/15	90% completed	
12/27			
1/11			
1/26			
1/13	1/18		
11/4			
2/14			
3/10			
12/15	2/19		
2/1			
1/19	2/13		$9,000 bond issue voted
12/15	2/19	60% completed	
1/15			
2/15			
2/2	3/16	60% completed	

CITY, VILLAGE, OR DISTRICT	COUNTY	TYPE OF PROJECT	ARCHITECT	COST
Orangeville	Barry	3 room school	Young	14,000
Ortonville	Oakland	Aud. and gym. 2 dr. r.	Madison	40,000
Palo	Ionia	Aud. and gym.	Wright NR	8,000
Perry	Shiawassee	Gym. and Classroom	Waters NR	28,000
Petersburg	Monroe	Remodeling	Grandolph NR	12,000
Pickford	Chippewa	4 room building	Holmes	22,000
Pinckney	Livingston	Gym. and 8 rooms	Holmes	70,000
Potterville	Eaton	Aud. and Gym.	Munison	7,000
Prescott	Ogemaw	Gymnasium	Holmes	25,000
Remus	Mecosta	4 additional rooms	Holmes	27,000
Rochester	Oakland	Remodeling H.S.	Madison	32,000
Rockland	Ontonagon	Gymnasium	Woodford NR	7,000
Romulus	Wayne	2 room addition	Holmes	7,000
Rose City	Ogemaw	Gym and new building	Bickel	94,000
Sand Lake	Kent	Gymnasium	Daverman	12,000
Sault Ste. Marie	Chippewa	Stadium and bleachers	Armstzen	31,000
Schoolcraft #6	Kalamazoo	1 room building	Pellett	3,500
Sherman No. 1	St. Joseph	One room building No. 5	State	4,000
Sheridan	Montcalm	Aud. and Gym.	Straight	16,000
Six Lakes	Montcalm	2 room addition	Gay	10,000
Stanton	Montcalm	Aud. and Gym.	Straight	9,000
Stanwood	Mecosta	Aud. and Gym.	Kuni	24,000
Stephenson	Menominee	Gym. and 6 class rooms	Hubert	60,000
Sterling	Arenac	2 room addition		3,900
St. Helen	Roscommon	2 room building	Holmes	10,000
Stockbridge	Ingham	4 room addition	Davenport	20,000
Sunfield	Eaton	11 room addition-Kellogg	Sarvis	50,000
Suttons Bay	Leelanau	Aud. and Gym.	Bauer	17,000
Taylor #6 Fr.	Wayne	2 room building	Vicary	9,000
Trenary	Alger	2 room addition	Gay	9,000
Tuscarora #1	Cheboygan	1 room addition	Thompson	5,000
Tustin	Osceola	Gym. and 2 rooms	Lyndon	30,000
Ubly	Huron	10 room building	Holmes	50,000
Vanderbilt	Otsego	6 room building	Cole	30,000
Vandalia	Cass	1 room addition	Haines NR	4,000
Vicksburg	Kalamazoo	Aud. and gym. 3 c. r.	Newlander	45,000
Vicksburg #6	Kalamazoo	1 room building	Pellett N.R.	3,500
Walled Lake	Oakland	Garage	Mench N.R.	3,000
Walhalla	Mason	1 room building #13	State	3,500
Warren	Macomb	Aud. and 4 class rooms	Madison	50,000
Wayland	Allegan	Aud. and gym.	Holmes	20,000
Webster School	Oakland	1 room addition	Heenan	8,000
Weidman	Isabella	Aud. and gym.	Gay	15,000
West Branch	Ogemaw	New H.S. building	Cowles	150,000
Whittemore	Iosco	Aud. and gym.	McKenzie	27,000
Wolverine	Cheboygan	Aud. and 7 class rooms	Gay	62,000
Wyoming Park	Kent	2 room addition	Allen	20,000
Ludington	Mason	Stadium	Knecht	69,520

DATE PREL. PLANS	DATE FINAL PLANS	PROGRESS AS OF APRIL 26/34	NOTES
2/20			School burned in Jan.
1/18			
12/15		Completed	
12/15	1/30	80% completed	
12/20		85% completed	
2/15			
1/15	3/23		Bond issue carried
1/29		30% completed	
12/25	2/23	95% completed	consolidated
12/1	2/26	85% completed	
2/3			
1/15			
1/18			
2/13			
2/19			
1/16			School burned
2/15			
12/15	1/31	90% completed	
1/28	3/13		
12/15			
3/7			
12/15	1/29	65% completed	
1/15			
1/25			
2/16			
1/21			
2/15			
3/8			
2/1			
2/13			
2/13			
1/23			
2/13			
2/6			Replace school burned
12/15	3/21	75% completed	
1/19			
3/14			
12/18	3/13	85% completed	
2/13			
1/20	2/20	90% completed	
1/17			
2/14			
2/13			
1/16			
3/28			

Table VII. Progress Report of Michigan CWA Airports. April 5th, 1934.

AIRPORT NO.	NAME OF CITY	% COMPLETE	APPROXIMATE AMOUNTS EXPENDED TO DATE	
			LABOR	MATERIAL & EQUIP-RENTAL
1	Battle Creek	90	10,317.58	1,490.04
2	Indian River	70	4,700.79	28.22
3	Cheboygan	60	10,641.70	2,337.71
4	Muskegon	100	5,685.00	2,103.25
5	Lansing	93	14,150.29	2,800.00
6	Owosso	75	12,981.25	3,184.22
7	Allegan	85	9,738.85	3,325.00
8	Marshall	50	4,872.00	405.50
9	Bellaire	50	2,675.00	340.00
10	Sturgis	40	4,774.70	2,016.42
11	Jackson	75	58,103.21	4,888.34
12	Northport	1	447.10	24.50
13	Grand Rapids	80	27,618.36	12,805.37
14	St. Ignace	60	5,222.40	1,119.55
15	Stambaugh	10	4,423.41	146.04
16	Laurium	60	22,784.52	1,014.01
17	Petoskey	80	4,336.35	5.15
18	Vanderbilt	90	2,023.00	900.00
19	Gladstone	77	16,480.91	3,000.00
20	Escanaba	50	20,500.00	4,000.00
21	Flint	75	189,907.87	42,333.35
22	Midland	60	6,526.79	2,382.10
23	Adrian	40	5,969.30	2,125.81
24	Sault Ste. Marie	40	3,655.80	1,783.15
25	Caro	75	6,898.09	1,638.20
26	Pontiac	50	4,566.78	1,081.60
27	Port Huron	35	4,542.14	98.00
28	Onaway	2	731.00	—
29	Traverse City	25	8,252.92	200.00
30	Mackinac Island	10	2,182.50	—
31	Hillman	0	None	
32	Frankfort	0	None	
33	Coldwater	0	None	
34	Harrison	0	None	
35	Detroit-Wayne County	95	130,000.00	41,000.00
36	Wayne County-Detroit Emergency Fields	97	43,214.15	2,742.56
37	Wayne County-Detroit Emergency Fields	93	8,232.33	376.67
38	Wayne County-Detroit Emergency Fields	96	13,598.43	827.25
39	Wayne County-Detroit Emergency Fields	95	13,874.81	815.22
40	Wayne County-Detroit Emergency Fields	95	7,814.43	941.28
	TOTAL		692,443.76	144,278.51
		Total Expended:	$836,622.27	
		Total Required:	301,895.50	
		Total:	$1,138,517.77	
		Total Approved:	$1,122,503.19	

| | AMOUNT REQUIRED TO COMPLETE | | |
LABOR	EQUIP. RENTAL	MATERIAL	REMARKS
5,000.00	710.00	200.00	
3,300.00	670.00	200.00	
6,300.00	1,280.00	300.00	
Completed	Completed	Completed	
1,912.50	1,500.00	1,000.00	
7,560.00	2,000.00	1,200.00	
2,640.00	1,000.00	150.00	
10,000.00	500.00	600.00	
1,080.00	160.00	40.00	
5,760.00	2,500.00	150.00	
18,912.00	3,000.00	300.00	
7,560.00	2,250.00	350.00	
7,688.00	1,000.00	700.00	
3,780.00	500.00	—	
9,360.00	4,700.00	300.00	
16,240.00	1,000.00	300.00	
2,600.00	350.00	150.00	
1,050.00	200.00	100.00	
3,840.00	600.00	200.00	
11,640.00	6,300.00	300.00	
49,188.00	4,000.00	1,500.00	
3,840.00	200.00	200.00	
3,240.00	850.00	150.00	
3,240.00	1,000.00	1,000.00	
1,440.00	400.00	100.00	
5,040.00	1,000.00	—	
5,040.00	2,200.00	600.00	
3,250.00	700.00	100.00	
7,620.00	3,000.00	150.00	
6,420.00	2,000.00	125.00	
3,250.00	900.00	100.00	
6,250.00	1,000.00	170.00	
7,560.00	2,500.00	200.00	
690.00	100.00	—	
4,000.00	—	—	
1,800.00	100.00	—	Algonquin
600.00	50.00	—	Shoemaker
800.00	50.00	—	Beatrice
1,000.00	100.00	100.00	Lyndon
500.00	50.00	50.00	Fair Grounds
240,990.50	50,420.00	11,085.00	
9 Old Airports improved.			
31 New Airports constructed.			

Lower Peninsula of Michigan that are more than 25 miles from a triangulation station or an accurate bench mark. However, these distances are too great to adequately supply property line surveys, topographical mapping, flood control projects, or other engineering work with suitable control. It is therefore readily seen that the extension of the surveys to furnish points carefully monumented at a reasonable distance apart is a project well worth while.

Inception of the Project: Organization

When the Civil Works Administration was established, the authorities in charge contacted the Bureau of the Coast and Geodetic Survey in Washington with reference to work of a technical nature that would furnish employment to engineers and other scientifically trained men who were at that time out of employment. Accordingly, the extension of the above control surveys was planned. Under this general plan, which was in operation in every state, we in Michigan worked, first under the Coast and Geodetic Survey direct, with personnel only furnished from the Civil Works Administration. A State Representative operating directly under the Coast and Geodetic Survey was later appointed.

General Conduct of the Work

Permanent bench marks consisting of reinforced concrete monuments weighing about 400 pounds were placed at convenient locations for the use of engineers and surveyors. These bench marks and traverse stations were on the average about 1 mile apart. In all, 979 of these monuments were placed on a total mileage of 960 miles was set, the monuments being placed in that section of the State most in need of such monumenting. After the monuments were set, leveling operations were carried on to determine the elevation above sea level of the above points. All such leveling is of a very high class, carefully checked and is tied in to the first order leveling of the United States Coast and Geodetic Survey. When computed, it is doubtful if an error more than 0.005 foot will exist between any two adjacent bench marks. In all, 1562 miles of leveling were accomplished. 715 miles of completed leveling was therefore done, because all lines were done at least twice, and some more than twice. In all, 821 miles of taping was done. This means that when the final computing is done, 378 of the 979 monuments will have their latitude and longitude determined.

The work of incidental office computation was made possible by the cooperation of several State Institutions: The Michigan State College, the University of Detroit, the

Michigan College of Mining and Technology and the University of Michigan. The Detroit Water Board and private engineers in Detroit furnished instruments at a nominal rental for use on this work. It was necessary to borrow, in all, at different times, about 30 transits at an estimated value of $12,000.00 and 30 levels at an estimated value of $6,000.00.

Merits of the Project

The main object of this project, that of furnishing useful work to a large body of so-called "white-collared" or technical men in need of employment, was accomplished in a creditable manner. While this type of work is normally not carried on during the winter months, yet, as the statistics show, a great deal was done. The work was uniformly of a high character.

A continuous source of employment for engineers and other trained men may be found in this work for a long time in the future, if desired. It is absolutely non-competitive, for it would not normally be performed by any private organization. When computed and the results furnished, it fosters other engineering work of a private nature. For this reason, no criticism as to the Government engaging in it can possibly arise. It is properly a Government function, either State or National, and it cannot properly be said to be "made work," for it is all something accomplished toward the ultimate ideal of control points set at such convenient distances that engineers and others needing such reference points can make use of them.

Health and Morale of Personnel

One of the most gratifying aspects of the whole project was the excellent health of the men employed. Sickness was much less prevalent than among men employed in the ordinary pursuits at that time of the year. The morale of the personnel was also high throughout the entire operation. Some of the better qualified men remained with the organization at what really amounted to a sacrifice in order that they might assist in this excellent work.

Accomplishments

From February 15th to April 1st a maximum of 338 men were employed. The materials, motor equipment etc., including gas, oil, cement, haulage, etc., occasioned an expenditure of $10,831.07. The total expended, including payrolls total up to April 1st, was $118,473.54. The total work accomplished may be summarized as follows:

- 979 monuments set
- 960 miles of monuments set
- 1562 miles of leveling done
- 715 miles of elevations determined
- 821 miles of taping done
- 578 miles of taping completed
- 765 angles repeated
- 308 miles of angles completed

It may be noted, also, that the survey for the proposed Mackinac Straits Bridge was included as a part of the Michigan control survey activity.

Rural and Community Sanitation

An important piece of sanitation in Michigan was accomplished through the Civil Works Administration by the introduction of a Federal Project sponsored by the U.S. Public Health Service, cooperating with the Michigan Department of Health. The enterprise was introduced about the middle of December when the Public Health Service and the State Commissioner of Health applied for approval of a project for improving sanitary conditions at schools. The prime object was to rebuild or replace all school privies which were not fly tight and rodent proof, or which did not properly dispose of sewage into the soil in such a manner that it could not affect the water supply, create a nuisance, or become a health hazard.

The Public Health Service furnished salary and travel expenses for two assistant state directors, travel expenses for 14 district supervisors, and a salary subsidy in lieu of travel expenses for all county supervisors on the project. Six district supervisors and all county supervisors received their salary through the CWA. Additional assistance was received through the generous offer of the Michigan Children's Fund and the Kellogg Foundation to "loan" their sanitary officers as district supervisors, not only in the counties in which they were operating, but also in adjoining counties. With this administrative and supervisory personnel established, active work on improving sanitation at schools commenced January 2. Office personnel and necessary desks and typewriters were provided through the Ingham County Administrator, and the State Department of Health provided the necessary office space.

Scope of the Sanitation Project

As it actually developed, the enterprise became a 3-point project which included:

1. School sanitation
2. Home, park, and resort sanitation
3. Sanitary surveys of schools

The construction of privies, under the first heading, has been mentioned above. These were built in accordance with specifications furnished by the U.S. Public Health Service, the design being based on long experience in the South where the Service has been doing extensive work of this nature. This phase was later expanded so as to embrace, in addition to sewage disposal work, the giving of advice by the supervisory forces, upon other matters having a bearing upon health, such as heating, lighting, ventilation, general sanitary conditions, and structural matters. As a result of the latter much work was done on school properties under other projects. Included were improved window arrangements, new floors, new basements, furnace installations, and the provision of drainage.

Under the second heading, above, rural and community sanitation on private property was undertaken. Through the police power granted to Health Departments for the elimination of nuisances and the improvement of the health of the community, the workers on this project were able to assist individuals in obtaining better sanitation. The individuals were required to furnish the material and, under the supervision of the county man, CWA laborers went on their property and erected the toilet facilities.

The third subdivision of the program consisted of sanitary surveys of schools, and in some cases included a complete survey of the physical school facilities of a given county. In Charlevoix county, for example, a thorough survey covering heating, lighting, ventilation, and structural and sanitary conditions was made. Further, the district supervisor of sanitation, with the cooperation of the county school commissioners and the county supervisors of this program, made a survey of all of the schools in the district comprising Genesee, Lapeer, Oakland, Macomb, and St. Clair counties. Of the 664 schools in the district, 426 were surveyed. 273 were found to lack proper pits in the privies, and 234 of these made application for privies of the approved type. 146 had septic tank systems, 58 had chemical toilets and 2 had cess-pools. In Genesee, Lapeer, and St. Clair counties, it was found that the general sanitary conditions at the schools as a whole could be rated only as poor, while in Macomb county the general rating was fair.

Difficulties Encountered on Sanitation Project

Due to the extremely cold weather which prevailed during much of the time, construction difficulties of unusual character had to be overcome constantly. In the Upper Peninsula it was necessary to clear away from 3 to 5 feet of snow before construction could start, and very frequently three to five feet of frost had to be penetrated in excavating the pit. Wherever possible, the construction of superstructures was carried on in barns, county highway garages, or other buildings, the use of which could be obtained gratis. All sorts of methods were employed for conveying the superstructure and floor slab to the point of erection. Sleighs, toboggans, wagons, and trucks performed this duty. Even the Coast Guard Cutter, "Escanaba," when called upon to deliver hay to starving cattle on Beaver Island, was pressed into service and carried four superstructures to the island. The county supervisor returned to the mainland by airplane, after erecting the privies—the only means of transportation between the two points.

Sanitation Accomplishments

As an index to what was accomplished through this program, the following data are pertinent. Privies were constructed at 882 schools, 101 homes, and 22 parks, resorts, etc. Further, 33 privies were repaired, 9 septic tanks were built, and 127 wells were repaired. 896 of the privies built had wood floors and risers while 43 used the concrete slab. This project required the services of 3,434 men. A total of 2,577 privies were built at homes and schools and in parks and resorts. They required the construction of 2,410 concrete or wood floors. During the same time a total of 296 other privies were repaired, 50 septic tanks were built, and 183 wells were improved by the application of sanitary principles. The project in its entirety gave employment to 7,775 men.

It is impossible to estimate the total amount of material which this program consumed, as both new and salvaged lumber was used and frequently the sand and gravel for the concrete floor and riser slabs was obtained from a local pit at a minimum charge, the hauling being done by the individual or by the laborers themselves, in order to keep working. Such materials as were purchased were furnished by the local CWA Administration, except when local boards had some funds available, inasmuch as the state project did not provide for any material purchases.

This project was essentially a sanitation program having considerable width of scope and touching upon schools, homes, resorts, and various public places. A large number of rural and consolidated schools received valuable aid from the sanitation standpoint, and health conditions in the individual homes and communities involved were definitely enhanced.

Appeal of the Sanitation Program

The appeal which is contained in this program can be summarized in a few of the statements which have come from the various counties. We are informed that in St. Joseph county at least 300 units could be built, while Van Buren wants at least 800 more. St. Clair county reports that people are realizing the necessity and importance of this work, and that at least 1,000 privies could be built if the program were continued. In Oakland county there is a resort area within five miles of Pontiac in which the county supervisor estimates that there are at least 1,000 open pit privies which should be replaced. Mason county has 150 orders on hand, ready to start, while Wexford county cannot fill the orders fast enough. In some localities the project appealed so strongly to the local authorities that they provided half of the material from the general village fund and the cost of the other half of the material was placed on the tax roll of the individual property to be benefited, so that sanitary conditions of the entire community could be improved. The outstanding county in this respect was Van Buren, where the villages of Bangor, Lawton, Lawrence, and Bloomingdale signed up one hundred percent for the program and three additional townships also asked for the program to cover the entire township.

Black Currant Eradication

The Michigan State Department of Agriculture and the Bureau of Plant Industry, U.S. Department of Agriculture, co-operated in the supervision of a CWA project designed to eradicate black currant bushes in Michigan, for the purpose of preventing blister rust.

The work extended into 32 counties, and consisted of mapping each county by township and indicating each separate premises in each township; of interviewing the owners to ascertain whether they had cultivated currants or gooseberries, and the variety and number of each; and of the eradication of any black currant bushes found, after securing the owners' consent.

The two departments mentioned above furnished the supervision of all work; assisted the local people in selecting foremen and employees; furnished all supplies and tools; and contacted the field forces regularly, through the supervisory staff, for the purpose of rendering assistance and guidance.

The work done differed in various counties because of varying topographical conditions. After February 15th it was necessary to curtail the work appreciably because of inability to secure the necessary man power.

The following work was accomplished in the counties affected:

Black Currant Bush Locations Found 751

Black Currant Bushes on these Locations 6536

Locations where Currants and Gooseberries other than black currants were found 5488

Currants and Gooseberries on those Locations 91,438

Owners Interviewed 47,638

Square miles of territory from which Black Currants were eradicated: (equivalent to

202 numerical townships). 7,290

Heavy blister rust infections are found in pine timber in Marquette county, and work was performed there as follows:

Areas Worked. 22

Blister Rust Cankers Pruned Out. 3,095

White Pine Trees Pruned 1,168

Acres of White Pine from which cankers were pruned. 995

Finally, the mapper of the State Department of Agriculture, with the assistance of one CWA worker, mapped 24 areas of white pine in Iron County, those areas involving a total of 2432 acres.

At the cessation of the program, the administrators of the different counties were asked to co-operate to the end that the Blister Rust black currant eradication project might be kept going in their counties. Under the plan suggested to them the State and Government will pay the foremen and furnish the transportation, and the counties will furnish the helper from their work relief rolls.

Cooperation was excellent throughout the project period, and it is hoped that all of the counties will work toward completion of the work. The State Department of Agriculture will give all possible assistance to the end that this may be done.

Highways

The improvement and construction of public highways and highway appurtenances constituted the largest single activity under the CWA in Michigan.[2]

The greater portion of this work was performed under the direction of local authorities, but work aggregating $3,986,410.58 upon over 2500 miles of highways was supervised by

---

2. 19% of all expenditures prior to February 15th.

the State Highway Department. Detailed statistics bearing upon this work in each county of the state are presented by the tabulation [in table VIII].

National Re-employment Service Project

The National Re-employment Service functioned as a Federal project. Its purpose was to register the unemployed in the counties under its jurisdiction and to assist in their placement upon Public Works projects, CWA projects, or in private enterprise. In effecting PWA and CWA placements, a convenient opportunity was afforded to adhere to the preferences set up for those organizations.

Registration and placements were as follows:

```
Unemployed registered in 73 counties........................................ 285,953
Unemployed placed with CWA ................................................ .63,891
Unemployed Placed with PWA & private enterprise............................. .14,354
                                                                             78,245
```

The above CWA placements, of course, represent the self-sustaining unemployed eligible for CWA after the first 50% of requirements had been met by the employment of relief clients. Of the total placed, 11,947 were veterans entitled to preference.

It is believed that the national re-employment service, financed by CWA funds, obviated serious complaints of discrimination, which could otherwise have developed in the placement of 78,000 persons.

Commencing Nov. 20th, an average weekly number of 235 persons was employed upon the national re-employment service activity. The total cost to March 31st was $101,200.48. Of this amount only 3.8% (or $3,852.51) was spent for incidental expenses, such as telephone and office supplies. A large benefit in the form of distributed wages to the project employees was therefore obtained, and this should be noted along with the services rendered.

State Welfare Department Projects

Three distinct projects of a fact-finding character were carried on by The State Welfare Department as a part of the CWA Program. CWA funds provided in this instance, in addition to needed employment, an opportunity for the State Welfare Department to accelerate materially a long-time program of study upon which to base future policies and developments in its work. The studies performed related to mothers' pensions, maternity care in

Table VIII. State Highway Dept. CWA Report.

PHOTO INDEX NO.	COUNTY	TOTAL MILEAGE	RELOC. OF COR. NO.	WIDENING GRADE & STRUCTURE	CU. YDS. EXC.	BRUSH & TRIM MILES	GRADE WIDENING DITCHING	GRAVEL RESURF. MILES	STUMPING FENCING MILES	BRIDGE REPAIR NO.
1	Ionia	5.5				400	2.5	3.0		
2	Antrim	4.0	3				1.0			
3	Benzie	2.9					2.9			
4	Charlevoix	7.0					7.0			
5	Emmet	4.6		2.9			1.7			
6	Grand Traverse	5.8					5.8			
7	Kalkaska	6.6			33000		6.5	0.1		
8	Lake	17.3		4.8				12.5		
9	Manistee	12.0		12.0						
10	Mason	4.3					4.3			
11	Missaukee	1.0					1.0			
12	Osceola	5.3					5.3			1
	Leelanau	*								
13	Wexford	56.5	1		30000		9.0		47.5	
14	Kent	97.2					17.5			
15	Montcalm	19.0					19.0			1
16	Muskegon	23.1					23.1			
17	Newaygo	19.6					19.6			
18	Oceana	25.0					25.0			
19	Ottawa	60.5					10.5			
20	Otsego	5.5			8550		1.7	0.3		
21	Cheboygan	13.4			26495		3.6			
22	Presque Isle	27.0			78906		7.9			
23	Montmorency	5.7			10500			4.3		
24	Alpena	20.6			12512		5.5			
25	Oscoda	13.4			615					
26	Ogemaw	21.9		0.2			15.0	1.0	5.0	
27	Arenac	20.3				17.5	2.3			
28	Crawford	5.0			15000		5.0			
29	Alcona	22.8					6.8	6.0		
30	Iosco	12.7		4.2				8.5		
31	Roscommon	10.4		5.4	5945			0.0		
32	Livingston	4.0		4.0						
33	Macomb	28.4					22.4			
34	Monroe	7.6					7.6			
35	Oakland	14.8					2.5			
36	Washtenaw	0.6		0.6						
37	Wayne	8.5		8.5						
38	Bay	2.0		2.0						
39	Clare	63.7		8.8						
	Genesee	*								
40	Gladwin	175.3		25.8						
41	Gratiot	44.7		15.9						

PLANTING TRIMMING MILES	STOCK-PILING CU. YDS.	GRUBBING SQ. RODS	CLEARING ACRES	FENCING MILES	GUARD RAIL MILES	DITCHING MILES	NO. OF MEN	MAN HOURS	PAYROLL	MATERIAL COST	TRUCK & TEAM COST
							3980	114975	52083.3		
							1237	28412	18610.7	2184.3	1271.1
							51	14439	6104.2	5.2	1253.9
							1682	41535	15955.4	12.0	1846.0
							53	24095	10070.0	484.5	758.0
							68	19049	9723.2	230.6	952.1
							2153	45162	18623.7	1354.0	3703.5
							1292	33667	12762.2	992.7	5176.9
	2000						110	50459	19051.8	552.6	4769.5
150.0							1682	42154	17823.5	502.6	2345.7
							90	9013	3663.3	405.9	512.9
	2000						2030	46752	19540.1	1093.1	1642.2
	2564						281	99439	41810.7	499.9	5135.8
80.0							11734	441653	214283.4	25472.8	
							5606	128416	51366.7	2961.0	
							11922	260027	130419.7	3909.7	
							6117	122174	50602.9	1852.7	
						25.0	4410	97130	40865.3	1808.5	
25.0									70816.8		
				1		2.5		10997	4335.5	541.6	1680.7
		4266	26.7	2.6		7.2		52527	21250.0	2734.9	
		3114	4.1			14.8	105	47275		1242.4	
		500			0.1	1.3		25995	10569.9	292.0	1546.6
		2111	17.3	3.6		11.5		58688	23923.8	4121.0	2201.5
		1980.6	12.4	0.8		0.2	90	4179	1812.4	426.2	77.5
	1700	120				0.7	156	11550	4620.0	588.0	
				0.5			78	11646	4658.4	115.3	
	2000						40	10104	4041.6	1716.2	
	2400			10.0			130	28884	11553.6	2147.3	
	6600			5.0			102	32550	13020.0	865.8	
	2720						86	22696	9078.4	1466.8	
							15	3330	1443.0	718.0	
						6.0	835	192912	108157.3	20046.8	
							421	59459	26071.6	4600.9	
11.5				0.8			88	14198	11218.3	2782.0	
							46	9836	4156.9	1152.3	
							341	264449	49250.4	7756.6	
							32	6935	3173.0	382.9	
54.9							256	79190	38487.4	1785.8	
94.0						56.0	226	67283	27504.2	4952.4	
28.7							247	89545	38022.1	5980.6	

PHOTO INDEX NO.	COUNTY	TOTAL MILEAGE	RELOC. OF COR. NO.	WIDENING GRADE & STRUCTURE	CU. YDS. EXC.	BRUSH & TRIM MILES	GRADE WIDENING DITCHING	GRAVEL RESURF. MILES	STUMPING FENCING MILES	BRIDGE REPAIR NO.
42	Isabella	64.7		64.7						1
43	Midland	482.0		8.7						2
44	Saginaw	33.2		6.7						
45	Shiawassee	6.6		6.6						
46	Huron	57.4					25.6			
47	Lapeer	28.4								2
48	St. Clair	28.8		3.7			18.1			2
49	Sanilac	49.3		22.7			52.0			1
50	Tuscola	47.9		3.8			32.6			1
51	Allegan	45.3				7.7	11.9	0.3		
52	Barry	27.5		27.5						
53	Berrien	57.5		10.0			22.5			
54	Cass	56.0								
55	Kalamazoo	29.5					29.5			
56	Van Buren	22.9					22.9			
57	St. Joseph	38.5					17.0	9.5		
58	Branch	4.0			18000			4.0		
59	Hillsdale	12.2		12.2						
60	Lenawee	15.0					15.0			
61	Clinton	24.0					24.0			
62	Eaton	63.0				42.0	11.0			
63	Ingham	24.5				11.0	13.5			
64	Jackson	6.6		6.6						
65	Calhoun	27.0		22.0		0.5				
66	Baraga	15.2		0.3			6.0	8.8		1
67	Dickinson	14.8					5.8	9.0		
68	Gogebic	37.2					37.2			
69	Houghton	69.0		6.0	120000		50.0	13.0		
70	Iron	33.8					15.0	6.3		
71	Keweenaw	7.0		7.0						
72	Marquette	64.2		4.2			60.0			
73	Ontonagon	20.9		3.9				20.0		
74	Alger	4.0					4.0			
75	Chippewa	12.6								
76	Delta	17.3		4.5		0.7	3.2	8.9		1
77	Luce	9.0	1				7.0			
78	Mackinac	2.5					2.5			
79	Menominee	38.7					6.0	21.7		
80	Schoolcraft	11.7		0.6			8.1	3		
	Mecosta	*								
	TOTAL	2515.1	5	316.7	359523	479.4	742.3	140.2	52.5	13

* No CWA work on highways

PLANTING TRIMMING MILES	STOCK-PILING CU. YDS.	GRUBBING SQ. RODS	CLEARING ACRES	FENCING MILES	GUARD RAIL MILES	DITCHING MILES	NO. OF MEN	MAN HOURS	PAYROLL	MATERIAL COST	TRUCK & TEAM COST
							519	78100	33590.6	2039.4	
83.5						390.0	453	118785	51563.4	1248.7	
						26.5	292	77410	35701.4	12179.7	
							157	55400	17981.9		
				23.3		8.5	1179	129836	52537.0	4341.0	
12.0				16.0		0.4	712	76447	30937.7	6643.4	
				7.0			798	38468	31295.7	7053.4	
				24.6			561	83294	30063.5	4608.7	
				11.5			1136	93443	37759.0	4515.9	
23.0						2.3	472	91662	40440.8	629.7	
							135	50480	28966.4	284.3	
						25.0	323	134326	76871.7	3495.7	
						56.0	175	52489	34599.3		
							651	204577	93643.8	17411.1	
							248	49589	22143.5	15.0	
						12.0	245	67080	46122.9	11563.0	
							42	7646	4075.6	403.3	
							167	41840	25032.7	2247.7	
							365	58190	30264.4	2046.6	
							113	45760	18611.9		
						10.0	177	59295	28075.7	2452.3	
							187	41580	58412.7	3588.2	
							124	33925	15121.0	801.3	
							286	64650	26024.2	385.2	
							7711	183890	77053.0	19578.0	
							2538	67940	41874.0	15056.0	
							11921	28410	127838.0	48201.0	
	11000						28225	685700	423807.0	63341.0	
12.5							7003	168010	99545.0	17246.0	
	2000						3849	90330	38852.0	2404.0	
							21434	501570	213576.0	50294.0	
							4050	100600	85824.0	7242.0	
							200	54517	22357.0	303.1	2404.2
							58	13502	5378.3	48.3	1239.2
							24738	263501	120900.5	16126.1	
				2.0			97	21808	8723.7	1379.9	
							615	15785	6585.1	558.6	
9.0						2.0	368	100392	42485.5	4591.6	12237.6
							210	101178	48601.6	36833.4	
584.1	34984	12091.6	60.5	108.7	0.1	658.0	180326	7119184	3453761.4	481894.4	50754.7

homes and hospitals, and private mental hospitals. Travelling expenses were furnished by the State Welfare Department. A brief description of these surveys follows:

Mothers' Pensions

No concrete knowledge concerning the functioning of the Mother's Pension Law, enacted in 1913, in each of the counties of the state has heretofore existed. Information was particularly needed as to the supervision set up in each county; the average pension grant per child; the standards set up for housing, food, medical care, and education; and the effect of the depression upon the income and living standards of Mother's Pension families.

Thirty-seven unemployed social workers were engaged to prosecute a state wide survey touching upon:

1. The method of administration and supervision of Mothers' pensions in each county.
2. Existing living conditions in pension family homes and the case records pertaining to them.
3. Special problems in those counties having apparently adequate records and supervision.

76 counties were covered, in which 4016 homes having 12,361 children were visited. A conference was held with the Judge of Probate for each county, inasmuch as the responsibility for Mothers' Pensions is vested in these judges, by law.

Many vital deficiencies in the operation of the Mothers' Pension program were disclosed by the survey. In some cases remedial steps have already been taken; in others such steps will be taken when possible; and in still others only legislative enactment can accomplish the desired result. It is clearly evident, in any event, that this survey, made possible by CWA, has and will result in great benefit to Michigan's fatherless childhood.

Maternity Care in Homes and Hospitals

All homes and hospitals offering maternity care in the state of Michigan are subject to inspection, license, and supervision by the State Welfare Department. Heretofore the department has had entirely inadequate information for the intelligent performance of its important duty of maternity home and hospital control.

Twelve registered nurses having special training in obstetrical care were engaged to execute a survey by means of which the State Welfare Department might be able to improve conditions relating to maternity homes and hospitals. The state was divided into 12 sections according to the number and location of hospitals. The existence of unlicensed hospitals (22% of the total number) was disclosed, as were conditions resulting in the revocation of 35 hospital and home licenses. Further, it was found possible to bring about significant improvements in medical service, nursing care, and child placing practices in a very large proportion of the institutions.

Private Mental Hospitals

Psychiatric social workers were engaged on this project to study generally the conditions existing in private mental hospitals, for the purpose of setting up new standards for licensing and supervision by the State Welfare Department. Fourteen hospitals were visited and valuable information was elicited. Some conditions necessitating a revocation of license were found.

Child Health Nursing

A project using the services of 107 unemployed nurses was carried on under the supervision of the Michigan Department of Health at the request of the U.S. Children's Bureau, for the purpose of promoting child health. One of the major objectives was to study malnutrition among children in relief families. The nurses worked in close co-operation with physicians, who contributed valuable services for a purely nominal fee when such were revealed as necessary. The activities of the CWA nurses on this project are summarized in the tabulation ["Summarized Report: Child Health Nursing Project"].

Conclusion

It should be emphasized that projects supervised locally, rather than by various state authorities such as mentioned in the accounts immediately preceding, comprised the bulk of CWA work in the state. This is true both numerically and as to the money involved.

It must be evident, from the facts related, that the large number of undertakings made possible of consummation in Michigan by the CWA were of a useful and desirable character.

SUMMARIZED REPORT
CHILD HEALTH NURSING PROJECT

January 28, 1934 to April 16, 1934. (incomplete)

VISITS

To county relief office 1209

To homes 23777

To schools 5777

To physicians 1415

To dentists 453

To nurses 745

Miscellaneous 3750

ANALYSIS OF HOME VISITS

Infant 7208

Preschool 15544

School 19441

Crippled children 502

Communicable disease 2081

Other 1156

Referred to physicians 3689

Referred to dentists 4682

Prenatal or Postnatal 619

SCHOOL ACTIVITIES

Physical examinations 5067

Dental examinations 8763

Height-weight 9458

Vision-hearing tests 6375

Inspections or assisting 58613

Tuberculin tested 10194

IMMUNIZATION

Number vaccinated 8052

Number given Toxoid complete 18199

Number Schick tested 2580

EDUCATIONAL

Talks other than to school child 201

Literature distributed:

Infant 7652

Preschool 11230

Communicable disease 20029

Nutrition 20018

Other 12613

Prenatal 406

Old Rapid River Bridge, Kalkaska, Michigan

New Rapid River Bridge, Kalkaska, Michigan, built under the CWA program

Fish hatchery at Baldwin, Michigan, constructed under State Department of Conservation specifications

Interior view of fish hatchery constructed at Paris, Michigan

Auxiliary (trout) fish hatchery, Paris, Michigan, construction supervised by Michigan Department of Conservation

Flood Control project, Lansing, Michigan

Dam constructed across River Raisin, Monroe County, Michigan

Stoning side slope of cut on Goguac Lake Road, Battle Creek, Calhoun County

Constructing retaining wall and dressing slope and surface, Battle Creek, Calhoun County

Monolithic combined sewer under construction, Muskegon, Michigan

Monolithic sewer construction, Muskegon, Michigan

Demolishing Battle Creek High School #1, Calhoun County, Michigan

Rural school undergoing remodeling under CWA, Calhoun County, Michigan

CWA widening of Seven Mile Road, Detroit, Michigan

Hippopotamus and African Bird exhibit building, Detroit Zoological Gardens, constructed through the CWA

CWA street widening and street lighting installation at new Post Office. Lafayette Boulevard, Detroit, Michigan

Shade trees planted as a CWA project, Melvindale, Michigan

South American Pampas Construction, Detroit Zoological Gardens

Wild life pond excavation at Belle Isle Park, Detroit. The mysterious statue unearthed received nationwide publicity

Gas tank at Detroit City Airport painted
by CWA workmen

Tunneling 12 feet below Grand
Trunk Railroad tracks, East
Lansing, Michigan, for Farm Tile
Drain Project

Preparing to lay drain tile, East Lansing Farm Drain Project

Municipal pier and breakwater construction, Traverse City, Michigan

Mecosta County Infirmary, Stanwood, Michigan. One of the outstanding pieces of CWA construction work in the state

CWA superintendent and foremen receiving first aid instructions in Michigan

CWA artist painting mural for press room, Detroit City Hall

CWA engineers planning city improvements and slum projects in Detroit

CWA symphony orchestra practicing in Detroit

CWA employees repairing books for Detroit Board of Education and library

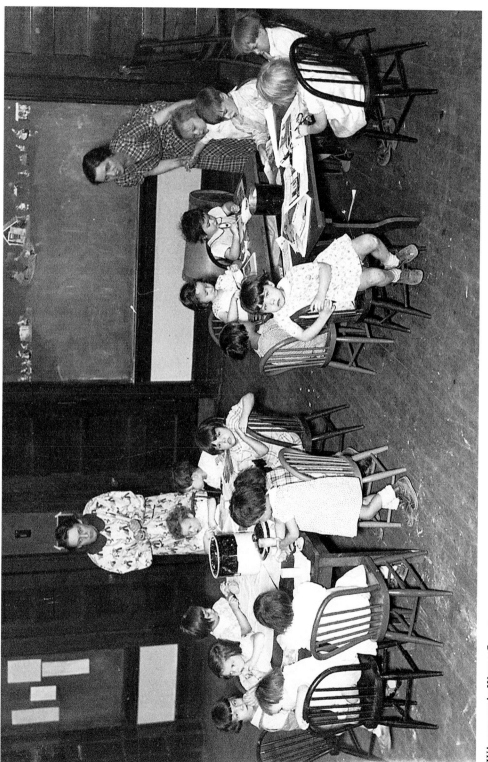

CWA nursery in Wayne County

Preparing CWA payrolls in Wayne County

CWA workers sewing clothing for Wayne County relief clients

Ingham County CWA float in parade staged on the 75th anniversary of the City of Lansing, May 18th, 1934, depicting examples of CWA work, etc. Float constructed by former CWA employees

CWA Administrative Activities

The present chapter is devoted to a brief consideration of certain phases of administrative effort arising out of the CWA program in Michigan, including labor relations and public relations.

Michigan CWA Safety Program

The Michigan Civil Works Administration, realizing its responsibility for returning CWA workers back to industry and their normal places in our economic life in a healthy, unimpaired physical condition, supported whole-heartedly the Federal CWA Safety program. All CWA operations were surrounded with a high standard of accident prevention service.

Scope of the Safety Program

The safety program which was developed for the Michigan CWA is explained in the following outline:

1. Organization, personnel, and general functions.

a. A State Safety Director and an assistant supervised and directed the safety work from the State Administration's office.

b. Five State District Safety Directors, with definite territories, periodically contacted the county administrators, assisted in county safety programs, and inspected CWA operations for dangerous conditions which might cause accidents.

c. Sixty-three full-time or part-time county safety inspectors, appointed by county administrators, and trained by district Safety directors, inspected and safe-guarded CWA operations in their respective counties.

d. Over 500 part-time or full-time safety inspectors, selected by their foremen, daily inspected and safe-guarded the particular job on which they were working.

2. Special safety undertakings

a. <u>First Aid Service</u>. All CWA employees were forcefully impressed with the necessity of applying immediate first aid attention to every minor cut, bruise, or injury, in order to prevent infections. The workers were particularly susceptible to infections because of their physical conditions. 1619 first aid kits were placed on as many CWA jobs. The effectiveness of the first aid service is attested by the fact that not a single fatality was reported due to an infection, following an injury.

b. <u>Red Cross First Aid Training Courses</u>. In order to provide proper training for those who administered first aid on each job, 50 Red Cross first aid training classes were conducted, giving instructions to 1207 CWA workers.

c. <u>Eye Protection</u>. Many CWA operations involved serious hazards to workers' eyes, due to flying particles of stone, gravel, frozen earth, concrete, and the like. To safe-guard the eyes, 1532 pair of goggles were provided. Their use no doubt saved many eyes.

d. <u>Safety Meetings</u>. A total of 252 safety meetings were held in various counties. These were attended by 9143 foremen and CWA workers.

e. <u>Safety Bulletins</u>. A total of 36 Safety Bulletins were prepared by the State Safety Director. The bulletins described the hazards of different types of CWA operations, and prescribed for their proper protection.

Accident and Fatality Record

3430 accidents of such severity that the injured person could not return to work the following day, were reported in Michigan on CWA operations. The frequency ratio of lost time accidents, based on a total of 58,000,000 hours worked, was 58.9. This ratio is higher than the frequency ratio of general industry, but it must be remembered that CWA operations were carried on under the most adverse weather conditions, and that many CWA employees, due to their subnormal physical condition and their inexperience in the work they were doing, were more susceptible to accidents than employees in industry.

It may be noted that out of those 3430 time losing accidents, 18.7% were caused by handling objects and materials; 16.2% were caused by falling objects; 15.4% were caused by hand tools; 13.8% were caused by falls of persons; and 10.2% were caused by stepping on and striking against objects.

A total of 20 men were killed on CWA operations. Of these 40% were caused by vehicles, street cars, trucks, automobiles, etc., while 30% were caused by falls of persons, and 15% were caused by falling objects. The use of explosives and hand tools each caused 5% of the fatalities.

Cost and Results of CWA Safety Work

The total cost of the CWA Safety program in Michigan approximated $25,000.00. This is less than $\frac{1}{10}$ of 1% of the total pay roll and is much less than is paid by general industry on safety work. It is estimated that general industry pays approximately ½ of 1% of its payroll for safety work.

There is no question but that the CWA Safety program resulted in the saving of many lives and in the prevention of many accidents. It also developed a safety consciousness in the minds of many thousands of its employees, who, as they go back to their places in industry or their various stations in life, will take with them a higher appreciation of the value of human life, and the necessity of its protection, through the great Gospel of Safety.

Compensation Division Activities

The Michigan CWA established the Compensation Division for the purpose of handling claims arising out of injuries sustained by (or the death of) CWA workers. A central office was deemed most advisable in order to insure prompt medical attention, uniform and efficient preparation of claims, and expeditious payment of the claims honored. The personnel consisted of a director, two claim examiners, two file clerks, and three stenographers. An Injury Clerk was designated in each county to discharge the duty of supervising the investigation of injuries, the arrangements for medical attention, and the preparation of formal claims.

A mass of claims for compensation and medical treatment, requiring immediate attention, arose almost before the state and local organizations were perfected. Many of those were incorrect or insufficient as to form.

Claims submitted by the counties to the state office were thoroughly examined, and classified. Forms improperly prepared were returned to the county for correction. When no compensation had been paid locally, but the case was obviously compensable, the claim was returned with instructions that compensation should be paid and necessary medical treatment authorized. A follow up system was utilized on all papers and forms returned to counties, so that claims would not be delayed in the event that papers were inadvertently laid aside or lost in the mail. Claims properly executed and complete in every detail were approved and sent to the United States Employees' Compensation Commission for official ruling.

An average of 50 new claims were filed in the State office daily during January and February. After March 1st those receipts had mounted to 80 per day. In addition, an average of 131 claims which had been returned to the counties for correction were re-submitted daily. At the end of March a total of over 225 old and new claims was being received daily.

At the end of February approximately 4600 claims were on hand in the counties, to be filed with the state office.[1] At this writing, claim counts as of April 1st are being filed and an estimate based on incomplete returns indicates that approximately 5500 unfiled claims were in the hands of the county authorities on that date.[2]

To and including the payrolls of March 8th, local payments of compensation amounted to approximately $25,000.

County administrations were confronted with many novel and difficult situations. Irregular work schedules, prejudiced witnesses, attempts by claimants to conceal pre-existing ailments, and inaccessible, isolated projects added considerably to their problems. All such matters were submitted to the State Division for explanation, interpretation and adjustment. County Administrations also met with considerable difficulty in completing claims on hand April 1st. Workmen from whom it was necessary to obtain statements had moved or left the county. The statement of the proper foreman was required on every claim; many of these men were not available. In some cases a Compensation Investigator was compelled to make several trips to distant points to secure a statement or signature.

In spite of these difficulties, it is anticipated that a high percentage of the unadjudicated claims will be submitted to the United States Employees' Compensation Commission within a few weeks.

Complaints typical of those that normally accompany such an enterprise were filed

---

1. The fact that the number of claims exceeds the number of accidents, previously discussed, results from the condition that the 3430 reported accidents included only those which caused a loss of time of one day or more, while the number of claims includes both claims for lost time and claims for medical attention growing out of injuries of such minor character as to entail less loss of time than one day.

2. Duplication exists between the two figures (4600 and 5500), for the reason that claims sent back to the counties for one reason or another enter into both totals.

by injured employees and others. Each of these required, as a matter of policy, correspondence and investigation—even though the complaints in nearly all cases were due to misunderstanding or lack of knowledge.

Contact was made between the State Compensation Division and county Administrations through the use of periodic bulletins, as well as through correspondence, telephone, and telegraph.

Correspondence Division

The Michigan CWA office received an avalanche of letters during its existence, touching in one way or another upon the CWA activity. The Correspondence Division, consisting of the director and six stenographers, was established for the purpose of dealing with this mail, and especially with those letters which registered complaints.

The mail received in January, February, and March was analyzed and classified in detail for the purpose of furnishing guidance to the state and local CWA authorities in Michigan. Statistics are therefore available for this period. The letters received during the three months above named numbered respectively 2132, 908, and 285; total 3325. The tabulation below presents further information concerning the origin and nature of this group of letters.

DIGEST OF CWA LETTERS RECEIVED DURING MONTHS OF JANUARY, FEBRUARY AND MARCH, 1934.

NO. OF LETTERS	WRITERS	OCCUPATION	SUBJECT OF COMMUNICATION
3,325	Men: 2,765	Laborer: 2,738	Complaint: 2830
	Women: 408	Clerical: 205	Asking information: 199
	Petitions: 91	Farmer: 138	Suggestion: 87
	Civic Group: 101		Request: 73
	Professional: 59		Praise: 73

NATURE OF COMPLAINTS

Protesting:

Failure to receive jobs....................................1,715

CWA salaries unfair or incorrect 382

Against being laid off 377

CWA jobs given to non-needy................................ 298

Miscellaneous 280

Discrimination against veterans 206

More than one in family holding CWA job....................... 163

Single men given CWA jobs 162

Political discrimination 120

Against Administration 119

Against reduction in hours and wages 98

Favoritism shown to farmers 85

Against graft 60

Against aliens being given preference 41

Discrimination against farmers 24

Favoritism shown union men 8

Favoritism shown non-union men 7

All letters were treated strictly on their merits and each was answered as promptly as possible. Some letters required merely a reply consisting of an explanation or some point of information, but many others required two or more letters. An example is found in complaints appearing to have an element of justification; these called for a reply to the complainant and a request for an investigation, addressed to the county administrator. It is therefore conservatively estimated that 6500 letters were sent out during the three months.

Complaint letters accounted for 87% of the total received, and 60.6% of all complaints protested inability to secure work under the CWA program. A lesser number claimed political discrimination, while still others showed evidence of animosity towards someone already on the CWA payroll. The retention of persons whose training and experience were such that they could not be replaced by any person who might qualify as needy, and who were rendered particularly useful for the efficient completion of the CWA project by those qualifications, also evoked some complaints.

Fortunately the correspondence Division was able to accomplish much more than the parrying of unjustified protests. Although many of the complaints came from so-called disgruntled individuals, many others were justified, and it was possible to secure numerous corrections. Because of the hasty organization of the CWA program, individuals had secured employment upon it who could not in any sense be construed as needy. When the attention of county administrators was called to specific instances, such individuals were laid off. In a number of cases skilled men were employed at skilled labor but were not being paid the rate of $1.20 per hour as specified by the federal administration. In other cases it was found that men had not been paid for work performed, and that remedy was delayed because the county administrative staff was unfamiliar with the procedure for making such a correction.

Purchasing

It was previously remarked [at the beginning of chapter IV] that the problem of putting the CWA into operation consisted of selecting projects, selecting men, and securing tools and materials to work with. It is natural, therefore, that the procurement of the tools, equipment, materials, and supplies necessary for the 12,000 CWA projects in Michigan constituted a very important phase of administrative activity.

Some of the problems encountered in meeting the material, tool, and other requirements of projects, and the approximate amount of money involved, have been mentioned heretofore [near the end of Chapter IV].

Organization

A central State (CWA) purchasing department was created for the purpose of instituting and maintaining an orderly and systematic procedure throughout the state in purchasing necessities, in paying for them, and in accounting for the funds expended. Each county administrator, in turn, appointed a bonded local purchasing agent.

The size of staff required to carry on the activities of the central purchasing office may be judged from the following data based on the payroll May 1st:

DIVISION	NO. OF PERSONS
Purchasing	127
Accounting	46
Board of review[3]	5
Statistical	19
Disbursing	107
Total	*304 employees*

It was expected that the Federal funds used for CWA purchases be accounted for in the manner prescribed by general Federal regulations governing procurements. Actually, however, the rush incident to launching work and the lack of familiarity with regulations, on the part of local authorities, resulted in extensive deviation from the Federal requirements. The vendors' claims for such purchases could, of course, not be approved by the state office. The resulting situation became so acute, both in Michigan and elsewhere, that President Roosevelt issued an executive order directing that all CWA purchases made prior

---

3. See post.

to February 15th, 1934, might be considered as emergency purchases and be exempted from the customary requirements, provided that a State Board of Review were constituted to examine and approve claims for materials, etc., purchased prior to that date and without full conformity to Federal regulations. Such a board was created in Michigan, March 6th.

Pressure of Work

The necessity facing each county administrator almost immediately upon receipt of his CWA employee quota—that of placing tools and materials on the job forthwith—resulted in the placing of great numbers of rush orders with dealers. The immediate response and helpful co-operation by the vendors proved of great assistance in minimizing delays on the job.

Because it was necessary that all vendors' claims pass through both the county and state offices before payment, however, bills could not be paid without some delay. Each voucher required the following attention in the county of its origin:

1. Check as to actual delivery of the goods.
2. Check as to correctness of the price.
3. Check as to proper vendor's claim affidavit.
4. Check as to vendor's NRA code compliance statement.
5. Check as to extensions of figures.
6. Approval of claim by County Purchasing agent.
7. Approval of claim by County Administrator.

After transmittal to Lansing, each voucher required examination and approval by the Purchasing Office, and, in many cases, an examination as to reasonableness of prices, by the Board of Review. Further, it was necessary for the Auditing and Accounting departments to check and enter for proper record; for the Statistical department to make entries designed as a basis for certain reports to Washington; and, finally, for the Disbursing office to examine and approve. Then and only then could the check be written and the vendor receive the money due to him.

Approximately 75,000 vouchers, for an average amount of about $110.00, were filed in the state office. The obvious result was both some delay in payment and an acute pressure of work. The office employees worked late into the night, without additional pay, in order that payments might be expedited as much as possible.

Some vendors were no doubt distressed by delay in payments, but, on the whole, they were extremely considerate. Their letters variously conveyed good will, impatience, consideration, condemnation, imploring appeals, and near financial tragedies. Not infrequently they would state "If I don't get my check next Monday, I'll go bankrupt," or "Let me see the color of a government check just once; then I'll pass it on to my creditors," or "the Government will put me in jail if I don't pay what I owe it; why in blazes don't you pay me?"

After creation of the Board of Review on March 6th, payments were accelerated greatly and much of the vendors' difficulties were relieved. The authorization for the payment of informal claims left as the only source of delay the physical limitation of the rapidity with which vouchers could be submitted, processed, and paid.

The greatest difficulty in arranging for the approval and payment of vouchers was encountered in the case of Detroit and Wayne County.

Present Status of Payments

On May 31st a total sum of $6,262,872.39 had been paid for materials. This is expected to represent very nearly 75% of the final total amount of claims. Payments are being made at the rate of about $100,000.00 per day.

Typical Local Purchasing—Ingham County

The following brief account of the (local) purchasing in Ingham County is presented as one typical of the experiences in most parts of the state.

The purchasing department of the Civil Works Administration in Ingham County was established about the first of December. For the two weeks prior to the department's inception, the various city and township officers in the county acted as purchasing agents for the procurement of tools, supplies, and materials for approved projects.

According to requirements of the Federal administration, the bids were made on forms furnished by the Federal Government. In case of bids of identical figures, the placing of the order was decided by lot. All bidders were of course required to comply with the provisions of the NRA code. Approximately two thousand requisitions and purchase orders amounting to about $200,000.00, were issued in Ingham county.

After the delivery of the tools or other materials, the reports of the vendors were signed either by the foreman or superintendent in charge of the project, or by the Work Director of the county. Upon receipt of this report, a voucher was prepared in quadruplicate and signed by the vendor. A statement that the vendor had complied with the code and was approved by the County Administration was incorporated in the voucher, which then passed through the process heretofore described, before payment was actually made.

Due to the fact that many thousands of vouchers were submitted, for payment, to one office almost simultaneously, considerable delay was encountered in paying the bills. Ingham County merchants of course objected to this delay. The condition improved greatly, however, after the creation of the State Board of Review on March 6th.

Because of the huge demand made by CWA activities, materials and supplies were extremely scarce in Ingham County. Delivery of tools was therefore delayed as much as two weeks, in some cases, and in others the manufacturers of tools were unable to fill orders within required time limits. There was, however, very little delay in the delivery of other materials.

Conclusion

The local purchasing agents, all things considered, did a thoroughly creditable and dependable job. A variation in conception is evidenced, however, by such events as the finding of one claim upon which three bids had been secured for two pounds of spikes (10 cts.), while the very next voucher (filed by another purchasing agent) stated that "emergency did not permit of securing bids" on $500.00 worth of lumber.

Public Relations & Publicity

By means of explanatory talks given by the officials of the State Emergency Relief Commission, before clubs and other gatherings interested in the accomplishments of CWA, and a public press very favorably inclined towards the program, public relations of the most pleasant kind were maintained throughout the life of the CWA.

The newspapers, both metropolitan daily and county weekly, gave freely of their space. The major part of the news published about CWA was kindly, and but few of the articles which reached print were censorious. It was particularly noticeable that the county weeklies were partial to the program—especially in regard to any part which affected their own home territory.

Sunday feature articles appeared in the metropolitan journals from time to time. These will prove of historical value, in addition to their immediate interest and usefulness. Seven capitol correspondents sent out a mass of constructive publicity. Papers having no correspondent at the capitol gave publicity to material furnished them by an ex-newspaper man employed by the Michigan State Emergency Welfare Relief Commission.

A particularly valuable series of articles bearing on CWA accomplishments appeared in the *Detroit News*. An example is reproduced on the pages immediately following.

Example of Michigan Publicity (Appeared in *Detroit News*, April 6, 1934).

FRUITS OF CWA LIVE ON THOUGH PARENT IS DEAD.

Miles of Pavements Improved, Buildings and Street Cars Refurbished,
New Trees Planted and Old Ones Saved.
By Donald Slutz.

Late last November, Detroit was electrified by the launching of the CWA program. Almost overnight, thousands of men were put to work and carloads of tools and equipment were rushed to project locations.

All departments of the City government, previously slowed down to bare maintenance operations, swung swiftly into action. Dozens of projects were prepared, approved, started. Unemployed men were registered, selected, assigned to jobs.

With a few weeks, no less than 45,000 Detroiters were drawing CWA paychecks.

Then the army of workers began to dwindle and finally, on March 31, was completely demobilized. Work halted. The CWA was done.

About four and one-third months had elapsed and during this period, the Federal Government had poured into Detroit nearly $14,000,000 for wages and tools and materials.

ENJOY FIRST RESPITE.

City officials, many of whom worked day and night, Sundays included, to keep the program moving, this week are enjoying their first respite and are looking back over those months of intense activity to measure the permanent physical improvements which the CWA brought to Detroit. Meanwhile, they are adjusting themselves to the new work-relief program that promises, in a small way, to replace the CWA.

It is difficult, these department heads find, to comprehend the extent to which the CWA has improved the City's "plant." The program was so vast, so elaborate and so extensive that only the high spots can be mentioned when officials begin to point with pride.

It would be virtually impossible, for example, to estimate the number of square yards of surface that were painted during the CWA period. The painter's brush fell on exteriors and interiors of buildings, street cars and buses, fences, street signs. The ceiling of the Council chamber, incidentally, was painted for the first time in 60 years.

MAJOR IMPROVEMENTS.

Before the program was done, Purchasing Commissioner Gorman had bought 77,974 gallons of paint.

Other major improvements which officials point to include the following:

Eighty miles of unpaved streets were graded and surfaced and 30,000 feet of street drainage equipment was installed.

Sections of 38 paved streets were widened in strips varying from one block to two miles.

The Rouge River, choked in several spots with brush and rubbish, was cleaned up, thus preventing possible flooding and destroying potential breeding areas for mosquitoes.

About 375 DSR street cars and 105 buses were completely overhauled, including repainting of bodies, rehabilitation of motors, reupholstering of seats and replacement of worn-out units.

Twenty miles of DSR car tracks were rebuilt, including the repairing of pavement between the tracks, thus making smoother riding for motorists as well as DSR patrons. Off-center tracks, such as those on Davison Avenue East, which caused numerous traffic accidents, were centered.

TREES PLANTED.

More than 16,500 trees were planted in City parks and along 46 miles of streets; 36,000 trees were trimmed; about 4,000 dead, diseased or dangerous trees were removed and 1,561 ailing trees were doctored. The new trees included 4,000 American elms that were planted on the east end of Belle Isle.

This reforestation work also included the removal from trees of 5,486 quarts of cocoons— or about 21,600,000 potential caterpillars.

Extensive improvements at the Airport, both to the grounds and the hangar, were completed.

Thirty-two sewer jobs, ranging from the building of manholes to the construction of a four-foot sewer under Second Boulevard between Philadelphia and Seward avenues, were finished.

And more than 350,000 school books were mended, recovered or otherwise rehabilitated.

There were dozens of other projects, large and a small, but this list offers an idea of what the CWA has meant to Detroit in physical improvements.

(End of *Detroit News* article).

Labor Relations

The Michigan Civil Works Administration endeavored to enforce the observance of the regulations of the Federal Civil Works Administration, whereby minimum wages of 50 cents and $1.20 per hour were established for unskilled and skilled labor, respectively.

Some tendency developed, on the part of local administrations, particularly in certain preponderantly rural sections of the state, to pay skilled labor a rate under the minimum. Every such violation which came to the attention of the state administration was corrected.

In some vicinities, as Detroit, for example, the wages paid were in excess of the minimum of 50 cts. and $1.20, for the reason that the local prevailing wage rates were determined to be in excess of these rate minimums. Employees on road projects outside of the corporate limits of municipalities were paid at rates established by the State Highway Department, but in no case less than 40 cts. per hour.

In some communities the prevailing wage rates were determined partly or solely by labor unions. In certain quarters adjustment boards, existing under various titles and constituted locally to hear labor grievances and advise administrators, figured in wage schedule determinations.

No strikes developed in Michigan and only one was seriously threatened. Many grievances, individual and collective, arose, however. The local administrations and the field representatives of the state office dealt with those, mainly. In the counties having adjustment boards, the latter rendered valuable assistance in this regard. Some county administrations established definite complaint departments to deal with grievances. Wage adjustments were made whenever justified.

Thousands of individual complaints were made by persons unable to obtain CWA work. A lesser number of complaints were made by employees protesting such matters as lay-off, unfair or incorrect wages, etc. Most individual wage rate complaints hinged upon the employee's status as a skilled tradesman. Every effort was bent to remedy all injustices, of whatever kind, to which attention was called. This matter has been touched upon previously in this chapter, under the heading <u>Correspondence Division</u>.

A considerable number of complaints regarding the giving or denial of preference to both union labor and farmers, was made. It is probable that farmers actually fared better in assignments, as to numbers, than a rigid interpretation of the rules required.

All in all, it must be said that labor relations on the CWA program were harmonious and successful in Michigan.

Engineering

This important phase of administrative and technical activity has been heretofore discussed, in Chapter IV. It is further alluded to in connection with the various projects discussed, and in the concluding chapter.

FERA Activities

The subject matter of this chapter deals with certain phases of the relief activity centered primarily in the FERA rather than in the CWA.

Women's Division

In October, 1933, the Federal Emergency Relief Administration created a women's division under the direction of Mrs. Ellen S. Woodward to handle emergency problems relating to women, with special emphasis on providing emergency facilities for destitute women and girls and stressing the necessity of meeting employment, food, clothing, and housing needs. Each state was requested to appoint a Director of Women's Work, and early in November when the CWA was being launched, a definite effort was made to include projects for the employment of women in the CWA plans. To further this activity, representative women from many women's organizations were requested to meet in Washington for "A White House Conference on Emergency Needs of Women," on November 20, 1933.

The Beginnings of the Women's Division

This meeting was attended by Mrs. Roosevelt, who has been a steady supporter of all efforts to provide employment for women. During the meeting, all National Women's Organizations were urged to get in touch with their state organizations and enlist their interest in helping the State Emergency Relief Commission to establish an effective Women's Work Division, and to assist in the planning of projects adapted to the needs of individual communities. A brief census of the types of work in which unemployed and needy women might find employment was made at the meeting.

Following the conference, each State Director of Women's Work was requested to call a general meeting of persons interested in women's work, and in Michigan such a meeting was held early in December. This meeting was attended by representatives from organizations interested in work for women, both public and private. The women's organizations of Michigan displayed a very keen interest in the problem in hand.

The above series of events led to the actual launching of women's work in Michigan. Many very desirable projects were submitted for approval in every field of activity in which women are interested, such as sewing centers, nursing service, visiting housekeeping, library work, and many others. Prominent projects undertaken include the Child Health Survey, employing 107 nurses, and the State Welfare Department project, both of which have been heretofore discussed.

Civil Works Service

All women provided employment were originally included in the CWA quota allowed each State. In Michigan this quota was practically filled before plans could be made for projects providing employment for women. Consequently, the number of women thus employed was very small in proportion to the total quota. When it became apparent that many projects were not eligible, under the ruling that CWA projects must be construction work, a separate division of Civil Works Service was created. These projects were, in general, especially adapted to the needs of women, but it was necessary to pay for them from Emergency Relief funds. Since Michigan had a very large relief load at this time, however, and the entire appropriation was needed for relief purposes, very few Civil Works Service projects were undertaken.

Extent of Women's Work

In March the following projects employing women were under way in Michigan:

2 Sewing Rooms, employing	224 women
5 Library & Education, employing	635 women
18 Studies, Surveys and Research, employing	316 women
14 Office Work, employing	117 women
39 Projects	Total employed 1292 Women

In addition, a number of women were employed in local Civil Works and Emergency Relief offices doing clerical work, and on various Federal Research Projects. All of these Federal projects were outlined in Washington, but the individuals carrying on the work were selected and supervised locally.

The number of women provided employment through CWA, CWS, and the Emergency Educational Program supervised by the State Department of Public Instruction, is as follows: January, 4073; February, 4349; March, 4506. This is a very small number out of the total CWA quota, since statistics show that women constitute ten per cent of the total registration of unemployed persons, both on the Unemployment Census of 1930 and the recent registration at the Federal Employment Bureaus.

Women's Work after CWA

Since the creation of the Work Division of the State Commission, April 1st, practically all the projects for women have been continued except those CWA projects that were abolished with the discontinuance of CWA. In many instances it has been necessary, for example, to replace women working on library repair projects who were not eligible as relief cases, by less skilled women from the relief rolls, but the work has gone forward in a modified form.

In Wayne County a very fine plan for employing women on sewing work has been worked out in co-operation with the Red Cross. The women on this project make surgical dressings for public hospitals, and do routine sewing. This project provides employment for several hundred women, and has the hearty support of the community.

The rural program necessitating payment in kind has made it very difficult to carry on women's work in the rural counties. Some plans have already been submitted for carrying on gardening activities using the services of women, and for canning centers to be established later in the summer season in co-operation with the Extension Division of the Home Economics Division at Michigan State College.

Teachers' Work Relief Program

The Michigan State Emergency Welfare Relief Commission, in co-operation with the State Department of Public Instruction (which includes the State Board for Vocational Rehabilitation), launched the "Emergency Program for Work Relief in Education" late in November, 1933. This activity was designed for the primary purpose of providing work for needy persons competent to give instruction or perform other incidental duties, and for the collateral purpose of accomplishing in some measure certain ends desirable from the educators' standpoint.

Scope of the Program

The Work Relief in Education program, more commonly referred to as the Teachers' Work Relief program, consists of the following (which is not exclusive):

1. <u>Rural education</u>. A school district having a population less than 5,000 persons is eligible for assistance in the form of teachers' salaries paid out of FERA funds, provided that the district is unable to keep the school open in spite of maximum efforts to raise local funds.
2. <u>Literacy classes</u>. Teachers may be provided to teach classes of persons over 14 years of age, who are unable to read or write with the ability of a fifth grade pupil. There were 76,800 illiterates in the state in 1930.
3. <u>Vocational education</u>. Trade extension and training opportunities are furnished unemployed adults who are in need of vocational training or adjustment in order to make them employable. Classes in home economics, agriculture, parent education, commercial subjects, trades, industry, and technical subjects (as architectural drawing, machine design, estimating, applied mathematics and science) are included. A minimum enrollment of 10 persons is required.
4. <u>Vocational rehabilitation</u>. This activity provides a service of vocational rehabilitation to physically disabled persons in need thereof and who cannot be accommodated through the regular rehabilitation program, and, further, it provides for the employment of needy persons of suitable background, for the purpose of effecting the rehabilitation work. Case workers and clerical assistants predominate among the work relief employees.

5. General adult education. Under this phase of the program, needy and qualified persons teach unemployed and other adults who are in need of further general education or workers' education. Activities include art courses, college courses (which do not duplicate available local facilities), general courses such as literature, etc., dramatic arts, immigrant education, hobby and club activities, musical training, physical training and recreation, and workers' education. The latter comprises studios in industrial organization, economic history, current economic problems, and public speaking and parliamentary law. A minimum enrollment of 10 persons is required.

6. Nursery schools. Emergency nursery schools provide educational guidance for children and health service and educational guidance for parents.

Control and Supervision

Teachers and others participating in this program as employees must be certified as eligible for work relief. Otherwise the local school authorities determine upon and select the personnel. They also provide all physical facilities, make general arrangements, and supervise the activity. The State Department of Public Instruction assists in the organization and supervision, however, and the state's system of higher education cooperates and gives counsel.

FERA funds are, with few exceptions, used only for personnel salaries and wages. A scale of rates graduated according to population applies uniformly throughout the state, except that salaries under the rural school phase of the program may be paid in accordance with the respective salaries paid prior to the closing of the schools, with a maximum of $100.00 per month. Salaries paid under the vocational rehabilitation program also depart from the uniform scale.

Magnitude of the Effort

The following tabulation indicates the number of persons employed upon the program as a whole each month to date, and the funds expended for the wages of these work relief employees:

	NO. EMPLOYED	AMT. SPENT
December, '33	40	1,617.15
January, '34	1793	57,323.80
February	2027	85,516.30
March	1901	76,618.81
April	1980	91,303.21

Student Aid

When announcement was made early in February that the Federal government had allotted some emergency funds to assist financially distressed students by means of providing for wages to be paid for services performed upon part-time jobs, practically every educational institution giving work of college grade in Michigan applied for this form of assistance.

Selection of Students

Each college administration caused to be constituted a special loan committee. These committees were charged with the duty of selecting the students to be assigned to the available part-time jobs.

Inability to complete the college year without assistance, or the degree of need approximating this state most closely, was the first basis of selection. An average scholastic grade of "C," or better, was a second requirement. Finally, acceptance of applications was subject to the restriction that the numbers of men and women assigned must bear a common ratio to the masculine and feminine student population, respectively, in each institution. The latter proved a very popular plan because theretofore women had found it very difficult to secure part-time employment.

Circumstances of Applicants

Investigation of the circumstances of the individual applicants for part-time employment under the student aid program revealed a general picture of the financial problems of a considerable section of college students in Michigan, and also a glimpse of the students' efforts to meet their problems.

The majority of students who applied had theretofore been financing their education almost wholly by their own efforts. Not uncommonly the parents had found it possible to contribute the amount of tuition charges, the student being obliged to attempt to provide all other necessities, such as board, room, clothing, books, and incidentals, by his own efforts.

The economic difficulties of the times had not only diminished the student's assistance from his parents; they had also rendered almost insuperably difficult the securing of normal part-time employment. Further, nearly all of the applicants had been forced into debt, the amounts varying from small sums to sums of more than $1,000.00. Michigan students were probably particularly hard hit, as compared with other states, in consequence of the distressing conditions arising out of the large sums of money impounded in closed banks.

The investigations showed clearly the hardships which the students were willing to subject themselves to in order to secure a college education. They revealed, further, that, in addition to those students who were on the point of being forced out of school, many others were being obliged to do without things necessary in order to derive the full benefits of the usual college opportunities.

Types of Work Performed

A survey of the student aid activity in Michigan disclosed that students assigned to clerical work headed the list. Those engaged upon janitorial work, research assistantships, and library duty followed in close order. In all, over 50 types of work were pursued. The nature of work performed In libraries, for example, is suggested by the following quotation from the report of one institution: "Nineteen girls are working part time in our college library. Nine are spending the few hours allotted at the circulation desk getting and taking care of books, picking up reserve lists of books, and similar work which is necessary in a well-kept library. Nine are working in the mending department where a great ultimate saving becomes possible in the repair of books and magazines and thus prolonging their usefulness. Another is working at the magazine desk, while still another is engaged in typing library cards and similar work, one of the girls having had three years experience before coming to college in a large city public library."

The officials of the educational institutions participating experienced little difficulty in finding suitable part-time positions upon which the students might be engaged. An accumulation of undone necessary work solved the question in many cases.

Results of the Program

Over 2500 students in 38 institutions of higher learning in Michigan have benefitted by the FERA student aid program. 1421 students had received aid before March 1st.

A considerable collateral benefit has inured to the educational institutions themselves. Personnel reductions necessitated by reduced budgets have been, in some measure, offset by the student employees engaged upon the many phases of campus work under the FERA plan. Future maintenance costs have been reduced by timely attention to the physical plants. Finally, the institutions have been enabled to accomplish necessary work which would in no event have been undertaken, except for the student aid program.

At the end of the winter semester, several institutions reported that some of the men and women receiving assistance through the FERA program had achieved ranking on the

Table IX. Part Time Jobs for College Students: Pay Roll Summary.

| | MONTH OF FEBRUARY | | | STATE OF MICHIGAN | |
HOURLY RATE	NUMBER OF HOURS	AMOUNT	PERCENT	NUMBER BENEFITED	PERCENT
$0.30	22464⅙	$6,739.21	64.66%	926	65.03%
0.31½	37	11.66	0.10	2	0.14
0.35	7196½	2505.86	20.72	242	17.00
0.37½	705	264.38	2.03	18	1.26
0.40	3114¾	1245.90	8.97	142	9.97
0.45	66⅔	30.00	0.19	2	0.14
0.50	1156½	578.28	3.33	92	6.46
TOTAL	34740⁷⁄₁₂	$11,375.29	100.00%	1424	100.00%
0.3275 Average Hourly Wage					

CLASS BENEFITED	NUMBER	PERCENT
Freshman	461	32.44%
Sophomore	291	20.48
Junior	261	18.37
Senior	279	19.63
Graduate	129	9.08

Note: Some students receive two or more rates per hour, so the number of students and number benefited will not correspond.

high scholastic lists of their respective institutions. Considering that the working student does not have as much time to devote to his studies as a non-working student, this fact is especially noteworthy. It is indicative of earnestness, serious-mindedness, and a real desire to achieve a college education, on the part of the needy students.

A gratifying improvement in the financial plight of the primary beneficiaries of the Federal student aid undertaking—the deserving students—is evident upon every campus. Without question of a doubt this project has made it possible for a large number of Michigan young people to continue educational pursuits which they otherwise would have been forced to abandon. It has given them more courage and hope and many have expressed a sincere feeling of gratitude for the Government's aid. Faith in the future of our country is being restored little by little by such moves as the distribution of funds for needy college students.

The tables on the three pages following contain data as to the exact types of work performed, the numbers aided, participating institutions, wage rates, etc.

Table X. Part Time Jobs for College Students: Pay Roll Summary.

MONTH OF FEBRUARY, STATE OF MICHIGAN

KIND OF WORK	NUMBER EMPLOYED	KIND OF WORK	NUMBER EMPLOYED
Athletic Assistant	10	Medical Office	2
Accompanist	1	Metallurgy	5
Campus Patrol	2	Miscellaneous	36
Clearing Land	3	Museum	6
Chemistry	5	Music	2
Civil Mining	5	Night Watchman	7
Clerical	375	Painter	7
Dining Room Help	59	Parking	4
Dormitory Assistant	8	Physics—Mathematics	5
Drawing	13	Research Assistant	116
Editorial	7	Reader	12
Electrician	10	Repair Work	12
Experimental	4	Receiving Room	4
Fireman	13	Secretarial	4
Filing	17	Shop Work	10
Forestry	3	Social	7
Gymnasium	4	Stenographer	60
Geology	5	Statistical	10
Hall Duty	1	Student Assistant	42
Janitorial	242	Student Foreman	1
Kitchen Help	24	Supervision	5
Laboratory Work	84	Switchboard	6
Library Work	102	Technician	24
Marking Papers	3	Washing	7
Mechanical	5	Working on Grounds & Bldgs.	55
Messenger	1	TOTAL	1455

Note: Some students perform two or more duties, so total number employed will not corresponded with total number of students.

Table XI. Part Time Jobs for College Students: Pay Roll Analysis.

MONTH OF FEBRUARY, STATE OF MICHIGAN, YEAR 1934

COLLEGE	PAY ROLL	NUMBER OF HOURS							AMOUNT PAID	
		0.30¢	0.31½¢	0.35¢	0.37½¢	0.40¢	0.45¢	0.50¢	0.30¢	0.31½¢
Adrian	$11.66		37							$11.66
Albion	277.54	858¾		57					$257.59	
Alma	362.26	1207							362.26	
Battle Creek	413.77	1379¼							413.77	
Bay City Junior	84.30	281							84.30	
Calvin	339.09			578¾		250		73		
Catholic Junior	79.70					199¼				
Central State Teachers	338.93	1129¾							338.93	
Detroit Institute of Technology	56.47	188¼							56.47	
Emmanuel Missionary	279.93	933							279.93	
Ferris Institute	52.20	25				38		59	7.50	
Flint Junior	139.26	464¼							139.26	
Grand Rapids Junior	231.07	770½							231.07	
Hillsdale	440.05	444		591		200		40	133.20	
Hope	580.00					1412½		30		
Ironwood Junior	255.00				680					
Jackson Junior	198.55	5		563					1.50	
Kalamazoo	390.51	1301¾							390.51	
Marygrove	525.00			943		150	66 2/3	210		
Michigan College of Mining	188.70	629							188.70	
Michigan State	1556.66	3808¼		965¾	25	160		5½	1142.50	
Michigan State Normal	2.70	9							2.70	
Muskegon Junior	66.75	222½							66.75	
Nazareth	165.00	550							165.00	
Western State Teachers	54.60	182							54.60	
Olivet	315.00	1050							315.00	
Port Huron Junior	61.80	206							61.80	
St. Joseph's	150.60	502							150.60	
Suomi	75.45	251½							75.45	
University of Detroit	1185.32			3386½						
University of Michigan	808.33	495		46½		685		739	148.53	
Wayne University	1136.18	3760½				20			1128.18	
Western State Teachers	492.91	1610⅓		28					483.11	
Spring Arbor Seminary	60.00	200							60.00	
TOTAL	$11,375.29	22464⅙	37	7196½	705	3114¾	66⅔	1156½	$6,739.21	$11.66

AMOUNT PAID					NUMBER BENEFITED							NUMBER BENEFITED PER CLASS				
0.35¢	0.37½¢	0.40¢	0.45¢	0.50¢	0.30¢	0.31½¢	0.35¢	0.37½¢	0.40¢	0.45¢	0.50¢	FR.	SO.	JR.	SR.	GRAD.
						2						1	1			
$19.95					46		3					19	11	8	11	
					24							2	6	4	12	
					28							6	5	6	11	
					15							10	5			
202.59		$100.00		$36.50			22		10		6	9	5	9	12	
		79.70							11			3	8			
					46							9	15	11	11	
					23							12	4	6	1	
					20							12	5	3		
		15.20		29.50	2				3		2	4	3			
					28							20	8			
					48							42	6			
206.85		80.00		20.00	10		18		4		1	8	9	10	6	
		565.00		15.00					43		1	8	12	10	14	
	$255.00							17				13	4			
197.05					1		15					11	5			
					30							8	7	6	7	2
330.00		60.00	$30.00	105.00			22		4	2	7	19	6	7	3	
					37							2	6	8	19	2
338.03	9.38	64.00		2.75	126		46	1	5		1	39	38	40	46	16
					1											1
					13							10	3			
					11							5		4	2	
					38							9	8	12	9	
					21							5	6	7	3	
					10							5	5			
					13							4	5	3	1	
					19							10	4			5
1185.32							107					40	24	19	24	
16.27		274.00		369.53	45		8		61		74	11	12	33	50	82
		8.00			173				1			85	32	20	16	21
9.80					94		1					18	21	35	21	
					4							2	2			
$2,505.86	$264.38	$1,245.90	$30.00	$578.28	926	2	242	18	142	2	92	461	291	261	279	129

CHAPTER VIII

CWA in Detroit and Wayne County

The CWA activities in the metropolitan area of Wayne County attained such magnitude as to warrant that special attention be devoted them in this report.

Organization

The Wayne County Commission consisted of James Fitzgerald, Detroit; Ruth Huston Whipple, Plymouth; and the Reverend Father Frederick Siedenburg, Detroit. John F. Ballenger served as administrative officer in charge of all Wayne County CWA activities, and William C. Markley and L. P. Cookingham filled the post of Deputy Administrators.

To facilitate the work undertaken, the county was divided into three parts, viz: the city of Detroit proper, the various other municipalities of the county, and the balance of the county area. The work in Detroit was under the direction of Lawrence G. Lenhardt; the work in the out-county municipalities came under the direction of L. P. Cookingham, Deputy Administrator; and work in the remainder of the county was directed by various county officials. The smaller municipalities and the townships ultimately placed much of their work in the hands of the County Road Commission and the County Drain Commission.

Project Selection

During the first days of the CWA period projects were selected with the primary view of putting men to work with minimum delay. Sewer repairs, street grading, paving repairs, and painting were types of work which readily met this requirement. These provided a ready means for absorbing a large volume of common labor, but could not be expected to fill the requirements for the entire CWA period. The problem of determining upon projects capable of supplying the necessary man-hours of work, and possible of completion within 90 days, for continuing the program, therefore remained to be solved.

The Detroit and Wayne County organizations had relatively little difficulty in perfecting plans for the more important projects eventually undertaken by them. The services of trained and competent men made it possible for them to find and launch suitable projects with dispatch.[1] The small municipalities and townships, lacking in proper guiding talent, however, encountered difficulty. This situation led to the establishment of a special department, under Mr. Cookingham, to plan projects for these communities, and also to the commitment of much of the work to the County Road Commission and the County Drain Commission, as previously mentioned.

By January 1st (1934) the classification of projects under way had been expanded to embrace nearly every phase of public works. Paving, sidewalk repair, painting, water main construction, street railway track replacement, and renovation of virtually every public building were in progress. In the jurisdictions of the two county commissions above named, abundant work was being found upon undertakings involving the grading of country roads, widening and cleaning of county drains, repairing and building sewers, maintaining public buildings, and the erection of necessary public buildings.

Projects Undertaken

A total of 50 projects were launched in the City of Detroit. These entailed an expenditure of $13,968,956.00, of which $3,775,950.00 was used for material, and the balance for labor. The following projects were included in the Detroit program:

---

1. The Department of Public Works and the Department of Parks and Boulevards, for example, assisted vitally in instituting and completing many of the most worthy projects in Detroit. An efficient City Purchasing Department contributed to the success.

PROJECTS	TOTAL EXPENDITURE	PROJECTS	TOTAL EXPENDITURE
Unpaved streets	$2,194,650.00	PLC (Public Lighting Com.)	88,500.00
Paving repairs	1,955,000.00	Small buildings	78,500.00
Sidewalks	111,000.00	Water Board	405,000.00
Sewers	545,000.00	Detroit Street Railway	3,275,000.00
Parks	1,550,000.00	Detroit Zoological Gardens	200,000.00
Building maintenance	945,000.00	Police Signals	39,000.00
Fire Department	410,417.00	Street signs	40,000.00
Police Department	85,000.00	Yard buildings and Yard repairs	150,000.00
Health Department	144,100.00	City Planning Commission	32,265.00
Department of Public Works	40,000.00	Plans and surveys	80,000.00
Library	103,600.00	PLC	170,000.00
Art	4,300.00	Emergency landing fields	118,000.00
Detroit City Airport	160,000.00	Rapid Transit	27,891.00
Water Board	209,583.00	Economic Plan Investigation	16,000.00
Board of Education	1,175,000.00	Woodward water main	5,500.00
Department of Recreation	422,000.00	Woodward PLC duct	14,850.00

The Detroit City Airport improvement affords a typical example of CWA work. With a total appropriation of $160,000.00 the entire interior of the huge hangar was painted; underground gasoline tanks were removed to less hazardous locations; obstructions bordering on the field were repainted to conform with Bureau of Aeronautics standards; new lighting equipment was installed; and additions to existing buildings were erected. All this work constituted necessary improvements but would have been impossible, except for the CWA, due to the strained financial condition of the city. Airport engineers planned and supervised the undertaking.

Another outstanding example of CWA work is found at the Detroit Zoological Gardens. Due to the large number of men available, improvements that normally would have required several years for completion were effected in the brief CWA period. These included the construction of buildings for housing animals, animal exhibition pens, a greenhouse, and an addition to the machine shops. The Zoo projects probably represent the most efficient CWA work performed in Wayne County.

One of the largest projects undertaken in Detroit centered upon the municipally owned street railway system. It was put in an excellent state of repair under the CWA program.

Selection of Employees

The rule requiring the first 50% of the CWA labor to be taken from the Welfare rolls, and the next 50% from the unemployed, was strictly adhered to in most cases. Exceptions were made, however, as in the instance of the Eloise Sewer Project. Here soil conditions 30 feet underground necessitated the hiring of experienced "Muckers."

A system of personnel records was established, through which it was found that men from practically all walks of life were numbered among those working in ditches and on roads with picks and shovels. Highly trained professional men such as engineers, lawyers, and school teachers were included, as were skilled mechanics. The leadership and supervision for the more important work which followed was provided by these professional and skilled men. Wage adjustments were made to conform with the nature of work done, with the result that CWA work in Detroit was in many instances more remunerative than factory work.

Investigation revealed a tendency for prospective CWA workers to attempt to secure assignment as skilled laborers. For example, over 40,000 men registered as painters, although that group normally numbers only about 7,000 in the Detroit area. The fact that painters were among the highest paid CWA employees, and possibly a fancied ability to conceal lack of skill in this type of work, offers a plausible explanation of this peculiar situation.

Difficulties Encountered

No enterprise such as the CWA undertaking could be expected to flourish without attendant obstacles and difficulties. Certainly these existed, but they were surmounted for the most part.

The quest for suitable projects in some parts of the county has been mentioned as an early problem. Another acute problem arose during the first rush when every available shovel in the county had been purchased and the shovel supply was quite depleted. The unexpected demand for materials also created a shortage which frequently delayed work and forced men to remain idle. Finally, the unusually severe winter hindered progress, particularly upon road work and street railway repairs.

These unavoidable hostile influences inevitably resulted in considerable inefficiency upon the CWA projects. Nevertheless they were completed on scheduled time in most instances.

Effects of the CWA in Wayne County

Within a week after the inauguration of the CWA program, 10,000 welfare clients and unemployed had been put to work. Men soft from idleness of perhaps two years duration and in some cases gaunt from hunger were being rehabilitated by earning wages more than sufficient for their immediate needs; others were being spared the necessity for rehabilitation in the near future.

A total of 41,803 CWA men were employed in the city of Detroit alone during the period of its existence while approximately 14,000 additional men found work in the county outside of Detroit. Approximately 20,120,000 man-hours of labor were performed throughout the period.

The effect of the CWA from an economic standpoint became apparent after its first week. The stimulation of business brought about by CWA material purchases was the first noticeable change. With the initial payroll both the large and small shopkeepers felt the improved business, for the major part of a large proportion of the first pay checks was applied on the grocery or butcher bill. By January 1st business throughout the city had felt the beneficial effects, and by the middle of January increased employment became noticeable as men left CWA work to go back to their previous occupations in factories, stores and offices. The improvement in conditions has been sustained since.

The most noticeable effect of the CWA, aside from providing food, clothing, fuel and shelter, for fully 15% of the population at the most critical period in the history of Detroit, was the remarkable rise in the morale of the people. Where a year before riots and violence were common, and revolution a common topic of conversation, confidence in the Government had been restored, and a new outlook on the future had apparently been inculcated. The renewed confidence and faith in the future of the United States is indicated in part by the fact that the Communist party was able to muster less than 100 followers for its demonstration in Detroit, during the month of March, while two years earlier as high as 30,000 followers were in evidence.

In Detroit and vicinity the official statistics show an increase of 134% in employment over a year ago, about ¾ of which has been gained since January 1st of this year.

Accomplishments and Results of the Michigan CWA

I t would be difficult to develop fully the subject suggested by the above title. This is true, firstly, because the more obvious and concrete benefits are extensive, and, secondly, because intangible benefits and tangible benefits somewhat difficult of measurement must be considered in any inclusive appraisal. The effort here is directed primarily toward the more obvious results of the CWA enterprise.

Secondary Accomplishments—the Work Done

Kind and Extent of Projects Consummated

The foregoing pages have conveyed a picture of the secondary or collateral attainments under the CWA program—that is the completed construction and other projects. The variety need not be discussed further. The extent of such work is best suggested by the dollars involved: $36,000,000.00 for labor and nearly $9,000,000 for materials Every section of the state has benefited through the completion of some link in this great chain of 12,000 CWA accomplishments.

Conformity of the Work to State and Local Needs

Definite evidence is not at hand to show that the work performed paralleled the needs of the state and local communities. However, the manner of project selection, the popular favor of the program, the selection, the popular favor of the program, the disappointments voiced upon cessation of the work, attests to the urgent necessity for many individual undertakings theretofore unduly delayed, and the patent merits of much of the completed work, all militate toward the conclusion that the work done was necessary and well worth while.

Project Status on March 31st

It is estimated that approximately 75% of all projects had been completed at time of the cessation of CWA work on March 31st. Considering the exceptionally inclement weather encountered, as discussed in Chapter I, and, further, considering that the work was discontinued a month earlier than originally proposed by the Federal government, the status of projects on March 31st would appear quite satisfactory. Many of the uncompleted projects had advanced so far as to render completion with local funds quite feasible; and most of the remaining projects have been or are being prosecuted under the work relief program which supplanted the CWA on April 1st.

Efficiency of Work Upon Projects

The efficiency attained on projects is conservatively judged as moderate or fair. Michigan climate, particularly in the northern sections of the state, is not conducive to the highest efficiency upon winter work. The particularly severe winter experienced this year naturally tended to detract from overall efficiency on all work subject to the influence of the weather. Delays in the delivery of tools and materials, and the resulting idleness, detracted further from the optimum efficiency. On the other hand, very good engineering practice, manifested in adequate supervision and close inspection by the regional engineers as well as in the worthy efforts of local engineering talent, promoted efficiency, conservation of funds, and high quality in the finished product.

Table XII. Civil Works Employment and Payrolls in Michigan.

WEEK ENDING	NUMBER EMPLOYED	PAYROLL FOR LABOR	WEEK ENDING	NUMBER EMPLOYED	PAYROLL FOR LABOR
November 16, 1933	343	$2,514.64	March 1, 1934	129,786	$1,701,951.64
November 23	33,430	$310,891.13	March 8	123,214	$1,688,445.38
November 30	60,727	$679,846.36	March 15	118,153	$1,590,736.35
December 7	89,522	$1,202,191.47	March 22	106,271	$1,484,416.26
December 14	118,104	$1,647,238.15	March 29	92,919	$1,320,527.10
December 21	154,018	$2,285,943.36	April 5	71,543	$932,272.46
December 28	161,167	$2,338,797.53	April 12	3,166	$75,138.23
January 4, 1934	162,685	$2,570,935.75	April 19	2,212	$50,858.18
January 11	167,533	$2,853,863.12	April 26	1,502	$34,043.95
January 18	167,286	$2,909,970.44	May 3	1,264	$28,085.24
January 25	165,244	$2,188,623.71	May 10	986	$22,942.36
February 1	148,225	$1,904,717.22	May 17	813	$19,415.33
February 8	148,852	$1,996,318.80	May 24	616	$15,894.12
February 15	145,287	$1,889,316.36	May 31	512	$12,402.26
February 22	139,375	$1,881,116.68	Total		$35,639,413.54

Primary Accomplishments

The primary intent of the CWA program was to assist, through the medium of adequate wages in return for honest effort, a large number of people who found themselves in either distressing or unfortunate economic circumstances. That this end was attained in Michigan is beyond doubt.

Wages Distributed and Numbers Aided

The tabulation above (Table XII) presents the approximate labor payroll by weeks, and the number of wage recipients. The figures are based upon weekly telegraphic reports and are, therefore, not precise. Accurate statistics for the entire period are, however, not available at this writing.

Effect on Relief Caseloads and Expenditures

The effect of the CWA in Michigan upon relief caseloads and expenditures may be surmised, at a glance, upon turning to the charts (i.e., diagrams) incorporated in Chapter II.

Moreover, statistics heretofore filed with the FERA in Washington show that, up to the last day of February, 99,300 resident families (containing 413,707 persons) had been removed from the relief rolls in the state subsequent to the inception of the CWA, for one reason or another. An additional 3,353 single men were removed in the same period.

More concretely, the following figures show the definite effect of CWA upon the relief case closings for a three month period:

	RELIEF CASES CLOSED			
	NOV.	DEC.	JAN.	FEB.
Because of CWA Employment	31,542	58,325	14,675	3,817
Because of other circumstances	7,193	11,651	20,200	15,898
Total	*38,735*	*69,976*	*34,875*	*19,715*
% closed because of CWA work	81.4	83.3	42.1	19.3

Further, 1261 out of 10,223 new relief cases opened in February, and 7,784 out of 23,439 cases reopened in the same month, are necessitated by the termination of CWA employment. The loss of CWA work therefore accounted for 12% of the new cases and 33% of the cases re-opened in that month.

Incidental Benefits

Certain accomplishments definitely incidental to the primary accomplishments may not pass without mention. The human values involved in the alleviation of distress (which was actually effected) are incalculable. The improvement in morale, both among CWA workers and citizens in general, was as remarkable as it was urgently needed.

Effect on Unemployment and Business

Statistics indicating the reduction in unemployment during the winter have been presented in Chapter II. The conclusion that the increased industrial and other normal employment was greatly assisted—if not caused by—the CWA is reasonable. The increased employment was particularly noticeable in the manufacturing area in southeastern Michigan.

A parallel—and logically so—improvement in business was in evidence soon after the inception of CWA. Merchants enjoyed the most advantageous Christmas business in several years, and the gain was sustained in large degree throughout the winter.

Administrative Accomplishments

The task of creating and building up such an organization as was necessary to handle the huge mass of detail work attendant upon CWA was an extraordinary feat in itself. In a recent address before a group of automobile executives in Flint, Michigan, Mr. Johnson brought gasps of amazement from those present when he told of placing 167,000 persons at work within a period of six weeks. An equal amount of time would be required by most of the large auto plants for a mere change of models, in spite of the existence of an organized and efficient force for handling the detail work.

Conclusion

The CWA venture was hastily conceived and hastily executed. The latter was possible because the substance of the President's order was substantially "put men to work," and the governing rules were in essence, "Pick a project, hire men, and start to work." The approval of projects was therefore virtually the only possible source of delay (aside from a dearth of tools); and since the spirit of the CWA readily caught on, all obstacles were surmounted with surprising facility.

Both the physical assets and the alleviation of unemployment distress, which were brought to the State of Michigan through the CWA program, were of extreme value. On the one hand, the state is richer by $45,000,000.00 worth of needed public improvements, which stand as worthy monuments to a bleak, dark period in American life when organized planning triumphed over seemingly insurmountable obstacles. More important, 167,000 needy persons were employed on an equitable basis and thus enabled to earn $36,000,000.00. The significance of the latter as a medium of eased welfare burden, improved business, and—most important—enhanced morale, independence, and self respect, is not readily overestimated.

The judgment must prevail that the CWA enjoyed the wide public favor with which it was endowed in Michigan because it definitely and satisfactorily alleviated a critical condition.

FINIS

The Living Legacy of the CWA

James R. Anderson

This report of progress outlines my supplemental research on the legacies of CWA projects in Michigan constructed or undertaken during the period November 1933 through April, 1934. Since early summer of 2018, I have made several trips around both the Lower and Upper Michigan Peninsulas tracing out the subsequent histories of a selection of aboveground CWA projects where public access was readily possible or obtainable. I visited the locations of several of the photographed projects shown in the CWA report, such as the Kalkaska County Rapid River Bridge and the Detroit Zoological Gardens, and talked with current staff members with knowledge, often quite limited, of project histories. Some, such as John Rogers, the manager of the Kalkaska County Road Commission, had extensive knowledge and detailed files.

The projects all met the urgent needs of their time, and their value has stood the test of time, even as traffic and population have grown and usage has shifted, for the more than eighty-five years since the CWA projects were undertaken. The first dramatic example of project value I witnessed is that the foundations of the badly needed Kalkaska bridge project, constructed and financed in 1934 under CWA auspices, are still intact and were utilized for a doubling of bridge traffic capacity in the 1980s. A striking before and after pair of pictures of the original CWA bridge is included in the photo gallery. Detailed views of the present-day bridge foundation in figures 1 and 2 show an example of the resilience of the CWA projects.

Figures 1 and 2. Rapid River Bridge, Kalkaska County. This view from east side, river level, shows the 1985 buttress (*foreground*) for the intact 1934 CWA bridge foundation. Source: Kalkaska County Road Commission Manager. Photos by author, May 2019.

Detroit Zoo

The financial situation of the zoo was dangerous by late 1931. William A. Austin described the formation of taxpayer "action groups" campaigning for privatization of the zoo to charge admission and make it a for-profit organization. The leader of the group publicly and notoriously threatened that "before the dreadful year 1931 was over, the people of Detroit might be eating the Swans and Monkeys."[1] Despite, or possibly because of, calls for admission charges, some 2.5 million people visited the zoo in 1932, a record. By the time the CWA came into existence in November 1933, the financial situation had worsened, although no animals or birds were eaten by hungry hunters.

The Detroit Zoo was rescued from potential financial failure at the depths of the Depression because it was an important beneficiary of CWA projects in two powerful respects. First, the CWA provided life-support project financing totaling $200,000 during late 1933 and 1934, when projects undertaken or underway in 1932 and early 1933, paid for by zoo revenues and various project gifts from Detroit and Michigan donors, had been completed and funds were exhausted. As the photo gallery illustrates, CWA funds provided labor and material costs for the construction of the Hippopotamus and African Bird Exhibit building. The building, so far as is known, has been in continuous exhibit use for more than eighty years, with occasional changes in the animal and bird exhibits featured in the structure, according to a zoo staff member I talked with in December 2018. The high quality of materials and construction in zoo structures and varied CWA structures still visible and in use throughout all sections of the state, ranging from northern Detroit to Copper Harbor, was a consistent feature of CWA projects

Second, although no one could know it in 1933, the CWA funds, which ended in March 1934, began nine years of continual federal support for zoo capital projects, especially construction and facility upgrades. Direct CWA funds were subsequently and generously augmented by grants from the Federal Emergency Relief Administration and the Works Progress Administration until 1942. Almost every structure or major improvement undertaken from 1933 to mid-1942 had substantial or partial federal funding through these three public works agencies. It is possible that the greatest single legacy, and probably most visited by the public, of the CWA in Michigan is the Detroit Zoo, for which federal investment made possible its financial survival and expansion as a public institution.

West Branch High School

My project legacy research since the end of spring 2019 focused primarily on northern Lower Michigan and the Western Upper Peninsula, the historic and continuing center of Michigan mining. My research began with a doubly rewarding trip to West Branch where I was welcomed and given substantial help by staff members of the Ogemaw County Historical Society, especially Sally Rea. This visit acquainted me with county level archival research and acclimated me to the extensive resources available at the county level. Second, I located the large high school structure, initiated in early 1934 with a $150,000 grant from the Michigan CWA, by far the largest school construction grant it awarded.

As the Ogemaw County school system has expanded and consolidated in recent decades, substantial additions have been built onto the original structure, and it has been converted to the core building of a middle school. A plaque inside the structure confirms construction of the building was completed in 1936, with additional funding from the Works Progress Administration. West Branch and surrounding communities have educated students in the building for more than eighty years.

Thanks in part to extensive additional materials on the Civilian Conservation Corps supplied by the Ogemaw County Historical Society staff, I also made a quick visit to the CCC camp at Higgins Lake, at the time under major renovation, which helped establish the local and regional context for Federal New Deal Programs in northeast Michigan. CWA, CCC, and other New Deal projects were sponsored mostly by local governments, with some sponsored or endorsed by state governments.

The Missing Upper Peninsula

Readers may take note of a significant bifurcation between the geographic focus of the main text of the CWA report and the gallery of photos. The main text has a statewide project focus, significantly including the Upper Peninsula. However, to my knowledge, none of the photos illustrate Upper Peninsula projects despite it being a highly significant area for CWA projects, because the collapse of the mining industry resulted in proportionately higher levels of unemployment and dire destitution than downstate industrial cities like Detroit. As my subsequent comments on project legacies will make clear, even federal officials such as Harry Hopkins took note of the extreme unemployment of the Upper Peninsula mining areas.

The highlight of my CWA legacy research was unquestionably the week of June 25–July 3, 2019, built around attendance at the Upper Peninsula History Conference in Escanaba June 28 and 29. My main mission was archival research and site visits to track the history and legacies of CWA projects. Some were referenced in the CWA report, and some I turned up in the course of archival and site research.

So far as I can tell, Upper Peninsula CWA projects, especially schools, highways, and

Figures 3 and 4. Main entrance to former West Branch High School, now a middle school. This project began with CWA funding and was completed under Works Progress Administration in 1936. Photos by author.

airports, were fairly represented or sampled in the main text of the report. My main observation, a tentative one because of limited but geographically focused sampling, is that CWA projects in the Upper Peninsula had long and often varied legacies, sometimes longer than their lower peninsula counterparts, simply because of less rapid population growth and slower economic transformation in the area, and because construction materials and craftsmanship were usually of exceptional quality and durability.

CWA Legacy in Western Upper Peninsula

Franklin D. Roosevelt's establishment of the CWA made front-page banner headlines in the Upper Peninsula, as well as across Michigan. For example, the *Escanaba Daily Press* (*EDP*) of Thursday, November 9, 1933, proclaimed in an eight-column banner headline, "New Relief Fund Promises Jobs to Four Million."

Legacies of CWA structures abound across the western Upper Peninsula, where unemployment reached more than 75 percent in most mining areas, bringing malnutrition, hunger, and desperation to the entire region. The projects were welcomed, widely and favorably reported, and helped prevent outright starvation or even death from the economic collapse of the Depression. I located several major projects and only limited time stood in the way of locating more of them. For example, the CWA undertook forty airport projects throughout the state, including thirty-one new airports. Projects undertaken and completed ranged from Wayne County to Laurium in Keweenaw, the heart of Michigan's Copper Country, decimated by the Depression.

Airports

The first legacy project I examined was an airport project in Escanaba. Utilizing archives of the City of Escanaba, Delta County, and especially the Delta County Historical Society, I was able to document that the city purchased property in December 1933 with a CWA grant for airport construction. The announcement of the site was announced in the *EDP* Wednesday, December 13, 1933. According to the CWA report, the airport was 50 percent completed by the end of March, with a CWA expenditure of $24,500.

The *EDP* reported frequently in the following days and weeks on CWA projects and employment. It accented or implied the vital and permanent importance of these projects. In public and governmental discourse, civil works projects always have had a long-range focus, without specification of exact life expectancy. The *EDP* published a banner headline "Civil Works Continue Until Spring" on Thursday, December 14, 1933. It followed this

Figures 5 and 6. Airport structure at Laurium, near Calumet, funded by CWA in 1934. Note the craftsmanship of the stonework. The sign on the west wall says Houghton County Airport, 1934. Photos by author.

story two days later, on Saturday, December 16, 1933, with another front-page report on the enormous success of the CWA: "Goal of CWA Reached; Jobs to 4 Million."

Control and administration of the airport, then called the Escanaba Municipal Airport, was transferred from the City of Escanaba to Delta County in July 1973, with relocation of the airport to the immediate south edge of Escanaba. To this day Delta County and the Central Upper Peninsula are well served by the Delta County Airport Authority, rooted in grants from the CWA and eventually other state and federal aeronautics authorities. The adjacent city of Gladstone also was granted funds by the CWA for construction of an airport project, although time did not permit tracking down its legacy. Delta County Historical Society staff members, who were extremely helpful to me in researching the Escanaba Airport project, assured me that the Gladstone airport was built and has since been incorporated into the County Airport.

Another airport was constructed at Laurium, adjacent to Calumet in Houghton County in the Central Keweenaw peninsula area, with a CWA expenditure of $23,800. For thirty years or more, it was Michigan's northernmost airport, serving four northwestern Upper Peninsula counties. The project was 60 percent completed by the end of March 1934, when the Michigan CWA was dissolved and merged back into the Federal Emergency Relief Administration. The airport was completed, and it has a dual legacy.

As the Laurium airport was outgrown, it was closed as part of the 1968 creation of the Houghton County Airport Authority, and its operations were transferred to the present Houghton County Memorial Airport, in Franklin Township some seven miles southwest of Laurium and Calumet. The Houghton County Memorial Airport inherited the distinction being of Michigan's northernmost airport.

The original Laurium airport hanger building was so sturdily constructed that it was then taken over by the Village of Laurium, probably around 1968, and is now in active service as the village's heavy equipment and maintenance garage (primarily for winter snow plowing). I was fortunate enough to be given a tour of the structure and the heavy equipment stored and maintained in it, by its gracious head mechanic on July 3, 2019. From outward and limited inside appearances, the building looks well fit for another half century of use, if it continues to receive sufficient preventive maintenance.

Keweenaw Peninsula Recreation Projects

The CWA was also involved with a least two major recreational projects in Keweenaw County, the northernmost county of Copper Country. Both were designed by county officials and the CWA as employment programs and economic diversification investments in Keweenaw County's tourism industry. Both have achieved lasting renown. One is the Brockway Mountain Drive; the other is the Keweenaw Park and Golf Course, which soon became known as the Keweenaw Mountain Lodge. Brockway Mountain Drive is famous to this day for its world-class long scenic vistas (see figures 9 and 10) overlooking Lake Superior to the north and eastward over the ridges, valleys, and inland lakes of the Keweenaw peninsula. The Keweenaw County Road Commission (KCRC) provided the driving energy and informed leadership for the nine mile scenic loop off M-26, the lakeshore state highway then in early stages of development.

Construction financing for the Brockway Mountain Drive spanned both the late Herbert

Figures 7 and 8. Brockway
Mountain Drive scenic panorama
with CWA stone fence. Photos by
author, June 2019.

Figure 9. Brockway Mountain Drive traffic at summit, late 1930s.

Hoover administration and the early New Deal, under Franklin D. Roosevelt. The KCRC applied for and received a loan of $30,000 to $35,000 from the Reconstruction Finance Corporation in late 1932 (KCRC minutes), and construction of the mountain drive began in spring 1933. The basic road, according to Paul LaVanway, was completed and opened for traffic in October, 1933, ahead of the winter season shutdown.[2] Employment averaged 150–200 men, some 20 percent of the family workforce of Keweenaw County at the time. Construction work on the road, suspended during the winter months, was completed in 1934, with less than $10,000 of additional direct grant funding from the CWA.

The road has been maintained and improved at intervals over the last eighty years. It continues to draw a steady stream of tourists from across Michigan and the United States every summer and fall. The extraordinary scenic vistas along the route bear glad witness to its famous legacy of beauty.

The Keweenaw Park and Golf Course, as it was originally known, is probably the most unusual and remarkable CWA project in Michigan, and may well be one of the most remarkable undertaken in the entire United States. It is a direct response to the desperate and often imaginative efforts reaching from the Keweenaw County Road Commission to the White House to create productive jobs for the 75.2 percent of the Keweenaw County population on relief at the time, highest in the nation. Harry Hopkins, one of Roosevelt's most important and trusted administrators of relief programs, and director of the Civil Works Administration, reported that Michigan's Copper Country had the highest relief load in the entire nation.

Figures 10 and 11. The Keweenaw Mountain Lodge main building, funded by CWA, has been in active use since 1934. Photos by author, June 2019.

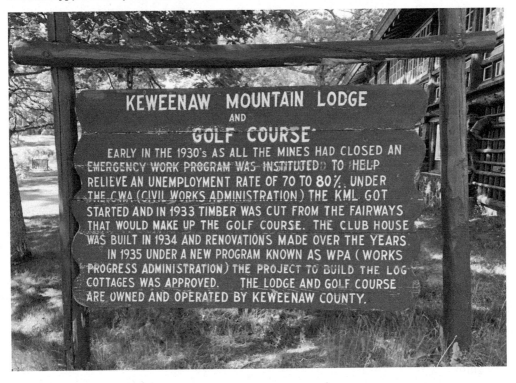

KEWEENAW MOUNTAIN LODGE
AND
GOLF COURSE

EARLY IN THE 1930's AS ALL THE MINES HAD CLOSED AN EMERGENCY WORK PROGRAM WAS INSTITUTED TO HELP RELIEVE AN UNEMPLOYMENT RATE OF 70 TO 80%. UNDER THE CWA (CIVIL WORKS ADMINISTRATION) THE KML GOT STARTED AND IN 1933 TIMBER WAS CUT FROM THE FAIRWAYS THAT WOULD MAKE UP THE GOLF COURSE. THE CLUB HOUSE WAS BUILT IN 1934 AND RENOVATIONS MADE OVER THE YEARS.
IN 1935 UNDER A NEW PROGRAM KNOWN AS WPA (WORKS PROGRESS ADMINISTRATION) THE PROJECT TO BUILD THE LOG COTTAGES WAS APPROVED. THE LODGE AND GOLF COURSE ARE OWNED AND OPERATED BY KEWEENAW COUNTY.

Without knowing of the forthcoming creation and funding of the CWA, KCRC member Ocha Potter, himself out of his job as superintendent of the closed down Ahmeek Mining Company and serving as volunteer head of the Road Relief Department, was developing plans for jobs for unemployed mine workers of Keweenaw County.

As LaVanway described the situation, Potter "received a telegram from the State Emergency Relief Office, asking for the submission of ideas for public projects suitable for funding under the CWA program. In response, Potter proposed a project which would employ hundreds—the construction of a publicly-owned golf course and clubhouse—what became known as the Keweenaw Park and Golf Course."[3]

The construction of this recreation project, literally shaped from a mountain side, began with CWA approval and funding in early 1934, continued with Federal Emergency Relief Administration (FERA) grant funding, and was completed as a Works Progress Administration Project. Eventually the development would take the name of the Keweenaw Mountain Lodge. The lodge operates to this day (see figures 10 and 11) as a vacation and golf resort, with a well-regarded restaurant.

In summary, a fascinating and hopefully representative sampling of CWA projects shows clear and sometimes striking legacies. All projects had a direct existence of at least thirty years; some, such as the West Branch High School, and the Escanaba and Laurium Airports, were incorporated into larger, more modern facilities. Some—such as the Detroit Zoo, the Rapid River Bridge in Kalkaska County, and the Keweenaw Mountain Lodge—have had continuous use since 1934. All met the employment and launch criteria for CWA projects, especially that "they should be socially and economically desirable." All the projects I have studied provide a forceful testament to their public value over the years since their inception or expansion under social and economic conditions of dire emergency.

■ NOTES

1. Quoted in William A. Austin, *The First Fifty Years, an Informal History of the Detroit Zoological Park and the Detroit Zoological Society* (Detroit: Detroit Zoological Society, 1974), 26. The Afterword material below relating to the Detroit Zoo is drawn from Chapter Three of this publication, titled "The Depression." The publication was located at the Local History Room, Royal Oak Public Library, around December 21, 2018.

2. Paul LaVanway, *The Brockway Mountain Drive Story* (Copper Harbor, MI: Published by the author, 2010).

3. Paul LaVanway, *The Keweenaw Mountain Lodge Story* (Copper Harbor, MI: Published by the author, 2010).